Second Language Acquisition
Theory and Pedagogy

Second Language Acquisition Theory and Pedagogy

Edited by

**Fred R. Eckman
Diane Highland
Peter W. Lee
Jean Mileham
Rita Rutkowski Weber**
University of Wisconsin–Milwaukee

LEA LAWRENCE ERLBAUM ASSOCIATES, PUBLISHERS
1995   Mahwah, New Jersey   Hove, UK

Copyright © 1995 by Lawrence Erlbaum Associates, Inc.
   All rights reserved. No part of this book may be reproduced in
   any form, by photostat, microfilm, retrieval system, or any other
   means, without the prior written permission of the publisher.

Lawrence Erlbaum Associates, Inc., Publishers
10 Industrial Avenue
Mahwah, New Jersey 07430

Cover design by Jan Melchior

Library of Congress Cataloging-in-Publication Data

Second language acquisition : theory and pedagogy / edited by Fred R.
   Eckman . . . [et al.].
      p.   cm.
   Selected proceedings of the twenty-second University of Wisconsin–
Milwaukee Linguistics Symposium, held October 8–10, 1993, on the UWM
campus.
   Includes bibliographical references and index.
   ISBN 0-8058-1687-9
   1. Second language acquisition—Congresses. 2. Language and
languages—Study and teaching—Congresses. I. Eckman, Fred R.
II. Linguistics Symposium of the University of Wisconsin–Milwaukee
(22nd : 1993)
P118.2.S435 1995
418—dc20   95-13550
                                                              CIP

Books published by Lawrence Erlbaum Associates are printed on acid-free
paper, and their bindings are chosen for strength and durability.

Printed in the United States of America
10 9 8 7 6 5 4 3 2

To the memory of
Robert D. Eckman and John C. Eckman
Fred Eckman

To John and Dan
Diane Highland

To Karen and Ben,
and to John Street, who let it all begin
Peter Lee

To my parents and my children
Jean Mileham

To Alice Rutkowski
Rita Rutkowski Weber

Contents

Acknowledgments

The papers in this volume were selected from those presented at the Twenty-Second University of Wisconsin–Milwaukee Linguistics Symposium on Second Language Acquisition Theory and Pedagogy, held October 8–10, 1993, on the University of Wisconsin-Milwaukee campus.

The editors would like to thank the following institutions for their generous support of the symposium:

University of Wisconsin–Milwaukee, Marquette Center
    for International Studies

College of Letters and Science

Center for the Improvement of Instruction

Intensive English as a Second Language Program

Department of Linguistics

Without the assistance that these units provided, the symposium, and this volume, would not have been possible.

—Fred R. Eckman
—Diane Highland
—Peter W. Lee
—Jean Mileham
—Rita Rutkowski Weber

Preface

Fred R. Eckman
University of Wisconsin–Milwaukee

A volume such as this one on second language acquisition (SLA) theory and pedagogy is, at the same time, a mark of progress and a bit of an anomaly. The progress is shown by the fact that the two disciplines have established themselves as areas of study distinct not only from each other but also from linguistic theory. This was not always the case, at least not in the United States. The anomaly results from the fact that this book deals with the relationship between L2 theory and pedagogy, despite the conclusion that there is currently no widely accepted theory of SLA (Long, 1993).

A few decades ago, the distinctness of SLA theory, L2 pedagogy, and linguistics was not clearly recognized. In the 1940s and 1950s, the school of American Structural Linguistics subsumed linguistic theory, language acquisition (including SLA), and language pedagogy under the same set of principles. The goal of American structuralism was to devise a set of procedures, such as segmentation, comparison-contrast, and classification, that, when applied to a corpus of data, would yield a description of the patterns exhibited by those data (Gleason, 1955; Hockett, 1958). These procedures were also assumed to be the principles used by a child or adult learner in acquiring the grammar of a language. From this position, it was a small step to the *audio-lingual method* (ALM), which held that a language could best be taught by presenting the learner with corpora (i.e., dialogues) and sets of pattern-practice drills that would assist the learner in segmenting, comparing, and classifying the various elements contained in the corpus. This, it was claimed, is how the learner would acquire the target language.

Although current research in SLA draws heavily on linguistics and uses many principles and concepts of linguistic theory to explain facts about SLA, the two disciplines are not considered to be one and the same. Constructs such as NL interference, parameter resetting, and affective filter are postulated as part of L2 theory but not as part of linguistic theory. The type of data considered relevant also differs between the two disciplines: Whereas linguists construct their theories solely on the basis of data from primary languages, SLA theorists analyze data from secondary languages (interlanguages).

The rise of SLA theory as a discipline in its own right has contributed greatly to our understanding of the nature of L2 acquisition. Given the advances that have been made in the field over the last two decades, we may be able to answer questions that previously could not even be formulated. However, two caveats are in order. As with any young discipline, there are far more questions than answers; and, as with any volume of this nature, it is not possible to deal with all, or even most, of those questions. Thus the chapters assembled in this volume attempt to address some of the more recent issues and questions in L2 theory and pedagogy.

The chapters have been grouped into five parts. The first considers questions about L2 theory and pedagogy at the macrolevel, from the standpoint of the L2 setting. The next two parts deal with the topic of input. Part II considers input in terms of factors that are internal to the learner, and Part III takes up the question of external factors affecting the input including the issue of whether points of grammar can be explicitly taught. The last two parts discuss learner output and production. Part IV deals with questions of certain complex, linguistic behaviors and the various external and social variables that influence learners. Part V deals with issues surrounding the teaching of pronunciation.

Gass' chapter begins Part I with a consideration of whether L2 teacher-training programs should require prospective teachers to take a course in SLA theory, and, if so, what the content of such a course should be. Drawing on several examples from the recent literature, Gass argues that teacher-training programs should offer courses in SLA theory that will provide the necessary background for the teachers to understand and evaluate SLA research. In Gass' words, teachers need to know enough about SLA theory to be able to read recent SLA literature and to play the "doubting game."

The chapter by Schinke-Llano in Part I takes up the topic of student–teacher interactions. Using a number of terms and constructs developed in Vygotskian psycholinguistics, she argues that much of current classroom practice needs to change so that the major responsibility for learning is shifted from the teacher to the learner. Interestingly, Schinke-Llano points out that some classroom practices, such as those advocated in the work of Long (1980) and Krashen (1982), already are consistent with Vygotskian philosophy.

Hastings' contribution argues for configuring L2 intensive programs so that students are tested and assigned to sequenced modules designed to focus on one language macroskill at a time, beginning with listening comprehension, proceeding to reading, then to writing, and finally to speaking. The rationale for this model, which is based heavily on the theoretical work of Krashen, is that the various skills are developmentally related and therefore constitute a natural sequence.

In the final chapter of Part I, Flynn and Martohardjono address what they see as the best way for SLA theory and L2 pedagogy to interact: Developments in each area should affect the other such that advances in SLA theory should have consequences for the L2 classroom, and the results of various pedagogical programs should impinge on the status of theoretical constructs and principles. The examples they use to illustrate their point are based on a Universal Grammar (UG) approach to SLA theory.

The chapters in the next two sections are concerned with the role of input. Those in Part II deal with "triggering" L2 learning through the manipulation of the input the learner receives. White and Bruhn-Garavito consider this question within the Principles and Parameters framework by testing the hypothesis that all of the structures related by a given parameter can be acquired through exposure to only one of those structures. The pedagogical consequences of this work are clear: The learner, *ex hypothesi*, should be able to acquire some structures without being directly exposed to them. Essentially the same topic is addressed by Hamilton and Croteau; they each test the ability of learners to generalize instruction in the acquisition of certain relative clause constructions. Both authors base their studies on the Accessibility Hierarchy (Keenan & Comrie, 1977). Croteau tested native speakers of English learning Italian; Hamilton used ESL learners but challenges the usual interpretation of the hierarchy. In Hamilton's view, the Accessibility Hierarchy can be construed as a principle pertaining to constituency rather than to grammatical relations.

In Part III, Larsen-Freeman lists ten myths about the teaching and learning of grammar and then offers arguments to dispel them. She discusses not only the contribution that SLA theory has to make to L2 pedagogy but also ways second language teaching can benefit L2 theory. She argues that it may well be fallacious to assume that untutored acquisition provides an appropriate model for L2 pedagogy.

After Larsen-Freeman's chapter, with its focus on the question of whether grammar should be taught, Bardovi-Harlig takes up the question of when structures should be taught. She asks whether parallels between the stages of acquisition in tutored and untutored learners are evidence for a natural acquisitional sequence. The results of her empirical study suggest that the effect of instruction is predictable on the basis of the stage of acquisition: Instruction will have no effect if the prerequisite stage has not been attained. Bardovi-Harlig also discusses the issue of whether formal accuracy improves as a result of instruction.

In the third chapter in Part III, VanPatten and Sanz take up the question of the type of grammar that should be taught and the type of learning processes the instruction should seek to affect. VanPatten and Sanz did an empirical study and found that "processing instruction," which uses structured input, has a positive effect for instruction that holds across a wide assortment of assessment tasks.

The next chapter in Part III is by Krashen. It represents a change of pace from the three previous chapters on grammatical instruction, though his chapter also deals with the role of input. Krashen argues for the *Reading Hypothesis*, that free, voluntary reading is the major source of literacy development. He argues against two alternatives: the *Instruction Hypothesis*, that literacy can be taught directly, and the *Writing Hypothesis*, that literacy comes from writing. He suggests that reading also helps people to understand spoken language, and he makes some specific proposals about what kinds of reading help people understand what kinds of discourse.

The final paper in Part III is by Ciccone. He argues for the role of authentic video in the L2 classroom. Basing his arguments on Krashen's work on comprehensible input, Ciccone relates the use of video to the enhancement of both listening and reading skills.

The last two parts of the book deal with factors affecting the learner's output. In Part IV, Cohen discusses a number of variables that affect a learner's production, including strategies learners use and the explicit teaching of complex verbal behavior. Cohen points out that studies have shown large gaps in learners' proficiencies. He suggests that learners may have to be explicitly taught some linguistic behaviors, such as apologies, which may be too demanding and too cultural specific to be learned solely through natural input. He also raises the question of whether learners should be taught to use certain learning strategies and thus to be conscious of and responsible for their learning processes.

Parker, Heitzman, Fjerstad, Babbs, and Cohen consider the nature of learners' use patterns in Foreign Language Immersion Programs (FLIP). They conducted an empirical study using classroom observations, interviews, and verbal-report techniques to determine the extent of NL and TL usage and the circumstances under which the learners switched languages. They found that in FLIPs, the TL plays a somewhat limited role in communication, and that the NL and TL are generally used for complementary tasks.

Tarone's contribution concludes Part III. She argues for the variationist's perspective on SLA data. According to this school of thought (Ellis, 1985, 1990; Tarone, 1988, 1990), L2 theory must consider data on intralearner variability as part of its theoretical domain. This view is counter to that of some other theorists, such as Gregg (1989, 1990), who have argued that SLA theory should abstract away from this type of variation. Tarone argues that it is necessary to consider data on variability in order to explain the mechanism by which second languages are learned. From a pedagogical standpoint, Tarone suggests that by isolating the external forces influencing intralearner variations, teachers can use these forces to enable the learner to generalize structures to other interactional contexts.

Part V, the final one of the book, treats L2 pronunciation. Paolillo's chapter considers the production of English /r/–/l/ contrasts by speakers of several Asian languages, and postulates two patterns by which learners acquire this contrast.

Paolillo argues that these two patterns correspond to two types of markedness: *language-specific markedness*, which reflects functional load, and *crosslinguistic markedness*, which reflects inherent difficulty.

Hammond adduces empirical results and arguments from several studies supporting the position that L2 pronunciation can be taught. Contrary to what some might suppose, this is not an obvious point. As Hammond notes, most of the communication-based pedagogies do not explicitly deal with the teaching of pronunciation.

The last chapter of Part V and the book is an empirical study by Hansen on the affects of acculturation on L2 pronunciation. Using the tenets of Schumann's Acculturation Model and building on the work of Oyama (1976), Hansen's results partly confirm Oyama's findings but also suggest that certain factors of acculturation also correlate with degree of accent in L2 pronunciation.

REFERENCES

Ellis, R. (1985). *Understanding Second Language Acquisition*. Oxford: Oxford University Press.

———. (1990). "A Response to Gregg," *Applied Linguistics* 11, 384–391.

Gleason, H. (1955). *An Introduction to Descriptive Linguistics*. New York: Holt, Rinehart & Winston.

Gregg, K. (1989). "Second Language Acquisition Theory: The Case for a Generative Perspective," *Linguistic Perspectives on Second Language Acquisition*, ed. by S. Gass and J. Schachter. Cambridge, England: Cambridge University Press.

———. (1990). "The Variable Competence Model of Second Language Acquisition and Why It Isn't," *Applied Linguistics* 11, 364–383.

Hockett, C. (1958). *A Course in Modern Linguistics*. New York: Macmillan.

Keenan, E., and B. Comrie. (1977). "Noun Phrase Accessibility and Universal Grammar," *Linguistic Inquiry* 8, 63–100.

Krashen, S. (1982). *Principles and Practice in Second Language Acquisition*. Oxford: Pergamon.

Long, M. (1980). *Input, Interaction, and Second Language Acquisition*. Doctoral dissertation, University of California, Los Angeles.

———. (1993). "Assessment Strategies for SLA Theories," *Applied Linguistics* 14, 225–249.

Oyama, S. (1976). "A Sensitive Period for the Acquisition of a Second Language," *Journal of Psycholinguisitic Research* 5, 261–283.

Tarone, E. (1988). *Variation in Interlanguage*. London: Edward Arnold.

———. (1990). "On Variation in Interlanguage: A Response to Gregg," *Applied Linguistics* 11, 392–400.

Part I

FACTORS AFFECTING THE L2 SETTING

Chapter 1

Learning and Teaching:
The Necessary Intersection

Susan M. Gass
Michigan State University

1. THE ROLE OF SECOND LANGUAGE ACQUISITION RESEARCH

In recent months there have been exchanges on SLART, the computer bulletin board devoted to issues related to second language acquisition (SLA).[1] The discussion started with what might seem like an innocent question concerning in part the value of an academic course in second language acquisition as part of an ESL teacher's graduate training. The mere fact that such a question was posed was, in my view, surprising, since it is difficult for me to imagine how the value of such a course could be questioned. Similar surprise was expressed by one of the respondents to the Second Language Acquisition Research and Teaching (SLART) discussion: ". . . the idea of an MATESOL degree without a course in second language acquisition is akin to a Medical degree without a course (or two) in anatomy!! Inconceivable" (April 28, 1993). Or another: "What a question to have to ask! I would like to think that every program does" (April 28, 1993). Or: "Would anyone seriously argue that knowledge of U.S. history is ancillary to American history teacher education?" (April 28, 1993).

This latter remark is of course akin to the comment about medical school and anatomy. In pondering these comments I began to think about other peda-

---

[1] I use the term *second language acquisition* to refer to the general field of learning a non-primary language, including what is commonly referred to as both second language acquisition and foreign language learning.

gogical issues, particularly those related to the teaching of other disciplines, such as science education or math education, both of which represent areas in which degrees are given. But what is the content of these degrees? Clearly, future teachers must know about science or math; a history teacher must know about history. However, this is not the correct analogy to the relationship between knowledge of acquisition and language teaching. For language teaching, the analogy is to a knowledge of the structure of the language being taught.

The relationship of the knowledge taught to the process of learning is, as I will argue, a crucial one, yet separate from the one that was being espoused on SLART. In this domain, the field of language pedagogy is far more sophisticated than in some of the other fields in which teaching degrees/certificates are awarded. In fact, in looking at books about math education, one finds that indeed information is imparted to prospective teachers about the phenomenon of learning. What is particularly striking is the fact that the theoretical foundation sounds very much like SLA in the 1970s. The following quote is from a 1987 anthology based on a conference that brought together cognitive scientists, math teachers, mathematicians, and math educators. The title of this particular article is "New Knowledge About Errors and New Views About Learners: What They Mean to Educators and More Educators Would Like to Know" (Maurer, 1987). It is reminiscent of Pit Corder's 1967 article "The Significance of Learner Errors." The article begins: "One of the insights of the cognitive science approach to learning theory is that many of the mathematics errors students make are systematic. These errors are bugs, like bugs in computer programs, not slips" (p. 165). And he goes on: "There *is* something new in today's statement that students make systematic errors. . . . Researchers are now able to predict a large number of the arithmetic mistakes that individual students will make—before the students work the assigned problems!" (p. 165). And: "What *is* important is the general insight these studies give into how students learn. Indeed, 'learn' may not be the best word to describe what happens; 'interpret' may be better" (p. 165). "All told, the research brings Good News and Bad News. The Good News is that, basically, students are acting like creative young scientists, interpreting their lessons through their own generalizations. The Bad News is that their methods of generalizing are often faulty" (pp. 165–166).

So in less than a page there are elements of *error analysis* (this precise term is used in scare quotes later in the paper), there is Krashen's *acquisition/learning distinction*, and there is *creative construction*. In the discussion that follows this article, arguments are presented that sound very much like arguments against pattern practice type drills. I won't go on to talk about the role learning theory plays in other disciplines but will only point out that the need to understand the nature of learning is not unique to our own pedagogical concerns; it is now beginning to extend to other content disciplines.

Freeman (1989) suggests that there are four components to teaching: knowledge, skills, attitude, and awareness. The present discussion focuses on knowledge, but the question is: knowledge of what? In my view, the response is two-pronged—knowledge of the structure of the language and knowledge about how people acquire that language. The difference between math education, for example, and general language teacher training is that the knowledge concerned with acquisition is a well-developed theoretical field for language, whereas it is not for math. I hope this is clear from my brief discussion of math education.

The debate about the value of SLA for teaching has not been limited to computer screens (cf. Flynn, 1990, 1991). Witness the difference in viewpoints expressed in the articles by Ellis (1993), on the one hand, and by Newmeyer and Weinberger (1988), on the other. Ellis' entire article argues for a particular type of syllabus—a structural syllabus. The basis for his argument is findings from research on second language acquisition. On the other hand, Newmeyer and Weinberger (1988), describing the relationship between pedagogy and acquisition, implied an unhealthy relationship: "The struggle of the field [SLA] to free itself from ties to pedagogy has been slow and arduous, and is still a long way from being totally achieved" (p. 41). Later they stated: "But the links between research and pedagogy are still not fully severed. Even many of the most theoretically-oriented papers in second language learning devote space to the presumed pedagogical implications and applications of the proposal discussed" (p. 42). But they also stated: "Nevertheless, the field of second language learning research shows every sign of shedding its legacy of direct involvement in pedagogical questions" (p. 42).

No doubt their comments were motivated in part by the need of an emerging discipline (SLA) to show its strength, vitality, and value. Nonetheless, their attitude toward the undesirability of a continuing relationship is apparent through their choice of words: "the struggle of the field to free itself," "the links are not fully severed," "the field . . . shows every sign of shedding its legacy." What I will argue here is that the need for a rapprochement is great, but that it can be done only by means of a full understanding of the field of SLA and of where the field does and does not relate to issues of pedagogy.

2. DEFINING SLA

Some of the debate centers around varying definitions of SLA. Some scholars have narrow definitions and include only a very limited range of subject matter in courses they teach in SLA. In fact, one person who was recently seeking advice on what to include in an introductory SLA course asked whether it would be necessary to include all that "input/interaction" stuff in the course. This would presumably be a course devoted primarily to UG issues, or at least to more formal approaches to SLA. But contrast this with another SLART statement: "Most students seem to like theoretical approaches with a direct influence on pedagogy. . . . Students are also interested in anything related to input and interaction. At the same time, most students here find sections of the course relating to a government and binding analysis of SLA rather unhelpful, and often PAINFUL (April 28, 1993).

Others take a broader view of second language acquisition, incorporating topics related to issues of UG, topics related to input/interaction, and those related to communication strategies as well as those related to variation, individual differences, and other matters. Therefore in looking at the relationship between acquisition and pedagogy, we must minimally decide what sort of acquisition we are dealing with. In a survey I conducted about a year ago, the results of which were presented at LARS in 1992, I found that what is included in SLA courses varies. The survey reported on 16 so-called SLA courses and found that a wide range of topics were dealt with: for example, eight dealt with UG as a part of the course, six with transfer, nine with learning strategies, four with individual differences, and even fewer with first language development, social and cultural factors, critical period, pidginization, fossilization, language teaching methods, vocabulary, and the role of instruction.

The books and articles used were equally varied and included books by McLaughlin, White, Ellis, Brown, Skehan, Larsen-Freeman and Long, Corder, Krashen, Grosjean, Rose, Beebe, and Odlin and articles by Lamendella, Lado, Schmidt, Andersen, Seliger, Long, Gass, Selinker, VanPatten, McLaughlin and Rossman, Schachter, Schumann, Ervin-Tripp, Bailey, Madden and Krashen, and Cummins. I mention this to give a general picture of the vastness of the field and the wide range of viewpoints about what should be included under the rubric SLA.

3. SLA AS A BASIS FOR EVALUATION

Not only must we debate the scope of acquisition phenomena, we must also debate the purpose of a language classroom. In my view a language classroom provides the most efficient means possible for enabling students to do what they cannot do on their own, or at least not as efficiently. In some sense, then, the language classroom is a shortcut, a notion I return to later.

What I explore in this chapter is the need for a basis for understanding the language classroom. It is my belief that SLA is one such basis, although it is not the only discipline that contributes to that understanding. My main point is that SLA is one of the fields that provides a basis for evaluating a language classroom. It is part of what I call the three E's of teaching: *Expectations* (Lightbown, 1985), *Experience* (which I do not discuss here), and *Evaluation*. How do we evaluate the language classroom? Or more specifically: How do we evaluate research that is applied to the classroom or that can potentially be applied to the classroom?

By evaluation I mean the assessment of whether what is being done in a language classroom is appropriate or not. The field of language pedagogy has in some ways been faddish. All too often with a paradigm switch in linguistics or SLA, teaching practices have been discarded without an appropriate evaluation of their value. As Bickerton (cited in Huebner & Ferguson, 1991, p. 3) stated in a 1983 paper:

> There is a pecking order within disciplines just as there is in barnyards. In linguistics, the theoretical linguist rules the roost; it is he who provides the descriptive models which, after a time-lapse of a few years, are applied to the description of natural languages by the working grammarians and phonologists on the next level down. Models that have been tried and found effective, or at least fashionable, on that level are then handed on, like second-hand clothing, to workers in the field of child language, and then, after another lapse of a year or two, they finally reach the second language acquisitionist, who is already well on the wrong side of the pure/applied line and has only language teachers to peck at.

Language teaching during the past 50 years or so has relied heavily on linguistic theory and on theories of learning. In the 1960s and 1970s teachers were trained in contrastive analysis. Among other things, they were often expected to write a contrastive analysis of a portion of the grammars of two languages. This was, of course, based on then-prevalent theories of language teaching, which in turn were based on earlier models of language and language learning. When the theoretical basis for contrastive analyses was shown to be inadequate, teaching based heavily on this model of language and learning went out of fashion as well. There was no concerted effort to evaluate the model in order to discover what parts of the model might be valuable for learning and ultimately for learners. Are repetition and drills totally unnecessary? Teachers were taught that repetition, drills, and memorization of dialogues are unnecessary and avoided them rather than evaluating their potential usefulness. Without an understanding of the SLA literature based on, for example, automaticity and restructuring, there is little context for understanding these methods. All too often we have used theories and assumed they were applicable to the classroom, and assumed invalidated theories were not applicable. In attempting to understand the relationship between SLA and the classroom, it is important to keep in mind that what learners do naturally cannot necessarily be induced in a classroom context (cf. Larsen-Freeman, this volume). Fifteen years ago Evelyn Hatch warned us about the need to "Apply with Caution" (Hatch, 1979, p. 123).

> Our field must soon be known for the incredible leaps in logic we make in applying our research findings to classroom teaching. When contrasts drawn between first and second languages showed differences and those differences seemed to match errors our students made in the classroom, we leapt to say that Contrastive analysis *alone* should form the basis of the language teaching curriculum. When so-called invariant word order of acquisition of morphemes was found, we made two leaps of logic—one to say that this was the best evidence for creative language acquisition process and a second, to say that this research shows that learners should just be

exposed to rather than be taught, the language. When we found traits shared by good language learners, we suggested that the curriculum should be altered to make sure everyone does what good learners do. We have looked at conversational analysis and declared that teaching materials should reflect true conversational data. No matter what the finding, we have taught ourselves to ask "What does this mean for the classroom teacher?" and made suggestions without careful thought.

And I would add, without careful evaluation, particularly from the point of view of evaluating before eliminating a particular teaching practice from our repertoire.

In what follows I present a number of examples from different areas of SLA study to show the potentiality for contradictory research findings and the need for teachers to be able to sort out and evaluate the information as they make pedagogical decisions. First I take an example from Universal Grammar (UG) based SLA. I discuss the kind of evidence learners need to formulate appropriate grammars. Perhaps the best example is the research done by Lydia White and her colleagues (e.g., Spada & Lightbown, 1993; White, 1991; White, Spada, Lightbown, & Ranta, 1991), in which she took a theoretical construct based on SLA work and investigated it in the context of the classroom. To briefly summarize the essential points, she reported work on adverb placement, in particular differences between French and English adverb placement. She said that French learners of English assume that a sentence such as "She eats bread" is a possible English sentence, but a sentence such as "She always eats potatoes" is not. This is because they adopt an L1 parameter value in their initial formulation of English adverb placement restrictions. Because positive evidence will inform these learners about possible English sentences, but not about impossible ones, she hypothesized that negative evidence would be effective in teaching the English rule system for adverb placement. This of course has been central for SLA and pedagogical research since teachers have adopted various positions regarding correction.

White's results are mixed, but in general they support the view that specific negative evidence is beneficial in leading learners to avoid Subject Verb Adverb Object (SVAO) order. However, tests one year later suggested that the learners did not retain what they had learned and reverted to their French constraints on adverb placement. Together with Martha Trahey, White conducted a follow-up study (Trahey & White, 1993) which was designed to determine the extent to which positive evidence alone would teach the English system. That is, is the notion of explicit correction necessary, or can correct adverb placement be learned through exposure only? In what has come to be known as the *input flood study*, it appears that exposure does have a positive effect on learners' acceptance of the grammatical SAV order, but it is not sufficient to rule out the ungrammatical English SVAO. In other words, positive evidence alone does exactly what one would predict: It ensures that learners understand that what is heard is grammatical, but it doesn't rule out the ungrammatical. For this, negative evidence is needed. We therefore have a relatively clear basis for pedagogical decisions. Or do we?

Yuan (1992) investigated the acquisition of reflexives by Chinese speakers learning English and by English speakers learning Chinese. A short explanation of the background of his study is necessary. In brief, there are various ways of interpreting reflexives in languages, based on the antecedent of the reflexive. In English, the following sentence is possible:

John thinks Bill$_i$ trusts himself$_i$

where *himself* can refer to Bill but not to John. In Chinese, on the other hand, in the same sentence,

Wang Ping$_i$ renwei Zhang Bo$_j$ xiangxin ziji$_{i/j}$
Wang Ping think Zhang Bo trust   self

self can refer to either Wang Ping or Zhang Bo. This latter phenomenon is known as *long-distance reflexivization*, but the English restriction is called *local reflexivization*.

What is the linguistic behavior of learners? Returning to the issue of positive and negative evidence, we might predict that English speakers learning Chinese would understand that Chinese allows both possibilities, because positive evidence is readily available. On the other hand, Chinese speakers learning English need to restrict their interpretation of English. This would presumably be a more difficult task because there is no positive evidence indicating that a more restrictive interpretation is necessary. Assuming that the Subset Principle is not operative in adult second language learning, one would need negative evidence to determine appropriate English reflexive use. In a large study involving 159 Chinese speakers learning English and 102 English speakers learning Chinese, Yuan tested exactly these constructions. The results are not unlike those of other studies of reflexives: The Chinese learners of English do in fact learn the appropriate English restrictions, but English-speaking learners of Chinese do not learn the appropriate Chinese interpretations. As can be seen in Fig. 1.1, the Chinese learners of English eventually (by Levels 6/7) learn that long-distance reflexivization is not possible in English, and that local interpretation is the only possibility. On the other hand, in Fig. 1.2, the English-speaking learners of Chinese have not learned even by Level 5 that long-distance reflexivization is possible.

So what is a teacher to do? Will negative evidence work? Is positive evidence enough? How can a teacher wade through and evaluate the literature? Assuming that methodology is not an issue in these studies, it is probably clear that negative evidence is sufficient in some cases but not in others; it is also clear that positive evidence will not suffice. But to see this, we must have a broad view of SLA which will allow us to evaluate the UG explanations and the more functional explanations for the asymmetry seen, for example, between English speakers learning Chinese and Chinese speakers learning English. And most importantly,

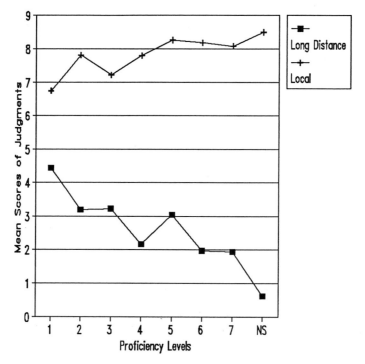

FIG. 1.1. Mean scores of judgments on local and long-distance reflexives by the seven EFL groups and native speakers of English.

we must have knowledge of how second languages are learned and consequently the tools for knowing how to test and interpret acquisition within a classroom setting. We must be able to understand that negative evidence, when dealing with learners' production of sentences, may necessitate corrective feedback, but when dealing with learners' interpretation of sentences, negative evidence may not be necessary.[2]

An additional aspect to be considered is the need for teachers to be trained to think about the nature of positive evidence. What evidence are learners exposed to? For example, with regard to adverb placement, theoretical predictions

[2]While it is beyond the scope of this chapter to provide an explanation for the differential behavior of Chinese- and English-speaking learners, a possible explanation may lie in the way general interpretation strategies are used by native speakers. English is a language highly governed by syntactic factors, whereas Chinese interpretation is more dependent on context. The reliance on context for interpretation may lead Chinese speakers to be able to use more contextual information in reflexive interpretation. English speakers, on the other hand, are not as easily able to "break free" from the syntactic constraints of language (for related arguments within the theoretical paradigm of the Competition Model, see Bates & MacWhinney, 1981; Gass, 1987; Harrington, 1987; Kilborn & Cooreman, 1987; Kilborn & Ito, 1989; Liu, Bates, & Li, 1992; MacWhinney, 1987; McDonald, 1987; McDonald & Heilenman, 1991; Sasaki, 1991; Wulfeck, Juarez, Bates, & Kilborn, 1986).

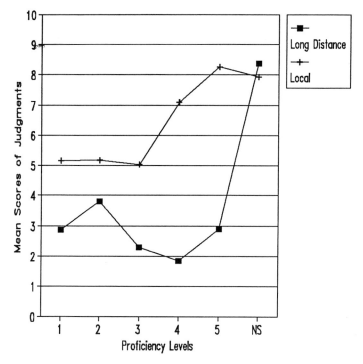

FIG. 1.2. Mean scores of judgments on local and long-distance reflexives by the five CFL groups and native speakers of Chinese.

are merely theoretical predictions; the reality of actual speech may be quite different, as was pointed out by Gass and Lakshmanan (1991) in a study of subject pronouns and by Lightbown and d'Anglejan (1985) in a study of textbook input versus actual native speaker usage.

  To take another example, consider input. Without a general picture of SLA, how can teachers evaluate the various claims about input? How can they evaluate the need for comprehensible input or input that is at the $i + 1$ level? How can they measure the claim for this need against the claim that what learners need is incomprehensible input, as White (1987) has claimed, or against the claim that non-understandings need to be created, as Varonis and Gass (1985) and Gass and Varonis (1994) have claimed? And what about input enhancement (Sharwood Smith, 1991, 1993)? Is there sufficient justification for form-focused instruction? What about VanPatten's (1995) notion of input processing—that is, "those strategies and mechanisms that promote form-meaning connections during comprehension" (VanPatten & Cadierno, 1993, p. 226)? At what point is it appropriate to provide instruction, and of what sort? Thus, understanding the nature of the SLA process leads one to ask the appropriate questions. Pedagogical theory or pedagogical practices not grounded in an understanding of SLA cannot hope to sort out the various pieces and place them in the context of the classroom and learners.

An important aspect of understanding the applicability of SLA research to the classroom comes from the area of replicability.[3] As Valdman (1993a, p. 505) stated:

> The way to more valid and reliable SLA research is through replication. Rerunning experimental studies under different conditions while maintaining central variables constant promises to eliminate much uncontrolled variance. If the same or another team of researchers fails to obtain nearly the same results on a second trial, then it may suspect that the key variables were not properly identified in the original study. In the case of naturalistic inquiry, replication neutralizes in large part the subjectivity inherent in this type of scientific endeavor. To be sure, in replication one loses the aura of glamour and the exhilaration of innovation. But it is a type of activity so basic to scientific inquiry and so prevalent in the so-called sciences that one wonders why it is so disdained in our field.

As a case in point, we consider the so-called Garden Path studies conducted by Tomasello and Herron (1988, 1989), Herron and Tomasello (1988, 1992), and Herron (1991). Their work was aimed at showing that explicit instruction, which could be a way of bringing a mismatch to a learner's attention, was beneficial only when that instruction occurred after a learner had been induced to make an error. Tomasello and Herron's goal was to determine the best point to deal with exceptions, to lay out the exception along with the rule itself, or to lay out the rule, allow the learner to make faulty generalizations (i.e., overgeneralizing), and then introduce the exception, thereby correcting the error made by means of a faulty generalization. The results showed that the second possibility led to more accurate results, that is, correction is more beneficial when learners are led down the garden path and are induced to make errors (with follow-up feedback) as opposed to being instructed on correct forms before making errors.

But what do teachers do with this information? We can imagine that these studies, most of which appeared in *French Language Review*, have become grist for the mill of those who want justification for correction. Although there may well be justification for correction in the classroom, it is not clear whether these studies provide the necessary justification. A familiarity with the SLA literature and an ability to evaluate research is once again critical. Not only are there numerous methodological difficulties that have been enumerated by Beck and Eubank (1991), there is an even more important difficulty, which teachers might discover on their own, and that is the problem of replication. Valdman (1993b) attempted to replicate the Garden Path studies. The fact that he was unable to achieve full replication is interesting from a number of perspectives. First, does

---

[3]An interesting step in recognizing the importance of replication in SLA is the newly created category of publications in the journal *Studies in Second Language Acquisition* titled "Replication Study." (See the editors' comments in 15:4 regarding the centrality of replication in understanding not only SL but also learning in a classroom setting.)

it mean that the garden path technique is not appropriate and that by using it teachers are in fact leading learners down another garden path? Teachers need to have the background to measure what is happening in the classroom against research findings. Is there something about the linguistic structures that were tested that might make replication difficult? Is there something about the methodology that was flawed? But equally as important is the question of how we evaluate the replication. How do we know when we have the right answer? Or are we between a rock and a hard place? As Diane Larsen-Freeman asked at the colloquium at which Valdman's data were presented, when we do replication, which one is the right answer? Do we need two out of three? Is it the best of five? The best of seven? With whom should replication be conducted? The same subjects? Comparable subjects? Of course, there are no easy answers. But teachers must have sufficient background to be able to evaluate the research that has been done. They need to be sensitive to the vagaries of research in the social sciences and to be sensitive to the students themselves and the classroom setting. They need to understand the fluid nature of research; and perhaps most important is the need to understand that SLA is at present in an exploration stage and, importantly, to understand the nature of exploration and their own role in contributing to that exploration.

4. SLA AS A PREDICTOR

Clearly, it would be ideal if SLA research could tell us where we can expect particular linguistic phenomena to take place. That is, are there stages that we can point to? Are these stages inviolable? What role does the native language play? How do UG principles relate to classroom practices? All of these have been debated extensively in the literature. But the responses are not always uniform. Where I think that SLA research may be able to make predictions is in the area of universals, but these would be universals in which structures are intrinsically related. This might involve either of two kinds of universals, functional universals or UG-based universals.

Gass and Ard (1984) proposed a framework for predicting the impact that certain kinds of universals would have on second language acquisition. We argued that universals that involve structural relatedness should have an effect on acquisition. Looking at this within a UG domain, we would argue that properties that cluster together in certain parameters should be ones that affect acquisition. I would like to extend this by arguing that these are precisely the areas that may be most amenable to pedagogical intervention and that pedagogical intervention may in fact be a means of manipulating structures to determine their relatedness (cf. Eckman, 1992, for similar arguments).

As I mentioned earlier, I believe the language classroom provides a shortcut for learners; it is also a place where information can be made available to learners in a digestible format or in a format that may not be available outside of the classroom. In this view, pedagogical research needs to understand which of learners' natural capabilities can be capitalized on in the classroom as they cannot be capitalized on outside of the classroom. Let me illustrate this with by now familiar SLA research, research on the Accessibility Hierarchy, which orders relative clause types into an implicational relationship (cf. Gass, 1979).

The question to be considered is: What would happen if through instruction a learner learned a more difficult relative clause position before learning an easier one. Would knowledge of the more difficult relative clause construction include knowledge of the easier relative clause positions? That would not be unexpected, because in some sense knowledge of a more difficult structure should incorporate knowledge of a related easier structure. There have been studies that lend support to this prediction. In Gass (1982), two groups of second language learners were given specific instructions on relative clauses. One group was instructed on subject and direct object relatives and the second group on the more difficult object-of-preposition relatives. After the period of instruction, both groups were tested on all relative clause types. The group that had received subject and direct object instruction only performed well on those two relative clause types but no others; the second group, however, performed well not only on the relative clauses they had been instructed on (object of preposition) but also on the relative clauses higher on the accessibility hierarchy (but not those that are lower).

A study by Eckman, Bell, and Nelson (1988) had similar findings. In their study there were four groups of learners, a control group and three experimental groups, each of which received instructions on one of three relative clause types: subject, direct object, and object of preposition. There were improvements for the three types of relative clauses, but the greatest improvement occurred in the group that was given instruction on the lowest position (the object-of-preposition group). The group with the next greatest improvement was the direct object group, and then the subject group, although the subject group showed greater improvement than the direct object group on the relative clauses on which they had been given instruction (subjects). Both of these studies suggest that learners' maximum generalization occurs from more marked structures to less marked ones. Generalization from less marked to more marked does not occur. Thus, in situations in which there is structural relatedness, acquisition relatedness also occurs. But does this mean that this should be directly translated into classroom practices? I don't think there is any great danger of this happening, because I have not seen massive changes in textbook orientation. But studies always beget studies, and this is no exception. Hamilton (1994, and this volume) continued and refined this line of investigation, finding that the domain of markedness generalization is limited to linguistic implicational hierarchies, exactly what I would predict and what Eckman's (1992) paper argues.

I argued earlier that the area of universals where implicational hierarchies dominate sheds light on the nature of second language acquisition. I am not suggesting that the area of UG related research where implicational hierarchies are not prevalent is not relevant. To the contrary, the area of parameters where properties cluster is a fruitful area of investigation for classroom research. The difficulty, as White (this volume) points out, is that parameters are not always stable. Nevertheless, I suggest that there are two types of parametric clusterings to be considered: those in which the properties are superficially related and those in which they are not. Given the model set forth in Gass and Ard (1984), we may predict that those parameters in which the properties are superficially related would have a greater effect on acquisition than those parameters in which the properties are not superficially related. In the same vein, the former would be more susceptible to pedagogical intervention as we have seen with relative clauses than the latter. There is some evidence that this is the case. In earlier research on what was known as the Pro-Drop parameter (White, 1985), a number of linguistic properties that were structurally unrelated were investigated. When these properties were looked at in a second language context, it appeared that they did not cluster in acquisition. Similarly, research by White (1991) on acquisition of adverb placement and questions suggests that instruction on questions does not affect adverb placement despite the fact that these structures are theoretically unified under the verb-raising parameter. This is precisely what would be predicted in the Gass and Ard model, because only overt structural relatedness is predicted to result in acquisition relatedness.[4]

The picture, however, is not as clear as it might be. White (this volume) discusses preliminary results from her research on reflexives. Both of the properties that she investigates (binding with subjects and long-distance binding) have to do with the interpretation of reflexives, so I would predict that they would co-occur in acquisition and that instruction on one would generalize to the other. Unfortunately, she did not find this in her preliminary results.

So far I have argued that language teachers do need a grounding in SLA, but if it is to be relevant to the classroom the grounding must be broad-based, given the multifaceted nature of the language classroom. I have also argued that the primary value of an SLA course lies in the intellectual background it provides teachers, enabling them to evaluate research rather than to apply it uncritically. This is not to say that we should return to the days when SLA researchers would feel compelled to tell practitioners what the implications were for the language classroom, for this leads to the uncritical acceptance by practitioners of research results. Rather, what I am arguing is that teachers need to have the tools to determine whether research findings are applicable.

---

[4]This is not to say that disparate parametric properties will never be learned, for this is clearly not the case. It only suggests that they will not be linked together in acquisition.

5. CONCLUSION

To return to the main purpose of this paper: Do teachers need an SLA course? They certainly do. But not all SLA courses are created equal, so what kind of course? I would argue that it is one that allows them to play the doubting game (Larsen-Freeman, 1983); one that allows them to question and evaluate SLA research and to decide whether it is applicable to the classroom; one that allows them to understand that there are different people in the classroom with different ways of approaching the process of learning. Although the SLA literature may tell us that negative evidence is necessary, that positive evidence is necessary, that grammar restructuring takes place, that language use becomes more automatic, and that indirect negative evidence is an inductive process (see Plough, 1994), it doesn't tell us how this relates to individuals. Teachers and researchers need to work in tandem to determine how SLA findings can be evaluated and be made applicable to a classroom situation, and to determine which SLA findings to use. Teachers need to have the foundation to do this in order to ask the right questions.

I have argued elsewhere (Gass, 1993) that to ensure the vitality of the field, SLA research must be relevant to something. This is not a novel idea. Many have argued that SLA research has important contributions to make to an understanding of the nature of language and human cognition. Yet despite our efforts, our general message does not appear to have extended beyond the parochial borders of second language teaching and second language acquisition. As Flynn and O'Neil noted, "the scope of linguistic theory remains unnecessarily limited due to the lack of integration of this significant body of data [SLA] into the mainstream of linguistic thought" (1988, p. 1). In a recent paper, Schachter (1993) argued cogently that the field of SLA needs to contribute to the field of language teaching. She pointed out that we have the opportunity "to shape language learning situations, language teaching approaches and classroom teacher/learner behaviours" (p. 180). I agree that this is the case, but believe that the field of SLA can contribute to this debate only if teachers themselves take an active role in the process and understand the issues surrounding acquisition. As Schachter suggested, "the most fruitful interactions come about when the concerns of second language teachers and second language researchers coincide" (p. 181). And there are many places where the concerns of both groups are the same: The issue of correction and negative evidence is one, the issue of individual differences is another, the issue of generalizations in grammatical acquisition is yet another, and the list goes on. It is my long-standing belief that teachers need SLA research and SLA research needs teachers.

Schachter characterizes the relationship as one resembling a Necker cube. Some see the field of Second Language Studies one way,[5] considering only the

---

[5]I use the term *second language studies* deliberately, rather than second language acquisition, because the term more aptly characterizes the intersection and the shared theoretical and practical concerns of both fields.

pedagogical implications, some see it another way seeing only the theoretical value, but both perspectives are there, and they are merely perspectives.

Our field touches on many areas of inquiry. Perhaps we have been overly concerned with the necessity of achieving "intellectual standing" with those scholars that count in academia and have thereby distanced ourselves from those in education. This has resulted in our not fully considering the rich possibilities of collaborative endeavors with language teachers. After all, as Schachter (1993, pp. 180–181) noted:

> The study of SLA is derived from the study of human behaviour. Models of SLA attempt to characterize what human beings do when in an SLA environment and why they do the things they do; as in first language acquisition, these models must make the correct predictions about what second language learners have available to them in terms of knowledge sources and learning procedures at the outset of the acquisition process. They must also make predictions consistent with what we know learner grammars are like at intermediate stages. Finally, they must offer us at least some insights on why SLA is not universally successful.
>
> What better place to observe people learning languages than in the classroom? The language classroom has been and should continue to be our experimental laboratory. It can be and should be the place where theory and practice have the most fruitful interaction, where our hypotheses can be tested and accepted, rejected or modified. Language classrooms are also the logical place for application to inform and shape theory development itself. In order for us to do this, we must request involvement from classroom teachers. We must inform them about the bases for particular hypotheses. We must interact with them in the development of appropriate teaching and testing materials. We must listen to them as they provide us with feedback on how the experiments have progressed and as they offer suggestions on making them more effective. We need to create a mindset in which both teachers and researchers view classroom as laboratories where theory and practice can interact to make both better practice and better theory.

This cannot be done unless both teachers and researchers have an understanding of the goals and needs of the other's field. Pedagogy cannot wait until SLA theory has it all worked out; SLA theory cannot wait until teachers have it all worked out. Teaching is by necessity constant experimentation, and teachers are therefore constant researchers. Teachers and researchers need to have a dialogue and SLA is the common language of that dialogue.

REFERENCES

Bates, E., and B. MacWhinney (1981). "Second Language Acquisition from a Functionalist Perspective: Pragmatics, Semantics, and Perceptual Strategies," *Annals of the New York Academy of Sciences Conference on Native Language and Foreign Language Acquisition*, ed. by H. Winitz, pp. 190–214. New York: New York Academy of Sciences.

Beck, M., and L. Eubank. (1991). "Acquisition Theory and Experimental Design: A Critique of Tomasello and Herron," *Studies in Second Language Acquisition* 13, 73–76.

Bickerton, D. (1983). Foreword. *A Longitudinal Study of the Acquisition of English*, ed. by T. Huebner. Ann Arbor, MI: Karoma.

Corder, S. P. (1967). "The Significance of Learners' Errors," *International Review of Applied Linguistics* 5, 161–170.

Eckman, F. (1992). "Secondary Languages or Second-Language Acquisition: A Linguistic Approach," Paper presented at the Second Language Research Forum, Michigan State University, East Lansing.

———, L. Bell, and D. Nelson. (1988). "On the Generalization of Relative Clause Instruction in the Acquisition of English as a Second Language," *Applied Linguistics* 9 (1), 1–20.

Ellis, R. (1993). "The Structural Syllabus and Second Language Acquisition," *TESOL Quarterly* 27 (1), 91–113.

Flynn, S. (1990). "Theory, Practice, and Research: Strange or Blissful Bedfellows?" *Georgetown University Round Table on Languages and Linguistics 1990: Linguistics, language teaching, and language acquisition: The interdependence of theory, practice, and research*, ed. by J. Alatis, pp. 112–122. Washington, DC: Georgetown University Press.

———. (1991). "The Relevance of Linguistic Theory for Language Pedagogy: Debunking the Myths," *Georgetown University Round Table on Languages and Linguistics 1991*, ed. by J. Alatis, pp. 547–554. Washington, D.C.: Georgetown University Press.

———, and W. O'Neil (eds.) (1988). *Linguistic Theory in Second Language Acquisition*. Dordrecht: Kluwer Academic Publishers.

Freeman, D. (1989). "Teacher Training, Development, and Decisionmaking: A Model of Teaching and Related Strategies for Language Teacher Education," *TESOL Quarterly* 23 (1), 27–45.

Gass, S. (1979). "Language Transfer and Universal Grammatical Relations." *Language Learning* 29 (2), 327–344.

Gass, S. (1982). "From Theory to Practice," *On TESOL '81*, ed. by M. Hines and W. Rutherford, pp. 129–139. Washington, DC: TESOL.

———. (1987). "The Resolution of Conflicts Among Competing Systems: A Bidirectional Perspective," *Applied Psycholinguistics* 8, 329–350.

———. (1993). "Second Language Acquisition: Past, Present and Future." *Second Language Research* 9 (2), 99–117.

———, and J. Ard. (1984). "L2 Acquisition and the Ontology of Language Universals," *Second Language Acquisition and Language Universals*, ed. by W. Rutherford, pp. 33–68. Amsterdam: John Benjamins.

———, and U. Lakshmanan. (1991). "Accounting for Interlanguage Subject Pronouns," *Second Language Research* 7 (3), 181–203.

———, and E. Varonis. (1994). "Input, Interaction, and Second Language Production," *Studies in Second Language Acquisition* 16 (3), 288–302.

Hamilton, R. (1994). "How Can Second Language Instruction Generalize to Forms Not Taught? Constraints on Implicational Generalization," *Language Learning* 44 (1), 123–157.

Harrington, M. (1987). "Processing Transfer: Language-Specific Strategies as a Source of Interlanguage Variation." *Applied Psycholinguistics* 8, 351–378.

Hatch, E. (1979). "Apply with Caution," *Studies in Second Language Acquisition* 2 (1), 123–143.

Herron, C. (1991). "The Garden Path Correction Strategy in the Foreign Language Classroom," *French Review* 64, 966–977.

———, and M. Tomasello. (1988). "Learning Grammatical Structures in a Foreign Language: Modelling Versus Feedback," *French Review* 61, 910–922.

———. (1992). "Acquiring Grammatical Structures by Guided Induction," *French Review* 65, 708–718.

Huebner, T., and C. Ferguson (eds.) (1991). *Crosscurrents in Second Language Acquisition and Linguistic Theories*. Amsterdam: John Benjamins.

Kilborn, K., and A. Cooreman. (1987). "Sentence Interpretation Strategies in Adult Dutch-English Bilinguals," *Applied Psycholinguistics* 8, 415–431.

——, and T. Ito. (1989). "Sentence Processing Strategies in Adult Bilinguals," *The Linguistic Study of Sentence Processing*, ed. by B. MacWhinney and E. Bates, pp. 257–291. Cambridge: Cambridge University Press.

Larsen-Freeman, D. (1983). *Second Language Studies*, ed. by K. Bailey, M. Long, and S. Peck, pp. 3–22. Rowley, MA: Newbury House.

Lightbown, P. (1985). "Great Expectations: Second Language Acquisition and Classroom Teaching," *Applied Linguistics* 6, 173–189.

——, and A. d'Anglejan. (1985). "Some Input Considerations for Word Order in French L1 and L2 Acquisition." *Input in Second Language Acquisition*, ed. by S. Gass and C. Madden, pp. 415–430. Rowley, MA: Newbury House.

Liu, H., E. Bates, and P. Li. (1992). "Sentence Interpretation in Bilingual Speakers of English and Chinese," *Applied Psycholinguistics* 13, 451–484.

MacWhinney, B. (1987). "Applying the Competition Model to Bilingualism," *Applied Psycholinguistics* 8, 315–327.

McDonald, J. (1987). "Sentence Interpretation in Bilingual Speakers of English and Dutch," *Applied Psycholinguistics* 8, 379–415.

——, and L. K. Heilenman. (1991). "Determinants of Cue Strength in Adult First and Second Language Speakers of French," *Applied Psycholinguistics* 12 (3), 313–348.

Maurer, S. (1987). "New Knowledge About Errors and New Views About Learners: What They Mean to Educators and More Educators Would Like to Know," *Cognitive Science and Mathematics Education*, ed. by A. Schoenfeld, pp. 165–187. Hillsdale, NJ: Lawrence Erlbaum Associates.

Newmeyer, F., and S. Weinberger. (1988). "The Ontogenesis of the Field of Second Language Learning Research," *Linguistic Theory in Second Language Acquisition*, ed. by S. Flynn and W. O'Neil, pp. 34–45. Dordrecht: Kluwer Academic Press.

Plough, I. (1994). "A Role for Indirect Negative Evidence in Second Language Acquisition." PhD dissertation, Michigan State University.

Sasaki, Y. (1991). "English and Japanese Interlanguage Comprehension Strategies: An Analysis Based on the Competition Model," *Applied Psycholinguistics* 12, 47–73.

Schachter, J. (1993). "Second Language Acquisition: Perceptions and Possibilities," *Second Language Research* 9 (2), 173–187.

Sharwood Smith, M. (1991). "Speaking to Many Minds: On the Relevance of Different Types of Language Information for the L2 Learner," *Second Language Research* 7 (2), 118–132.

——. (1993). "Input Enhancement in Instructed SLA: Theoretical Bases," *Studies in Second Language Acquisition* 15 (2), 165–179.

Spada, N., and P. Lightbown. (1993). "Instruction and the Development of Questions in L2 Classrooms," *Studies in Second Language Acquisition* 15 (2), 205–224.

Tomasello, M., and C. Herron. (1988). "Down the Garden Path: Inducing and Correcting Overgeneralization Errors in the Foreign Language Classroom," *Applied Psycholinguistics* 9, 237–246.

——. (1989). "Feedback for Language Transfer Errors: The Garden Path Technique," *Studies in Second Language Acquisition* 11, 385–395.

Trahey, M., and L. White. (1993). "Positive Evidence and Preemption in the Second Language Classroom," *Studies in Second Language Acquisition* 15 (2), 181–204.

Valdman, A. (1993a). "Editorial," *Studies in Second Language Acquisition* 15 (4), 505.

——. (1993b, August). "Foreign Language Classroom Learning Research: Apply with Caution!," Paper presented at Colloquium on Classroom Research, Association Internationale de Linguistique Appliquée (AILA), Amsterdam.

VanPatten, B. (1995). "Cognitive Aspects of Input Processing and Second Language Acquisition: On the Relationship Between Form and Meaning," *Studies in Language Learning and Spanish Linguistics in Honor of Tracy D. Terrell*, ed. by P. Hasheimpour, R. Maldonado, and M. van Naerssen, pp. 170–183. New York: McGraw-Hill.

————, and T. Cadierno. (1993). "Explicit Instruction and Input Processing," *Studies in Second Language Acquisition* 15 (2), 225–243.

Varonis, E., and S. Gass. (1985). "The Comprehensibility of Non-Native Speech: A Model for Negotiation of Meaning," *Applied Linguistics* 6 (1), 71–90.

White, L. (1985). "The 'Pro-drop' Parameter in Adult Second Language Acquisition," *Language Learning* 35, 47–62.

————. (1987). "Against Comprehensible Input: The Input Hypothesis and the Development of L2 Competence," *Applied Linguistics* 8, 95–110.

————. (1991). "Adverb Placement in Second Language Acquisition: Some Effects of Positive and Negative Evidence in the Classroom," *Second Language Research* 7 (2), 133–161.

————, N. Spada, P. Lightbown, and L. Ranta. (1991). "Input Enhancement and L2 Question Formation," *Applied Linguistics* 12, 416–432.

Wulfeck, B., L. Juarez, E. Bates, and I. Kilborn. (1986). "Sentence Interpretation Strategies in Healthy and Aphasic Bilingual Adults," *Language Processing in Bilinguals: Psycholinguistics and Neurological Perspectives*, ed. by J. Vaid. Hillsdale, NJ: Lawrence Erlbaum Associates.

Yuan, B. (1992). "Long Distance and Short Distance Reflexives in Second Language Acquisition," Unpublished manuscript, University of Edinburgh.

Chapter 2

Reenvisioning the Second Language Classroom: A Vygotskian Approach

Linda Schinke-Llano
Millikin University, Decatur, Illinois

1. INTRODUCTION

According to the late Soviet semiotician and psychologist L. S. Vygotsky (1896–1934), play enables a child to become what he or she is not; it creates a zone of proximal development (ZPD) in which the child explores not-yet-acquired adult roles and values that are socioculturally appropriate (1978). As such, play precedes development. In the following pages, I invite all of us to "play," to explore our individual and collective zones of proximal development for the teaching of second languages in the hope that we can collaboratively reenvision the second language classroom. By reexamining the purpose of second language teaching and learning—specifically the roles of teachers and students and the relationships between them—we can, in turn, better understand the nature of activity that needs to exist both within the classroom and beyond.

Admittedly, recommendations of a review or change of classroom practices are neither new nor unique. In general education, for example, people have suggested fewer teacher-fronted activities, and we have witnessed the advent of cooperative learning and the whole-language approach to reading. In second language education, we have been told to abandon drills and to focus on the learners, providing them with as many opportunities as possible for interaction, specifically negotiated interaction. Although presumably both our general education classes and our second language classes are the better for such innovations, there is a sense that we still lack a framework that is consistent, coherent, and cohesive enough to encompass all that we know or think we know about the second language acquisition (SLA) process.

1.1. Vygotskian Concepts

One theory that offers great potential for providing these needed qualities is that forwarded by Vygotsky and his followers. Although their analysis of cognitive and linguistic development is not new, its applicability to SLA theory and practice has only recently begun to be explored (see Schinke-Llano, 1993). In order for one to appreciate fully the significance of Vygotskian thought to the SLA process, several concepts need to be elaborated. First and foremost, this is a sociocultural theory; it holds that human development cannot be viewed independently of its social context. Rather, development occurs as the result of meaningful verbal interaction, that is, of dialogic relationships between novices and experts in the environment, be they parents, older peers, or teachers (Vygotsky, 1962, 1978). The theory recognizes the nonlinear nature of development: Learners both progress and regress as they develop. It focuses on processes and changes, not on products and states; and it acknowledges that each stage of development subsumes the previous one and that potentially development never ceases.

Critical to this development is the notion of the zone of proximal development, mentioned earlier, which is "the distance between the actual developmental level as determined by independent problem solving and the level of potential development as determined through problem solving under adult guidance or in collaboration with peers" (Vygotsky, 1978, p. 86). In order for learners to progress through the ZPD, they must move from *object-regulation* (a stage in which the facts of the environment control the learner) to *other-regulation* (in which an "expert" mediates by providing strategies) and finally to *self-regulation* (in which the learner controls the activity) (Wertsch, 1979).[1] Important to the emergence of self-regulation is the use of private speech (or private dialogue, as Wertsch, 1980 refers to it); such vocalized inner speech surfaces in times of psychic stress and represents an effort on the part of the individual to regain control of the task situation (McCafferty, 1992, 1993).[2] As a learner progresses from object-regulation to other-regulation to self-regulation, the activity thus moves from an interpsychological plane to an intrapsychological plane. In fact, as Vygotsky claims, "Every function in the child's cultural development appears twice: first, on the social, and later on the individual level; first, *between* people (*interpsychological*) and then *inside* the child (*intrapsychological*)" (1978, p. 57). Inherent in this view of development is the notion that thought and language are not "inner and outer manifestations of the same mental phenomenon, but really two distinct cognitive operations that grow together uniquely in the human animal" (Fredericks, 1974, p. 283).

---

[1]Examples of these stages include a child's attempting to put together a puzzle but instead using the pieces as play soldiers or objects to throw in the air (object-regulation); the mother's telling the child where to put each piece (other-regulation); and the child's putting the puzzle together without assistance (self-regulation).

[2]In the example given in Footnote 1, the child may use private speech, such as "The red piece goes there," to aid his or her self-regulation.

2. CLASSROOM APPLICATIONS

If we extrapolate the concepts just discussed to the topic of our focus—second language acquisition—we can readily accept Tharp and Gallimore's claim that "teaching can be said to occur when assistance is offered at points in the ZPD at which performance requires assistance" (1988, p. 31). Thus, our task as second language instructors is not to deliver to learners tidy bundles of information on the subjunctive in Spanish, the *passé simple* in French, or irregular verbs in English. In other words, to use Freire's (1970) analogy, we are not to use the "banking" approach to teaching; we should not view ourselves as depositors of informational currency in the empty accounts of students' minds. Rather, as second language instructors, we need to view our classroom as the social organization that it is (Gallimore & Tharp, 1990), and we need to participate in dialogic activity with learners so that they may achieve cognitive and linguistic self-regulation in ways that are socioculturally appropriate.[3] In short, our task is to enable learners to find their "voice, their speaking personality, the[ir] speaking consciousness" (Holquist & Emerson, 1981, p. 434). Thus, "learning a language, first or second, is the struggle to construct one's *voice*" (Lantolf, 1993).[4] Said another way, our job is not to teach ESL or Russian or Swahili as an object but rather to enable learners to participate in dialogic activity using ESL or Russian or Swahili as a tool.

At first glance, this recommended change seems merely semantic, the replacement of one set of labels by another. On further analysis, I believe the change represents pervasive differences in conceptualization. Similarly, on a theoretical level, these ideas may seem both attractive and plausible; on a practical level, however, they may appear daunting. Admittedly, an "easier said than done" reaction is understandable. Fortunately, a growing body of evidence from both first and second language development suggests that teaching and learning based on Vygotskian concepts are not only possible but highly effective and therefore desirable.

2.1. First Language Evidence

First language evidence that Vygotskian-based activities promote desired learning comes to us from several countries and from several areas of linguistic and cognitive development. In reading, for example, Clay and Cazden reported the success of the Reading Recovery program in New Zealand in which interactional support "maximize[s] the growth of the child's intrapsychological functioning"

---

[3]Note that the term *dialogue* is not employed, lest the traditional L2 activity of memorizing a previously written interchange be thought of. Rather, a dialogic activity is one in which two interlocutors engage in meaningful communication, the purpose of which is to move the interlocutor of lesser ability to a higher level in the ZPD through mediation from the more skilled interlocutor.

[4]For a discussion of voice, see Bakhtin (1981, 1984, 1986) and Wertsch (1991).

(1990, p. 219). Because of its tenet that oral as well as written language is learned best in context of use, the whole language approach to reading utilizes what is, in essence, a Vygotskian emphasis on the mediational role of the teacher and the increasingly independent role of the learner (Goodman & Goodman, 1990). Evidence of the viability of Vygotskian concepts in the development of children's writing, which Vygotsky designated a "complex cultural activity" (1978, p. 118) comes from McLane's (1990) study of an after-school program for low-income inner-city children, aged 6 to 8; McNamee's (1990) work with Head Start children and their parents; and Moll and Greenburg's (1990) case studies of the social histories of two households. Additionally, work done with 3rd through 5th grade social science students in Denmark demonstrates that the use of materials that are sensitive to the learners' ZPDs and that acknowledge individual differences in both rate and manner of learning results in qualitative changes to their problem-solving capabilities (Hedegaard, 1990).

2.2. Second Language Evidence

In addition to first language evidence, we now have an emerging body of second language literature, both supportive of and demonstrative of the efficacy of Vygotskian concepts in achieving desired learning. Van Lier in his writings on contingency, for example, incorporated Vygotskian thought when he claimed that the quality of contingency in conversation is essential for the alteration of social interaction to language development (1992; see also van Lier, 1993). In their study of bilingual dictionary accessing skills of university students at three levels in Spanish, Lantolf, Labarca, and den Tuinder (1985) demonstrated that bilingual dictionaries are of pedagogical use only to students at a self-regulatory stage of development. In a more recent study, Lantolf and Aljaafreh (1993) examined the effects of negative feedback in second language acquisition and report a developmental progression in the learners from other-regulation to self-regulation. Similar movement is seen in the use of private speech by second language learners (McCafferty, 1992, 1993). Finally, studies conducted on both first- and second-language learners argue that overregulation on the part of teachers engaged in joint cognitive activities precludes the achievement of self-regulation for the learners (Schinke-Llano, 1986, 1994).

2.3. Additional Considerations

Because most of the studies just cited focus on the teacher, a likely reaction is this: Realistically how can one teacher in a class with numerous students possibly attend to each one's current ZPD and enter into dialogic activity on an individual basis? In short, because class size militates against such tailor-made approaches, what is the well-intentioned second language instructor to do? Fortunately, mounting evidence shows that both peer teaching and collaborative learning are viable complements to teacher-student dialogic activity. Certainly Vygotsky (1978) recognized the value of dialogic activity between a learner and a more competent peer. Forman and Cazden (1985) further pointed out that not only does the novice benefit from dialogue with a more experienced peer, but the tutor also benefits because explaining helps to internalize knowledge.

In peer collaboration, although scant research exists regarding the intellectual benefits to the participants, Perret-Clermont (1980) hypothesized that peer work creates cognitive conflict which fosters cognitive restructuring and growth. Tudge (1990) recommended the use of peer collaboration, because in the process of joint problem-solving activity, culturally appropriate development occurs.

If we accept the concept that the purpose of teaching is to enable learners to progress through their ZPDs, to move from functioning on an interpsychological plane to functioning on an intrapsychological plane, then it behooves us to reconsider the potential benefits of other kinds of activities beyond the usual teacher-student interaction or even peer tutoring or peer collaboration. Activities outside the classroom, such as obtaining information from teachers or other students or interviewing community members, take on new significance in a Vygotskian framework. Certainly many second language teachers already incorporate such activities into their repertoire but often solely so students may "get practice" or "meet native speakers." In a Vygotskian paradigm, such activities enable the learner to utilize the new language as a tool in the process of becoming self-regulatory. Further, although I know of no research using a Vygotskian approach to analyze the benefits of interactional video and interactional software programs, such research would be useful. Finally, given this reconceptualization of the second language classroom, we need to reconsider assessment. Rather than evaluating achievement, namely, the lower boundary of the ZPD, we need to focus on measuring the amount of assistance necessary when learners face problem-solving activities selected from higher in their ZPDs (Brown & Ferrara, 1985). The more assistance needed, that is, the more other regulation needed, the more distant the learner is from achieving self-regulation in the activity designated and the less advanced the learner is in second-language development; in contrast, the less mediation needed, the more self-regulating the learner is and the more advanced in second-language development.

3. CONCLUSION

Grappling with Vygotskian theory can sometimes be frustrating, much like dealing with a video camera that slips in and out of focus. On the one hand, haven't we already been doing appropriate activities in our second language classrooms—namely, peer work, small-group activities, and "beyond the classroom" work? On the other hand, isn't it impossible to conceive of a classroom in which each learner's ZPD is measurable, much like a daily barometer reading? The answer to both queries is affirmative. As I have claimed elsewhere (Schinke-Llano, 1993), key aspects of our current SLA theory, such as Krashen's (1982) $i + 1$, Long's (1980) negotiated interaction, and the more recent focus on task-based learning, are indeed compatible with a Vygotskian approach. Nevertheless, work in general education highlights the challenges of constructing and implementing individual assessment plans. I would argue, however, that reenvisioning the second language classroom from a Vygotskian perspective is both logical and efficacious. As I have stated, Vygotskian theory is sociocultural; as such, it subsumes SLA theories that are solely linguistic and acknowledges the inherent social nature of the classroom itself. Not only is the theory developmental but it also recognizes the ebb and flow of linguistic and cognitive development; it goes beyond those theories that focus on the linearity of development or that view language acquisition as the learning of discrete elements. Although we have evidence from both the Baby Talk and the Foreigner Talk literature that more competent speakers accommodate their speech to those perceived to be less competent, there are also claims that overaccommodation or prolonged accommodation (i.e., other-regulation) can negatively affect both cognitive and linguistic development. An excellent means of both monitoring and preventing those tendencies is to keep ourselves ever cognizant of our purpose and role as instructors—to enable learners to move from other-regulation to self-regulation. Such a focus, in turn, helps clarify the utility of various activities, both inside and outside the classroom, and of assessment procedures.

As Tharp and Gallimore claim, "teachers, like their students, have ZPDs" (1988, p. 190). As second language instructors in social interaction with one another, we can collectively move through our own zones of proximal development and, as a result, better enable our second language learners to move through theirs. We can provide them with the tools necessary to develop their unique voices in their second language and culture.

ACKNOWLEDGMENT

I would like to thank Millikin University, whose Hardy Distinguished Professorship of English allowed me the release time to write this paper in addition to working on various other projects.

REFERENCES

Bakhtin, M. (1981). *The Dialogic Imagination: Four Essays by M. M. Bakhtin*, ed. by M. Holquist, trans. by C. Emerson and M. Holquist. Austin: University of Texas Press.
———. (1984). *Problems of Dostoevsky's Poetics*, trans. by C. Emerson. Minneapolis: University of Minnesota Press.

———. (1986). *Speech Genres and Other Late Essays*, ed. by C. Emerson and M. Holquist, trans. by V. W. McGee. Austin: University of Texas Press.

Brown, A., and R. Ferrara. (1985). "Diagnosing Zones of Proximal Development." *Culture, Communication, and Cognition: Vygotskian Perspectives*, ed. by J. Wertsch. Cambridge: Cambridge University Press.

Clay, M., and C. Cazden. (1990). "A Vygotskian Interpretation of Reading Recovery." *Vygotsky and Education: Instructional Implications and Applications of Sociohistorical Psychology*, ed. by L. Moll. Cambridge: Cambridge University Press.

Forman, E., and C. Cazden. (1985). "Exploring Vygotskian Perspectives in Education: The Cognitive Value of Peer Interaction." *Culture, Communication, and Cognition: Vygotskian Perspectives*, ed. by J. Wertsch. Cambridge: Cambridge University Press.

Fredericks, S. (1974). "Vygotsky on Language Skills." *Classical World* 67, 283–290.

Freire, P. (1970). *Pedagogy of the Oppressed*. New York: Seabury.

Gallimore, R., and R. Tharp. (1990). "Teaching Mind in Society: Teaching, Schooling, and Literate Discourse." *Vygotsky and Education: Instructional Implications and Applications of Sociohistorical Psychology*, ed. by L. Moll. Cambridge: Cambridge University Press.

Goodman, Y., and K. Goodman. (1990). "Vygotsky in a Whole-Language Perspective." *Vygotsky and Education: Instructional Implications and Applications of Sociohistorical Psychology*, ed. by L. Moll. Cambridge: Cambridge University Press.

Hedegaard, M. (1990). "The Zone of Proximal Development as Basis for Instruction." *Vygotsky and Education: Instructional Implications and Applications of Sociohistorical Psychology*, ed. by L. Moll. Cambridge: Cambridge University Press.

Holquist, M., and C. Emerson. (1981). Glossary for *The Dialogic Imagination: Four Essays by M. M. Bakhtin*, ed. by M. Holquist, trans. by M. Holquist and C. Emerson. Austin: University of Texas Press.

Krashen, S. (1982). *Principles and Practice in Second Language Acquisition*. Oxford: Pergamon.

Lantolf, J. (1993). "Sociocultural Theory and the Second Language Classroom: The Lesson of Strategic Interaction." Paper presented at the Georgetown University Roundtable of Linguistics, Washington, DC.

———, and A. Aljaafreh. (1993). "Negative Feedback and L2 Learning in the Zone of Proximal Development." Paper presented at the American Association for Applied Linguistics Conference, Atlanta, Georgia.

———, A. Labarca, and J. den Tuinder. (1985). "Strategies for Accessing Bilingual Dictionaries: A Question of Regulation." *Hispania* 68, 858–864.

Long, M. (1980). *Input, Interaction, and Second Language Acquisition*. Ph.D. dissertation, University of California, Los Angeles.

McCafferty, S. (1992). "The Use of Private Speech by Adult Second Language Learners: A Cross-Cultural Study." *Modern Language Journal* 76, 179–189.

———. (1993). "A Sociocultural Approach to Private Speech." Paper presented at the American Association for Applied Linguistics Conference, Atlanta, Georgia.

McLane, J. (1990). "Writing as a Social Process." *Vygotsky and Education: Instructional Implications and Applications of Sociohistorical Psychology*, ed. by L. Moll. Cambridge: Cambridge University Press.

McNamee, G. (1990). "Learning to Read and Write in an Inner-City Setting: A Longitudinal Study of Community Change." *Vygotsky and Education: Instructional Implications and Applications of Sociohistorical Psychology*, ed. by L. Moll. Cambridge: Cambridge University Press.

Moll, L., and J. Greenberg. (1990). "Creating Zones of Proximal Development." *Vygotsky and Education: Instructional Implications and Applications of Sociohistorical Psychology*, ed. by L. Moll. Cambridge: Cambridge University Press.

Perret-Clermont, A. (1980). *Social Interaction and Cognitive Development in Children*. New York: Academic Press.

Schinke-Llano, L. (1986). "Foreigner Talk in Joint Cognitive Activities." *Talking to Learn: Conversation in Second Language Acquisition*, ed. by R. Day. Rowley, MA: Newbury House.

———. (1993). "On the Value of a Vygotskian Framework for SLA Theory and Research." *Language Learning* 43, 121–129.

———. (1994). "Linguistic Accommodation with LEP and LD Children." *Vygotskian Approaches to Second Language Research*, ed. by J. Lantolf and G. Appel. Norwood, NJ: Ablex.

Tharp, R., and R. Gallimore. (1988). *Rousing Minds to Life: Teaching, Learning, and Schooling in Social Context*. Cambridge: Cambridge University Press.

Tudge, J. (1990). "Vygotsky, the Zone of Proximal Development, and Peer Collaboration: Implications for Classroom Practice." *Vygotsky and Education: Instructional Implications and Applications of Sociohistorical Psychology*, ed. by L. Moll. Cambridge: Cambridge University Press.

van Lier, L. (1992). "Not the Nine O'Clock Linguistics Class: Investigating Contingency Grammar." *Language Awareness* 1, 91–108.

———. (1993). "Contingency Grammar." Paper presented at the Twenty-Seventh Annual Teachers of English to Speakers of Other Languages Conference, Atlanta, Georgia.

Vygotsky, L. (1962). *Thought and Language*, ed. and trans. by E. Hanfmann and G. Vakar. Cambridge, MA: MIT Press.

———. (1978). *Mind in society: The Development of Higher Psychological Processes*, ed. by M. Cole, V. John-Steiner, S. Scribner, and E. Souberman. Cambridge, MA: Harvard University Press.

Wertsch, J. (1979). "The Regulation of Human Action and the Given—New Organization of Private Speech." *The Development of Self-Regulation through Private Speech*, ed. by G. Zivin. New York: Wiley.

———. (1980). "The Significance of Dialog in Vygotsky's Account of Social, Egocentric, and Inner Speech." *Contemporary Educational Psychology* 5, 150–162.

———. (1991). *Voices of the Mind: A Sociocultural Approach to Mediated Action*. Cambridge, MA: Harvard University Press.

Chapter 3

The FOCAL SKILLS Approach:
An Assessment

Ashley J. Hastings
University of Dallas

1. INTRODUCTION

The FOCAL SKILLS (FS) approach is a relatively recent development in language program design. The basic intent of FS is to accelerate the acquisition of intermediate-level language proficiency by maximizing the efficiency of instruction; this is supposed to be accomplished by carefully placing each student in a sequence of skill-focused modules in which comprehensible input and communication are stressed. Since FS is now being used by several intensive English programs, it is both possible and desirable to evaluate the approach empirically.

In Section 2 of this chapter, I explain the key features of the FS approach, contrasting it with the *standard model* (SM, an informal label referring to the program design features that characterize many intensive ESL programs in the United States). In Section 3, I present the results of various studies that compare the learning outcomes of students in FS and SM programs. In the concluding section I discuss these results and their implications.

2. FOCAL SKILLS AND THE STANDARD MODEL

2.1. The Standard Model

Before explaining the FS approach, I will outline the key features of the SM. This will provide a frame of reference with which the distinctive characteristics of FS can be contrasted. It should be understood that the SM is an abstraction, not a detailed description of any particular program.

2.1.1. SM Program Structure

In a typical intensive preuniversity ESL program, students progress through a series of levels (usually about six). Ordinarily, all the levels are structured in much the same way, with balanced amounts of time devoted to listening, reading, writing, speaking, and grammar (Fig. 3.1). Thus, while the work becomes more difficult as the student progresses through the program, its general nature remains fairly constant.

2.1.2. SM Placement

A variety of placement instruments may be used to place incoming students; these may include standardized global proficiency tests such as TOEFL®, in-house test batteries that measure separate skills, and so forth. Continuing students may be placed by the same system as incoming students, by their grades in previous work, or by a combination of these methods. In some SM programs, each student is placed in the same level for all skills; in other programs, *split placements* may be permitted, allowing a student to be placed in different levels for different skills.

Placement can pose dilemmas and paradoxes in a SM program. It is not uncommon for a student to be stronger in one skill than another. For example, a student may have Level 2 listening/speaking ability and Level 4 reading/writing ability. In a program that places students in one level across the board, such a student can be placed in Level 3 as a reasonable compromise; but then some of the work will be too easy and some will be too difficult. If the program uses split placements, the student can be placed in Level 2 listening/speaking and Level 4 reading/writing. However, split placements can lead to very heterogeneous groupings as far as collateral skills are concerned. For example, the Level 4 reading/writing class may have students with listening/speaking abilities ranging over several levels, making oral communication in the classroom rather problematic. Also, students with split placements are likely to finish some parts of

LEVEL 1	LISTENING	SPEAKING	READING	WRITING	GRAMMAR
LEVEL 2	LISTENING	SPEAKING	READING	WRITING	GRAMMAR
LEVEL 3	LISTENING	SPEAKING	READING	WRITING	GRAMMAR
LEVEL 4	LISTENING	SPEAKING	READING	WRITING	GRAMMAR
LEVEL 5	LISTENING	SPEAKING	READING	WRITING	GRAMMAR
LEVEL 6	LISTENING	SPEAKING	READING	WRITING	GRAMMAR

FIG. 3.1. Structure of a standard model intensive ESL program.

the program before other parts, causing scheduling headaches for themselves and their advisors.

2.1.3. SM Pedagogy

Most SM ESL programs in the United States employ an eclectic pedagogy. A general characterization is difficult, but it would probably be fair to say that certain broad features are prevalent. There is a tendency to favor synthetic, interventionist syllabi, in which the language is presented in fragments that are sequenced and controlled by the teacher (Long & Crookes, 1992).[1] Detailed syllabi are often constructed in which each level has its own agenda for each skill, and each skill is subdivided into smaller components. Language components such as vocabulary, grammar, and pronunciation are often taught in discrete units, each accompanied by various types of drills, exercises, and other relatively artificial activities. This general pedagogical orientation calls for specialized instructional materials, which are available from a number of publishers.

2.2. The FOCAL SKILLS Approach

2.2.1. Functional Skill Integration

The basic idea underlying the FS approach is that the macroskills—listening, reading, writing, and speaking—form complex and shifting patterns of functional interrelationships during the course of L2 acquisition, especially when the target language is also the language of instruction (Fig. 3.2). At a given stage of development, a skill may be dependent or autonomous. Dependent skills can be subdivided into focal and emergent skills, and autonomous skills include the categories of foundational and instrumental skills.

A *dependent skill* is one which a language acquirer is not yet able to use with relative ease. Such a skill has great potential for development if sufficient input is provided. An *autonomous skill*, on the other hand, is relatively well developed; it can contribute to the development of other skills, and it will continue to develop without special attention through normal language use.

A focal skill is the focus of intensive efforts to develop it as rapidly as possible. For example, a FS program has a Listening Module in which all of the work is aimed at accelerating the students' progress in listening comprehension.

Instrumental skills can be used as tools when focusing on another skill. For example, listening comprehension is instrumental in the Reading Module of a FS program, because the teacher always conducts class discussions in the target language.

---

[1]In this context, *synthetic* means that the student must resynthesize the language out of the fragments provided by instruction.

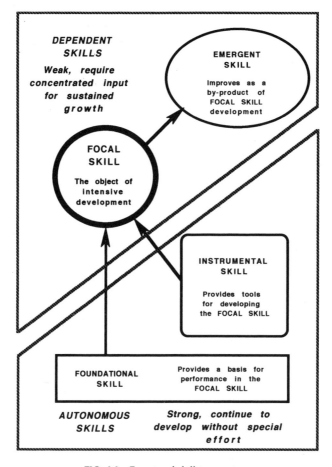

FIG. 3.2. Functional skill integration.

A foundational skill provides a basis for performance in another skill. For example, reading is foundational for writing, because the elements that a person can appropriately produce in writing will generally be a subset of the elements that the person can recognize and understand when reading.

Emergent skills are those that develop as a consequence of growth in their foundational skills. For example, since listening is foundational for speaking, we expect speaking proficiency to improve if listening comprehension improves.

2.2.2. FS Program Structure

The guiding program design principle of FS is to create a sequence of skill-focused instructional modules configured in such a way as to take the greatest possible advantage of the functional skill relationships. The instructional modules are organized around the FS Proficiency Assessments, an ordered series of skill

The FOCAL SKILLS Approach

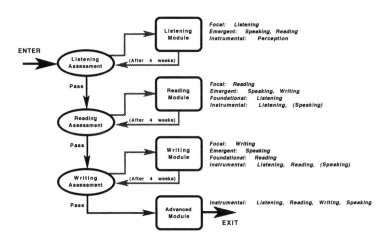

FIG. 3.3. The FOCAL SKILLS program structure.

assessments. The relationships between the modules, the skills, and the assessments are illustrated in Fig. 3.3.

The *Advanced Module* is not actually a FS module because it has no designated focal skill. This module functions as a transitional stage for advanced students, providing whatever additional work they need before leaving the intensive ESL program. The Advanced Module could be set up like an advanced level in a SM program, or it might have any other format; this depends entirely on the needs and circumstances of the program and its students.

It will be noticed that no modules focus on speaking or grammar. The FS approach relies mainly on acquisition rather than direct instruction for these aspects of language (Krashen, 1985, p. 2). One of the Electives (discussed later) may offer grammar instruction for students who request it, and individualized instruction can be provided in the Writing Module to help students learn certain "editing" grammar rules that are not readily acquired (Krashen, 1992, p. 28).

The FS modules meet for only 3 hours a day (75% of the instructional day). The fourth hour is devoted to Elective Courses. These Electives are entirely separate from the regular curriculum. An Elective is anything related to the study of English that a teacher wants to teach and students want to take, from grammar to poetry reading. Students select freely from the currently available offerings; they are allowed to change their Elective at weekly intervals.

2.2.3. FS Placement

The placement system, which consists solely of the Listening, Reading, and Writing Assessments (see Fig. 3.3), is designed to ensure that every student's time will be spent as productively as possible, focusing on skills that particularly need improvement. It ensures that the students in each module have the appropriate foundational and instrumental skills to accelerate their progress in the focal skill of the module. It allows them to spend as much time as they need in each module and then move on at the end of any 4-week period, as soon as they have reached criterion in the focal skill. It also allows them to skip any module that they do not need. Exactly the same criteria used for placing incoming students are used for placing continuing students: the skill assessments. Teachers do not assign grades or determine which students pass their classes.

New students are first tested for listening comprehension. The Listening Assessment identifies students whose listening proficiency is less than that of the average Level 4 student in a typical six-level SM program. Students who cannot demonstrate this level of listening comprehension must enter the Listening Module; they will have a chance every 4 weeks to pass the test and move on. All students who pass the Listening Assessment, whether on their first or a subsequent try, take the Reading Assessment next. This test requires about a Level 5 reading ability to pass; those who are below this standard take the Reading Module and are retested every 4 weeks. After passing the Reading Assessment, students must take the Writing Assessment, with a passpoint comparable to the ability of a Level 6 student. Any student who has passed all three assessments is placed in the Advanced Module.

The FS placement system may be thought of as a method of determining which skill has the highest acquisition potential at a given point in time for a given student. A skill with high acquisition potential is a good candidate to be a focal skill, since there is likely to be a large return for time spent. High acquisition potential is associated with two factors. First, any foundational and instrumental skills must be well established (the conditions that enable rapid development must be present). Second, the skill itself must be relatively weak (there must be ample room for growth).

This placement system avoids the pitfalls associated with SM programs (2.1.2). An unambiguous, motivated placement is determined for every student, and the question of compromise or split placements does not arise.

2.2.4. FS Pedagogy

Pedagogically as well as structurally, the FS approach differs in important respects from most SM programs. The modules of a FS program are not very much like the levels and classes of a SM program. Both the groupings of students and the curricular objectives of the modules are determined by principles that differ rather sharply from those that govern SM programs. Accordingly, it is not surprising that many features of standard ESL pedagogy are not well suited to the needs of FS teachers and students.

The pedagogical techniques of FS are relatively simple in concept and straightforward in application. The dominant themes are comprehensible input and communication. The pedagogical design of each FS module aims primarily at creating opportunities for the exchange of meaningful, topic-centered language: as much as possible, of the highest possible quality, at the appropriate levels of difficulty, through the appropriate channels, with due regard for the focal, foundational, and instrumental skills of the module. The target language itself serves as the medium of instruction, not as the topic. In general, the FS pedagogy can be characterized as analytic and noninterventionist. The language is presented in intact chunks and the teachers and students can share in decision making (Long & Crookes, 1992).[2] Vocabulary, grammar, and other language components are allowed to develop naturally. There are no syllabi of subskills and no artificial exercises. Within these broad guidelines, teachers are encouraged to create and share their own pedagogical ideas.

Excellent FS materials are readily available from ordinary sources such as video stores, bookstores, periodicals, and libraries. Some specialized ESL materials can be used in FS, but they play a modest role. The Listening Module relies mainly on video movies and realia. Students in the Reading Module have enough background in the language to deal with the types of light reading materials advocated by Krashen (1993, pp. 46–64). Writing students can read more advanced materials, which serve as input and stimuli for their writing projects. Teachers and students generally collaborate in the choice of materials and topics; these are not imposed from above.

3. EMPIRICAL COMPARISONS

Because the FS approach is so different from the SM, it is important to compare learning outcomes. If FS offers an effective option for program design, the profession at large needs to be informed of this. If, on the other hand, FS students are suffering any disadvantages, corrective action needs to be taken as quickly as possible.

The research reported here must be regarded as providing only tentative answers to the questions raised. An opportunistic strategy has been followed in gathering data, taking advantage, whenever possible, of test results that were generated for program-internal purposes, and causing as little inconvenience as possible for the students, teachers, and administrators of the programs involved. In some cases, quite small numbers of subjects contributed data, and the conditions under which measurements took place could not be completely standardized. Variables such as age, sex, and national/linguistic background were not recorded in most instances and are not controlled for; however, the student populations of the various programs are probably not too dissimilar.

---

[2]*Analytic* means that the pedagogy relies on the student's ability to analyze the language as an integral part of the acquisition process.

3.1. Skill Acceleration

One of the basic assumptions of the FS approach is that the acquisition of a skill can be significantly accelerated if students with high acquisition potential in the skill spend 3 hours a day in classes that focus on the skill. In order to test this assumption, an investigation of short-term gains in skill was made, using data from the programs designated FS1 and SM1.

The FS Proficiency Assessments were used to measure progress in both programs. These tests have been found to have satisfactory reliability (Hastings, 1992a) and high correlations with TOEFL (Hastings, 1992b). The Listening Assessment is recorded on tape; each of the 60 items consists of a dialogue followed by a yes/no question. The Reading Assessment consists of 20 paragraphs, each followed by three yes/no questions, for a total of 60 items. The Writing Assessment is a 12-paragraph, 120-item C-Test. Scores are expressed as percentages; the Listening and Reading scores are adjusted for guessing. Parallel forms of the instruments were used as pre- and posttests.[3]

The FS Proficiency Assessments were given in SM1 during the first and seventh weeks of the 1993 spring semester. There were seven levels of classes, from pre-1 through 6. Each student took only one of the three tests. Students in Levels Pre-1 and 1 took the Listening Assessment; those in Level 2 took either the Listening or the Reading Assessment; and students in the top four levels took either the Listening, the Reading, or the Writing Assessment. The FS1 data came from regular testing in the Listening, Reading, and Writing modules during the beginning 4-week periods of the 1992 fall semester, the 1993 spring semester, and the 1993 summer session. Students took only the test appropriate to their current module.

Because of the selective effects of the FS placement procedure, the pretest means of the students in the two programs were quite different; this made the comparison of their gain scores difficult to interpret. To remedy this, the data from the SM1 program were truncated by discarding subjects whose pretest scores were outside the range of the FS1 program scores and then truncating further as needed to match the FS program data as nearly as possible. Because the interval between pre- and posttests differed in the two programs, the raw gain scores were divided by the number of weeks (six at SM1, four at FS1) to find the weekly gains. The FS1 students had much larger weekly gains on all three tests (Table 3.1).

---

[3]Although it might be suspected that the use of the FS tests would bias the comparison in favor of the FS students, this is probably not the case. The contents of these instruments are not related in any way to the material covered in the modules: they are proficiency assessments, not achievement tests. The tests are never practiced, previewed, or reviewed, and items are never discussed with the students. During the time of this study, the FS students had no more exposure to or preparation for the tests than the comparison group did.

TABLE 3.1
Accelerated Skill Gains

Test	Group	N		Pretest	Posttest	Weekly Gain	Effect Size
Listening	FS1 Listening Module	74	M	20.8	43.0	5.6	1.81
			SD	18.8	26.9	4.6	
	SM1	42	M	20.7	27.0	1.0	
			SD	20.7	25.0	2.5	
Reading	FS1 Reading Module	49	M	32.9	48.4	3.9	1.04
			SD	15.6	20.8	4.4	
	SM1	37	M	32.8	40.2	1.2	
			SD	15.0	18.2	2.6	
Writing	FS1 Writing Module	24	M	57.6	66.2	2.2	1.08
			SD	10.2	11.9	2.4	
	SM1	27	M	57.4	61.3	0.7	
			SD	6.1	9.5	1.4	

A t-test for independent samples was performed; all of the differences in weekly gain scores are statistically significant ($p < .001$ for Listening and Reading; $p < .02$ for Writing).[4] Furthermore, the effect sizes are all quite large.[5] It seems safe to conclude that skill acceleration is indeed being achieved in the FS modules. But this finding does not guarantee that FS students make higher skill gains overall, because it is possible that the other skills lie dormant while the focal skill is being accelerated. In the next section I examine this issue.

3.2. Emergent Skill Development

The concept of *emergent skills* is important in the program-design philosophy of FS. It is assumed that Listening students will make some gains in reading, and perhaps in writing as well, and that Reading students will develop some writing ability, even though they do not do any work aimed specifically at those skills until they have reached the modules that focus on them. But do skills actually emerge in this way? If they do, then FS students are in effect enjoying "free" skill gains that come about as beneficial by-products of work focused on another skill. On the other hand, if skills do not emerge as assumed, then the rapid gains in the focal skill may be largely offset by a lack of progress in the other skills, resulting in little or no overall advantage.

---

[4]SPSS Release 4.0 for Macintosh was used for the statistical analyses in this study.

[5]The effect size is computed by subtracting the SM1 mean gain score from the FS1 mean gain score and then dividing the difference by the standard deviation of the SM1 gain scores. I am indebted to Stephen Krashen for pointing out the usefulness of effect size in comparisons of this kind.

TABLE 3.2
Emergent Skill Gains

Test	Group	N	Pretest	M Weeks	Weekly Gain
Reading	FS Listening Module	37	30.9	8.8	1.5
	SM1	50	30.5	6.0	1.3
Writing	FS Listening, Reading Modules	33	39.1	8.5	1.4
	SM1	38	39.2	6.0	1.5

In the FS1 program, new students normally take all three skill assessments, giving us pretest scores in all the skills. Thereafter, they take only the test for their current module until they pass it; then they take the next assessment in the sequence. Students who are still in the program at the end of the semester often retake the entire battery (although some do not). From these sources, we can obtain a certain amount of information about the development of emergent skills in FS programs. Emergent skill gains were computed and divided by the number of weeks between pre- and posttest. The weekly gains are shown in Table 3.2 and are compared with the weekly gains of matching groups of the SM1 students.

The FS1 students' emergent skill gains are virtually identical to the gains of the SM1 students. It appears that rapid progress in a focal skill is indeed accompanied by respectable gains in emergent skills, as the FS program design assumes.

However, these short-term studies of accelerated and emergent skills do not necessarily tell us how well FS students do over longer periods of time, especially when the skills are considered together rather than separately. The next section presents the results of a semester-long study that addressed the question of global skill development.

3.3. Global Skill Development

Two FS programs (FS1 and FS2) and one standard program (SM2) participated in this study. The FS Proficiency Assessments were administered at the beginning and end of the 1992 spring semester in all three programs; all the students took all the tests.[6] In the two FS programs, the interval between pre- and posttests was 16 weeks; it was 15 weeks in the SM2 program. Gain scores were computed and expressed as mean weekly gains. The gains in the two FS programs were virtually identical, so their data were combined for comparison with the SM2 data (Table 3.3).

---

[6]Scores from FS program students who began the semester in the Advanced Module were not included in this study, since they did not participate in any of the actual FS modules.

TABLE 3.3
Global Skill Gains

Test	Group	N		Pretest	Posttest	Weekly Gain	Effect Size
L, R, W	FS1, FS2	46	M	98.1	166.3	4.3	1.75
			SD	65.3	53.2	2.3	
	SM2	17	M	98.7	116.4	1.2	
			SD	54.7	71.8	1.8	

The weekly gains of the FS students are significantly greater than those of the SM2 students ($p < .001$); the effect size is also quite large. This result suggests that FS students make good progress in global proficiency over the course of a semester regardless of which module they are initially assigned to.

3.4. TOEFL Gains

The Test of English as a Foreign Language (TOEFL) is a well-regarded and widely used measure of global English proficiency that affects the careers of many thousands of international students every year. It is therefore important to determine whether FS students make satisfactory progress on this measure. The study reported in this section compares TOEFL gain scores of students in FS1 and SM2.

The SM2 students are required to take the institutional TOEFL as a placement/exit instrument at the beginning and end of every semester; this comparison uses data from 1991–1992. FS1 normally offers the institutional TOEFL on a voluntary basis only at the end of each semester. For this study, the TOEFL was administered to all the FS1 students during the 2nd and 16th weeks of the 1992 fall semester.[7] TOEFL gain scores were computed and expressed as weekly gains to compensate for the unequal intervals at the two institutions. The results are displayed in Table 3.4.

The FS1 students had somewhat higher weekly gains, although the difference falls short of significance ($p = .195$) and the effect size is rather small. These findings suggest that FS students do at least as well as typical SM program students, as far as TOEFL gains are concerned.

3.5. Other Comparisons

The comparisons examined so far have involved global proficiency and the specific language skills addressed by the FS modules. A number of other skills and language components, including vocabulary, grammar, speaking, and com-

---

[7]As in the previous study, scores from students who began the semester in the Advanced Module of the FS program were not included.

TABLE 3.4
TOEFL Gains

Test	Group	N		Pretest	Weekly Gain	Effect Size
TOEFL	FS1	27	M	428.3	3.0	.22
			SD	46.1	2.6	
	SM2	75	M	427.6	2.4	
			SD	47.0	2.5	

position, are not the focus of any FS module. Are FS students deficient in these areas? In this section I present evidence bearing on this question.

3.5.1. Vocabulary

The FS approach assumes that vocabulary is acquired through exposure to comprehensible input. Since the main business of the modules is to provide such input, no special vocabulary work is deemed necessary. Many SM programs, however, devote considerable time and energy to vocabulary instruction. The SM1 program follows this approach, using special vocabulary textbooks, exercises, and quizzes. Ruffu and Rogal (1993) examined the rates of vocabulary growth in the FS1 and SM1 programs. They found that the FS1 students had slightly higher vocabulary gains, although the difference was not significant. This finding implies that the FS policy of allowing vocabulary to be acquired naturally is at least as successful as the SM practice of focused vocabulary work.

3.5.2. Grammar

Grammar is another area where the FS approach relies on acquisition through comprehensible input rather than explicit instruction. The most direct evidence available at this time concerning FS students' acquisition of grammar comes from their gain scores on TOEFL Section 2 (Structure and Written Expression). We can compare these with the corresponding scores for the SM2 students, who studied grammar as part of their curriculum. As in the case of the total scores, the FS1 students had somewhat higher weekly gains on Section 2 than the SM2 students, but the difference was not statistically significant. The evidence suggests that FS students acquire grammar at least as well as students in SM programs.

3.5.3. Speaking

Like vocabulary and grammar, speaking is simply allowed to emerge in the FS approach. There is no speaking module, and students are not ordinarily called on to do any practice or demonstration speaking; rather, they are given opportunities to speak voluntarily as a natural part of classroom interaction. Standard programs such as SM1, however, usually devote part of their regular curriculum to focused activities in which students are expected to practice various aspects of speaking. The speaking abilities of FS1 and SM1 students were compared at the end of the 1992 fall semester, using a sentence repetition test (SRT).[8] Only the Level 6 students (the most advanced) at SM1 took the SRT, so they were compared with the students in the Advanced Module at FS1. The FS1 mean score was slightly higher, but the difference was not significant. This finding suggests that FS students learn to speak as well as students in SM programs.

3.5.4. Composition

The FS Writing Assessment (described earlier) measures a student's command of the lexical, grammatical, and orthographic aspects of the written language, but it does not test composition writing ability. FS students do not even begin to work on writing until they reach the Writing Module. Even then, their writing is generally informal, self-directed, and exploratory. We would therefore not expect them to be as adept at timed, topic-controlled composition writing as students in a SM program where composition is taught at all levels.

The SM2 program uses a TWE-type essay as part of its placement/exit testing. The same essay prompt and time limit used in SM2 in December 1992 were used at FS1 and SM1, in order to investigate differences in the composition abilities of FS and SM students. The SM students had somewhat higher mean scores (3.2 vs. 2.8 on a 6-point scale). The FS Advanced Module students had a mean score of 3.6, only slightly lower that the SM Level 6 students (3.8).

It is known that composition scores are closely correlated with global proficiency measures such as the TOEFL (Jacobs, 1987, p. 87); in our sample, the correlation coefficient between the composition scores and the TOEFL scores was .81. Composition is probably a partially emergent skill in the terminology of this paper. By the time FS students reach the Advanced Module, they appear to have developed composition skills nearly the equal of their SM counterparts, even without any focused instruction.[9]

4. DISCUSSION AND CONCLUSIONS

All of the comparisons presented here must be interpreted with caution. The samples were small, background variables were not controlled for, and the con-

---

[8]SRTs have been found to correlate very well with other measures of speaking ability, including oral interviews; some of the correlations range as high as .92 (Radloff, 1991). The SRT used here was created specifically for this study and is not a refined or well-documented instrument; however, on the basis of limited data, its internal reliability index is good (.92), and its correlation with TOEFL (.70) is comparable to correlations cited by Radloff between SRTs and other global proficiency measures.

[9]If desired, FS programs can easily provide composition training and practice as part of the Advanced Module, or as an Elective for students in any module.

ditions under which the tests were administered were not as standardized as one might wish. The FS tests were administered before classes began in the FS programs but well into the first week of classes in the SM programs. For this reason, the pretest scores in the FS programs may have been somewhat depressed by the fatigue, disorientation, and anxiety of newly arrived students; this may have given the gain scores in the FS programs an extra boost. The same factors may have operated to elevate the TOEFL gains in program SM2. Since the FS tests have a special function in FS programs, they cannot be regarded as ideal instruments for comparisons between FS and SM programs. TOEFL scores may also be a questionable basis for comparing programs: Many students resort to special courses and self-help materials designed to improve their performance on the TOEFL, and this might tend to obscure differences between programs. The other measures used here (vocabulary estimate, SRT, writing sample) are also open to a variety of criticisms. It is clear that a fully satisfactory comparison of the FS and SM approaches would require a larger number of subjects and a carefully designed study using more appropriate instruments.

However, the comparisons presented in this paper are not without interest. Taken together, the results make sense in terms of the goals and assumptions of the FS approach. The FS approach is designed to accelerate progress in listening, reading, and writing without sacrificing growth in the other language skills and components. All of the evidence that is available at this time suggests that these design objectives have been achieved: FS wins the comparisons that it is supposed to win and holds its own in the other comparisons. Although each of the informal studies presented in this paper can be questioned on methodological grounds, they do seem to converge in their support of the basic design features of the FS approach. Perhaps these preliminary results will attract the attention of other researchers who can contribute to a more rigorous and comprehensive examination of the questions raised here.

At the very least, our comparisons give us no reason to believe that FS students do any worse than students in SM programs. This in itself may come as a surprise to some. The following precepts are widely held in the field:

- All skills must be taught at all levels.
- Grammar, vocabulary, and speaking must be taught explicitly.
- Elaborate syllabi and textbooks are essential.
- Students need to do exercises and drills.

Those who embrace these precepts might expect trouble to follow if any one of them was violated. Abandoning all of them simultaneously would presumably be considered an invitation to certain disaster. Yet the FS approach has done just that. One skill is focused on at a time; grammar, vocabulary, and speaking are allowed to emerge; there is no point-by-point syllabus; and few if any special textbooks, exercises, or drills are used. Furthermore, only 75% of the instructional time is devoted to the regular FS curriculum; the students choose how to spend the balance of the time. In spite of these radical departures from the common wisdom, FS seems to produce results that are at least as good as those of SM programs that obey all of the standard precepts and use all of the available time for the planned curriculum. Those who are interested in alternative ways of teaching languages may find the FOCAL SKILLS approach worth exploring.

ACKNOWLEDGMENTS

I would like to thank Fred Eckman, Stephen Krashen, and the anonymous reviewers for their very helpful comments on an earlier draft of this paper.

Two FS programs and two SM programs contributed data to these studies: FS1 and FS2, at the University of Wisconsin-Milwaukee and Mississippi State University, and SM1 and SM2, at the University of North Texas and Wayne State University. I would like to thank Gaye Childress, Peter Lee, Bruce Morgan, and Harold Smith for their assistance with the data from their institutions.

REFERENCES

Hastings, A. J. (1992a). "The FOCAL SKILLS Placement Tests: Reliability Estimates." (FSR/UWM ESL. Report No. 1). Milwaukee, WI: the University of Wisconsin.
———. (1992b). "The FOCAL SKILLS Placement Tests: Correlations with TOEFL." (FSR/UWM ESL Report No. 2). Milwaukee, WI: the University of Wisconsin.
Jacobs, H. (1987). "Test of written English." Reviews of English Language Proficiency Tests, ed. by J. C. Alderson, K. J. Krahnke, and C. W. Stansfield, pp. 86–88. Alexandria, VA: TESOL.
Krashen, S. D. (1985). The Input Hypothesis: Issues and Implications. New York: Longman.
———. (1992). Fundamentals of Language Education. Torrance, CA: Laredo.
———. (1993). The Power of Reading: Insights from the Research. Englewood, CO: Libraries Unlimited.
Long, M. J., and G. Crookes. (1992). "Three Approaches to Task-Based Syllabus Design," TESOL Quarterly, 26(1), 27–56.
Radloff, C. F. (1991). Sentence Repetition Testing for Studies of Community Bilingualism. Arlington, TX: Summer Institute of Linguistics and University of Texas, Arlington.
Ruffu, R., and J. Rogal. (1993). "Approaches to Vocabulary at Two IEPs: What's the Difference?" Paper presented at the Fifteenth Annual TEXTESOL Convention, Dallas, TX.

Chapter 4

Toward Theory-Driven Language Pedagogy

Suzanne Flynn
Massachusetts Institute of Technology

Gita Martohardjono
Queens College/CUNY

1. INTRODUCTION

In recent years, theory-driven second language (L2) acquisition research and L2 pedagogy have become increasingly dichotomized. This is unfortunate, because it is clear that a systematic examination of how developments in each of these areas interact constitutes a critical step in building a comprehensive account of L2 learning.

Our purpose in this chapter is to build upon and extend previous discussion of these issues (e.g., Flynn, 1991a, 1991b, in press; Gair, 1992; White, 1990). More specifically, we will attempt to begin to identify and explore specific areas of current linguistic theory and the associated acquisition research that we believe have consequences for language pedagogy.

1.1. Background

As is well known, recognition of the fact that theory, research and practice are intimately related is not new. For example, as noted by Gair (1992, p. 1), during World War II, the military as well as many civilians needed to be "trained effectively and in the shortest time possible in the use of a wide variety of languages, many of them exotic." To do this, the government sought the help of the American Council of Learned Societies, which in turn contacted the Linguistic Society of America (LSA). As a result, many neo-Bloomfieldian linguists became involved in writing texts and developing materials to teach the various languages that they were commissioned to deal with. Even Bloomfield himself worked on a text for spoken Dutch, as well as one on Russian.

The approach to language and language learning assumed in this work became more formalized in the articulation of Contrastive Analysis (CA), first by Fries (1945) and later by Lado (1957). Within this context, language learning in general consisted of the learning of a fixed set of habits over time. L2 learning involved the added component of transfer in that it was argued that the L2 learner attempted to transfer the linguistic habits from the first language (L1) to the L2. Where the L1 and the L2 matched, positive transfer took place, and where they did not, negative transfer ensued. Although this is an oversimplified account of CA, what is important is that linguistic theory, namely structuralism, as well as a theory of learning, namely behaviorism, were productively paired in an attempt to understand L2 learning in order to develop sound pedagogical materials and practices.

The demise of behaviorism as an explanatory account of the language learning process and the movement away from structuralism within linguistic theory did not immediately sound the death knell for the relationship between theory, research, and practice. With the advent of transformational grammar, the 1960s also witnessed many attempts to link linguistic theory to language learning and use.

Continued investigation along these lines resulted in the development of Creative Construction (CC) (Dulay & Burt, 1974). This work built directly upon proposals made within a generative account of language and made one of the first attempts to link L2 acquisition with L1 acquisition in a very direct way. Specifically, CC claimed that L1 acquisition and L2 acquisition were essentially the same processes in that they were both guided by the same set of innate language principles for language. Development of this work also resulted in an important linkage of theory and language practices in the work of Dulay, Burt, and Krashen (1982). Although we have suggested elsewhere (Flynn, 1985) that some of the conclusions drawn were premature in the context of the existing data, the work nonetheless represented an important attempt to relate theory and practice.

Disillusionment, skepticism, and disregard of any possible relevant interactions among theory, research, and practice began to emerge when it was discovered that the proposals made within early models of generative theory did not have the psychological reality initially envisioned (see extended discussion in Flynn, 1993).[1] For example, working within a transformational model of generative linguistics, many researchers hypothesized that the comprehension, and perhaps even acquisition, of sentences was affected by the number of grammatical rules or transformations employed in a sentence's derivation. This was essentially the Derivational Theory of Complexity (DTC) (see discussion in Fodor, Bever, &

---

[1]Much of the discussion in this section of the chapter can also be found in Flynn, 1993.

Garrett, 1974). After much psycholinguistic testing of the DTC, it was empirically shown that structures involving fewer transformations were not always easier to acquire or process than those involving more transformations. This finding proved devastating to many researchers attempting to establish a link between linguistic theory and a psychology of the mind.

At the same time that psycholinguists' hopes for establishing the "reality" of a transformational grammar were temporarily undermined, the theory began to evolve and change quite rapidly; in fact, this is still the case. Although the leading ideas of Chomsky's theory have remained constant, the changes in detail have often proved quite frustrating for those attempting to understand the theory and make connections across the relevant domains. What has resulted is that many language pedagogues and researchers on L2 acquisition believe that linguistic theory has little or no relevance for their respective enterprises. There are also many linguists and researchers who also share this belief.

2. UNIVERSAL GRAMMAR

These earlier failures were principally the function of not having the "right" formulation of a theory of language, namely the "right" theory of UG. However, because UG is a theory of cognition as well as a theory of grammars, it seems only natural that we should once again attempt to understand its relevance for language learning and language pedagogy. In this chapter we argue that recent developments in the theory of UG make it more conducive to such application (see e.g. Cook, 1991; Flynn, 1991a, 1991b, in press; Gair, 1992; Gass, this volume; Rutherford, 1987; Sharwood-Smith, 1981; White, 1990, this volume).

As is well known, UG consists of (i) a universal computational system which is commonly referred to as linguistic competence, and (ii) a system of parameters associated with the lexicon that account for linguistic variation. One goal of linguists and language researchers is to understand what is universally specified and what is language specific. The universally specified is hypothesized to be given as a part of our biological endowment, and it presumably does not have to be learned; that which is language specific has to be learned and presumably may be taught in some manner. Although this might seem to be a trivial task, it is a very complicated one because even when we have specified what needs to be learned, we need to establish the various learning mechanisms that underlie the acquisition of the language-specific aspects of a particular target language. For example, the processes underlying the determination of values of lexical parameters might differ significantly from those used to learn such language-specific rules as "do support" for English. If different learning mechanisms are involved, then presumably the teaching interventions must also vary.

To illustrate several ways in which we have begun to isolate what is universal and what is language specific in terms of empirical L2 research, we will briefly outline several programs of research and highlight their implications for language pedagogy. Specifically, we will consider results from experimental L2 acquisition studies that focused on: (a) Parameter-setting, (b) Lexical feature assignment, and (c) Functional Categories.

2.1. Different Parameter Values

Research has suggested that one area in which learning is involved concerns parameter setting. Results of several studies (e.g. Flynn, 1983, 1987; Flynn & Espinal, 1985; Flynn & Lust, 1990; Thomas, 1991) indicate that where parametric values of the L1 and the L2 match, language acquisition is enhanced in comparison to the case in which the parametric values of the L1 and the L2 do not match. One explanation advanced for this pattern of results is that in the matched case, learners do not need to assign a new value to the parameter; thus, no new learning is needed with respect to the value of the parameter, although learning may take place with respect to the instantiation of a particular parameter in terms of language-specific structures.

What is important for our present purposes, however, is that where the L1 and the L2 differ in parametric values, the new value must be learned in some sense and it therefore becomes relevant for language teaching. These results have emerged most saliently in studies of the acquisition of head-initial languages by speakers of head-final L1: head direction in this case is defined in terms of the direction of the head of the complement phrase (CP), C^0, and the adjunction direction that learners correlate with it. A left-headed C^0 correlates with right branching; a right-headed C^0 correlates with left branching. "In this formulation, embeddings of sentence (CP) adjuncts are under either NP or S heads. These include relative clauses in complex NPs and adverbial subordinate clauses in complex sentences" (Flynn & Martohardjono, 1994, p. 322). (See also Flynn, 1987, in press; Lust, 1994.)

The results of these studies indicate that speakers of Spanish, a head-initial language, have significantly less difficulty with complex sentence structures in English that instantiate head initiality than do their Japanese counterparts, whose L1 is head final, learning English as a second language. The speakers were tested in an elicited imitation task on sentence structures such as those exemplified in 1. The sentences varied with respect to the preposing and postposing of the subordinate clause in relation to the main clause. Preposed structures correspond to head-final structures, and postposed clauses to head-initial structures.

(1) *Preposed and postposed subordinate adverbial clauses*

    a. *Preposed:* When the actor finished the book, the woman called the professor.

    b. *Postposed:* The worker called the owner when the engineer finished the plans.

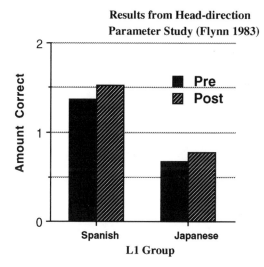

FIG. 4.1. Experimental studies on head direction (comp-direction).

The results are shown in Figure 4.1.

Moreover, an examination of the nature of the errors made by the Japanese speakers, especially at the lowest level of English as a second language (ESL) competence, indicated that the principal locus of error for these speakers is at points where the structures tested manifest rightward directionality. For example, Japanese speakers at the low level often were able to repeat only the main clause of the subordinate sentence structures administered. This finding suggests that these speakers were unable to embed; in other words, they had difficulty with the right-branching structure of English. However, in going from the low to mid levels of ESL competence, there is a significant decrease in the number of one-clause repetitions made across the sentence types tested. This suggests that the Japanese speakers were gradually developing control of embedding in English in accord with its properties as a right-branching language.

The results outlined in this section are interesting because they isolate the role of parameters in L2 acquisition and at the same time specify how parameter setting might work in L2 acquisition. They also isolate in a profoundly interesting and important way one aspect of language that has to be learned during acquisition. It is important to bear in mind that this is not an obvious empirical result; there are several other logically possible learning sequences that are also plausible for the L2 acquisition process but do not occur.

2.2. Canonical Government Direction

Results of a related second study indicate another important area of language that must be learned, viz. lexical-head direction. That is, in addition to determining the head direction for a target-language grammar on the basis of a configuration of the CP, L2 learners must also establish the head direction for lexical categories such as the verb phrase (VP), noun phrase (NP), prepositional phrase (PP), etc. In an elicited imitation study that investigated the acquisition of restrictive relative clauses for Spanish, Japanese, and Chinese speakers learning English as an L2, results indicated, not surprisingly, that the Spanish speakers outperformed the Japanese and Chinese speakers, mainly because of the comp head-direction parameter setting shared by Spanish and English, as indicated by the studies discussed earlier. What was surprising, however, was that the Japanese speakers, and not the Chinese speakers, performed very poorly on sentences that involved a gap in object position in the relative clause (2b) in comparison to their performance on sentence structures that involved a gap in subject position in the relative clause (2a). More precisely, as shown in Fig. 4.2, in the subjects' elicited imitations of sentences such as 2a and 2b, the Japanese speakers performed significantly better on relative clause structures in which the relative clause gap was a subject, not an object. In fact, Japanese speakers, in their elicited imitations of sentences such as 2b, would convert the *object* gap to a *subject* gap, as illustrated in 3.

(2) *Relative clause sentence structures*
   a. *Subject Gap:* The student [who Ø called the gentleman] answered the policeman.
   b. *Object Gap:* The diplomat questioned the gentleman [who the student called Ø].

(3) *Conversion of an Object Gap to a Subject Gap*
   Stimulus: The diplomat questioned the gentleman whom the student called.
   Response: The diplomat questioned the gentleman *who called the student.*

The explanation proposed for these results related to the UG claim that relative clauses contain an empty category, namely a variable that must be interpreted in relation to the head noun phrase. The argument is that there are certain linguistic requirements on the occurrence of null categories of that type, viz. canonical government. English and Chinese are head-initial in VPs and are thus standardly assumed to have proper government of objects (and thus also canonical government, as in Kayne, 1983) to the right, allowing empty categories in that position that are not properly licensed under more general conditions concerning the occurrence of these gaps in certain positions. These requirements cannot be met in Japanese for a structural position to the right of a verb, as English requires for the object position. However, this is not the case for Chinese, which does allow such elements in the object position; this fact follows from the head-initial structure of the VP in Chinese. Thus, what the Japanese speaker must learn is the permissibility of a null element in a specific position in accord with a parameter setting of English even though elements of that type occur in

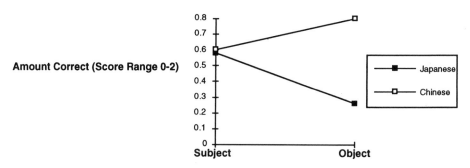

FIG. 4.2. Amount correct for subject and object gap relative clauses.

Japanese relative clauses as well, because the two languages match on the occurrence of such elements in subject position (see Flynn & Brown, 1989; Gair, Flynn, & Brown, 1994). Thus, results indicate that the Japanese speakers, and not the Chinese speakers, must learn this about English.

2.3. The Need to Relearn Subcategorization Features

A third important research contribution concerns subcategorization. Results of studies investigating the acquisition of "control" by L2 learners of English indicate that in the acquisition of the structures in 4, L2 learners did not transfer their L1 knowledge in acquiring these structures, even when the L1 would have provided them with the right answer. That is, (i) L2 learners do not transfer their L1 knowledge about the referent for the null element (PRO) in the infinitive structures exemplified in 4a even when L1 provides the correct referent (Cooper, Olshtain, Tucker, & Waterbury, 1979; d'Anglejan & Tucker, 1975); and (ii) L2 learners prefer infinitives to tensed that clauses even when such structures are marked or nonexistent in L1 (Flynn, Foley, & Lardiere, 1991).

(4) *Study on control structures*

    a. *Infinitives:*
        i. John promised Henry Ø (PRO) to go to the store. (Subject Control)
        ii. John reminded Henry Ø (PRO) to go to the store. (Object Control)
    b. *Finites:*
        i. John promised Henry that he will go to the store. (John, Henry, other)
        ii. John reminded Henry that he will go to the store. (John, Henry, other)

More specifically, results of two earlier studies (Cooper, Olshtain, Tucker, & Waterbury, 1979; d'Anglejan & Tucker, 1975) indicate that L2 learners performed significantly better on object control structures (4aii) than on subject control structures (4ai). That is, L2 learners were able correctly to identify the referent for PRO in the object-control sentences more often than for the subject-control sentences. Importantly, no evidence was found that the L2 learners tested attempted to translate or to map the L1 language structures onto those of the target language even when the L1 would have provided the correct interpretations for the subject-control verbs. Like L1 learners of English (see review in Cohen-Sherman, 1983, and Sherman & Lust, 1993), the L2 learners interpreted *promise* as an object-control verb even when the first language would have given them the correct answer for an interpretation task.

In a more recent study, Flynn, Foley, and Lardiere (1991) found that regardless of the grammatical status of infinitives and tensed "that " clauses in the L1, L2 learners significantly prefer infinitives (as in 4a) over the finite clauses (as in 4b) in their productions in early stages of acquisition. This preference was found regardless of the status of infinitives and finite clauses in the L1. In fact, in the L1s of the speakers tested, Chinese, Japanese, and Spanish, only Spanish unequivocally instantiates infinitive structures. Nevertheless, all three groups performed better in elicited imitations of infinitive structures even when the infinitives and the finite clauses were equated in number of words and syllables. In fact, when speakers were given the structures in 4b to produce, they converted these structures to the corresponding infinitive structures exemplified in 4a.

These results are important because they suggest that transfer from the L1 is not operating in the acquisition of subcategorization features of L2 lexical items; learners must learn anew the lexicon along with its relevant features and subcategorization properties. Furthermore, learners must establish anew in the L2 the mechanisms controlling structural derivations. Both of these areas of "learning" are important for our discovery of what we can assume about the knowledge base of the L2 learner and what needs to be learned.

2.4. Wh-Movement

Research in the acquisition of syntactic Wh-movement has further helped identify areas of grammar which must be learned. Here again, it appears that parameter setting adds to the complexity of the acquisition task.

(5) EXPERIMENTAL STUDIES ON WH-MOVEMENT (Li, 1993; Martohardjono, 1992; Martohardjono & Gair, 1993; Uziel, 1991; White, 1992)

    a. Cross-linguistic variation: +/– overt Wh-movement
        English: + Wh-fronting   What do you like_ ?
        Chinese: – Wh-fronting   Ni shihuan sheme?
                        You like what?

    b. Structures involved:
        Relative Clauses: The woman who drove the car saw the light.

Adjunct Clauses:	The man ordered the soup after the waiter came.
Wh-Island Clauses:	Sue knows where Pat hid the candy.
Noun Complements:	John believed the rumor that his neighbor stole a car.

The studies cited in 5 all converge in showing that universal constraints such as Subjacency and the Empty Category Principle (ECP) are accessible to L2 learners, even if these constraints are not instantiated in the same way in the L1 as suggested in the results in 6. To illustrate, from an acquisition perspective, the sentence types tested in all of these studies can broadly be said to fall into two categories: Strong and Weak movement structures. Strong structures are those that produce strong movement violations because they instantiate crosslin-guistically 'invariant' UG principles, e.g. nodes that are barriers in every language (examples are relative clauses and adjunct clauses); weak structures are those that typically produce weak movement violations because they are instantiations of either parameterized UG knowledge or language-particular knowledge (examples are certain types of Wh-islands and noun complements).

The particular parameter involved in Wh-islands and noun complements is that the most deeply embedded Inflection Phrase (IP) constitutes an extra barrier in English-type languages. In addition, the acquisition of Noun Phrase Comple-ments (seen in 5b) requires language-particular knowledge of subcategorization: some nouns, like *fact*, select a phrasal complement; others, like *rumor*, do not. In short, from an acquisition perspective, these sentence types present a more complex learning task than the instantiation of sentences involving relative clauses and adjunct clauses.

(6) RESULTS FROM WH-MOVEMENT (Martohardjono, 1992, 1993)

L1		Mean Percentage Correct			
		Relative Clause	Adjuncts	Wh-Islands	Complements
Chinese	S[1]:	76	94	67	42
	O[2]:	66	82	32	33
Indonesian	S:	84	88	75	32
	O:	89	91	37	39
Italian	S:	88	91	61	75
	O:	95	93	57	54

Interestingly, however, the degree of success in which various sentence types affected by these constraints are mastered seems to be modulated by the different steps involved in the acquisition of these structures. Not surprisingly, results from the majority of the Wh-movement studies show that learners seem to have more difficulty with structures involving parameterized and language-particular knowledge, as can be seen e.g. in 7 (taken from Martohardjono, 1993).

(7) Rejection of Strong and Weak Violations in Johnson (1988), White &
Juffs (1992), Li (1993)

Johnson, 1988	RC	79%	Strong
	NC	54%	Weak
	Wh-islands	50%	Weak
White & Juffs, 1993	RC	86%	Strong
	Sentential Subject	86%	Strong
	Adjunct Clauses	88%	Strong
	That-trace	39%	Weak
Li, 1993	RC	76%	Strong
	Sentential Subject	79%	Strong
	Wh-islands	52%	Weak

2.5. Functional Categories

In our most recent experimental study on the acquisition of functional categories
(Epstein, Flynn, & Martohardjono, 1993a, 1993b, 1993c, 1994; see also Eubank,
in press; Schwartz, 1993; Schwartz & Sprouse, 1991; Vainikka & Young-Scholten,
1992, 1993), we seem to have isolated two other sources of complexity for both
children and adult L2 learners of English: namely, type of derivation and number
of boundaries involved in a derivation. In this study we included a variety of
sentence types manifesting lexical material (either morphemes or words) in the
Inflection Phrase (IP) and the Complementizer Phrase (CP). The sentences we
tested for IP contained tense morphemes, modals, progressives, and negation. The
sentences we tested for CP were topicalization, RCs, and Wh-questions.

(8) Functional category study with child and adult L2 learners of English
Examples of stimulus sentences:
IP

a. Present tense:
The nervous professor inspects the broken television.

b. Past tense:
The nervous doctor wanted a new lawyer in the office.

c. Modal
The little girl can see a tiny flower in the picture.

d. Progressive
The clever student is inspecting the expensive basket.

e. Negation
i. The elderly grandfather is not picking the blue flower.
ii. The happy janitor does not want the new television.
CP

f. Topicalization
i. Breakfast, the wealthy businessman prepares in the kitchen.
ii. The pencil, the talented architect says is expensive.

g. Relative Clauses
   The lawyer slices the vegetables which the father eats.
h. Wh-questions
   i. Which young girl erases the tiny picture in the notebook?
   ii. Which secret message does the young girl find in the basket?

Using an elicited imitation task we found that adult learners whose native language was Japanese had a higher error rate on the structures involving CP (sentences f–h) than on those involving IP (sentences a–e). What is the difference between these two types of structures, that is, between IP and CP structures? Can the result be predicted by current linguistic theory? Although movement is involved in the instantiation of both IP and CP structures, the particular *type* of movement differs for the two: Movement to SpecCP involves long-distance maximal movement; movement to I^0 involves short-distance head movement. As you can see in Fig. 4.3, adult L2 learners seem to have more difficulty with CP than with IP.

Furthermore, the number of boundaries crossed in a derivation also seems to increase complexity in acquisition. For example, if we look at error rates within topicalizations, we find that complex topicalizations involving two clauses had a higher error rate than simple topicalizations involving only one clause. This was true even though word and syllable lengths were held constant across the two types of sentences. Results from this study thus suggest that derivational complexity is another source of difficulty in acquisition and that learning might be enhanced by additional instruction.

To summarize, we have shown that in the search for universals constraining acquisition, UG-based SLA research has also proven quite fruitful in identifying

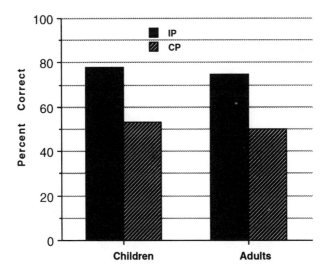

FIG. 4.3. IP vs. CP sentence types: Japanese adults and children.

those areas of grammar where the acquisition task is rendered more complex and which might therefore benefit from additional pedagogical support: we have isolated several such areas in language learning, namely when parameter setting needs to take place, when language-specific lexical learning has to occur (by this we do not mean learning the words in the L2, but much more complex tasks, such as lexical feature assignment) and subcategorization, and when structures are generated by increased derivational complexity.

3. PEDAGOGICAL IMPLICATIONS

The original goal of UG-based L2 acquisition research was to compare L2 acquisition to L1 acquisition and to learn whether there is any grammatical knowledge underlying L2 acquisition which does not need to be learned by L2 learners because it is made available to them by the language faculty. Today most of the research strengthens this hypothesis. The findings we have discussed also demonstrate that the UG research paradigm has proven fruitful in identifying those areas of language learning which do present additional levels of complexity for the L2 learner. This implies that such areas constitute precisely the areas of grammar that are most likely to benefit from additional pedagogical support.

We have described three specific areas of grammar that are candidates for such support: grammatical structures affected by differential parameter settings in the L1 and the L2, structures involving lexical items that require language-specific feature assignment, lexical subcategorization, and structures that are generated by increased derivational complexity. As UG-based research continues to be done, additional areas of difficulty in L2 grammar learning will undoubtedly be identified. Furthermore, new research strategies will have to be devised to determine the precise nature of the pedagogical support that is needed to affect the learning of these areas of grammar. Some obvious questions arise: Will explicit instruction in the grammatical structures themselves be efficient as a strategy? If surface transfer from the L1 does not really occur, precisely how does L1 knowledge interact with L2 acquisition? How can L1 knowledge be used to enhance L2 acquisition? Much of the research in L2 pedagogy has tried to answer these types of questions; however, our suggestion in this chapter is that theory-driven research, and in particular UG-based research paradigms, can and should guide us in building efficient language-teaching methodologies.

CONCLUSIONS

We have argued that UG-based SLA research has afforded us a clearer and more precise picture of what needs to be learned than we had previously. These findings can and should be developed into a principled language pedagogy. Having isolated these areas, we now need to experiment with different pedagogical practices in order to determine whether those areas are amenable to enhanced focus and whether this will facilitate language learning.

ACKNOWLEDGMENTS

We would like to thank the editors of this book as well as the anonymous reviewers for important feedback and suggestions for revision. We also thank the participants at the 22nd Annual University of Wisconsin at Milwaukee Linguistics Symposium for their questions and comments concerning our claims. We have revised our chapter in light of all this valuable input.

REFERENCES

Cohen-Sherman, J. (1983). *The Acquisition of Control in Complex Sentences: The Role of Structural and Lexical Torfacs*, Doctoral dissertation, Cornell University.

Cook, V. (1991). *Second Language Learning and Language Teaching.* London: Edward Arnold.

Cooper, R., E. Olshtain, R. Tucker, and M. Waterbury. (1979). "The Acquisition of Complex English Structures by Adult Native Speakers of Arabic and Hebrew," *Language Learning* 29, 255–275.

d'Anglejan, A., and Tucker, R. (1975). "The Acquisition of Complex English Structures by Adult Learners," *Language Learning* 25, 281–296.

Dulay, H., and M. Burt. (1974). "Natural Sequences in Child Second Language Acquisition." *Language Learning* 24, 37–53.

———, and S. Krashen. (1982). *Language 2.* London: Oxford University Press.

Epstein, S., S. Flynn, and G. Martohardjono. (1993a). "Explanation In Theories of Second Language Acquisition." Paper presented at Workshop on Recent Advances in Generative Approaches to Second Language Acquisition, MIT.

———. (1993b). "Evidence for Functional Categories in Japanese Child and Adult Learners of English as a Second Language." Paper presented at Second Language Research Forum, University of Pittsburgh.

———. (1993c). "The Full Access Hypothesis in SLA: Some Evidence from the Acquisition of Functional Categories." Paper presented at the International Association for Applied Linguistics (AILA), Amsterdam.

———. (1994). "Contrasts and Similarities in Child and Adult Sla: Some Evidence from the Acquisition of Functional Categories." Paper presented at Boston University Conference on Language, Boston University.

Eubank, L. (In press). "Optionality and the 'Initial State' in L2 Development." *Language Acquisition Studies in Generative Grammar,* ed. by T. Hoekstra and B. Schwartz. Amsterdam: John Benjamins.

Flynn, S. (1983). "A Study of the Effects of Principal Branching Direction in Second Language Acquisition: The Generalization of a Parameter of Universal Grammar from First to Second Language Acquisition." PhD dissertation, Cornell University.

———. (1985). "Principled Theories of Second Language Acquisition," *Studies in Second Language Acquisition* 7, 99–107.

———. (1987). *A Parameter-Setting Model of L2 Acquisition: Experimental Studies in Anaphora.* Dordrecht, Netherlands: Reidel.

————. (1991a). "Linguistic Theory and Foreign Language Learning Environments." *Foreign Language Research in Cross-Cultural Perspective*, ed. by K. R. de Bot, Ginsberg, and C. Kramsch. Amsterdam: John Benjamins.

————. (1991b). "The Relevance of Linguistic Theory to Language Pedagogy: Debunking the Myths." *Georgetown University RoundTable on Language and Linguistics 1991*, ed. by James E. Alatis. Georgetown: Georgetown University Press.

————. (1993). "Marriage for Life: Theory, Research and Practice," *Georgetown University RoundTable on Language and Linguistics 1993*, pp. 148–161, ed. by James E. Alatis. Georgetown: Georgetown University Press.

————. (in press). "Parameter Setting in Second Language Acquisition." *Handbook for Second Language Acquisition*, ed. by T. Bhatia and W. Ritchie. New York: Academic Press.

————, and O. Brown. (1989). "Three Patterns of Development in Adult Second Language Learning." Paper presented at the Boston University Conference on Language, Boston University.

————, and I. Espinal. (1985). "Head/Final Head/Initial Parameter in Adult Chinese L2 Acquisition of English," *Second Language Acquisition Research* 1, 93–117.

————, C. Foley, and D. Lardiere. (1991). "Who's in Control? Adult L2 Acquisition of Control Structures." Paper presented at the Second Language Research Forum, University of Southern California, Los Angeles.

————, and B. Lust. (1990). "A Note in Defense of Parameter Setting in L2 Acquisition: A Response to Bley-Vroman and Chaudron," *Language Learning* 40, 419–449.

————, and G. Martohardjono. (1994). "Mapping from the Initial State to the Final State: The Separation of Universal and Language Specific Properties," *Syntactic Theory and First Language Acquisition*, Vol. 1, ed. by B. Lust, G. Harmon, and J. Kornfilt. Hillsdale, NJ: Lawrence Erlbaum Associates.

Fodor, J., T. Bever, and M. Garrett. (1974). *The Psychology of Language.* New York: McGraw Hill.

Fries, C. (1945). *Teaching and Learning English as a Foreign Language.* Ann Arbor: University of Michigan Press.

Gair, J. (1992). "Linguistics, L2 Acquisition Research, and Pedagogical Applications: Restoring the Link." Paper presented at SALA XIV, Stanford University.

————, S. Flynn, and O. Brown. (1994). "Why Japanese Object to L2 Objects." Unpublished manuscript, MIT/Cornell University.

Johnson, J. (1988). *Critical Period Effects on Universal Properties of Language: The Status of Subjacency in the Acquisition of a Second Language.* Doctoral dissertation, University of Illinois.

Kayne, R. (1983). *Connectedness and Binary Branching.* Dordrecht, Netherlands: Foris.

Lado, R. (1957). *Linguistics Across Cultures.* Ann Arbor: University of Michigan Press.

Li, L. (1993). "Adult L2 Accessibility to UG: An Issue Revisited." Paper presented at the workshop on Recent Advances in Generative Approaches to Second Language Acquisition, MIT.

Lust, B. (1992). "Functional Projection of CP and Phrase Structure Parameterization: An Argument for the Strong Continuity Hypothesis." Paper presented at the Cornell Symposium, Ithaca, NY.

Martohardjono, G. (1992). "Wh-movement in the Acquisition of a Second Language." Workshop on the Acquisition of Wh-movement, University of Massachusetts.

————. (1993). *Wh-movement in the Acquisition of a Second Language: A Cross-linguistic Study of Three Languages with and without Overt Movement.* Doctoral dissertation, Cornell University.

————, and J. Gair. (1993). "Apparent UG Inaccessibility in Second Language Acquisition: Misapplied Principles or Principled Misapplications." *Linguistics, L2 Acquisition, and Speech Pathology*, ed. by F. Eckman. Amsterdam: John Benjamins.

Rutherford, W. (1987). *Second Language Grammar: Language and Teaching.* London: Longman.

Schwartz, B. (1993). "Lexical and Functional Categories in L2a: A Principled Distinction for Explaining 'Transfer'?" Paper presented at the Conference on Recent Advances in Generative Approaches to Second Language Acquisition, MIT.

————, and R. Sprouse. (1991). "Word Order and Nominative Case in Nonnative Language Acquisition: A Longitudinal Study of (L1 Turkish) German Interlanguage." Paper presented at First Biannual Conference on Applied Linguistics at Michigan State University.

Sharwood-Smith, M. (1981). "Consciousness Raising and the Second Language Learner," *Applied Linguistics* 2, 159–168.

Sherman, J. C., and B. Lust. (1993). "Children Are in Control," *Cognition* 46, 1–51.

Thomas, M. (1991). *Universal Grammar and Knowledge of Reflexives in a Second Language*. Doctoral dissertation, Harvard University.

Uziel, S. (1991). *Resetting Universal Grammar Parameters: Evidence from Second Language Acquisition of Subjacency and the Empty Category*. Master's thesis, MIT.

Vainikka, A., and M. Young-Scholten. (1992). "The Development of Functional Projections in L2 Syntax." Paper presented at the Annual Winter meeting of the Linguistic Society of America, Philadelphia.

————. (1993). "X'-theory in L2 Acquisition." Paper presented at a conference on Recent Advances in Generative Approaches to Second Language Acquisition, MIT.

White, L. (1990). *Universal Grammar and Second Language Acquisition*. Amsterdam: John Benjamins.

————. (1992). "Subjacency Violations and Empty Categories in L2 Acquisition." *Island Constraints*, ed. by H. Goodluck and M. Rochemont. Dordrecht: Kluwer.

White, L., and A. Juffs. (1993). "UG Effects in Foreign Language Learners." Paper presented at the MIT workshop on Recent Advances in Generative Approaches to SLA, MIT.

Part II

INPUT: INTERNAL FACTORS

Chapter 5

Input, Triggers, and Second Language Acquisition: Can Binding Be Taught?

Lydia White
McGill University

1. INTRODUCTION

In order to arrive at a theory of L2 acquisition, it is essential to have a theory of what it is that the learner acquires; in other words, a theory of language (a linguistic theory) is necessary (Gregg, 1989; White, 1989). Furthermore, language pedagogy is, in its turn, affected by our theories of language and language acquisition, although it is not necessarily the case that linguistic theory or second language acquisition (SLA) theory will have direct pedagogical implications. Indeed, the relationship between linguistic theory or SLA theory and language pedagogy is like the relationship between other "pure" and "applied" sciences: the pure theory may turn out to have significant applications, but it is not usually developed with applications in mind. However, with more than a decade of UG-oriented second language (L2) research behind us, particularly research that has looked into the question of whether UG is available to L2 learners, more and more of this research addresses the question of whether L2 input can still trigger principles and parameters of UG, raising the question of the role of L2 input in and out of the classroom and the effectiveness of different kinds of pedagogical intervention in triggering properties of UG. An advantage of applying linguistic theory to SLA and to issues of language pedagogy is that the theory makes specific claims about the nature of language and hence testable predictions about the nature of interlanguage and the relationship between a mental grammar and input.

Researchers working on Universal Grammar (UG) in second language acquisition accept the premise that first language acquisition is mediated by a system of innate principles and parameters. The motivation for postulating a construct like UG is that adult linguistic competence is too complex to have been derived solely from the linguistic input (Baker & McCarthy, 1981; Hornstein & Lightfoot, 1981). It is important to note, however, that theories of acquisition that presuppose UG do not assume that linguistic input plays no role in acquisition, although this is often misunderstood. Rather, the claim is that input alone is insufficient to account for acquisition. In this framework, first language (L1) acquisition is assumed to proceed on the basis of naturalistic positive evidence (utterances in the input that children are exposed to) interacting with innate principles and parameters of UG. The input data "trigger" properties of UG (Lightfoot, 1989, 1991), causing UG parameters to be set without the necessity for learning to take place. Although parameters are part of UG, an L1 acquirer learning a particular language cannot know in advance what the appropriate parameter setting is for that language. Here the input is crucial: certain properties of the input will determine that a particular parameter setting is required—this is triggering. The parameter is set up to "expect" certain properties in the input. The assumption for L1 acquisition is that triggering is always done by positive input. Negative data (information about ungrammaticality) are assumed to play no role.

2. RESETTING PARAMETERS: POSITIVE AND NEGATIVE INPUT IN L2 ACQUISITION

In recent years there has been considerable theoretical discussion of the effects of different kinds of L2 input on the interlanguage grammar. From the perspective of L2 learnability, researchers have examined whether parameters of UG can be reset by positive L2 input, whether the L2 classroom provides appropriate input, and whether negative evidence plays a role (Felix & Weigl, 1991; Schwartz, 1993; Schwartz & Gubala-Ryzak, 1992; White, 1987, 1989, 1991a, 1991b).

In a number of experimental studies, the kind of input available to the L2 learner has been controlled for, with some subjects receiving negative evidence, some receiving explicit positive evidence, and others receiving naturalistic positive evidence (Trahey & White, 1993; White, 1991a, 1991b, 1992). These studies look at the operation of a parameter of UG, namely the verb-raising parameter of Emonds (1978) and Pollock (1989). White (1991a, 1991b) shows that francophone learners of English incorrectly assume that English, like French, allows raising of the main verb over an adverb, one of a cluster of properties associated with the parameter. As a result, French-speaking learners of English accept and produce sentences like (1) where the adverb intervenes between verb and object (SVAO word order):

(1) Mary takes usually the metro.

My colleagues and I conducted a series of studies investigating francophone students (in Grades 5 and 6, aged 11–12) in intensive English as a second language (ESL) programs in Quebec, Canada (White, 1991a, 1991b). One group received 2 weeks of instruction on adverbs, including explicit positive and negative evidence on English adverb placement, that is, evidence about sentences like those in (1). Another group received no instruction on adverbs; instead they received instruction on another aspect of English, namely question formation. Subjects were pretested immediately prior to the experimental treatment, post-tested immediately thereafter, and tested again 5 weeks later, on a variety of tasks. Results show that both groups started out with the L1 parameter setting, accepting and producing SVAO order in English. Only the group that received explicit instruction and negative evidence on adverb placement revealed knowledge of the impossibility of SVAO order in English. White (1991a) concluded that negative evidence might be necessary to trigger parameter resetting in SLA, in contrast to the situation in L1 acquisition (but see Schwartz & Gubala-Ryzak, 1992, for an alternative account).

In a related study, Trahey and White (1993) examined whether an "input flood" of positive evidence in the L2 classroom is sufficient to lead to parameter resetting. Subjects were exposed to input containing positive evidence of sentence types like (2):

(2) Mary usually takes the metro.

Such sentences are possible in English, where the main verb does not raise, but not in French, where the verb must raise. In other words, sentences like (2) are a consequence of the English value of the verb-raising parameter. The assumption made by Trahey and White is that such sentences provide the learner with positive evidence that English verbs do not raise; hence, they should (indirectly) also provide the learner with evidence that sentences like (1) are ungrammatical in English. To test whether such positive evidence would be effective in parameter resetting, another group of francophone children was exposed for 2 weeks to an input flood of specially prepared materials containing English adverbs used naturalistically. Subjects showed a dramatic increase in use of the grammatical English order subsequent to the input flood but little or no decline in use of the ungrammatical SVAO order. These results suggest that positive L2 input did not trigger parameter resetting.

3. REFLEXIVE BINDING

In this chapter I discuss another situation where current linguistic theory provides testable hypotheses about the role of input as a trigger in SLA, namely cross-linguistic differences in the behavior of reflexive pronouns. Languages differ as to whether reflexives must be bound to a local antecedent (i.e. within the same clause) or whether long-distance binding is permitted. As shown in (3), in English only local binding is permitted, whereas in languages like Japanese, the antecedent of a reflexive can be local or nonlocal.

(3) a. Mary$_i$ blamed herself$_i$

  b. *Mary$_i$ thought that Susan blamed herself$_i$

  c. The nurse asked the patient$_i$ about herself$_i$

In English, Mary (the subject) can be the antecedent of the reflexive in sentences like (3a) but not in (3b). In Japanese, on the other hand, Mary can be the antecedent of the reflexive in (3b) as well as (3a). In fact, the Japanese equivalent of (3b) is ambiguous, with either Mary (subject of the higher clause) or Susan (subject of the lower clause) as potential antecedents of the reflexive. Another difference between the two languages is shown in sentences like (3c). In languages like English, (3c) is ambiguous: the reflexive can have either the subject (*the nurse*) or the indirect object (*the patient*) as a potential antecedent. In Japanese, on the other hand, zibun requires subject antecedents, so the interpretation where the indirect object is the antecedent of the reflexive is not possible.

Recent analyses of binding account for the cross-linguistic differences by assuming that there are two types of reflexive anaphors (Cole, Hermon, & Sung, 1990; Pica, 1987; Progovac, 1993). One kind is the morphologically complex phrasal anaphor (XP), like English *himself, herself*; the other is the morphologically simple head anaphor (X^0), like zibun in Japanese. Each anaphor type has certain properties associated with it, in fact a cluster of properties that are assumed to fall out from UG. I omit from discussion here the various theories that account for these phenomena and concentrate only on the reflexes of the anaphor types: XP (phrasal) anaphors are morphologically complex (containing a pronoun and a morpheme meaning 'self'), require local binding, and allow binding to subject and nonsubject. X^0 (head) anaphors are morphologically simple (consisting of the morpheme 'self'), allow long-distance binding, and require binding to a subject.

There has been considerable research in recent years on reflexive binding in SLA (Finer, 1991; Finer & Broselow, 1986; Hirakawa, 1990; Thomas, 1991) which has been concerned mostly with the role of the Subset Principle, on the assumption that reflexive binding involves two parameters proposed by Wexler and Manzini (1987), namely the Governing Category Parameter and the Proper Antecedent Parameter. Current theories, however, assume that: (a) Governing categories are not parameterized—instead, differences in binding domains are a consequence of properties of XPs versus heads (see Bennett, 1994, for research on properties of XP vs. head reflexives in SLA); and (b) Long distance binding and the requirement of only subject antecedents are linked, rather than falling out from two independent parameters, as on the Wexler and Manzini model (see Christie & Lantolf, 1993, and Thomas, 1995, for research that explicitly looks at whether these properties cluster in interlanguage grammars).

In current theories, then, there is a connection between long-distance binding and the impossibility of binding to object, because these are part of a cluster of properties that are assumed to be linked as a consequence of properties of UG. Such a cluster can be exploited experimentally in SLA, to test issues relating to triggering. Returning to the sentences in (3), nonlocal binding like (3b) is disallowed in English, whereas binding to an object is allowed, as in (3c). Japanese has the opposite properties: nonlocal binding is possible but binding to a non-subject is not. Consider Japanese learners of English. Assuming that they transfer the head anaphor type from the L1 to the L2, a number of incorrect assumptions about English are predicted; specifically, Japanese learners should assume that English allows long-distance binding and subject orientation only.

What properties of English L2 input could reveal to an L2 learner that such assumptions are incorrect? As far as long-distance binding is concerned, there is a potential problem. Local binding is possible in Japanese as well as long-distance, so that if the Japanese learner of English hears sentences like (3a), or (3b) in a context that indicates that the local antecedent is appropriate, this will not be sufficient to show that long-distance binding is ruled out. In this case, negative evidence might be required. In the case of binding to nonsubjects, on the other hand, there is potential positive evidence, in the form of sentences like (3c) in the input, in a context where the reflexive is bound to the indirect object rather than the subject.

Given the purported cluster of properties associated with anaphor type, positive input on one aspect of the cluster should have effects on other aspects of the cluster. In the aforementioned case, then, positive evidence that English allows binding to objects should show the L2 learner that long-distance binding is prohibited. Another kind of positive evidence that might serve the same purpose is the morphological form of the reflexive itself. If English reflexives are analyzed by L2 learners as morphologically complex, which might be revealed by the fact that the form of the pronoun varies, as in *himself, herself, ourselves*, and so on, then, once again, they should realize that an XP anaphor is involved and hence that long-distance binding is prohibited.

In this chapter I report on a pilot study investigating these issues, in particular investigating whether positive evidence from one aspect of a cluster of properties can trigger knowledge of some other part of the cluster. The following hypotheses motivated this research:

1. Japanese-speaking learners of English will initially assume that English has a morphologically simple X^0 anaphor and hence that long-distance binding is permitted but binding to objects is not.
2. Providing positive evidence that English in fact allows binding to objects (either explicitly or implicitly) should lead to knowledge not just that binding to objects is possible but also that long-distance binding is impossible.

4. PILOT STUDY

4.1. Method

Subjects for the experiment were 30 adult learners of ESL, 19 francophone and 11 Japanese speaking, in a 6-week-long intensive ESL summer program (at the School of English at Queen's University, Ontario, Canada). Subjects took an "in-house" proficiency test which assessed them at the intermediate level. In addition, there was a control group of 20 adult native speakers of English.

Most of the Japanese subjects were in Canada specifically to attend the summer school, but three of them had been in Canada for periods ranging from 6 months to 1 year. None of them had ever visited any other English-speaking country. Their mean age on first exposure to English at school was 12.72 years (range 11–15 years). Their mean age on first using English for communication was 19.63 (range 16–28). The francophone subjects were from Quebec, with the exception of one who was from France. Like the Japanese-speaking subjects, they were in Ontario to improve their English; the mean amount of time they had ever spent out of Quebec (either in English-speaking Canada or in the United States) was 5 weeks (range 0–4 months). Their mean age on first exposure to English was 10.38 years (range 8–14 years). Their mean age on first using English for communication was 15.82 (range 10–20).

As described above, Japanese differs from English in having an X^0 anaphor. (It also has an XP anaphor, with properties similar to English; this anaphor, however, is much less frequently used than the X^0 anaphor and is more formal.) There are two kinds of reflexives in French: phrasal anaphors, like lui-même, and reflexive clitics, like se. Although superficially somewhat like English reflexives, French phrasal reflexives are used only emphatically. Reflexive clitics are more common; these have no equivalent in either English or Japanese and do not pattern with either the XP anaphor type or the X^0. Reflexive clitics require local antecedents, like phrasal reflexives; at the same time, some researchers argue that they are (defective) heads (Kayne, 1989).

Subjects were divided into three treatment groups. The first group ($n = 11$: 4 Japanese and 7 francophones) received explicit grammar instruction on English reflexive pronouns. This treatment lasted for 4 weeks, with three 20-minute sessions per week spent on reflexives. In some of these sessions, the main focus was on the grammar of reflexives; in others, reflexives were reviewed while some other aspect of English grammar was the main focus. Subjects were taught various properties of reflexives, including the fact that their morphological form varies depending on number and gender and that a reflexive may have a nonsubject as antecedent. They were not taught anything about long-distance binding; in other words, they received no negative evidence that long-distance binding is prohibited in English. Their input, then, might be characterized as being explicit positive data. The second group ($n = 11$: 6 Japanese and 5 francophones) was a reading group.

They received no explicit grammar instruction on reflexives. Instead, they read passages (and did related comprehension exercises) into which had been inserted examples of sentences involving reflexives, including some reflexives bound to subjects, and others to objects. They had three 20-minute sessions per week with reading material of this type, over a period of 4 weeks. Their input could be characterized as naturalistic positive data, although it was written rather than spoken input. The third group ($n = 8$: 1 Japanese and 7 francophones) was neither taught about reflexives nor read any materials involving reflexives, i.e., they received no special treatment.[1] As far as their English proficiency was concerned (as measured by the in-house proficiency test), an ANOVA shows that there were no significant effects for treatment group ($f = .776, p = .471$) or L1 ($f = 2.679, p = .1147$), and no interaction ($f = 1.391, p = .268$).

Subjects were pretested at the beginning of the ESL program. They then underwent the treatment. At the end of the ESL program, they were posttested. Testing involved two different tasks. The first was a self-paced grammaticality judgment task, which consisted of 32 monoclausal sentences, half of which were ungrammatical. Two versions of the test (with the same sentences in different orders) were used, to control for ordering effects. This task was not designed to look at subjects' knowledge (or lack thereof) of local versus long-distance binding facts in English. Rather, the majority of the test sentences (28) (involving binding to the subject) were included to investigate whether the ESL learners knew gender and number agreement properties of English reflexives. Four of the sentences involved binding to objects, to see if the learners would allow this. Examples are given in (4):

(4) a. Mary looked at herself in the mirror.
    b. The boy sprayed herself with paint by mistake.
    c. The girls hurt herself in the accident.
    d. John asked Mary all kinds of questions about herself.

The second task was a truth-value judgment task, designed to ascertain whether the L2 learners knew that English disallows long-distance binding and allows binding to objects. Truth-value judgment tasks have been used in L1 acquisition research (e.g. Crain & McKee, 1986). An advantage of these tasks is that one can indirectly get a grammaticality judgment without the subject having to focus on the form of the sentence to be judged. This methodology is particularly useful in the case of young children; the methodology usually involves spoken language, which is often accompanied by pictures or scenes to provide a context.

---

[1]In fact, all subjects took grammar and reading classes during the summer course. However, the students who received the grammar treatment in our study did not get any exposure to reflexives in their reading classes; conversely, the group exposed to the reading treatment were not taught reflexives in their grammar classes.

In this study, the truth-value task was adapted for use with adult L2 learners. (For other studies using truth-value story tasks to investigate knowledge of binding principles in SLA, see Bruhn-Garavito, this volume; Thomas, 1995.) Written stories were used, each followed by a comment. Subjects had to read each story and then indicate whether the comment was true or false. All the comments were grammatical English sentences; their appropriateness depended on the context provided by the story. The task consisted of 40 stories. Half of the stories had the reflexive bound to a masculine subject and half to a feminine one; no plural reflexives or first- or second-person reflexives were used. There were two versions of the task (with the same stories in different orders), to control for ordering effects; the task was self-paced.

Knowledge of reflexive binding was tested with the following sentence types: 16 monoclausal sentences, 8 involving binding to the subject and 8 to the object; 16 biclausal sentences, to investigate whether subjects assumed long-distance binding was possible, 8 with a finite embedded clause and 8 with a nonfinite one; 8 monoclausal sentences testing for use of linear-order strategies (such as picking the most recently mentioned NP as the antecedent of the reflexive). For each type tested, half of the stories required the answer 'true' and the other half 'false', to guard against the possibility of response biases.

Examples of the different story types are given below. Example (5) provides a case of binding to the subject of a monoclausal sentence. If the learner interprets English reflexives correctly, the comment on the story is true.

(5) Monoclausal binding to the subject (true):
A man was looking for someone to work in his restaurant, so he put an advertisement in the newspaper. Bill sent the man a letter about his experience and qualifications.

Bill sent the man a letter about himself.   (T) (F)

Binding to nonsubjects is investigated with stories like that in (6). Here, a learner who knows that binding to objects is permitted is expected to choose 'true'. The comment would be false only if the learner incorrectly assumed unavailability of binding to object.[2]

(6) Monoclausal binding to the object (true):
Susan wanted a job in a hospital. A nurse interviewed Susan for the job. The nurse asked Susan about her experience, her education, and whether she got on well with people.

The nurse asked Susan about herself.   (T) (F)

---

[2]Stories were piloted on native speakers of English. In many cases, native speakers rejected binding to objects, even when it was grammatical and when the pragmatics of the context heavily biased the interpretation in favor of the object. The stories that were used in the testing were all ones in which native speakers did accept binding to object.

The possibility of long-distance binding is examined using stories like (7) and (8). In (8), the correct answer is 'false'. Subjects' treatment of these sentence types is of particular interest; the comment could be true only if the learner incorrectly assumed long-distance binding to be possible in English.

(7) Nonfinite biclausal (true):
    Susan talked to a friend about her husband who gets violent when he drinks. Susan's friend suggested that Susan should go in the bedroom and lock the door when her husband was drunk.
    Her friend advised Susan to lock herself in the bedroom.   (T) (F)

(8) Finite biclausal (false):
    Johnny and a little boy were playing with matches. Johnny lit a match and then dropped it on the little boy's leg. The little boy went screaming to his father and told him what had happened.
    The little boy said Johnny burned himself.   (T) (F)

An example of a story testing for use of linear-order strategies is provided in (9). The rationale for these stories is that if learners consistently choose the closest NP to the reflexive as the antecedent, they will appear to know that English permits only local binding. These stories are designed so that the closest NP is not, in fact, the antecedent of the reflexive. Learners who have mastered the relevant properties of English are expected to identify these as false.

(9) Monoclausal linear order (false):
    Susan went to the drugstore. While she was there, a woman walked to the counter and stood beside Susan. The woman wanted to smell some perfume. She pressed the spray button of the perfume bottle and the perfume went all over Susan.
    The woman beside Susan sprayed herself with perfume.   (T) (F)

4.2. Results

Mean accuracy scores on the grammaticality judgment task are presented in Table 5.1, where accuracy is defined as correct acceptances of grammatical sentences and rejections of ungrammatical ones. The mean accuracy score of the control group was 31.45 (out of a total of 32 sentences). The subjects were already quite accurate in their knowledge of agreement properties of English reflexives before any treatment. A series of ANOVAs conducted on these results show that there were no significant effects for treatment ($f = .926$, $p = .41$) or language ($f = .359$, $p = .555$) on the pretest, and no interaction ($f = 1.525$, $p = .238$). Similarly, on the post-test there were no significant effects for treatment ($f = 1.302$, $p = .291$) or language ($f = .08$, $p = .78$), and no interaction ($f = .334$, $p = .719$). A comparison between the pretest and post-test performance of the three treatment groups on all

TABLE 5.1
Grammaticality Judgment Task: Mean Accuracy Scores by L1 and Treatment

Treatment	Test	French	Japanese
Grammar	Pretest	23.29	24.0
	Posttest	26.29	24.25
Reading	Pretest	28.0	24.33
	Posttest	28.8	26.5
No treatment	Pretest	23.71	31.0
	Posttest	28.57	31.0

sentences shows that there was a significant improvement overall in the perform-ance from pretest to posttest ($f = 6.514$, $p = .017$). In the case of the sentences involving binding to objects (which was specifically taught to the grammar group), only the grammar group showed a significant improvement in their acceptance of these sentences ($f = 5.755$, $p = .035$).

Turning now to the results from the truth-value judgment task, the overall results are presented in Table 5.2, again as a mean accuracy score, where accuracy is defined in terms of appropriate answers of *true* or *false* to the comments on the stories. The control group's mean accuracy score was 38.05 (out of a total of 40 stories).

ANOVAs show that on the pretest there were no significant effects for treatment ($f = .077$, $p = .926$), or for language ($f = 2.068$, $p = .163$), and no interaction ($f = 2.077$, $p = .147$). On the posttest there were no significant effects for treatment ($f = .762$, $p = .478$) or language ($f = .688$, $p = .415$); the interaction approaches significance ($f = 3.019$, $p = .068$). The lack of effects for L1 is somewhat surprising, given the fact that only Japanese allows long-distance binding and the French phrasal anaphor was presumed to behave similarly to the English one. This issue will be further considered in Section 5. In view of the small numbers of subjects in each L1 and of the fact that there was only one Japanese-speaking subject in the no-treatment group, L1 will not be con-sidered in subsequent analyses; rather, the results will be analyzed in terms of treatment only.

TABLE 5.2
Truth-Value Judgment Task: Mean Accuracy Scores by L1 and Treatment

Treatment	Test	French	Japanese
Grammar	Pretest	30.57	30.25
	Posttest	31.57	29.25
Reading	Pretest	33.8	27.0
	Posttest	35.8	28.17
No treatment	Pretest	31.57	31.0
	Posttest	31.0	36.0

A comparison between the pretest and posttest performance of the three treatment groups on the various binding possibilities tested in the story task is presented in Table 5.3. It is noticeable that there are few significant differences between the three treatment groups (grammar, reading, no treatment) or the two tests (pretest, posttest). In particular, there is no interaction between treatment and test, i.e. no indication that any treatment led to improvement in the subjects' knowledge of English reflexive binding. This is true whether we look at all truth-value responses or individually at the various binding structures included in the test. The only cases showing significant improvement from pretest to posttest were finite biclausal sentences where the response was 'true' and sentences testing linear responses where the response was 'true'. In the former case, these responses were the ones that accepted the local antecedent. In the latter case, the response of 'true' was the one that picked the antecedent that was not linearly the closest to the reflexive.

The structures that are of particular concern in this study are those involving monoclausal sentences with binding to the object where 'true' is the correct response (Mono-Obj [T]) and those involving biclausal sentences with long-dis-

TABLE 5.3
Truth-Value Judgment Task: Mean Accuracy Scores by Sentence Types

Sentence Types	Test	Grammar	Reading	No Treatment	F Treatment	F Test	F TxT
All	Pre	30.46	30.09	31.5	.129	1.045	.445
	Post	30.73	31.64	31.63			
Mono-Subj (T)	Pre	3.46	2.91	3.75	2.66	2.32	.676
	Post	3.46	3.18	4.0			
Mono-Subj (F)	Pre	3.73	3.45	3.5	1.278	1.434	.125
	Post	3.64	3.18	3.25			
Mono-Obj (T)	Pre	2.91	3.18	3.25	.079	.076	.724
	Post	3.27	3.27	2.88			
Mono-Obj (F)	Pre	3.46	4.0	3.63	.379	.063	2.599
	Post	3.73	3.64	3.88			
Bi-finite (T)	Pre	2.91	3.09	3.25	.003	4.218*	1.086
	Post	3.64	3.46	3.25			
Bi-finite (F)	Pre	2.73	2.36	2.0	.118	.05	2.176
	Post	2.00	2.73	2.75			
Bi-nonfinite (T)	Pre	3.36	3.27	3.75	.395	.843	.836
	Post	3.46	3.09	3.13			
Bi-nonfinite (F)	Pre	2.27	2.27	1.13	2.35	.051	2.664
	Post	1.36	2.46	1.88			
Linear (T)	Pre	2.82	3.09	3.63	.386	4.49*	5.975**
	Post	3.55	3.82	3.0			
Linear (F)	Pre	2.82	2.46	3.63	3.368	0.149	.941
	Post	2.64	2.82	3.63			

Note. T = true, F = false, mono = monoclausal, bi = biclausal, subj = subject, obj = object.
*$p < .05$. **$p < .01$.

tance binding where 'false' is the correct response (Bi-finite [F] and Bi-nonfinite [F]). The hypotheses tested in this study predict that the possibility of long-distance binding is connected to the impossibility of binding to objects and that by providing input indicating that binding to objects is possible in English, one should be able to eliminate nonlocal binding from the interlanguage grammar. We now look in more detail at the results relevant to binding to objects and long-distance binding.

The first issue to consider is whether it is indeed the case that learners reject binding to objects and accept long-distance binding. To address these questions, the three treatment groups' pretest responses to monoclausal sentences where the appropriate response is 'true' were compared for cases involving subjects (Mono-Subj [T]) and objects (Mono-Obj [T]). Learners who responded 'true' in the former case were accepting binding to a local subject, whereas 'true' in the latter case indicates binding to an object. Both are possible in English. Native-speaker controls showed no significant difference in their 'true' responses in these cases, and neither did the experimental groups, at either the pretest or the posttest, suggesting that L2 learners do not in fact reject binding to object (or at least were not doing so at the point in their L2 development that they had attained when initially tested).

As far as the responses to biclausal sentences are concerned, on both the finite and the nonfinite biclausal sentences, one can compare responses to stories where the comment is true with those where the comment is false. If learners allow only local binding, they should be equally accurate on both types. If they accept nonlocal binding, on the other hand, they should be less accurate in the cases where the response was 'false'. Indeed, on the pretest, for the finite biclausal sentences, the experimental groups were significantly less accurate at rejecting long-distance binding than at accepting local binding, $f(2, 27) = 7.3, p = .0118$. A similar effect showed up for the nonfinite biclausal sentences, $f(2, 27) = 44.926, p = .0001$. The control group, on the other hand, showed no significant difference in their accuracy to the 'true' or 'false' responses, in either the finite or nonfinite cases.

Similar results obtained on the posttest; that is, the experimental groups were significantly less accurate at rejecting long-distance binding than at accepting local binding, both on finite biclausal sentences, $f(2, 27) = 15.968, p = .0004$, and on nonfinite ones, $f(2, 27) = 20.295, p = .0001$. A further interesting finding on the posttest, though not on the pretest, is that the subjects were significantly more likely to accept long-distance binding out of nonfinite clauses than finite ones, $f(2, 27) = 5.04, p = .0332$, which replicates other results reported in the literature (e.g., Finer & Broselow, 1986; Hirakawa, 1990).

5. DISCUSSION

On the face of it, the results are rather discouraging, since neither of the initial hypotheses was supported. First of all, there were no effects due to the L1; the Japanese-speaking learners of English and the francophones behaved similarly on the pretest and the posttest.[3] The francophones proved to be no more accurate on long-distance binding than the Japanese speakers, even though only Japanese allows nonlocal binding. Several explanations of this are possible. One is that the francophones recognize that the L2 does not have a reflexive clitic but assume that the English reflexive is nevertheless a head (because reflexive clitics are heads), thus permitting nonlocal binding. Another possibility is that the L1 does not have direct effects on binding in the interlanguage (Flynn, 1987). In that case, one has to explain why long-distance binding is permitted. It could perhaps be argued that the X^0 anaphor is the unmarked case.

Second, the pretest results suggest that lack of binding to objects and the possibility of nonlocal binding may not have been linked in the interlanguage grammars of these learners. Subjects allowed binding to objects as well as nonlocal binding both before and after the experimental intervention, suggesting a mixture of properties of XP and X^0 anaphors. It is possible that results in Table 5.3 could conceal the fact that individual subjects do indeed behave as predicted, rejecting binding to objects and allowing long-distance binding. The data from individual subjects show that only two subjects (one francophone and one Japanese speaker) fall into this pattern. (It should also be noted that there are a number of languages that allow both X^0 and XP anaphors, Japanese being one of them. In such cases, binding of the XP anaphor to a local object is permitted.)

Another problem is that it has not been demonstrated that the L2 learners in fact analyze the reflexive as an X^0. In the grammaticality judgment task, they were quite accurate on gender and number agreement in the reflexive, suggesting that they may be sensitive to the morphological complexity of the English reflexive. It is, therefore, not at all clear that the theory of reflexive binding assumed for this study in fact provides an account of the interlanguage grammar of our subjects.

The third failure is the failure of the experimental treatments. There was almost no improvement from the pretest to the posttest and no differences depending on treatment (either explicit or implicit) or the lack of treatment. There was certainly no indication that positive evidence on binding to objects triggered knowledge of the impossibility of long-distance binding.

There are a number of reasons why the experimental treatments might have failed: controlled classroom input, even if contriving to be positive rather than negative, does not necessarily contain the crucial triggering properties. Indeed, we do not necessarily know what the relevant triggers are, so that the triggers assumed above may not, in fact, have been triggers at all. It is possible that an alternative trigger could be provided to learners by concentrating on the complex

---

[3]On the other hand, it might be argued that no differential effects due to L1 should be expected if one takes into account the fact that Japanese does have an XP reflexive as well. See Lakshmanan and Teranishi (1994) for arguments that the Japanese XP reflexive is transferred by Japanese-speaking learners of English.

morphological form of the English reflexive, although, as already mentioned, the results from the grammaticality judgment task suggest that the L2 learners tested here already had some sensitivity to this property. Roeper and Weissenborn (1990) argue, somewhat controversially, that each parameter has a unique trigger. It could be that this study did not hit on the appropriate unique trigger.

Alternatively, as discussed previously if the properties assumed to be linked are not in fact linked in the learner grammar, it is hardly surprising that teaching one property (or ensuring that it occurs in the input) has no effect on some other property. Another factor is that the intervention was very short (four hours spread over four weeks) and might simply have been insufficient. After all, the idealization of instantaneous setting is clearly an idealization even in L1 acquisition, so that more time may have to be allowed for resetting in SLA. Further evidence that time might be a factor is that the grammar teaching did not appear to have effects even on binding to objects, which was specifically taught (except in the grammaticality judgment task, where the grammar group did show significant improvement).

Finally, a few comments are in order about the truth-value judgment task. In many respects, this task is a major improvement over traditional judgment tasks, since it allows one to probe the learner's unconscious knowledge of reflexives without asking for an explicit judgment of the form of a sentence. It might be argued, however, that the stories were too difficult and that subjects were guessing or had a response bias to accept any kind of reflexive binding. In fact, this is not at all the case. Subjects were quite accurate at rejecting cases where the reflexive had no antecedent in the sentence although there was an antecedent in the discourse context provided by the story (Mono-Subj [F] and Mono-Obj [F]). Nevertheless, it would be worth developing the truth-value task such that subjects do not have to read the context stories but rather hear them or see pictures or scenes that act out the events.

6. CONCLUSION

It has been claimed that positive L2 input is sufficient to bring about changes in the interlanguage grammar (Krashen, 1985); this has rarely been tested with specific hypotheses. In this study, the specially contrived positive input (both to the grammar group and to the reading group) did not prove to have any particular effects on interlanguage reflexive binding, even when it was naturalistic (as to the reading group); the grammar and reading groups performed no better and no worse than the group that received no special treatment (who were also exposed to positive input but not input that placed any emphasis on reflexives). As we have seen, there are a number of potential reasons for this, which can be further investigated, for example by increasing the length of the experimental intervention and including larger subject groups. However, even if further study should lead to the same results, it is important to note that our understanding of the nature of interlanguage competence and the relationship of grammars to input, including pedagogical input, can be increased as much by negative results as by positive ones.

ACKNOWLEDGMENTS

The pilot study reported here was developed with the assistance of a number of research assistants: Susan Bennett, Cindy Brown, Dongdong Chen, Makiko Hirakawa, Alan Juffs, Philippe Prévost. Two deserve special mention: Joyce Bruhn-Garavito initiated and developed the truth-value judgment story task, and Joe Pater arranged the teaching and testing and did some of the teaching himself. I would like to thank the School of English of Queen's University, Kingston, Ontario, for their cooperation in allowing us to conduct this research, as well as the students and teachers who participated. I would also like to thank Margaret Thomas and Noriaki Yusa for comments and suggestions. This research was supported by SSHRCC grant No. 410-92-0047 to Lydia White and by FCAR team grant No. 94-ER-0578 to Lisa Travis, Mark Baker, Nigel Duffield, and Lydia White.

REFERENCES

Baker, C. L., and J. McCarthy (eds.) (1981). *The Logical Problem of Language Acquisition*. Cambridge, MA: MIT Press.

Bennett, S. (1994). "Interpretation of English Reflexives by Adolescent Speakers of Serbo-Croatian." *Second Language Research* 10, 125–156.

Christie, K., and J. Lantolf. (1993). "Bind me up, Bind me down: Evidence for UG from Reflexives." Paper presented at the Workshop on Recent Advances in Second Language Acquisition, MIT, Cambridge, MA.

Cole, P., G. Hermon, and L.-M. Sung. (1990). "Principles and Parameters of Long-Distance Reflexives," *Linguistic Inquiry* 21, 1–22.

Crain, S., and C. McKee. (1986). "Acquisition of Structural Restrictions on Anaphora." Proceedings of NELS 16. Graduate Linguistics Students Association, University of Massachusetts at Amherst.

Emonds, J. (1978). "The Verbal Complex V'-V in French." *Linguistic Inquiry* 9, 151–175.

Felix, S., and W. Weigl. (1991). "Universal Grammar in the Classroom: The Effects of Formal Instruction on Second Language Acquisition." *Second Language Research* 7, 162–180.

Finer, D. (1991). "Binding Parameters in Second Language Acquisition." *Point Counterpoint: Universal Grammar in the Second Language*, ed. by L. Eubank. Amsterdam: John Benjamins.

———, and E. Broselow. (1986). "Second Language Acquisition of Reflexive-Binding." *Proceedings of NELS 16*. Graduate Linguistics Students Association, University of Massachusetts at Amherst.

Flynn, S. (1987). *A Parameter-Setting Model of L2 Acquisition*. Dordrecht: Reidel.

Gregg, K. (1989). "Second Language Acquisition Theory: The Case for a Generative Perspective." *Linguistic Perspectives on Second Language Acquisition*, ed. by S. Gass and J. Schachter. Cambridge: Cambridge University Press.

Hirakawa, M. (1990). "A Study of the L2 Acquisition of English Reflexives," *Second Language Research* 6, 60–85.

Hornstein, N., and D. Lightfoot (eds.) (1981). *Explanation in Linguistics: The Logical Problem of Language Acquisition.* London: Longman.

Kayne, R. (1989). "Null Subjects and Clitic Climbing." *The Null Subject Parameter*, ed. by O. Jaeggli and K. Safir. Dordrecht: Kluwer.

Krashen, S. (1985). *The Input Hypothesis: Issues and Implications.* London: Longman.

Lakshmanan, U., and K. Teranishi. (1994). "Preferences Versus Grammaticality Judgments: Some Methodological Issues Concerning the Governing Category Parameter in SLA." *Research Methodology in Second Language Acquisition*, ed. by S. Gass, A. Cohen, and E. Tarone. Hillsdale, NJ: Lawrence Erlbaum Associates.

Lightfoot, D. (1989). "The Child's Trigger Experience: Degree-0 Learnability," *Behavioral and Brain Sciences* 12, 321–375.

———. (1991). *How to Set Parameters: Arguments from Language Change.* Cambridge, MA: MIT Press.

Pica, P. (1987). "On the Nature of the Reflexivization Cycle." *Proceedings of NELS 17.* Graduate Linguistics Students Association, University of Massachusetts at Amherst.

Pollock, J.-Y. (1989). "Verb Movement, Universal Grammar, and the Structure of IP," *Linguistic Inquiry* 20, 365–424.

Progovac, L. (1993). "Long-Distance Reflexives: Movement-to-Infl vs. Relativized Subject," *Linguistic Inquiry* 24, 755–772.

Roeper, T., and J. Weissenborn. (1990). "How to Make Parameters Work: Comments on Valian." *Language Processing and Language Acquisition*, ed. by L. Frazier and J. de Villiers. Dordrecht: Kluwer.

Schwartz, B. (1993). "On Explicit and Negative Evidence Effecting and Affecting Competence and 'Linguistic Behavior'," *Studies in Second Language Acquisition* 15, 147–163.

———, and M. Gubala-Ryzak. (1992). "Learnability and Grammar Reorganization in L2A: Against Negative Evidence Causing the Unlearning of Verb Movement," *Second Language Research* 8, 1–38.

Thomas, M. (1991). "Universal Grammar and the Interpretation of Reflexives in a Second Language," *Language* 67, 211–239.

———. (1995). "Acquisition of the Japanese Reflexive *Zibun* and Movement of Anaphors in Logical Form." *Second Language Research* 11.

Trahey, M., and L. White. (1993). "Positive Evidence and Preemption in the Second Language Classroom." *Studies in Second Language Acquisition* 15, 181–204.

Wexler, K., and R. Manzini. (1987). "Parameters and Learnability in Binding Theory." *Parameter Setting*, ed. by T. Roeper and E. Williams. Dordrecht: Reidel.

White, L. (1987). "Against Comprehensible Input: The Input Hypothesis and the Development of L2 Competence," *Applied Linguistics* 8, 95–110.

———. (1989). *Universal Grammar and Second Language Acquisition.* Amsterdam: John Benjamins.

———. (1991a). "Adverb Placement in Second Language Acquisition: Some Effects of Positive and Negative Evidence in the Classroom," *Second Language Research* 7, 133–161.

———. (1991b). "The Verb-Movement Parameter in Second Language Acquisition," *Language Acquisition* 1, 337–360.

———. (1992). "Long and Short Verb Movement in Second Language Acquisition," *Canadian Journal of Linguistics* 37, 273–286.

Chapter 6

L2 Acquisition of Verb Complementation and Binding Principle B

Joyce L. S. Bruhn-Garavito
McGill University, Montreal, Quebec

1. INTRODUCTION

Within the Principles and Parameters theory of grammar (see e.g. Chomsky & Lasnik, 1993), first language acquisition is viewed as the change from an initial state to the steady state that is the mature grammatical competence of the individual. This competence includes the blueprint not only of what is possible but of what is impossible in the language. It is a basic tenet of this theoretical framework that the initial state is equivalent to universal grammar (UG), which restricts the possible kinds of grammar available for acquisition. UG is genetically determined and uniform for all members of the human species. The child's exposure to natural language (primary linguistic data) triggers the setting of the appropriate parameters for the language being acquired.

One piece of evidence for this is the fact that the properties of the grammar appear to be severely underdetermined in the input available to the child (see White, 1989). A theory of language acquisition that assumed the child's initial state was that of a *tabula rasa* (some hypothesis-testing approaches) would have to explain how the child arrives at the complex underlying system that constitutes an adult competence on the basis of such scant and often contradictory evidence. Furthermore, research has shown that children do not receive negative evidence, and even if they do, they are incapable of making use of it. Without negative evidence and without UG, it is unclear how children would correct a hypothesis that was not compatible with the language being acquired or how they would acquire knowledge of what is not possible in the language.

It is a matter of some controversy, however, whether this process may be repeated in a similar fashion by older learners. Does the initial state of adults approaching a new language consist of UG plus their native language(s), or only their native language(s)? In the latter case, is UG available through the native language? This would limit the acquisition process to "natural" languages but might make it difficult ultimately to reset parameters. Or is UG made completely opaque to the learner, perhaps by the native language itself or the emergence of other processing systems?

The problem of second language acquisition is nevertheless similar to that of first language acquisition if we consider the nature of the input: It seems clear that the input will underdetermine the grammar in the same way as in first language acquisition, assuming of course that the learner ultimately acquires a complex underlying grammar (White, 1989). There is some evidence that this is the case. White and Genesee (1992), for example, showed that near-native speakers of English obey UG principles as native speakers do.

On the other hand, it has been argued that there is a crucial difference in the input to second language learners: the availability to second language learners of negative and explicit evidence. White (1991) has suggested that in some cases negative evidence may be needed to help reset parameters. Against this position, Schwartz (1993) claimed that negative and explicit evidence can never lead to any type of restructuring of the linguistic module of the mind because such evidence is not processed by this module. This type of input is available directly to the "central processing systems" and therefore cannot lead to the resetting of a linguistic parameter.

It seems that another argument for this position can be made if we take into consideration the characteristics of explicit data. If "natural" input underdetermines the complex target grammar, explicit input does so even more. Our understanding of language is still very tentative and most language teachers have at their disposition considerably less than the total of current linguistic thought: they usually must manage with quite traditional and prescriptive grammars.

If we assume for the sake of argument that learners do produce UG violations, it is unclear whether they can make use of corrections. Furthermore, there is some evidence that teachers' corrections are often misleading, inconsistent, and unclear.

In this chapter I look at a particular instantiation of Principle B of the Binding Theory in the acquisition of Spanish as a second language by adult learners. My objective is to ascertain whether some learners' performance shows evidence of certain underlying grammatical principles and the specific grammatical consequences of these principles, in spite of receiving explicit input which is incomplete and misleading. I show that this is indeed the case.

2. BACKGROUND

2.1. Verb Complementation and the Subjunctive

UG-based research into second language acquisition has only recently begun to show interest in the acquisition of the lexicon and how it may lead to consequences in the syntax. Perhaps this is because it is only in the last few years that linguistics itself has been willing to face this problem. However, given the fact that the lexicon "feeds" into the syntax, it is obvious that any differences in the subcategorization frame or similar theoretical construct may have enormous repercussions on the structures generated.

A realization of this relationship—between the lexicon, on the one hand, and the resulting structure in relation to principles of grammar, on the other—can be seen in the case of verb complementation. In the Romance languages, verbs may take complements in the infinitive, the indicative, and the subjunctive. Rochette (1988) argued for three types of complementation. Propositional verbs (*croire* 'to believe', *savoir* 'to know') s-select (i.e. select the semantic type) *proposition*, which is structurally realized by CP. Effective verbs (*pouvoir* 'to be able to', *commencer* 'to begin') s-select an *action*, which projects only a VP. A defective inflection (INFL) lacking tense and agreement (AGR) may be projected to I'. Of interest to this chapter is that the emotive verbs (*vouloir* 'to want to', *préférer* 'to prefer') are characterized as having an infinitival or a subjunctive complement. They select the semantic type *event*, which is realized as the projection of Infl. These are –Tense because it is argued that the presence of +Tense implies an operator in the complementizer phrase (Comp).

The structures are given in (1):

(1) SUBJUNCTIVE   INFINITIVE

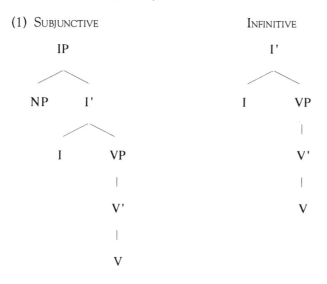

A well-known characteristic of the verbs that take complements in the sub-junctive is that the subject of the lower clause cannot corefer with the subject of the main clause. Rochette (1988) (see also Kempchinsky, 1986; and Picallo, 1985, who argue something similar on different grounds) has argued that because there is no CP in the embedded clause, there is no barrier to government, and therefore the governing category is in fact the matrix clause. If the embedded subject were coindexed with the matrix subject, we would have a violation of Principle B of the Binding Theory, which states that a pronoun must be free in its governing category (Chomsky, 1988).[1]

In Spanish, examples of this may be found in (2):

(2) a. *Quiero   ir   a la   fiesta.*
       want-1st to go-INF to the party
       'I want to go to the party.'

  b. *Quiero   que vayas   a la   fiesta.*
       want-1st that go-2nd-SUBJ to the party
       'I want you to go to the party.'

  c. pro$_i$ *quiero que* pro$_{i*/j}$ *vaya   a la   fiesta.*
       want-1st   that go-1st*/3rd-SUBJ to the party
       'I want me*/him/her to go to the party.'

Therefore, the fact that in many embedded clauses that take the subjunctive the subject must be disjoint from the matrix clause subject results straightfor-wardly from the type of verb complementation. However, it is not correct to say that every time we find an embedded clause in the subjunctive we have this obviation effect. There are at least two cases where it does not hold: when the embedded verb is a modal and when the subjunctive is found in an adjunct clause.

According to Rochette (see also Picallo, 1985), modals must project a CP because they must have an operator in Comp. To explain the possibility of a Comp position, Rochette suggests "there is a kind of reverse selection operating from the head Infl of the complement that would require the presence of the sentential operator, thus creating a Comp position" (1988, p. 276). Whether this is the correct explanation or not, the fact is that the subject of the embedded clause may corefer with the main subject in the case of modals, as can be seen in Example (3).

(3) Pro$_i$ *espero   que* pro$_{i/j}$ *pueda   hablar   con él   hoy.*
       hope-1st   that I/s/he will be able to speak with him today
       'I hope to be able/that I/s/he will be able to speak with him today.'

---

[1]If the subjects are full NPs, we have a violation of Principle C.

However, it is important to keep in mind that the infinitive is always possible in these sentences when there is coreference, and this may indeed be the preferred structure:

(4) Pro *espero   poder   hablar   con   él   hoy.*
       hope-1st to be able to speak with him today
       'I hope to be able to speak with him today.'

The second case, that of adjuncts, has not been the subject of much research, but the reason for the possibility of coreference is clear: we find a CP in these clauses, a CP that is most probably the site of the subordinating adverbial.

(5) Pro$_i$ *voy a llamarte* [CP *cuando* [IP pro$_{i/j}$ *llegue.*
       will call-1st you   when   arrive-1st/3rd-SUBJ
       'I will call you when I/he/she arrive/s.'

2.2. The Subjunctive, Disjoint Reference and Explicit Knowledge

It is a well-known fact that the subject of a subjunctive dependent clause cannot corefer with the subject of the matrix clause. It is mentioned as a condition for use of the subjunctive in almost all grammar-based textbooks. Furthermore, if a student should violate this rule (which is not very often, in my experience) the error will be corrected. Teachers questioned at the institutions where I carried out my research invariably affirmed this was the case.

However, there is only one textbook that I know of, *Pasajes* (Bretz, Dvorak, & Kirschner, 1992), which states that adjunct clauses introduced by an adverbial conjunction (*cuando* 'when', *en cuanto* 'as soon as', etc.) may take the subjunctive even when the subjects corefer (the infinitive is impossible).

Furthermore, that modals also function in a way different from other verbs is not only not mentioned, it is not recognized as a fact by most teachers and textbooks. When asked, seven out of eight teachers said they would correct a sentence such as (3). One teacher said she would not, but she would try to avoid the problem because it was better not to have exceptions to the rules. Five teachers told me these sentences were incorrect in Spanish because they violated the rule of the subjunctive. However, as we shall see, all but one of the native-speaker control group accepted coreference with the verb *poder*.[2]

The case of the subjunctive and disjoint reference seems to be a good example of explicit rules that are incomplete and often in error, passed from grammar books and teacher to learners. The question is, do learners acquire the correct

---

[2]The exception happened to be a teacher who explained to me that the sentences made sense but were "incorrect" in Spanish. This linguistic analysis also led the person in question to reject sentences with *cuando*, although they cannot be said any other way!

structures in spite of this misinformation?[3] If the answer is yes, this could be taken as an indication that the learner has access to UG. It would not, however, indicate whether UG is accessed directly or through the native language, if we take s-selection by verbs and Principle B of binding to apply across languages.

To summarize, then, the question that I attempt to answer in this chapter is whether some learners are able to go beyond what they are explicitly taught to attain a grammar of the subjunctive in relation to Principle B of Binding Theory that is compatible with principles of UG and more in line with a native speaker's adult competence.

3. METHODOLOGY

3.1. Subjects

The subjects were 17 university students and 10 adult learners in the continuing education program. All were enrolled in advanced classes: literature and advanced grammar for the university students, Level IV (the highest level) of Continuing Education. They were given a background questionnaire which, unfortunately, not all the subjects filled out completely. However, it was possible to determine native language and other languages spoken, as well as the kind of contact the subjects had with Spanish. This is mainly in the university, formal setting.

The subjects were taken from advanced classes because the objective of this study was to see whether learners are ultimately capable of performing at a native speaker's level in the structures studied. This does not mean that the learners' academic level implied they had reached nativelike competence, but the likelihood of finding subjects who have is higher in these groups.

There were 13 speakers whose first language was French and 8 whose first language was English. Four learners identified two first languages: English/French, Italian/English, Greek/English, Silesian/Polish. One was Vietnamese, one Italian.

However, all the subjects spoke English and French well, and many spoke other languages: German, Afrikaans, Zulu. These subjects were either language majors or highly interested in languages, but not linguistics.

There was also a control group of 12 subjects whose native language was Spanish. As with the second language learners, they also spoke French and/or English as second languages.

3.2. Method of Testing

Methodology is a serious problem in testing the acquisition of anaphora, as has been shown by Crain and his associates (see, e.g., Crain & McKee, 1985) for first language acquisition and by Thomas (1991) for second language acquisition.

---

[3]In fact, the frequency of structures in the subjunctive that permit coreference cannot be too high either, particularly in the case of the modals. Recall that the infinitive is the preferred form.

Tests involving the interpretation of sentences (e.g., by act-out or picture identification tasks) point only to preferences on the part of the subject, preferences that may be strong enough to override the subject's perception of possible ambiguities. In other words, the fact that one interpretation is chosen does not necessarily mean that the other is excluded.

In order to solve this problem in first language acquisition, Crain and his associates (see, e.g., Crain, 1982; Crain & Fodor, 1988; Hamburger & Crain, 1982) have developed a methodology based on truth-value judgment tasks: the subject is asked whether a sentence uttered by one of the characters accurately describes an action carried out by an experimenter. In this way, a certain interpretation is forced on the subject, who is then free to reject it if it is not valid.

In the present study, a similar test was developed for adults. It was also a truth-value judgment task, but it was a written test. The learner was presented with a short story describing a particular situation. One of the characters mentioned in the situation then said something and the subject had to indicate whether what was said was a reasonable response given the situation. In all cases the sentence presented to be judged was grammatical in isolation but could become inappropriate in the context given.

In total there were 50 sentences (and their corresponding situations) to be judged, 20 with embedded clauses in the subjunctive, 10 infinitivals, 10 indicative, and 10 that were a hodgepodge of all types mainly meant as distractors.

In Spanish the third person and the first person of the present subjunctive verb forms are the same. In the test, the first person was used in the matrix clause and the subject of the subjunctive was always pro (a null pronoun). The situation always called for an interpretation in which the pro coreferred with the matrix subject, the first person. However, in 10 of these sentences coreference was not possible; it was ruled out by Principle B of Binding Theory, according to which, as I mentioned earlier, a pronoun must be free in its governing category (Chomsky, 1988). The only possible reference for the embedded pro is some third person. Therefore it was expected that these 10 sentences would be judged inappropriate, as can be seen by the following example.

(6) *Mencha cumple años el viernes. Desea recibir muchos regalos.*
    Mencha dice:
    Quiero que reciba muchos regalos.   (sí)   (no)

    It is Mencha's birthday on Friday. She wants to get a lot of presents.
    Mencha says:
    I want that pro get-SUBJ a lot of presents.   (yes) (no)

In the remaining 10 embedded clauses coreference was possible because there was a CP barrier, as explained previously: They included a modal (*poder*) (see 7a) or are adjunct clauses introduced by *cuando* (see 7b).

(7) a. *María le pide a Pepe que le ayude pero Pepe tiene que*
   disculparse porque está ocupado.
   Pepe dice:
   Siento mucho que no pueda ayudarte.   (sí)   (no)

   Maria asks Pepe to help her but Pepe must excuse
   himself because he is busy.
   Pepe says:
   I regret very much that pro not be able-SUBJ to
   help you.   (yes) (no)

   b. *Paquita se va de viaje y su mamá está preocupada.*
   Paquita dice:
   No te preocupes. Te mandaré un telegrama cuando
   llegue.   (sí)   (no)

   Paquita is going on a trip and her mother is worried.
   Paquita says:
   Don't worry. I will send you a telegram when pro
   arrive-SUBJ.   (yes) (no)

If learners accepted all 20 of these sentences, they could not be said to have captured the basic nature of the subjunctive. If they rejected all 20, they would be following the rules as taught, and explicit knowledge could be said to play a major role in their comprehension of Spanish.

If they rejected the first 10 and accepted those sentences where coreference was theoretically possible, this would have been evidence that they were performing as native speakers and had gone beyond what they had been taught, perhaps guided by principles of UG.

In sentences where the dependent clause is infinitival, coreference is obligatory: the matrix subject controls the embedded subject. Five of the ten sentences which had an infinitival dependent clause were correct in that the situation called for coreference, as in example 8a, but five were not correct because the context demanded disjoint reference; a subjunctive would have been the appropriate response (see Example 8b).

(8) a. *Amalia tiene que dar una conferencia a las tres y el tráfico*
   está muy pesado.
   Amalia dice:
   Espero llegar a tiempo.   (sí)   (no)

   Amalia has to give a lecture at three and the traffic
   is very heavy.
   Amalia says:
   I hope to arrive on time.   (yes) (no)

b. *La enfermera tiene que hacer mucho trabajo hoy, pero el*
médico está desocupado.
El médico dice:
Siento tener tanto trabajo. ¿Puedo ayudarte?   (sí)   (no)

The nurse has a lot to do today but the doctor
is free.
The doctor says:
I regret to have (having) so much work. Can I help you?   (yes)   (no)

These sentences were intended to test whether the learners were aware of
the distinction between the subjunctive and the infinitive: in other words,
whether they had the two structures given in 1 and 2.

The ten sentences that included dependent clauses in the indicative were all
appropriate in the context given: five showed coreference, five did not. These
sentences were included to test whether the learners distinguished the indicative
from the subjunctive, in that a dependent clause in the indicative always includes
a CP and is therefore never governed by the matrix clause. The pronoun is free
and may or may not be disjoint.

(9) a. *Gustavo y Clara hablan de política. Gustavo no está*
de acuerdo con Clara.
Gustavo dice:
Opino que no tienes razón.   (sí)   (no)

Gustavo and Clara are talking about politics.
Gustavo does not agree with Clara.
Gustavo says:
I believe that you are wrong.   (yes)   (no)

b. *Guillermo va en carro camino a la casa de una amiga. Hay*
un accidente en la carretera. Guillermo mira el reloj.
Guillermo dice:
Veo que no voy a llegar a tiempo.   (sí)   (no)

Guillermo is in a car on his way to a friend's house. There
is an accident on the road. Guillermo looks at his watch.
Guillermo says:
I see I will not be on time.   (yes)   (no)

Finally, there were 10 sentences that contained a variety of structures but
that could be judged inappropriate mainly from the vocabulary or the ordering
of the items. These served to focus the subjects' attention on the meaning and
to provide balance and rule out the possibility of a bias toward accepting all
structures.

(10) *Susana va a ver al médico porque está muy gorda.*
      El médico le dice:
      Creo que debe comer más.   (*sí*) (*no*)

      Susana goes to see the doctor because she is very fat.
      The doctor says:
      I believe you should eat more.   (yes) (no)

In all there were 25 sentences where the correct response was to reject the
sentence: 10 subjunctive clauses where coreference was ruled out by Principle
B, 5 infinitivals where coreference was grammatically obligatory (control) but
the context called for no coreference, and 10 distractors. There were also 25
sentences where the correct response was to accept: 10 subjunctive sentences,
5 with a modal in the subjunctive, 5 in adjunct position; 5 infinitivals where
coreference was appropriate according to the context; and 10 indicatives—5
with coreference, 5 without.

4. RESULTS

4.1. The Control Group

Tables 6.1, 6.2, and 6.3 present the results of the test for the control group. As
can be seen, there was almost unanimous rejection of the subjunctive with
coreference where this was theoretically disallowed, and acceptance for the sentences with the modal or an adjunct. As was mentioned previously (n. 2), one
subject rejected all of the latter. Three other subjects rejected one sentence each
with the modal. This explains the lower percentage for this category. The control
group also performed as expected on the infinitive, the indicative, and the
distractors.

TABLE 6.1
Percentage of Accurate Responses by the NS Control Group

Total	95.83
Correct sentences (in the context)	94.33
Incorrect sentences (in the context)	97.33

TABLE 6.2
Correct Responses by the NS Control Group According to Complement

Subjunctive	Infinitive	Indicative
92.91%	97.50%	97.50%

TABLE 6.3
Percentage of Correct Responses by the NS Control Group
According to Coreference Possibilities

Subj. +C U	Subj. Modal +C G	Subj. Adjunct +C G	Inf. +C G	Inf. −C U	Indic. −C G	Indic. -C G	Distract. U
97.50	85.00	91.66	96.66	98.33	98.33	96.66	98.33

Note. Number of subjects was 12. +C: coreference; − C: no coreference; G: correct response to accept sentence; U: correct response to reject sentence.

4.2. Spanish L2 Learners

The results for the L2 learners are presented in Tables 6.4, 6.5, and 6.6. The nonnative speakers performed in a similar fashion to the native speakers except in two areas: the subjunctive in complement clauses without a modal and infinitival clauses where the situation called for disjoint reference between the subject of the lower clause and the matrix clause. In other words, about one half of the responses failed to reject coreference when a subjunctive was present and about one fourth failed to reject lack of coreference when an infinitival was

TABLE 6.4
Percentage of Accurate Responses by the L2 Group

Total	80.15
Correct sentences (in the context)	88.88
Incorrect sentences (in the context)	71.40

TABLE 6.5
Percentage of Correct Responses by L2 Group
According to Type of Complement

Subjunctive	Infinitive	Indicative
67.00	81.48	91.48

TABLE 6.6
Percentage of Correct Responses by the L2 Group
According to Coreference Possibilities

Subj. +C U	Subj. Modal +C G	Subj. Adjunct +C G	Inf. +C G	Inf. −C G	Indic. −C G	Indic. -C G	Distract. U
49.26	85.92	87.40	88.15	74.81	95.55	87.40	91.85

Note. Number of subjects was 27. +C: coreference; − C: no coreference; G: correct response to accept sentence; U: correct response to reject sentence.

present, in spite of having been explicitly taught that this was not possible. It is not a question of a bias toward accepting everything, because the distractor sentences were rejected 91.85% of the time. I return to this later.

Recall, however, that the object of the present study was to determine whether it is possible to master verb complementation and its relation to binding. From a purely ideal point of view, even one learner who has done so clearly and uncontroversially should be enough to show that it is possible. It is therefore necessary to look at the individual learners to see whether any of them performed as native speakers. Table 6.7 shows a frequency distribution of the L2 subjects' performance rates on the test as a whole.

In the literature it has traditionally, though somewhat arbitrarily, been assumed that a score above 90% indicates mastery. I will therefore turn now to the five learners who obtained between 91% and 100% on the test. Table 6.8 gives the percentage scores for these students according to the type of complementation; Table 6.9 gives the scores in the different subtypes. As can be seen, these five subjects performed similarly to native speakers with regard to the acceptance or rejection of coreference between subjects in all three types of complementation. They also showed mastery of the different possibilities with regard to the subjunctive: they accepted coreference when a modal was present or the subjunctive was in an adjunct clause and rejected it in all other cases.

It could be argued at this point that these learners all spoke French and were therefore simply transferring the surface grammar from French into Spanish. This claim does not hold water for several reasons. In the first place, the structures in question are not identical in French and in Spanish. Either the infinitive or

TABLE 6.7
Performance of L2 Speakers

%	Frequency
91–100	5
81–90	4
71–80	14
61–70	4

TABLE 6.8
Percentage of Correct Responses According to Complement
by Subjects Whose Total Scores Surpassed 90%

Subject	Native Language	Subjunctive	Infinitive	Indicative
102	French	95	90	100
125	French	95	90	100
131	French	100	100	80
133	English	90	100	100
134	Silesian/Polish	95	100	100

TABLE 6.9
Percentage of Correct Responses by L2 Subjects Whose Total Scores
Surpassed 90% According to Coreference Possibilities

Subject	Subj. +C U	Subj. Modal +C G	Subj. Adjunct +C G	Inf. +C G	Inf. −C G	Indic. −C G	Indic. +C G	Distract. U
102	100	100	80	80	100	100	100	100
125	90	100	100	80	100	100	100	100
131	100	100	100	100	100	100	80	100
133	90	80	100	100	100	100	100	100
134	90	100	100	100	100	100	100	100

Note. +C: coreference; −C: no coreference; G: correct response to accept sentence; U: correct response to reject sentence.

the indicative may be used in French where the subjunctive is used in Spanish. It seems in particular that French does not permit coreference of the subject of a subordinate subjunctive and the indirect object of the main clause, as Spanish does. This may be because movement of the direct object clause is possible in Spanish but not in French (see Bruhn-Garavito, 1992). In French the subject of the subordinate clause is therefore c-commanded by the indirect object and Principle B takes effect. Compare the French Examples 11a and 11b with the Spanish Examples 11c and 11d.

(11) a. *Je te demande d'aller au bureau.*
   I you ask   *de* to go to the office
   'I am asking you to go to the office.'

   b. **Je te$_i$ demande que tu$_i$ ailles au bureau.*
   I you ask   that you go-SUBJ to the office
   'I am asking you to go to the office.'

   c. *Yo te pido ir a la oficina.* (Possible, but infrequent)
   I you ask to go to the office
   'I am asking you to go to the office.'

   d. *Yo te$_i$ pido que* pro$_i$ *vayas a la oficina.*
   I you$_i$ ask that pro$_i$ go-SUBJ to the office
   'I am asking you to go to the office.'

French is similar to Spanish in that the subject of a subjunctive modal permits coreference, as in 12a, but not in other cases, as in 12b.

(12) a. *Je crains que je ne puisse t' aider.*
   I fear that I not can you help
   'I fear that I cannot help you.'

b. *Je crains que j' aille   par avion.
   I fear   that I go-SUBJ by plane
   'I fear to go by plane.'

However, French is quite different when it comes to adjunct clauses. Spanish uses the subjunctive in adjunct clauses whenever the action of the embedded clause is anticipated in relation to the main clause. As in English, the future can never be used:

(13) Pro$_i$ te   veré   cuando pro$_i$ vaya (*iré)   a la casa.
     Pro you will see when   pro go   (*will go) to the house
     'I will see you when I go (*will go) to the house.'

French uses the future indicative in these sentences. It is possible that French never permits the subjunctive when there is a full CP, but Spanish does.

(14) a. Je te   verrai   quand j' irai   chez toi.
        I you will see when I   will go to your place
        'I will see you when I go to your place.'
     b. *Je te   verrai   quand j' aille   chez toi.
        I you will see when I   go-SUBJ to your place
        'I will see you when I go to your place.'

Therefore, when subjects rejected coreference with the subjunctive in complement clauses but accepted it in adjuncts, they could not be transferring from French. These subjects also gave appropriate responses to the indicative, so they were quite aware of the difference between these two moods.

Finally, although it is impossible to rule out some effects from French in the ultimate acquisition of the structures in question, given the small number of learners who met our criterion (though notice that one of the five was a native speaker of English and one was Polish), it is possible to show that at an earlier stage of acquisition transfer doesn't seem to work at all. As can be seen in Table 6.15, four out of the ten speakers who accepted coreference where it was not possible 90% of the time or more were native speakers of French. They were, in fact, accepting interpretations which are ungrammatical in French.

(15) a. *Pro$_i$ quiero   que pro$_i$ reciba   muchos regalos. (Test sentence 3)
        Pro$_i$ want-1st that pro$_i$ receive many   gifts
        'I want to receive many gifts.'
     b. *Je veux   que je reçois   beaucoup de cadeaux.
        I want-1st that I receive many   gifts
        'I want to receive many gifts.'

Tables 6.10, 6.11, and 6.12 show that the overall scores for native speakers of English are similar, though slightly lower, than scores for native speakers of French. Only the answers of subjects who categorized themselves as native speakers of one or the other language were tabulated in these tables. Bilinguals and native speakers of other languages were excluded. However, recall that all the subjects spoke at least some French.

To summarize this section, I claim that a group of learners show mastery over the relation between verb complementation and Principle B of Binding and that this mastery cannot be accounted for by the role of explicit input or simple surface transfer from the native language. As I mentioned earlier, however, I am not excluding the possibility that UG is being accessed through the native language.

TABLE 6.10
Correct Responses by L2 Group as Whole and
by Native Speakers of French and English

	L2 Group	French	English
	N = 27	N = 13	N = 8
Total	80.15	81.23	77.00
Correct sentences (in context)	88.88	88.30	85.50
Incorrect sentences (in context)	71.40	74.15	68.00

TABLE 6.11
Percentages of Correct Responses by L2 Group as a Whole and by
Native Speakers of French and English by Type of Complement

	L2 Group	French	English
	N = 27	N = 13	N = 8
Subjunctive	67.00	69.61	64.00
Infinitive	81.48	85.38	77.50
Indicative	91.48	91.53	88.75

TABLE 6.12
Percentage of Correct Responses by L2 Group as Whole and Native Speakers
of French and English According to Coreference Possibilities

	Subj. +C U	Subj. Modal +C G	Subj. Adjunct +C G	Inf. +C G	Inf. −C G	Indic. −C G	Indic. +C G	Distract. U
Total	49.26	85.92	87.40	88.15	74.81	95.55	87.40	91.85
French	55.38	86.15	81.53	90.76	80.00	95.38	87.69	90.00
English	43.00	75.00	95.00	80.00	75.00	92.00	85.00	90.00

Note. Total N = 27; French N = 13; English N = 8. +C: coreference; −C: no coreference; G: correct response to accept sentence; U: correct response to reject sentence.

In the next section I discuss subjects who did not meet the criterion for mastery.

4.3. L2 Learners: Nonmastery

The main points of difficulty for the Spanish L2 learners, as we have seen, are disjoint reference in subjunctive clauses and lack of it in infinitivals. Table 6.13 shows a cumulative frequency for subjunctive clauses only. The subjects seem to concentrate at the extremes: 11 between 80% and 100% correct responses, 11 between 80% and 100% incorrect responses. There are only 5 subjects who seem to be intermediate. This is an interesting result which suggests that acquisition may be triggered by something in the input. This cannot be negative or explicit evidence because, as we have seen, it tends to be incomplete and confusing. Furthermore, the learner's background in Spanish was very similar for all the subjects. They mainly acquired Spanish in a formal, foreign setting. The background questionnaire shows that some had traveled for a few weeks to Spanish-speaking countries, but their main contact was at the university.

It is nevertheless clear that hardly any of the subjects were actually performing according to the rules as taught. However, as can be seen in Table 6.13, there were 7 subjects who met a criterion of 90% on correct responses to the subjunctive. These subjects were 102, 124, 125, 127, 131, 133, 134. Of these we examined 5 who exhibited overall mastery of the structures studied. Table 6.14 shows the scores for the remaining 2. Although they rejected coreference where it was impossible, they also rejected it where it should have been possible, in the same way that 2 of the native speakers did. The explanation given by the native speakers was in terms of conscious rules. It is not farfetched to suppose that the explanation is similar here. (One of these learners also did poorly on the distractors. I have no explanation for this.)

TABLE 6.13
Cumulative Frequency for Disjoint Reference with the Subjunctive

Score	Frequency
10	4
9	3
8	4
7	1
6	0
5	2
4	1
3	1
2	1
1	8
0	2

TABLE 6.14

Percentage of Correct Responses by Additional L2 Subjects Whose Score on Disjoint Reference Surpassed 90% According to Coreference Possibilities

Subject	Subj. +C U	Subj. Modal +C G	Subj. Adjunct +C G	Inf. +C G	Inf. −C G	Indic. −C G	Indic. +C G	Distract. U
124	100	10	100	80	80	80	80	50
127	100	0	0	100	100	80	100	100

Note. +C: coreference; −C: no coreference; G: correct response to accept sentence; U: correct response to reject sentence.

We turn now to those learners who seemed to violate Principle B in subjunctive sentences. Table 6.15 shows the results in the different categories for these learners. Note that coreference between subjects in subjunctive embedded clauses was accepted in all cases.

The question we are now faced with is whether these learners were violating principles of UG at this stage in their acquisition of Spanish. The most plausible answer is that they were not and that the problem lay in their acquisition of the morphology and the special nature of the subjunctive. The characteristics of the verb moods studied here are +Tense, +AGR for the indicative tenses; −Tense, −AGR for the infinitives; and −Tense, +AGR for the subjunctive. The subjunctive is considered tenseless because its tense seems to depend on the tense of the main verb. However, it is incorrect to say that it is completely featureless regarding tense in all cases (see Bruhn-Garavito, 1992). In Spanish and French there seems to be a further division of verbs (and their complements)

TABLE 6.15

Percentage of Correct Responses by L2 Subjects Whose Score on Disjoint Reference Was at or Below 10% According to Coreference Possibilities

Subject & L1	Subj. +C U	Subj. Modal +C G	Subj. Adjunct +C G	Inf. +C G	Inf. −C G	Indic. −C G	Indic. +C G	Distract. U
101 E	10	100	100	80	80	100	100	100
106 F	10	100	100	100	100	100	100	90
107 F	10	80	100	100	60	100	80	100
108 F	10	100	100	100	60	100	100	90
110 E	10	100	100	80	100	80	100	100
118 E	10	80	100	100	10	100	80	100
122 O	10	100	100	100	0	100	100	100
128 B	10	100	100	100	100	100	80	90
109 F	0	100	100	100	40	100	80	80
105 E	0	100	100	80	80	80	100	100

Note. E: English; F: French; O: other; +C: coreference; −C: no coreference; G: correct response to accept sentence; U: correct response to reject sentence.

into those verbs that totally absorb the tense features of the subjunctive (as shown for French in Examples 16a and 16b, and for Spanish in 16c and 16d) and those that permit the features [+ or − past] in relation to the tense of the main verb (as shown in Examples 16e, 16f and 16g for French, and Examples 16h and 16i for Spanish). In the latter class French sometimes permits the indicative and Spanish becomes more flexible as to coreference.

(16) a. *Je veux que tu viennes.*
   I want that you come-SUBJ
   'I want you to come.'

   b. **Je veux que tu sois venu.*
   I want that you have come-SUBJ
   'I want you to have come.'

   c. *Quiero que vengas.*
   want-1stp that come-2ndp.-SUBJ-pres.
   'I want you to come.'

   d. **Quiero que hayas venido.*
   want-1stp that have come-2ndp.-SUBJ-perf
   'I want you to have come.'

   e. *Je crains que tu viennes trop tard.*
   I fear that you come-SUBJ too late

   f. *Je crains que tu sois venu trop tard.*
   I fear that you have come too late

   g. *J' espère que tu viendras.*
   I hope that you will come-fut.

   h. *Espero que vengas.*
   hope-1stp that come-2ndp.-SUBJ-pres.
   'I hope that you will come.'

   i. *Espero que hayas venido.*
   hope-1stp that have come-2ndp.-SUBJ-perf.
   'I hope you have come.'

If we add to this the possibility of infinitivals that show agreement features, such as those found in Portuguese, it becomes obvious that −Tense is a simplification. There seem to be at least two possibilities: [−Tense, +tense features] and [−Tense, −tense features]. It is possible that the subjunctive with verbs like *vouloir/querer* (indirect commands) which is −tense features is some type of infinitive with agreement morphology. If this is so, then we may suppose that L2 learners do not interpret the subject of the lower clause as pro in these sentences, but rather as a case of PRO controlled by the main verb. In other words, they have remarked only on the feature −Tense and not on the feature +AGR. Agreement is, as a matter of fact, slightly less robust in the subjunctive than in the indicative in Spanish. If we exclude informal *tú*, we have the same form for all three singular verb persons. In 17, pro could be 'I' (*yo*), 'you' (*Ud.*) or 'he, she' (*él, ella*).

(17) pro *Quiere que* pro *venga.*
pro wants that pro (I, you, he, she) come

There is, in fact, some indication that these learners may have been confusing the subjunctive and the infinitive: Note the relatively high proportion of errors in the rejection of disjoint reference in infinitivals. Table 6.16 shows the cumulative frequency for this group. Recall that the percentage of error for this category was 75% (see Table 6.6). Although the distribution is different from that of the subjunctive in that there were not a great many learners at the lower end of the scale, it is still surprising that even three should accept disjoint reference with an infinitival between 90% and 100% of the time. It seems, then, quite reasonable to suppose that there was confusion about what the different verbal forms stand for. The learners had not clearly sorted out the morphology, and this in spite of being advanced learners of Spanish. They did not clearly differentiate the forms that take pro and those that take PRO, resulting in a sort of chameleon nature for both.

Another option is to suppose that the learners were not aware of the −Tense feature of the subjunctive and had noted only that it is +Agreement. In this case, they were using the subjunctive as equivalent to the indicative, which might mean they were taking Spanish to be a language like Mohawk, where only CP complements are allowed (see Ikeda, 1991). We cannot tell if this is the case, because the test did not include subjunctive sentences with disjoint reference. However, if it is true, it would again show that there is a problem in the misleading grammatical descriptions being taught. Learners are told there are four "tenses" in the subjunctive, and few books (Bretz, Dvorak, & Kirschner, 1992 again being the exception) point out the fact, and provide practice in it, that an 'imperfect' subjunctive is past only in that it is dependent on a past matrix clause, but that it can actually refer to a future action. The full realization of this may be the trigger that leads to the ultimate acquisition of verb complementation in Spanish.

TABLE 6.16
Cumulative Frequency for Disjoint Reference with the Infinitive

Score	Frequency
5	11
4	6
3	6
2	1
1	2
0	1

5. SUMMARY

In this chapter I have looked at the acquisition of Principle B of Binding in the domain of verb complementation. Verbs that project a full CP will permit either coreference or disjoint reference between the lower and higher subjects. However, verbs that project only an IP disallow coreference between subjects (when the subject is pro) given that the governing category is the matrix clause. My main objective has been to ascertain whether at least some advanced learners perform as native speakers in spite of conflicting evidence from explicit input. I have tried to show that it is possible to suppose that for these learners UG is available in some way.

I believe this research should be continued with larger groups, because the number of learners who have attained mastery is so small. It would also be interesting to look at groups that are less bilingual than this group in order to be able to completely rule out influence from French. Finally, the search for the trigger that causes the learner to acquire full mastery of these structures should be continued.

ACKNOWLEDGMENTS

I gratefully acknowledge the support of SSHRCC grant No. 410-92-0047 to Lydia White, without which this research would not have been possible. I would also like to thank Lydia White for her personal support and encouragement.

REFERENCES

Bretz, M. L., T. Dvorak, and C. Kirschner. (1992). *Pasajes: Lengua.* New York: McGraw-Hill.
Bruhn-Garavito, J. (1992). " '*Dire de*' vs. '*decir que*': Some Types of Verb Complements in French and Spanish." Unpublished manuscript, McGill University, Montreal.
Chomsky, N. (1988). *Lectures on Government and Binding.* Dordrecht: Foris.
———, and H. Lasnik. (1993). "Principles and Parameters Theory." *Syntax: An International Handbook of Contemporary Research,* ed. by J. Jacobs, A. von Stechow, W. Sternfell, and T. Vennemann. The Hague: Mouton.
Crain, S. (1982). "Temporal Terms: Mastery by Age Five," *Papers and Reports on Child Language Development* 21, 33–38.
———, and J. Fodor. (1988). "Competence and Performance in Child Language." Unpublished manuscript, City University of New York.
Crain, S., and C. McKee. (1985). "Acquisition of Structural Restrictions on Anaphora." *Proceedings of the North Eastern Linguistic Society,* 16, University of Massachusetts, Amherst, MA.
Hamburger, H., and S. Crain. (1982). "Relative Clause Acquisition." *Language Development, Volume 1,* ed. by S. Kuczaj. Hillsdale, NJ: Lawrence Erlbaum Associates.
Ikeda, E. (1991). *Sentential Complementation in Mohawk.* Master's thesis, McGill University, Montreal.
Kempchinsky, P. (1986). *Romance Subjunctive Clauses and Logical Form.* PhD dissertation, University of California, Los Angeles.

Picallo, C. (1985). *Opaque Domains*. PhD dissertation, City University of New York, New York.

Rochette, A. (1988). *Semantic and Syntactic Aspects of Romance Sentential Complementation*. PhD dissertation, MIT, Cambridge, MA.

Schwartz, B. (1993). "On Explicit and Negative Data Effecting and Affecting 'Competence' and 'Linguistic Behaviour,'" *Studies in Second Language Acquisition (SSLA)* 20, 147–163.

Thomas, M. (1991). "Universal Grammar and the Interpretation of Reflexives in a Second Language," *Language* 67, 211–239.

White, L. (1989). *Universal Grammar and Second Language Acquisition*. Amsterdam: John Benjamins.

———. (1991). "Adverb Placement in Second Language Acquisition: Some Effects of Positive and Negative Evidence in the Classroom," *Second Language Research* 7(2), 133–161.

———, and F. Genesee. (1992). "How Native is a Native Speaker?" Paper delivered at Boston University Conference on Language Acquisition.

Chapter 7

The Noun Phrase Accessibility Hierarchy in SLA: Determining the Basis for Its Developmental Effects

Robert L. Hamilton
University of South Carolina

1. INTRODUCTION

1.1. Competing Accounts of Noun Phrase Accessibility in SLA

The field of second language acquisition (SLA) has enjoyed a profitable relationship with formal linguistics throughout the years, a relationship that most would agree is beneficial and even necessary for the development of SLA theory. However, the adoption of formal constructs by SLA theorists is often done without rigorously testing the applicability of those constructs to the second language (L2) context, potentially resulting in situations in which theorists maneuver to make L2 data fit the constructs rather than ensuring that the constructs fit the data.

In this chapter I argue that this has occurred in the application to SLA of Keenan and Comrie's (1977) Noun Phrase Accessibility Hierarchy (NPAH). The NPAH as originally proposed was understood to be a hierarchy of grammatical relations (GRs) whose universal status enjoyed substantial typological support. Keenan and Comrie developed the NPAH in the nascent years of Relational Grammar, which takes GRs such as subject (SU), direct object (DO), and so forth as syntactic primitives from which configurational structure is derived. This theory contrasted with Chomsky's Standard Theory, in which just the reverse was true; that is, configuration (i.e., dominance and precedence relations between constituents in phrase structure) was considered primitive and GRs were considered derivative (e.g., the subject is defined as the "NP imme-

TABLE 7.1
The Noun Phrase Accessibility Hierarchy

Subject (SU)	*The man who knows the woman*
< Direct Object (DO)	*The man that the woman knows*
< Indirect Object (IO)	*The man that the woman gave a pencil to*
< Oblique (OBL)	*The desk that the woman put the pencil on*
< Genitive (GEN)	*The man whose pencil the woman took*
< Object of Comparative (OC)	*The man that the woman is taller than*

Note. < means "is more accessible than."

diately dominated by S" [Chomsky, 1965, p. 71]). The levels of the NPAH as realized in English relativization are shown in Table 7.1.

Keenan and Comrie's proposal that the GRs of the NPAH are implicationally related was understandably attractive to theorists just beginning to investigate markedness in SLA. One body of research in particular showed that L2 learners generally found relative clause formation easier on NPs higher in the hierarchy (i.e., the less marked GRs such as SU) than on those lower in the hierarchy (Doughty, 1991; Eckman, Bell, & Nelson, 1988; Gass, 1979, 1980, 1982, 1983; Hyltenstam, 1984; and Pavesi, 1986).[1] Although most of these researchers aimed to explore the pedagogical implications of the NPAH rather than to confirm the formal constructs in question, nonetheless the claim was implicit that GRs successfully account for these L2 data.

Alternative accounts of the NPAH L2 data have been proposed, however, that draw on configuration rather than GRs as the relevant explanatory construct. Wolfe-Quintero (1992) and Hamilton (1994) have suggested that the varying difficulty of the different relative clause types is due to the degree of phrasal discontinuity set up by Wh-extraction in each type. Thus, for example, SU relativization in English may be easier to acquire than DO relativization because the extraction site for DO is more deeply embedded in phrase structure—extraction from VP within IP for DO, but only from IP for SU. The same holds for relativization of DO versus IO or OBL, the latter types in English typically involving extraction from PP within VP within IP. Berent (1993, 1994) offered a similar account in terms of the number of maximal projections crossed by the Wh-operator in relativization.

A configurational account of the data is more than just a plausible alternative to the GR account, however, because it can elegantly explain certain recurring anomalies in the NPAH L2 studies that a GR account is forced to consider modifications by "language specific properties" (Gass, 1979, p. 339) or "local factors" (Pavesi, 1986, p. 50) to an otherwise universal hierarchy. Thus, relativization of the IO and OBL positions was not dissimilar in the way predicted by the NPAH in Doughty (1991), Gass (1980), Hyltenstam (1984), and Pavesi (1986).

[1]This is based on pretest scores; gain scores in the instructional studies (Doughty, 1991; Eckman, Bell, & Nelson, 1988; Gass, 1982) are not directly relevant.

Most of these researchers attributed this to the fact that both the IO and OBL NPs in these studies occur in PPs; note, however, that this constitutes an appeal to identity of phrase structure (i.e., configuration). Similarly, the surprisingly high accuracy scores of learners on Genitive (GEN) relativization in both Gass (1979, 1983) and Doughty (1991) can be accounted for configurationally when we note that (a) the Wh-extraction site in GEN relativization varies according to the phrase structure position of the possessed NP; and (b) virtually all of the GEN sentences in Gass' and Doughty's tasks involved possessed SU or DO NPs (Doughty, 1988, pp. 197–209; Gass, 1979, p. 341).[2] Thus, GEN relativization of the possessor of a subject involves movement of the entire subject NP (including possessor NP) from [Spec,IP] just as normal SU relativization does, and GEN relativization of a possessor of a direct object moves the entire direct object from V-complement position, precisely as DO relativization does. This is illustrated in (1); (1a) depicts GEN of a subject and (1b) GEN of a direct object relativization:

(1) a. *the woman*$_i$ [*whose*$_i$ *hat*]$_j$ [$_{IP}$ t$_j$ [$_{VP}$ *is red*]

  b. *the woman*$_i$ [*whose*$_i$ *name*]$_j$ [$_{IP}$ *we* [$_{VP}$ *know* t$_j$]

It is no surprise, then, that Gass' and Doughty's learners found GEN relativization about as difficult as SU and DO relativization, if learners were sensitive to the configuration of the extracted NP rather than to the GEN nature of the NPs involved (cf. Gass, 1979, p. 341). Indeed, Fuller (1983) presented experimental evidence that L2 English learners find GEN formed on SU relatives easier than GEN of DO, which in turn is easier than GEN of OBL. Hawkins (1989) adduced similar evidence for L2 French, showing that learners acquire the correct relativizer morphology for GEN of SU relatives before GEN of DO relatives (the latter involving a more deeply embedded extraction site, as in English).[3]

---

[2]The greater difficulty of GEN in Hyltenstam (1984) and Pavesi (1986) may be task related, because both counted only pronoun resumption rates on the same elicited oral-production picture task.

[3]Though the configurational approach of Wolfe-Quintero (1992) and Hamilton (1994) adopted here is based on underlying phrase structure, Tarallo and Myhill (1983) and Hawkins (1989) proposed an alternative to the GR account based on the linear surface order of constituents. This surface order account derives from data in Tarallo and Myhill (1983, p. 63), which showed that though learners are less likely to accept ungrammatical resumptive pronouns with SU relatives than with DO relatives, this effect only obtains when the L2 in question is a right-branching language like English (i.e., in linear order the SU position is closer than the DO position to the coreferential head noun). In left-branching languages like Chinese and Japanese, in which the DO position is closer to the head, the data showed that resumptive pronouns are less likely to be accepted with DO relatives (23% acceptance with DO, 49% with SU). This finding led Tarallo and Myhill to suggest that it is not the GR value of an NP but rather the linear proximity between the head noun and this NP which determines the difficulty of relativization. It is not clear, however, that Tarallo and Myhill's data truly support their proposal when one considers the performance of their learners on IO and OBL relatives in left-branching languages. That is, the same data reveal a rate of pronoun resumption acceptance in relativization on IOs (42%) and OBL objects of *with* (50%) which is similar to the rate for SU relatives (49%), though the SU position is less proximate to the head noun than either the IO or OBL positions.

1.2. The Present Study

A configurational account for the NPAH data in SLA is arguably more parsimonious than the GR account, then, because it uses one mechanism (i.e., phrase structure) to explain those results that are predicted as well as those not predicted by the NPAH, whereas the GR account must appeal to at least two mechanisms (the universal GR hierarchy and various language-specific factors).[4] In this study, I attempted to further test these two accounts by measuring learner sensitivity in English relativization to the configurational distinction associated with argument PPs versus adjunct PPs and the GR distinction between IO and OBL NPs, while controlling for intervening variables that may have been present in previous studies.

I chose these particular GR and configurational values for several reasons. The IO/OBL distinction represents perhaps the most significant division of GRs in Relational Grammar, that between term relations (SU, DO, and IO) and all oblique objects (Perlmutter & Postal, 1983). The IO/OBL distinction is typologically well motivated and plays a crucial role in relational analyses of numerous languages (e.g., Aissen, 1983; Bickford, 1987; Dryer, 1983). Moreover, it is the only GR distinction in English relativization relevant to the NPAH for which configuration can be held constant (in this chapter both IOs and OBLs are in argument PPs). The argument/adjunct distinction was chosen for similar reasons; that is, unlike phrase structure distinctions varying on the XP level (e.g., subject vs. direct object NPs), learner performance on arguments versus adjuncts can be measured without the interference of covarying GR values (in this chapter the OBL value is held constant for arguments vs. adjuncts). The distinction between argument and adjunct PPs has configurational correlates, because adjuncts are traditionally held to attach higher than arguments in phrase structure, though the precise attachment site has been debated (e.g., Culicover & Wilkins, 1984; Oehrle, 1976; Radford, 1988, pp. 237–239).[5]

The main hypotheses of this chapter, then, are twofold:

---

[4]Though Hawkins (1989) also argues for the supremacy of a configurational account over a GR account of the NPAH findings, he does not explicitly appeal to parsimony as the deciding factor between the two accounts as I have here. Instead, he argues that a configurational approach is better (simply) because it can explain acquisition differences such as the variable GEN findings discussed above, which are based on parsing difficulties rather than mapping from different GR values. Though I agree that configuration can account for such parsing difficulties, this fact does not fully counter the claims by Gass (1979) and Pavesi (1986) that the GEN findings and similar anomalies are nothing more than language specific exceptions to the universal GR hierarchy. That is, a GR account does not exclude the possibility of independent parsing difficulties, since presumably *any* account of language acquisition must assume the operation of a parser at some level. The configurational account is superior not because it appeals to parsing difficulty, but because by appealing *only* to parsibility (and not to GRs as well) it is more parsimonious.

[5]Larson (1988) abandoned the traditional phrase structure distinction between arguments and adjuncts in dual object constructions; however, this move has been strongly criticized by Jackendoff (1990a).

Hypothesis One (H1): learners *will* perform significantly differently on relativization of NPs in argument versus adjunct PPs, other factors being constant. *Hypothesis Two (H2)*: learners *will* *not* perform significantly differently on relativization of IO versus OBL prepositional objects, other factors being constant.

If confirmed, these results will suggest that L2 learners approach English relativization sensitive to configuration but not to GR values, thus supporting the configurational accounts of the NPAH data in SLA.

2. METHOD

2.1. Subjects

The subjects for this study were 98 L2 learners of English enrolled in three ESL programs. Forty-six subjects were from the English Program for Internationals at the University of South Carolina (MTELP mean = 73, s = 16.6), 16 were from the English Language Training Institute of the University of North Carolina at Charlotte (MTELP mean = 77, s = 7.9), and 36 were from the English Language Institute of the University of Alabama (TOEFL mean = 486, s = 39; MTELP scores not available).[6] Altogether 12 intermediate-to-advanced ESL classes participated in the study, these classes being selected *in situ* on the basis of their general proficiency range. The subjects included 60 males and 38 females from a variety of language backgrounds including Japanese (n = 37), Arabic (n = 15), Korean (n = 15), Spanish (n = 9), Chinese (n = 6), and nine other languages with less than 5 speakers each in the study.

2.2. Task and Administration

Each subject was administered a sentence-combination task requiring formation of various relative clause types, including two types representing the configurational distinction between prepositional object (i.e., [NP,PP]) targets of relativization in argument versus adjunct PPs, and two types representing the GR distinction between IO and OBL [NP,PP] targets (see Appendix A). In the following examples the values in focus for each distinction are asterisked; the thematic value of each [NP,PP], using Jackendoff's (1990b) labels, is also listed following its configurational and GR values:

---

[6]TOEFL scores were available for only 19 subjects in the Alabama group. The mean and standard deviation reported is based on these subjects.

Configurational Distinction (between types A and B):
    Type A (Argument*/OBL/Location):
    This is the desk.   *I laid my pen on the desk.*
    Combined: *This is the desk that I laid my pen on.*
    Type B (Adjunct*/OBL/Location):
    She drove the bus.   *I did my homework on the bus.*
    Combined: *She drove the bus that I did my homework on.*

GR Distinction (between types C and D):
    Type C (Argument/IO*/Beneficiary-Goal):
    This is the boy.   *I passed the ball to the boy.*
    Combined: *This is the boy that I passed the ball to.*
    Type D (Argument/OBL*/Goal):
    She left the party.   *I took my friends to the party.*
    Combined: *She left the party that I took my friends to.*

The sentences were designed so that their syntax and relevant morphology differ only with respect to the configurational or GR distinction being tested. Thus, all of the NP targets of relativization for all sentence types are [NP,PP], all sentence types contain a direct object preceding the PP, and all of the intended relative clauses are right-embedded. Additionally, the selection of prepositions was controlled for each distinction (e.g., types A and B testing the configurational distinction both use *on*). Finally, as much as possible, the configurational, GR, and thematic values for the target NPs were allowed to vary only in regard to the distinction being tested for a given sentence type. The exceptions are sentence types C and D, which vary in terms of their thematic values (i.e., Beneficiary-Goal vs. Goal), as well as in terms of the GR distinction being tested (i.e., IO vs. OBL). In view of this, the Beneficiary-Goal versus Goal distinction was independently tested with sentence types E and F to discover if it would constitute an intervening variable in the comparison of types C and D (which proved not to be the case—see Section 3). Note that Jackendoff (1990b) allows an NP to have multiple thematic values, the Beneficiary role being dominant in Beneficiary-Goal NPs.

Thematic Distinction (between types E and F):
    Type E (Adjunct/OBL/Beneficiary-Goal*):
    You know the woman.   *I cooked a cake for the woman.*
    Combined: *You know the woman that I cooked a cake for.*
    Type F (Adjunct/OBL/Goal*):
    This is the party.   *I baked cookies for the party.*
    Combined: *This is the party that I baked cookies for.*

Thus, an additional hypothesis of the study is:

Hypothesis Three (H3): learners *will not* perform significantly differently on relativization of Beneficiary-Goal versus Goal objects, other factors being held constant.

Concerning the values assigned to the NPs in this study, argument status of an NP is indicated by its being existentially entailed by the verb or being obligatory in surface structure (cf. Pinker, 1989, pp. 40–41). The IOs are identified by their ability to undergo dative shift, unlike most OBLs. Though the benefactive OBLs in the Type E sentences behave like IOs in this regard, unlike IOs, they cannot further passivize from initial object position for many English speakers (Blake, 1990, pp. 6, 161). Thematic values have been assigned subjectively (as is typical in the literature) but accord with Jackendoff (1990b).

Because five tokens of each sentence type were needed to ensure the statistical validity of the results, two parallel versions of the sentence combination task were designed rather than having one excessively long instrument. One version included five sentence pairs for each of the sentence types A, B, E, and F (i.e., those exemplifying the configurational and thematic distinctions) plus five distractor pairs; this version was administered to the South Carolina subjects ($n = 46$). The other version contained five pairs for each type C, D, E, and F (i.e., the GR and thematic distinctions) plus five distractors; this version was given to the UNC-Charlotte and the Alabama subjects ($n = 52$).[7] Each version, then, contained 25 randomly ordered sentence pairs.

Subjects were allowed 25 minutes to complete the task and were given these directions orally and in writing:

> Please combine the two sentences. Make one good English sentence. Do not leave out any information, and do not change the meaning. If you do not know the meaning of a word, raise your hand and the teacher will tell you. Do not use the words *or*, *and*, or *but*. Instead, use the words *who*, *whom*, *that*, or *which*. Always begin with sentence A.

The tasks were administered by the learners' own ESL teachers, who were given strict guidelines but were not told the study's theoretical purpose.

2.3. Scoring

Responses were scored incorrect if they violated the directions, evidenced avoidance of the target structure, or were otherwise ungrammatical (with some exceptions to be discussed later).[8] One typical error involved beginning with

---

[7]The only substantial difference between the two groups taking each version of the task was the proportion of native Japanese speakers in each (26%, $n = 12$, in the South Carolina subjects; 48%, $n = 25$, in the UNC-Charlotte and Alabama subjects). The ratio of males to females was virtually equal (29:17 vs. 31:21). A two-tailed t test showed no significant difference in MTELP means between the two pools of subjects for whom MTELP scores were available ($SE = 3.145$; $T = 1.272$; $df = 60$).

[8]One subject's data for the A and B sentence types were incomplete and were thus omitted from the scoring because of his failure to complete the test in the allotted time. The C and D sentence type data for four other subjects were omitted since these subjects misread a particular sentence on the test, establishing an unintended coreference (creating a center-embedded relative clause). For example:

sentence B rather than A (violating the directions). This probable form of avoidance always resulted in a more easily relativizable NP type (i.e., SU or DO; cf. Gass, 1980; and Schachter, 1974), as in (2):

(2) *She drove the bus.   I did my homework on the bus.*
    I did my homework on the bus that she drove.

Both the configurational and the GR accounts of the NPAH predict the likelihood of such avoidance, SU and DO being easier to relativize than IO and OBL in both configurational and GR terms, as discussed earlier.

A second typical error was passivization of the NP target of relativization. Again, this is a form of avoidance, because it always results in relativization of a SU, the most easily relativizable NP type in both configurational and GR terms:

(3) *This is the boy.   The girl sang a song for the boy.*
    *This is the boy who was sung a song by the girl.

Another type was omission of the preposition. This is clearly ungrammatical for sentence types A, B, D, and F and is marginal at best for Types C and E:[9]

(4) **This is the party that I baked cookies. (Type F)*
    ?She brought the child that he made a toy. (Type E)

A fourth type of error was substitution of a different preposition for the target preposition. This involved a change of meaning, in violation of the directions:

(5) *She brought the child.   He made a toy for the child.*
    *She brought the child to whom he made a toy.

Another error type involved the use of a resumptive pronoun or noun:

(i) *Everyone likes the store.   They took me to the store.*
   Everyone who likes the store took me to the store.
Omitting these data ensured that no statistical measurement would be made on a sentence type represented by less than five tokens.

[9]An informal survey of six English native speakers confirms that preposition omissions in type C and E sentences are judged as moderately or severely ungrammatical: on a scale of 1 to 5, 1 indicating "awful" and 5 "fully acceptable," the mean judgment (out of 18 total judgments for each sentence type) was 2.1 for Type C preposition omissions and 1.6 for Type E (cf. Bardovi-Harlig, 1987, p. 404, n. 6). Moreover, in the present study the mean frequency of preposition omission for Type C versus Type D sentences as well as for E versus F sentences was not significantly different on paired t tests ($MD = 0.048$, $s = 1.173$, $T = 0.296$, $p > 0.77$ for C vs. D; $MD = 0.071$, $s = 0.922$, $T = 0.767$, $p > 0.45$ for E vs. F). This suggests that learners approach these sentence types in the same way as far as factors contributing to preposition omission are concerned; scoring such responses as grammatical for one sentence type but not the other would obscure this fact.

(6) *She brought the child that he made a toy for him.

Some learners resorted to a nonrelative-clause strategy, most often an adverbial clause using where or when. This was considered an error because in every case it required disregarding the directions to use who, whom, which, or that (a form of avoidance).

(7) This is the house where the girl brought her bags.

Finally, an incomplete response or no response was counted as an error. On the other hand, responses not counted as incorrect included spelling errors, omission of determiners, incorrect relative marker morphology (e.g. who for whom), and omission of relative markers (the latter grammatical in the case of relativization on prepositional objects).

3. RESULTS

Two-tailed paired t tests were administered to measure the difference in subjects' accuracy scores for each of the three distinctions being tested. One t test measured the South Carolina subjects' scores on Type A versus B relative clauses (i.e., the configurational distinction), another measured the UNC-Charlotte and Alabama subjects' scores on Types C versus D (i.e., the GR distinction), and two additional t tests measured each of these groups' scores on Types E versus F (i.e., the thematic distinction; recall that these sentence types were included on both task versions). The two groups' thematic scores were treated separately in the manner of a replication study so as to more conclusively determine whether the thematic distinction functioned as an intervening variable in the testing of the GR distinction. Descriptive statistics and the results of the t tests are shown in Table 7.2.

Of the four paired t tests, Table 7.2 shows that only the one measuring learners' performance on the configurational distinction approached a significant probability value ($p > .051$, given a .05 alpha level). This strong statistical trend tentatively suggests that the subjects were sensitive to the configurational difference in relativization on objects in argument PPs (Type A) versus adjunct PPs (Type B), other factors being held constant. Of the two types, argument relativization proved to be easier than adjunct relativization for 11 of 16 learners whose scores exhibited a nonzero difference between the two types. In contrast to the results for the configurational distinction, Table 7.2 shows that the performance of those subjects tested for the GR distinction between IOs and OBLs and for the thematic distinction between Beneficiary-Goals and Goals was not significantly different for either distinction (the results on the thematic distinction being replicated).

TABLE 7.2
Paired t Tests

Type	Mean	s	SE	T	$p > |T|$
Configurational Distinction ($n = 45$)					
A	4.378	1.319			
B	4.067	1.643			
Diff A/B	0.311		0.155	2.010	0.051
Grammatical Relation Distinction ($n = 48$)					
C	3.354	1.885			
D	3.188	2.018			
Diff C/D	0.167		0.156	1.071	0.290
Thematic Distinction (South Carolina subjects; $n = 46$)					
E	4.087	1.314			
F	4.217	1.349			
Diff E/F	0.130		0.166	0.780	0.437
Thematic Distinction (Alabama, UNC-Charlotte subjects; $n = 52$)					
E	3.731	1.827			
F	3.577	1.851			
Diff E/F	0.154		0.168	0.916	0.364

Note. n = number of subjects (cf. fn. 8). s = standard deviation. SE = standard error of means. T = T value.

4. CONCLUSIONS

These findings tentatively suggest that second language (L2) learners of English are sensitive to configurational differences in the various types of English relativization in such a way as to affect their interlanguage performance but are not sensitive in the same way to hierarchically relevant distinctions in either grammatical relations (GRs) or thematic roles. Though these findings do not necessarily challenge the validity of GRs or thematic roles as constructs in syntactic theories of Universal Grammar (there is considerable typological evidence for their validity), the findings do support the argument presented earlier that Keenan and Comrie's Noun Phrase Accessibility Hierarchy (NPAH) is not, on its GR interpretation, as parsimonious an explanation of the L2 relativization data as is phrase structure/configuration (seen either on an abstract level as the X-bar component of UG or simply in terms of phrasal continuity) (see Berent, 1993, 1994; Hamilton, 1994; and Wolfe-Quintero, 1992). The anomalous findings in earlier NPAH-associated studies, considered by some researchers at the time to be language-specific intrusions into an otherwise universal hierarchy of GRs, may be seen in retrospect as indications of the configurational basis on which L2 learners approach the various types of relativization.[10]

---

[10]This is not to discount the role that other factors (e.g., morphological) might have in determining the relative difficulty of various types of relativization.

However, my results of the present study must be interpreted tentatively for several reasons. First, though a strong statistical trend (.051) suggested that learners are sensitive to the argument/adjunct distinction, the alpha level (.05) was, strictly speaking, not reached. Second, the argument/adjunct distinction, though it has strong configurational correlates, is not strictly configurational in nature. Thus, it may be that an NP's thematic relatedness to the verb (or lack thereof), rather than the NP's phrase structure attachment site per se, is responsible for learners' differing performance on relativization of sentence Types A versus B. For these reasons this study needs to be replicated and the hypotheses should be tested in additional contexts that may more definitively demonstrate learner sensitivity to configurational factors. For example, a configurational account of the NPAH data in SLA would predict that L2 learners of purportedly nonconfigurational languages such as Japanese would not find relativization on one NPAH position harder than relativization on another, if other factors are held constant (Fred Eckman, personal communication, October 8, 1993). This would assume, of course, that there is sufficient theoretical basis for positing configurational equivalence in the given language between the NPAH positions in question.

Perhaps more important than the ramifications for an understanding of the NPAH in SLA, the present study's findings highlight the need for L2 researchers to design highly controlled ways to test the suitability of constructs borrowed from formal linguistic theory as explanators for SLA data. Regardless of the amount of typological or theory-internal support there is for a formal construct, there is no guarantee that L2 learners will be sensitive to that construct, at least not in ways relevant to the descriptive or explanatory purposes for which L2 theorists may use it. Crucially, the suitability of such a construct cannot be shown simply by demonstrating that particular L2 data are compatible with an explanation that utilizes the construct, because alternative accounts that draw on other constructs may be compatible with the data as well. Beyond compatibility, it needs to be demonstrated that the construct in question has predictive power even when alternative accounts of variation in the data are unavailable (e.g., because of manipulation of the linguistic context so that the values of alternative constructs are held constant). In my study the GR construct appears to have come up short in this respect, and the results suggest that a more economical account of the NPAH data may be one that draws instead on configuration as the salient construct.

ACKNOWLEDGMENTS

I would like to thank Stan Dubinsky for sparking the idea for this chapter and for his supportive input on earlier drafts. I would also like to thank Jerry Berent, Fred Eckman, Dean Mellow, Kate Wolfe-Quintero, and Helmut Zobl for their

helpful comments on various aspects of this research. Finally, I am grateful to
the directors, teachers, and students of the three ESL programs who participated
in this study.

REFERENCES

Aissen, J. (1983). "Indirect Object Advancement in Tzotzil." *Studies in Relational Grammar 1*, ed.
by D. Perlmutter. Chicago: University of Chicago Press.

Bardovi-Harlig, K. (1987). "Markedness and Salience in Second-Language Acquisition," *Language
Learning* 37, 385–407.

Berent, G. (1993). *Noun Phrase Accessibility and Relative Clause Learnability*. Manuscript.

———. (1994). "The Subset Principle in Second-Language Acquisition." *Research Methodology in
Second-Language Acquisition*, ed. by A. Cohen, S. Gass, and E. Tarone. Hillsdale, NJ: Lawrence
Erlbaum Associates.

Bickford, J. A. (1987). *Universal Constraints on Relationally Complex Clauses*. PhD dissertation,
University of California at San Diego.

Blake, B. (1990). *Relational Grammar*. New York: Routledge.

Chomsky, N. (1965). *Aspects of the Theory of Syntax*. Cambridge, MA: MIT Press.

Culicover, P., and W. Wilkins. (1984). *Locality in Linguistic Theory*. Orlando, FL: Academic Press.

Doughty, C. (1991). "Second Language Instruction Does Make a Difference: Evidence From an
Empirical Study of SL Relativization," *Studies in Second Language Acquisition* 13, 431–69.

Dryer, M. (1983). "Indirect Objects in Kinyarwanda Revisited." *Studies in Relational Grammar 1*, ed.
by D. Perlmutter. Chicago: University of Chicago Press.

Eckman, F., L. Bell, and D. Nelson. (1988). "On the Generalization of Relative Clause Instruction
in the Acquisition of English as a Second Language," *Applied Linguistics* 9, 1–20.

Fuller, J. W. (1983). "Relative Clause Comprehension and the Noun Phrase Accessibility Hierarchy."
Paper presented at the Seventeenth Annual TESOL Convention, Toronto.

Gass, S. (1979). "Language Transfer and Universal Grammatical Relations," *Language Learning* 29,
327–44.

———. (1980). "An Investigation of Syntactic Transfer in Adult Second Language Learners."
*Research in Second Language Acquisition: Selected Papers of the Los Angeles Second Language
Acquisition Research Forum*, ed. by R. Scarcella and S. Krashen. Rowley, MA: Newbury House.

———. (1982). "From Theory to Practice." *On TESOL '81: Selected Papers from the Fifteenth Annual
Conference of Teachers of English to Speakers of Other Languages*, ed. by M. Hines and W.
Rutherford. Washington, DC: TESOL.

———. (1983). "Second Language Acquisition and Language Universals." *The First Delaware
Symposium on Language Studies: Selected Papers*, ed. by R. Di Pietro, W. Frawley, and A. Wedel.
Newark: University of Delaware Press.

Hamilton, R. (1994). "Is Implicational Generalization Unidirectional and Maximal? Evidence from
Relativization Instruction in a Second Language," *Language Learning* 44, 123–57.

Hawkins, R. (1989). "Do Second Language Learners Acquire Restrictive Relative Clauses on the
Basis of Relational or Configurational Information? The Acquisition of French Subject, Direct
Object and Genitive Restrictive Relative Clauses by Second Language Learners," *Second Language
Research* 5, 156–188.

Hyltenstam, K. (1984). "The Use of Typological Markedness Conditions as Predictors in Second
Language Acquisition: The Case of Pronominal Copies in Relative Clauses." *Second Languages:
A Cross-Linguistic Perspective*, ed. by R. Andersen. Rowley, MA: Newbury House.

Jackendoff, R. (1990a). "On Larson's Treatment of the Double Object Construction," *Linguistic
Inquiry* 21, 427–56.

———. (1990b). *Semantic Structures*. Cambridge, MA: MIT Press.

Keenan, E., and B. Comrie. (1977). "Noun Phrase Accessibility and Universal Grammar," *Linguistic Inquiry* 8, 63–99.

Larson, R. (1988). "On the Double Object Construction," *Linguistic Inquiry* 19, 335–91.

Oehrle, R. (1976). *The Grammatical Status of the English Dative Alternation*. PhD dissertation, MIT, Cambridge, MA.

O'Grady, W. (1987). *Principles of Grammar and Learning*. Chicago, IL: University of Chicago Press.

Pavesi, M. (1986). "Markedness, Discoursal Modes, and Relative Clause Formation in a Formal and an Informal Context," *Studies in Second Language Acquisition* 8, 38–55.

Perlmutter, D., and P. Postal. (1983). "Some Proposed Laws of Basic Clause Structure." *Studies in Relational Grammar 1*, ed. by D. Perlmutter. Chicago: University of Chicago Press.

Pinker, S. (1989). *Learnability and Cognition: The Acquisition of Argument Structure*. Cambridge, MA: MIT Press.

Radford, A. (1988). *Transformational Grammar: A First Course*. New York: Cambridge University Press.

Schachter, J. (1974). "An Error in Error Analysis," *Language Learning* 27, 205–14.

Tarallo, F., and J. Myhill. (1983). "Interference and Natural Language Processing in Second Language Acquisition," *Language Learning* 33, 55–76.

Wolfe-Quintero, K. (1992). "Learnability and the Acquisition of Extraction in Relative Clauses and Wh-Questions," *Studies in Second Language Acquisition* 14, 39–70.

APPENDIX A

Sentence Pairs Used in Sentence Combination Tasks

Type A: Argument/OBL/Location
We left the table.	I placed the money on the table.
My friend mailed the letter.	I put a stamp on the letter.
The student wanted the paper.	The teacher put a grade on the paper.
This is the desk.	I laid my pen on the desk.
This is the chair.	She set her coat on the chair.

Type B: Adjunct/OBL/Location
She drove the bus.	I did my homework on the bus.
My wife found the bug.	I dropped a book on the bug.
We found the train.	I lost my bag on the train.
This is the sofa.	The boy took a nap on the sofa.
This is the highway.	He drove his car on the highway.

Type C: Argument/IO/Beneficiary-Goal
Everyone likes the teacher.	I gave a present to the teacher.
We watched the student.	The teacher handed the paper to the student.
This is the boy.	I passed the ball to the boy.
I know the woman.	He offered the money to the woman.
This is the child.	I told a story to the child.

Type D: Argument/OBL/Goal
| Everyone likes the store. | They took me to the store. |
| She left the party. | I took my friends to the party. |

We found the beach.	She sent the children to the beach.
This is the house.	The girl brought her bags to the house.
This is the country.	I mailed a postcard to the country.

Type E: Adjunct/OBL/Beneficiary-Goal

You know the woman.	I cooked a cake for the woman.
This is the man.	I bought a book for the man.
She brought the child.	He made a toy for the child.
This is the boy.	The girl sang a song for the boy.
Everyone likes the teacher.	She brought flowers for the teacher.

Type F: Adjunct/OBL/Goal

I remember the trip.	My son took a pillow for the trip.
I watched the game.	She brought a camera for the game.
This is the party.	I baked cookies for the party.
This is the meeting.	He wrote a speech for the meeting.
No one likes the class.	I read a book for the class.

Chapter 8

Second Language Acquisition of Relative Clause Structures by Learners of Italian

Karen C. Croteau
California State University, Sacramento

1. INTRODUCTION

I have tested the implications for second language acquisition of a theory of relative clause description set forth by Keenan and Comrie (1977). Several studies have previously tested the implications of this theory for learners of English as a second language. I conducted this study on learners of Italian as a foreign language using techniques similar to those of previous studies.

1.1. Theoretical Background

The Noun Phrase Accessibility Hierarchy (NPAH) was developed by Keenan and Comrie (1977). They proposed a hierarchy of grammatical relations beginning with subject at the highest level and continuing with direct object > indirect object > object of preposition > genitive > object of comparison, which is the lowest level. In surveying a large number of languages, they found that if a language can relativize at a given position on the hierarchy, it will also allow relativization at higher positions. For example, if a language allows relativization from the OP (object of preposition) position (e.g., *Here's the book that you were asking about*), it will also allow relativization from IO (indirect object), DO (direct object), and SU (subject) positions (e.g., *Here's the boy who called*). Thus, an implicational relationship exists through the Hierarchy such that relativization on a lower position implies, for any language, the acceptability of relativization on a higher position, but not vice versa. In other words, the hierarchy involves a series of markedness relationships from SU (least marked) to Object of Comparison (OC) (most marked). However, a language may not allow relativization all the way down the hierarchy.

Quite separately from this, Zobl (1983) discusses the "projection problem" in second language acquisition. He notes that first language learners attain more knowledge than there is direct evidence for in the input data, and suggests that a similar ability exists in second language acquisition. Specifically, exposure to a marked property of a language may be enough for a learner to develop competence with a related, unmarked property.

1.2. Previous Studies

Several studies have been conducted to test the implications of Keenan and Comrie's NPAH for second language learning. Two studies demonstrate that L2 learners of English find higher positions on the Hierarchy easier to produce. Gass (1979) found that adult learners of English as a second language were able to relativize the higher positions more easily than the lower positions with the exception of the GEN Pavesi (1986) studied two groups of Italian learners of English. One group learned English in a high school classroom ("formal learners"). The other group consisted of "street" learners who were exposed to English through work, home, or recreation. Pavesi found that the formal group produced a greater number of marked forms than the informal group.

The subjects in these studies acquired their knowledge of English relativization in the course of different personal histories. When these histories are not known precisely, it is difficult to determine which factors may have led to their differential ability with different relative clause types. However, more controlled experimental studies have suggested that a kind of projection device operates in relative clause acquisition: if a person acquires knowledge of more marked (complex) relative clause structures (such as OP), knowledge of less marked structures comes along "for free."

Gass (1982) compared two groups of students. The control group learned SU, GEN, and all forms of Object relativization through a standard textbook. The experimental group learned relativization only on the OP position. She found that the experimental group generalized their learning to other positions on the NPAH. Put differently, students who were taught relative clauses that were formed by relativizing positions lower on the hierarchy were able to generalize their knowledge to positions higher on the hierarchy.

Eckman, Bell, and Nelson (1988) took this idea a step further and created three experimental groups in which each group was taught to relativize at a different level. The groups contained L2 learners of English who learned to form the subject (SU), direct object (DO), or object of preposition relative (OP) clauses. The OP group appeared to yield the best results; they produced fewer errors on all levels (one error in OP structure, four in DO, and none in SU) than any of the other groups.

Doughty (1991) believed that the way students are taught relativization is an important factor to consider before inferences can be made about the projection model. One of her instructional techniques—the *rule-oriented group*—was based on a traditional view of language acquisition. The subjects in this group were provided instruction through rules and "on-screen sentence manipulation." The sentence given contained a matrix clause and a relative clause formed on the OP. The instructions were to reduce the sentence to two sentences—a "decomposition" of the original sentence. Then the subjects observed on the computer screen a "recombination" of the two sentences which resulted in the original sentence with the matrix and OP relative clauses (Doughty, 1991). The experimental groups received instruction on OP relativization through a computer program that administered the lessons and practice tasks. The results indicated significant gains for experimental groups—they were successful in acquiring OP relativization and projecting this knowledge up the Hierarchy.

To summarize, Keenan and Comrie's study indicates that languages exhibit a hierarchy such that, if they can form relative clauses from a given position, then they can also form relative clauses on all higher positions. Pavesi shows that learners of English as a second language appear to favor higher positions, producing relative clauses at such positions more readily and frequently. Finally, Gass, Eckman, and Doughty demonstrated that if people learn how to relativize a lower, more marked position, they appear to project that knowledge to higher, less marked positions. Although this projection model has been tested several times on learners of English, it has not been tested much on learners of other languages. In this chapter I report the results of testing the model on L2 learners of Italian.

In this study, "homework packets" were designed in a rule-oriented instructional style modeled after Doughty's (1990). (See Appendix A) Three experimental groups were taught relativization using this method through homework packets that taught DO, OP, or GEN relativization. I hoped that if I controlled factors that may affect the acquisition of Italian relativization, the study would yield reliable answers to whether the implications of the NPAH—that subjects taught lower positions would relativize to higher positions and that subjects taught higher positions would not relativize to lower positions—are supported.

1.3. Italian Relative Clause Structures

SU and DO relativization in Italian is very similar to English relativization. The relative pronoun is the link in the two ideas expressed. For example,

(1) *Come si chiama la ragazza che suona il piano?*
   'What is the name of the girl *who* is playing the piano?'

The first idea, *Come si chiama la ragazza* 'What is the name of the girl', and the second, *suona il piano* 'is playing the piano', are linked with the pronoun *che*. In

Italian, *che* represents the English counterparts *who, whose, whom, which,* and *that.*

Relativization of OP is a little more complex for SL learners. Prepositions cannot be stranded at the end of the sentence, like

(2) Antonella is the person whom I am going with.

Prepositions must precede the relative pronoun, which in this case is *cui* (i.e., pied piping is obligatory in Italian):

(3) *Antonella è la persona con cui vado.*
    'Antonella is the person with whom I am going.'

The GEN is probably the most difficult relative clause type for native English learners to acquire because it does not resemble English relativization of the GEN at all. In English we typically use the pronoun *whose* as a possessive relative pronoun. In Italian a definite article (*il, i, la, le*) must be placed before the pronoun *cui.* This appears between the two ideas expressed:

(4) *Preferisco il cane il cui collare è rosso.*
    'I prefer the dog whose collar is red.'

See Appendix A for a sample homework packet.

2. METHOD

2.1. Subjects

Sixty-five undergraduate students that were enrolled in third-quarter Italian classes at the University of California, Davis served as voluntary participants. There were 20 students in the DO group, 24 in the OP group, and 21 in the GEN group. A preliminary survey determined whether the students had experience with Italian or any other language. This precaution was taken in case any of the students were already familiar with relative-clause structure rules of Italian or other languages that may have similar rules. No students were excluded from the study.

2.2. Materials

The preliminary survey determined how long the students had been studying Italian and their opportunities to use the language. The survey also determined all students' native language, their proficiency in English, and their background in other languages. This was done to ascertain the homogeneity of the subject pool.

The pretest and posttest were parallel forms of the same test. (See Appendix B.) Each test consisted of a sentence combination task with 19 items. For every question in Test A there was a corresponding question in Test B. The questions were altered by changing the words (such as nouns, verbs, articles, etc.) but the same sentence structure was maintained. This was done to prevent the subject from learning the sentence through a practice effect. There were five SU, four DO, five OP, and five GEN relative clause sentence combination tasks for each test. (After administration of the pretest, an error was found in one of the direct object sentences. This sentence and its corresponding sentence on the other test were discarded.) Students were asked to combine two sentences into one, all-encompassing sentence by attaching the second sentence to the first.

The homework packets were made as similar to each other as possible. Each of the three homework packets began with the definition of a relative pronoun (in English) along with the definition of the relative pronoun the students would be using to combine the sentences.

The "lesson" was modeled after Doughty's rule-oriented method. First a sample sentence was presented. Then the sentence was broken down into the two ideas that were expressed. The student was presented with a step-by-step explanation of the changes a sentence had to undergo to utilize the relative pronoun properly. Each lesson ended with an explanation of mandatory relative pronoun markers in Italian as opposed to optional markers in English.

There were ten practice questions followed by an answer key for the students to correct their mistakes. The questions were broken down into five sentence-combination tasks and five grammaticality judgment tasks. (See Appendix A.)

2.3. Design and Procedure

The subjects were asked to fill out the preliminary survey and complete the pretest to the best of their ability. The pretests were scored, students were matched as closely as possible to scores similar to theirs, and then they were randomly assigned to one of three groups. The homework packets were distributed the next day and students were asked to complete the assignment without the aid of any dictionaries, textbooks, or other students. Practice questions were included in the homework packet following the lecture part of the instructions. An answer key was also included for students to check their answers.

Test scoring had to be altered because some students did not learn the term for a relative pronoun that was higher or lower on the hierarchy than the one they were taught. Therefore, the sentence was considered correct if the student used the appropriate sentence structure, even if the relative pronoun used was incorrect. This rule was used on both the pre- and posttests, but it was especially significant on the posttest.

One week after the pretests were administered, students completed the post-test. Students who did not complete the homework assignment were asked not to take the posttest at that time, and other arrangements were made so that they could continue to participate in the study.

The study was a 3 × 2 × 4 (homework packet type × pre-/posttest × relative-clause type) mixed design with the test factor and relative-clause type repeated. As was explained earlier, the homework packets taught relativization of DO, OP, and GEN relative clauses. The test factor consisted of a pretest and posttest. Four relative clause types were measured on the pre- and posttests: SU, DO, OP, and GEN.

3. RESULTS

A three-way analysis of variance (ANOVA) revealed two significant main effects, one significant two-way interaction effect and a significant three-way interaction effect (see Table 8.1). There was a significant effect of test factor (i.e., the results of the pretest vs. the results of the posttest), $F(1, 62) = 51.55$, $p < .001$, a significant effect of clause type (i.e., how each of the groups did on each relative clause), $F(3, 186) = 62.97$, $p < .001$, a significant effect of homework packet by clause type, $F(6, 186) = 14.02$, $p < .001$, a significant interaction effect of test factor by clause type, $F(3, 186) = 3.60$, $p < .05$, and a significant three-way effect of homework packet by clause type by test factor, $F(6, 186) = 22.43$, $p < .001$. The means and standard deviations for all factors are reported in Table 8.2.

Each of the homework packets was individually analyzed to locate significant differences. For each of the homework packet groups, there was a significant two-way interaction of test factor by clause, $F(3, 57) = 12.17$, $p < .001$ (for the DO group), $F(3, 69) = 13.73$ (for the OP group), and $F(3, 60) = 23.41$, $p < .001$. Pairwise comparisons were run within the homework groups testing for significance on each relative clause type, using the original error term from the three-way ANOVA. (See Figures 8.1, 8.2, and 8.3.) Within the DO homework group, there were increases from pre- to posttest on the SU relative clause and

TABLE 8.1
ANOVA for Homework Packet by Test Factor by Relative Clause Type

Source of Variation	df	MS	F
Homework (A)	2	492.96	0.16
Test Factor (B)	1	40,996.15	51.55**
Relative Clause (C)	3	46,219.99	62.97**
A × B	2	962.24	1.21
A × C	6	10,291.79	14.02**
B × C	3	1,945.75	3.60*
A × B × C	6	12,139.91	22.43**

*$p < .05$; **$p < .001$.

TABLE 8.2
Means and Standard Deviation

	Pretest							
	S		DO		OP		GEN	
	M	SD	M	SD	M	SD	M	SD
DO	48.50	32.20	37.25	32.06	26.00	31.85	.00	.00
OP	52.50	31.21	33.33	30.00	18.33	32.26	.00	.00
GEN	55.48	32.48	33.10	24.26	24.76	35.16	.00	.00

	Posttest							
	S		DO		OP		GEN	
	M	SD	M	SD	M	SD	M	SD
DO	81.00	29.36	79.00	31.69	32.00	39.68	.00	.00
OP	54.17	40.64	52.29	43.69	80.00	33.36	.00	.00
GEN	40.95	37.67	29.52	35.95	28.57	40.28	63.81	39.30

the DO relative clause, $F(1, 6) = 20.12$, $p < .01$, and $F(1, 6) = 32.59$, $p < .01$, respectively. The OP homework group had significant results on DO and OP relative clauses, $F(1, 6) = 16.01$, $p < .01$ and $F(1, 6) = 85.23$, $p < .001$, respectively. The GEN group had significant increases only in the GEN relative clause, $F(1, 6) = 77.00$, $p < .001$.

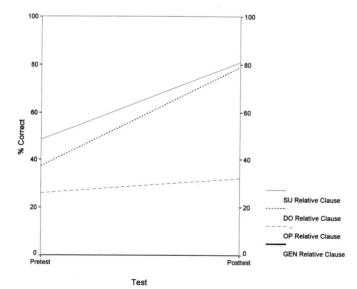

FIG. 8.1. DO homework packet.

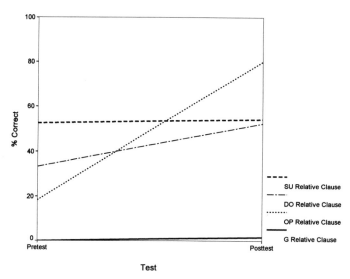

FIG. 8.2.   OP homework packet.

4. DISCUSSION

The results from the Omnibus Analysis indicate a significant main effect of test factor. This suggests that scores change between the pretests and posttests, that is, the subjects learned something from the homework packet. There was also a significant main effect of clause structure, that is, the performance of subjects on relative clauses was statistically different on the two tests. The three groups

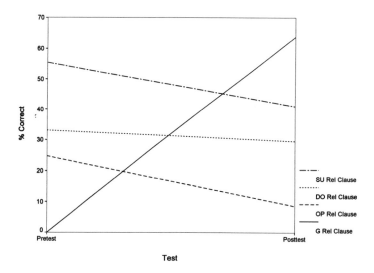

FIG. 8.3.   GEN homework packet.

were organized in such a way that they would be as equal as possible; therefore, there was no significant main effect of homework packet groups and thus there were no significant differences between the groups on the pretest.

The three-way interaction effect indicates that (a) teaching the students in the rule-oriented method may be an effective way to teach relativization, (b) ability to perform on the clauses varies depending on the type of clause, and (c) students show significant changes in ability from pretest to posttest. According to the analyses, the homework groups did not differ from one another statistically at the SU level and the DO level on the posttests, but they *did* differ from one another at the OP and GEN levels, indicating that some groups (i.e., the OP and GEN groups) did better on the lower levels of the hierarchy. This was predicted by a projection model of the NPAH. But this does not mean that all the groups were capable of generalizing to the higher levels. Refer to Table 8.3 for an overview of the actual results.

There is no question that the homework groups did better in the lesson they were assigned. The DO homework group clearly improved their knowledge, as can be seen in the significant increase between the pretest and the posttest.

The students in the OP group were interesting in that they improved significantly on OP and DO relative clauses, but not on SU, as predicted. This "fizzling out" of knowledge is somewhat apparent in Doughty's (1990) study as well: Her experimental groups had only 11–20% gains compared to 31–39% gains on the level on which they were taught.

The subjects who were taught GEN relativization had the highest percentage increase (about 63%) in the relative-clause type they were taught. But their knowledge of OP relative-clause types increased only slightly (~4%) and even decreased for SU (~ −15%) and DO (~ −4%) relative clause knowledge. (Possible reasons for this will be discussed later.) On the basis of this information, I have come to the conclusion that the GEN homework group did not learn to relativize up the Hierarchy.

Subjects in the GEN Homework group did worse on the SU and DO relative clauses on the posttest than on the pretest. They appeared to have over 50% and 33% accuracy rates on the pretest, indicating that some may have had a good understanding of SU and DO relativization. Because Italian relativization of the GEN is very different from the English relativization, perhaps subjects tried to transfer knowledge of the Italian GEN and disregarded their previous

TABLE 8.3
Summary of the Results of the Second Part of the NPAH Theory

		Relative Clause Type		
Group	Subject	Direct Object	Object of Preposition	Genitive
DO	X	X		
OP		X	X	
GEN				X

understanding of higher level relativization from L1 knowledge. Posttest responses indicated this was true in many cases.

A final note on the GEN relativization: other studies appear to have had problems with the GEN relative clauses as well. Gass found "the easiest position to relativize was the SU position with the lower positions more difficult . . . , with the genitive as an exception" (1979, p. 339). Gass (1982, p. 138) stated ". . . [learners] did relativize what they had been taught to other positions, with the exception of the genitive." Finally, Pavesi (1986) explained that her subjects found it easier to relativize the OC position than the GEN position (which is higher on the Hierarchy). Given this history with English relativization of the GEN, the results for Italian relativization are not surprising.

In trying to understand the results, we should remember that these subjects were foreign language learners, not second language learners. More than likely these students were not exposed to the language in the same way as L2 learners are. L2 learners—consciously or unconsciously—may acquire relativization of a less-marked position from some minimal exposure to appropriate examples, but that opportunity for minimal exposure may not have been available to these foreign language learners. Thus, these learners may have had little or no experiential base from which to learn unmarked Italian relativization. More research needs to be conducted on minimum exposure to unmarked forms.

5. CONCLUSION

I conducted this study in order to test the projection model on a language other than English, but the results were not meant to be generalized to other languages. I suggest that the theory be tested on other languages—especially those that do not relativize clauses in a way similar to English.

In conclusion, my study had mixed results. Because the NPAH hypothesis has two distinctive parts, each part should be considered on its own. First, the hypothesis suggests that if a person is taught to relativize at a higher position on the NPAH, generalization to a lower position will not occur. None of the groups demonstrated the ability to generalize to a lower position than they were taught. Second, the hypothesis predicts subjects will be able to perform well on positions higher than the one they were taught. This was true in some cases. Those taught DO relativized to the SU position. Those taught OP relative clauses relativized to the DO, but not the SU, position. And those taught GEN did not relativize to any higher positions at all.

ACKNOWLEDGMENTS

I would like to thank Fred Marshall for his advice, his teaching, his comments on this chapter, and his constant support. My thanks to Antonella Bassi for her help with the Italian translation and for the use of her students. I also thank Ron Cowen and Fred Eckman for their comments and support.

REFERENCES

Doughty, C. (1991). "Second Language Instruction Does Make a Difference," *Studies in Second Language Acquisition* 13, 431–469.

Eckman, F., L. Bell, and D. Nelson. (1988). "On the Generalization of Relative Clause Instruction in the Acquisition of English as a Second Language," *Applied Linguistics* 9, 1–11.

Gass, S. (1979). "Language Transfer and Universal Grammatical Relations," *Language Learning* 29, 327–344.

———. (1982). "From Theory to Practice." On *TESOL '81*, ed. by M. Hines and W. Rutherford. Washington, DC: TESOL.

Keenan, E., and B. Comrie. (1977). "Noun Phrase Accessibility and Universal Grammar," *Linguistic Inquiry* 8, 63–99.

Pavesi, M. (1986). "Markedness, Discoursal Modes, and Relative Clause Formation in a Formal and an Informal Context," *Studies in Second Language Acquisition* 8, 38–55.

Zobl, H. (1983). "Markedness and the Projection Problem," *Language Learning* 33(3), 293–313.

APPENDIX A

Relative Clauses (Genitive)

<u>Vocabolario</u>
relative pronoun—(who, whose, whom, which, that) link one clause to another
il/la/i/le + cui—relative pronoun meaning "whose"

Lezione

Hanno parlato al vicino il cui cane abbaia tutta la notte.
'They spoke to the neighbor whose dog barked all night.'

There are 2 ideas expressed in the previous sentence:

[1]Hanno parlato al vicino / [2]il cui cane abbaia tutta la notte
"cui" refers to "*the neighbor*":
Hanno parlato al vicino / il (vicino) cane abbaia tutta la notte

. . . and it belongs later in the sentence. It really completes the second clause:

Hanno parlato al vicino / il cane <u>del vicino</u> abbaia tutta la notte

So the two sentences/ideas underlying the original sentences are:

Hanno parlato al vicino *and* il cane abbaia tutta la notte

Two sentences referring to the same person or thing can be combined by using the reverse procedure:

Hanno parlato al vicino. Il cane del vicino abbaia tutta la notte.

First, identify the two uses of the same noun or phrase and underline them:

Hanno parlato <u>al vicino</u>. Il cane <u>del vicino</u> abbaia tutta la notte.

Then move the underlined noun in the second sentence to the beginning of the second sentence:

Hanno parlato al vicino. (del vicino) Il cane _____ abbaia tutta la notte.

Now remove the underlined noun in the second sentence.

Hanno parlato *al vicino*. Il cane abbaia tutta la notte.

Insert the relative pronoun after the determiner (il, la, le, i) that starts the second sentence:

Hanno parlato al vicino il cui cane abbaia tutta la notte.

Frasi Far Practica

A Combine the two sentences into one using the relative pronoun 'cui'.

1. A Il professore rimprova (*rimproverare = to reprimand*) lo studente.
   B Il compito dello studente è in ritardo.
2. A La polizia ha trovato la donna.
   B Ho urtato (*to collide with*) la macchina della donna.
3. A La facoltà di chimica ha domandato all'uomo di fare una conferenza.
   B La ricerca dell'uomo ha vinto un premio (*award*).
4. A Questo è il gatto.
   B La coda (*tail*) del gatto è bianca.
5. A L'artista dà una lezione.
   B Studiamo le sue opere (*works*) questa settimana.

B Correct the following sentences.

1. L'amico cui libro Guglielmo ha preso in prestito ha telefonato.
2. Non conosco la regista (*movie director*) il film ha vinto un premio.
3. Il professore la classe si riunisce alle due è interessante.
4. La città la popolazione è diminuita recentemente hanno bisogno di attirare (*to attract*) li turisti.
5. Molti immigranti (*immigrants*) recenti lingua madre (*native*) è lo spagnolo abitano al sud e all'ovest degli Stati Uniti.

Soluzioni

A

1. Il professore rimprova lo studente il cui compito è in ritardo.
2. La polizia ha trovato la donna la cui macchina ho urtato.
3. La facoltà di chimica ha domandato all'uomo la cui ricerca ha vinto un premio di fare una conferenza.
4. Questo è il gatto la cui coda è bianca.
5. L'artista le cui opere studiamo questa settimana dà una lezione.

B

1. add 'il' before 'cui'
2. add 'cui' after 'il'

3. add 'cui' before 'classe'
4. add 'cui' before 'popolazione'
5. add 'la cui' before 'lingua'

APPENDIX B

Test A

DIRECTIONS: Combine the following sentences into one, all-encompassing sentence by attaching the second sentence to the first.

01. Samuele ha ricevuto una lettera.
    La lettera è arrivata alle cinque.
02. Il ragazzo guida una Corvette.
    Il ragazzo abita accanto.
03. Quest'uomo è il candidato.
    Preferisco questo candidato.
04. La musica è bella
    Voi ascoltate la musica.
05. Ho afferrato la palla.
    Il giocatore ha calciato la palla in porta (goal).
06. "Una Bianca Nubile" ("Single White Female") è un film.
    Tutti parlano del film.
07. Mostrami (show me) lo scrittore.
    Hai sentito parlare dello scrittore.
08. Lui è l'uomo.
    Il suo cappello è nella mia macchina.
09. Questo è il cameriere.
    Il servizio del cameriere è magnifico.
10. Ecco il treno.
    La locomotiva (engine) del treno non funziona più.
11. Dov'è la casa?
    Il recinto (fence) della casa ha bisogno di essere riparato (repaired).
12. Non conosco la regista.
    Girano il film della regista all'università questa settimana.
13. Dov'è la ragazza?
    Uscirai con la ragazza.
14. È la signora.
    Andiamo a teatro con questa signora.

15. Hai parlato alla professoressa?
    La classe ha mandato i fiori alla professoressa.
16. Ho mangiato i dolci.
    Mio padre mi ha portato i dolci.
17. È la donna?
    La donna recita a teatro o al cinema.
18. Aspettiamo l'autobus.
    L'autobus deve passare di qui tra dieci minuti.
19. Quello è il ragazzo.
    Il ragazzo è venuto a casa mia ieri.

Part III

INPUT:
EXTERNAL FACTORS

Chapter 9

On the Teaching and Learning of Grammar: Challenging the Myths

Diane Larsen-Freeman
MAT Program, School for International Training, Brattleboro, Vermont

1. INTRODUCTION

There are a number of myths in circulation today about the teaching and learning of grammar. The following are but ten of them:

1. Grammar structures are meaningless forms. They are the skeleton, the bones of the language.
2. Grammar consists of arbitrary rules; the acquisition of the rules is also a somewhat arbitrary process.
3. Grammar structures are learned one at a time.
4. Grammar structures operate at the sentence and subsentence levels only.
5. Grammars are complete inventories; they explain all the structures in a language.
6. Grammar is an area of knowledge like vocabulary (as opposed to a skill like reading, writing, speaking, or listening).
7. Grammar is acquired naturally; it doesn't have to be taught.
8. Learners will eventually bring their performance into conformity with the target language; error correction is unnecessary.
9. All aspects of grammar structures are learned in the same way.
10. Grammar teaching and learning are boring.

I will mercifully stop at ten; there are others, and I am sure readers will have their own lists as well. It is no doubt also true that some would not agree with my assessment of these as myths. Bearing in mind the theme of this book, *Second Language Acquisition Theory and Pedagogy*, I will use second language acquisition (SLA) research and theory to demonstrate that certain of these are indeed myths. SLA theory will be invoked to refute numbers 1–3. SLA theory has also, in my opinion, contributed several items to the list. I will discuss these as well (Nos. 7–9). Then, in the spirit of reciprocity, I will consider what SL pedagogy can contribute to SLA theory. Next, I will point to some areas where I believe a collaborative effort between theorists and pedagogues would be welcome. Finally, I will conclude with an important caveat concerning the application of SLA theory. To begin with, then, how has SLA theory helped to counter some of these myths?

2. COUNTERING MYTHS 1–3

2.1 Myth 1: Grammar Structures Are Meaningless Forms

Perhaps this myth is a holdover from structural linguistics, in which forms in a language were described without appeal to meaning. As forms, grammatical structures were characterized by their morphology and syntax alone. Judging from a survey of pedagogical materials, I think it is clear that this assumption persists today. Textbooks introduce learners to grammatical structures by delineating their formal properties. It is not uncommon today, for example, to find materials introducing ESL/EFL students to the passive voice in English by demonstrating how a passive sentence is derived from its active counterpart. The transformationalists' regard for the autonomy of syntax is manifest in this purely form-based description. Similarly, the follow-up to such an introduction is often a series of exercises in which students are instructed to transform active sentences into passive ones. To my mind, such an introduction to the passive voice is very misleading. Passive and active sentences sometimes have different meanings and always serve very different purposes. Moreover, the long-term challenge in acquiring the passive voice in English is not learning how to form it, but rather learning when to use it, that is, learning which discourse contexts favor the passive voice and which do not.

The reason I say that SLA research can refute Myth 1 is that quite early on in the evolution of the SLA field it was pointed out that the acquisition of the form of a grammatical structure was incomplete without the concomitant acquisition of its function. Wagner-Gough (1975) was the first, I believe, to make this point in print. Her subject, Homer, a five-year old Farsi speaker, used the *-ing* morpheme very early in his acquisition of English, as did the other subjects being reported on in the morpheme acquisition studies at the time. What Wagner-Gough noticed in Homer's performance, however, was that he used *-ing* not only for its target function but also to signal an imperative function. Other researchers that expanded on this theme were Andersen (1977), who demonstrated the folly of talking about the acquisition of the English article as though it were one structure, thus obscuring its many semantic uses; Bahns and Wode (1980), whose German-speaking subject used *didn't* for some time as a past-tense marker before he used it as a negator; and Huebner (1980), whose Hmong-speaking adult subject used a general Wh-question marker (*waduyu*) for all Wh-question words (e.g., *Waduyu kam from?* for *Where are you from?* and *Waduyu kam?* for *Why did you come?*) It is obvious, then, that one cannot talk about the acquisition of a form unless its function is also considered. Indeed, it is often said these days that the language acquisition process is all about learning to map form on function or form and meaning.

I think it is worth pointing out that when we elect to use two terms in tandem as a shorthand—form and function, or form and meaning—we should never lose sight of the fact that there are really three dimensions with which we need to be concerned: form, meaning, and function (use) (Larsen-Freeman, 1991). To return to the passive for our example, we can clearly see that there are three dimensions that must be mastered before any learner can be said to have acquired it. Its form requires a 'be' verb (the final auxiliary verb), a past participle, a transitive main verb, and when present, the 'by' preposition before the agent. We also should acknowledge its meaning as conferring focus on the theme or receiver of the action, rather than the agent, as happens in canonical word order, and the fact that passive sentences may convey a meaning different from that of the active voice with the same agent and theme. Finally its use: When or why is it used instead of the active voice? The answers are numerous: when the theme is the topic, when the agent is unknown or redundant or when one wishes to conceal it, etc.

Thus, with some impetus from SLA research and a little reflection, we have come to realize that grammatical structures are more than forms; therefore, their acquisition must entail more than learning how to form the structures. It must also include learning what they mean and when and why to use them as well. This awareness is extremely important from a pedagogical standpoint, of course, because as language teachers will attest, the learning challenge for students is not accuracy alone but meaningful and appropriate use as well. As such, grammar teaching does not mean merely teaching forms and it is certainly not limited to teaching explicit form-based rules.

2.2. Myth 2: Grammar Consists of Arbitrary Rules; Their Acquisition Is Also a Somewhat Arbitrary Process

I am afraid arguing against the first half of this myth will take me too far from my foregrounded objectives in this chapter, i.e. discussing the process of teaching and learning grammar. Suffice it to say that much of the apparent arbitrariness of grammar rules is dispelled when we look at language from a discourse perspective, that is, viewing language from this perspective helps us to see why the rules are the way they are. For the second half of this myth, I summarize what the SLA theory of interlanguage (Selinker, 1972)—which has been so fundamental to our understanding of the language acquisition process for the past two decades or so—has to say about the arbitrariness of the process.

Far from being arbitrary, learner interlanguages are thought to exhibit a fair degree of systematicity and order. Systematicity does not mean that learners use structures in a targetlike manner from their first exposure. What it does mean is that like natural languages, interlanguages (ILs) appear to be rule governed. There is variability in learner performance, to be sure, but it is typically systematic, that is, learners use certain forms erroneously by target-speaker standards but consistently as a response to certain extralinguistic factors such as task demands (Hulstijn & Hulstijn, 1984; Larsen-Freeman, 1975); topic, setting, and interlocutors (Bell, 1984), attention to form (Tarone, 1988), and planning time available (Crookes, 1989). There does seem to be some random or free variation, such as when a learner produces *no go* and *don't go* within moments of each other under seemingly identical conditions (Ellis, 1985). In fact, there is a fair degree of synchronic variability. Structures do cooccur with temporally and developmentally earlier constructions, and yet change over time follows established paths.

Many explanations for these developmental paths have been put forth, running the gamut from psychological explanations such as the shedding of speech-processing strategy constraints (Clahsen, 1987; Pienemann, 1985), and the invoking of Slobin-like operating principles (Andersen, 1988), to environmental ones having to do with factors in the input such as frequency of occurrence, perceptual saliency, or factors arising out of interaction with speakers of the target language (Larsen-Freeman, 1975; Lightbown, 1983; Long, 1980), and to linguistic ones having to do with markedness directionality (Eckman, 1981) and Universal Grammar (UG) principles and parameter resetting (e.g., Bley-Vroman, 1986; Flynn, 1987; Schachter, 1988; White, 1985). Continuing with our story of interlanguage I will address Myth 3.

2.3. Myth 3: Grammar Structures Are Learned One at a Time

IL theory posits that progress is not linear. Language acquisition is not a matter of steadily accumulating structural entities (Rutherford, 1987, p. 4). Backsliding is common, giving rise to so-called U-shaped behavior (Kellerman, 1985). Development is gradual, but occasionally there is a fundamental overhaul or restructuring of the underlying grammar (McLaughlin, 1990). A good example of this type of restructuring is reported in the work of Meisel, Clahsen, and Pienemann (1981). They reported that learners of German in their study would sometimes omit items that the learners had previously appeared to master. The omissions involved certain forms over which learners had to move other forms. McLaughlin (1990) speculated that this apparent backsliding resulted from a temporary restructuring of the system that involved an omission of certain elements to allow for the development of other elements. Thus, the acquisition of structures is interdependent and not a matter of simple aggregation.

3. SLA THEORY: HELPING US TO UNDERSTAND GRAMMAR LEARNING AND TRANSFORM TEACHING

As was just seen, SLA theory has been helpful in challenging the first three myths about the learning of grammar. Before moving on, I would like to underscore the significance of the contribution of SLA theory to the understanding of the learning of grammar. Although the description of SLA that I have just given may seem commonplace by now, remember that in the historical context in which it arose, SLA was a radical departure. Before SLA researchers began looking at learning and the learner in the early 1970s, both had been virtually ignored, at least in modern times. So even if this description of the SLA process does not withstand the test of time, SLA theory has already performed a great service for second language pedagogy by helping us to see learners as rightful partners in any pedagogical enterprise.

This view of language acquisition has influenced language pedagogy in encouraging learner-centered teaching. Learner centeredness, combined with the shift to a focus on communicative competence, has helped to transform the language teaching field dramatically in the past twenty years. Instead of an explicit focus on language itself, there has been an emphasis on learners' expressing their own meanings through language. This in turn has led to a greater tolerance for errors in learners' performance and the creation of opportunities for learners to use the language in more authentic and spontaneous ways (Lightbown & Spada, 1990, p. 430).

4. A MEGAMYTH AND THE REFLEX FALLACY

Another application of an SLA theory to pedagogy has been the claim that learners can develop greater communicative abilities through instruction that more closely resembles the characteristics of a "natural," that is, untutored, environment. It has been argued by Krashen (1982, 1985) and others that given suitable exposure to the target language, SLA can proceed in much the same manner as child language acquisition, where a learner's performance gradually approximates and then matches the environmental input. This is a radical reconceptualizing of second language pedagogy, to be sure. But although we appreciate that SLA theory forces us to reexamine long-standing assumptions about second language pedagogy, it would be prudent to interject a note of caution. It seems to me that the biggest myth of all, a megamyth if you will, is the assumption that what works in natural language acquisition should automatically become the pedagogy of the classroom. It may turn out to be effective, but this should not be assumed a priori.

Whether or not there are fundamental differences between tutored and untutored acquisition processes (currently a contentious issue), why should it be assumed that features of natural acquisition are superior to those that occur in instructional settings? In a recent study, for example, Buczowska and Weist

(1991, p. 548), whose subjects were Polish adults learning English in Poland, reported that "in the domain of temporal location, tutored L2 learners do not follow the course of acquisition that is prototypical for L1 learners or untutored L2 learners, and deviations from the untutored L2 pattern [in L2 teaching] can facilitate rather than impede the acquisition process."

Indeed, I would strenuously object to the assumption that because certain conditions exist in naturalistic acquisition, our objective as teachers should be to emulate them to the best of our abilities. I have called this "the reflex fallacy." "The fallacy lies in the assumption that teaching is an involuntary reflex of natural acquisition such that what is present and natural in untutored acquisition should be present in abundance in classroom instruction, and what is absent in natural acquisition should be prohibited in the classroom" (Larsen-Freeman, 1990, p. 262). The goal of SLA theory is to identify what is minimally necessary for SLA to occur. What is minimally necessary for SLA to take place outside the classroom does not automatically constitute the most effective means of learning in the classroom (Cohen, Larsen-Freeman, & Tarone, 1991). One would hope that effective teaching would accelerate the natural process. "The basis of schooling is the assumption that nature can be improved on by artifice" (Widdowson, 1992). Yet sometimes SLA researchers have taken the unwarranted step of proscribing or prescribing pedagogical practices on the basis of their findings from untutored acquisition (Larsen-Freeman, 1990). As a teacher, I do not ask myself what is minimally necessary for my students to learn but rather what I can give my students that will maximize their learning. It is important that SL teachers know about SLA theory so they can complement natural processes, but their job is to stimulate learning rather than to emulate acquisition.

I believe that there are a few myths that have arisen from the reflex fallacy. It is to these that I will turn next.

5. CONTRIBUTING TO THE MYTHS

5.1. Myth 7: Grammar Is Acquired Naturally; It Doesn't Have to Be Taught

Taken at face value, the first half of Myth 7 is demonstrably true. Some untutored L2 learners are successful acquirers of second language grammars, and SLA theory does need to account for their success.[1] Nevertheless, this item deserves the myth designation because not all untutored learners successfully acquire L2 grammars. Moreover, even if all learners were successful in acquiring L2 grammars without grammar instruction, the second half of Myth 7 is not an inevitable consequence. It does not necessarily follow that grammar should not be taught.

---

[1]The same could be said, of course, for the successful acquisition of second language grammar by tutored language learners. Some succeed, but by no means all.

As I have argued previously, pedagogy cannot be wholly informed by reductionist explanations of natural acquisition. In light of the discussion just completed, a better question would be, what value is there, if any, in teaching grammar or of focusing on form, as it has come to be called?[2] Are learners who receive grammar instruction better off than those whose attention is not drawn in any way to the formal features of the code? My interpretation of the research conducted so far yields an affirmative answer to this question.

Research providing evidence that meaning-focused instruction alone does not necessarily lead to grammatical accuracy comes from the much-studied Canadian French immersion programs. "These programs are referred to by Krashen (1984) as 'communicative programs par excellence' since the focus is almost exclusively on meaning through subject-matter instruction rather than on the form of the language itself" (Lightbown & Spada, 1990, p. 431). Much good has come from these programs. Young classroom learners who receive this content-based instruction develop productive repertoires in French. It has been demonstrated, however, that although children learn to speak French fluently, their accuracy in French syntax and morphology is still far below what one might expect of learners who have spent several years immersed in the second language (Harley & Swain, 1984). "Less salient morphosyntactic features of the target system, incongruent with the L1 and/or not crucial for comprehension or for getting meaning across may fail to become intake" (Harley, 1993b, p. 11), possibly because of the self-reinforcing nature of peer interlanguage. "Indeed, some observers have concluded that French immersion is the best demonstration of the inadequacy of CLT" (Hammerly, 1987; see also Lightbown & Spada, 1990, p. 431), since students become "dysfunctional bilinguals who can convey messages but do so very ungrammatically" (Hammerly, 1992, p. 215). In fact, it is considered enough of a problem in Canada that "the improvement of immersion children's oral and written grammar has been identified as a major priority by immersion educators . . ." (Day & Shapson, 1991, pp. 26–27).

It is not my intent to detract from the success of immersion education. Indeed I have already asserted that much good has been achieved through it. It seems reasonable, however, to seek ways to address its inadequacy while preserving the good that has come from it.[3] My position is that the acknowledged weakness of immersion education can be overcome by selective form-focused instruction. Research has already been initiated by Harley (1989), Day and Shapson (1991)

---

[2]An unfortunate appellation, in my opinion, given that the acquisition of grammar involves more than the acquisition of form.

[3]At the Symposium, Krashen commented that what's wrong with immersion can be corrected by giving students more of the same, i.e. more comprehensible input, not by resorting to form-focused instruction. It is ironic that Krashen advocates doing more of the same when he has previously faulted others for giving the same advice: "Some researchers have simply assumed the effectiveness of error correction. When correction fails, they simply call for more, or more consistent correction. Language acquisition simply does not work that way" (Krashen, 1991, p. 417).

and Lyster (1993) in French immersion programs which shows that form-focused instruction makes a positive impact on the IL development of students who have had several years of communicative language use. In the Day and Shapson study, for example, the experimental group of Grade 7 early French immersion students performed significantly higher on accuracy in the use of conditionals than a control group who had played no linguistic games with conditionals and had not received any metalinguistic instruction, as had the experimental group. Other studies that have corroborated the value of form-focused instruction, or "input enhancement" activities, to use Sharwood Smith's (1991) term, are Gass (1982), Pienemann (1984), Zobl (1985), Eckman, Bell, and Nelson (1988), Tomasello and Herron (1988, 1989) (but cf. Doughty, 1991; Ellis, 1989; Lightbown, 1991; Spada & Lightbown, 1993; Valdman, 1993; White, 1991; White, Spada, Lightbown, & Ranta, 1991; Zhou, 1992). Although admittedly some of these endorsements are weakened because they could not demonstrate a long-term effect for instruction (e.g. Harley, 1989; White, 1991), it does not necessarily follow that focus on form does not affect the learners' internalized language systems, as Schwartz & Gubala-Ryzak (1992) concluded. As Harley (1993b) observed, alternative interpretations of the forgetting are possible.[4]

Moreover, Krashen (1991) did accept the Lightbown and Spada (1990) study as demonstrating an effect for form-focused instruction. In a post hoc description of some specific classroom events and outcomes, Lightbown and Spada used a modified version of the COLT (Communicative Orientation to Language Teaching) instrument to collect observational data on four classes of French-speaking students. The macrolevel analyses indicated that all four classes were primarily communicative in their approach and that classroom interaction focused on meaning most of the time. However, the four teachers differed from each other in terms of the total amount of time they gave to form-focused activities.

> In class 1, where the most form-focused instruction was provided, the learners were most accurate in their use of the progressive -ing, were more likely to use the presentational forms preferred by native speakers (*there is* rather than *you have*), and were at a more advanced stage with their use of possessive determiners. Students in class 4 had the lowest accuracy on all the features examined in the analysis of spontaneous language samples. The teacher in this class was the only one who virtually never focused—however briefly—on grammar. (Lightbown & Spada, 1990, p. 443)

It should be noted, however, that students in class 4 showed no disadvantage in their overall performance.

---

[4]Among the explanations Harley (1993b) offered are that the instruction may have been lacking in some way because it was not oriented toward the students' communicative needs and because the target of instruction may have been too infrequent in subsequent class use to reinforce what learning had taken place. Harley (1993a) offered some guidance for a kind of form-focused instruction that may prove helpful. In any event, I would concur with Harley that in the future research methodology must include an assessment of long-term retention.

Why is form-focused instruction effective in dealing with morphosyntax? Perhaps it is because focusing student attention facilitates intake. Certainly this is what Schmidt (1990) reported for his own acquisition of Portuguese in Brazil. Schmidt was convinced that he usually noticed forms in the out-of-class input only after they were taught—and only then did he begin to acquire them. According to Schmidt, "Noticing is the necessary and sufficient condition for converting input to intake" (1990, p. 129). Indeed in terms of information-processing theory, it is necessary for learners to attend to the forms they are learning. So giving increased salience to forms, especially perceptually nonsalient forms, is one possible explanation for form-focused instruction being helpful. Other reasons might be that with form focus, learning transfer from marked to unmarked forms is facilitated (more on this later), and provision of negative evidence might help to destabilize an incorrect rule (Long & Crookes, 1992). With respect to negative evidence, I turn to the next myth.

5.2. Myth 8: Learners Will Eventually Bring Their Performance into Conformity with the Target Language. Error Correction Is Unnecessary

There is currently a debate in the field over whether negative evidence (e.g., a teacher's correction of a learner's utterance) is needed. Krashen (1981 and elsewhere) has argued that the only data necessary for acquisition are the actually occurring linguistic forms provided by native speakers in communicative situations. The universal grammar (UG) model for SLA adopts this same theoretical premise. Learners are thought to be equipped with a set of principles that constrain their hypotheses such that the only data necessary for acquisition are actually occurring linguistic forms. Mere exposure to these "positive" data are thought to trigger the appropriate setting of a parameter in the case of L1, or to reset the L1 parameter in the case of L2 (Schachter, 1986, p. 221). This position has arisen out of the need for UG theorists to explain "how it is that learners can avoid being trapped in an overgeneralization from which escape without provision of disconfirming evidence would theoretically not be possible" (Rutherford, 1993, p. 4), part of the so-called logical problem.

However, some UG theorists have come to believe that negative evidence may play a more significant role in L2 acquisition than was first hypothesized. White (1987), in her discussion of Krashen's input hypothesis, argued that comprehensible input in and of itself does not eliminate overgeneralizations. A native speaker of French who treats English like French will produce utterances such as those in (1) if the speaker relies on positive evidence alone:

(1) a. John drank his coffee slowly.

   b. Slowly, John drank his coffee.

   c. John slowly drank his coffee.

   d. *John drank slowly his coffee.

There is nothing in positive evidence from English to inform the learner that the last example is ungrammatical. Hence, White asks, how can learners learn of the nonoccurrence of a particular possibility if they have no access to negative evidence? It is worth noting that White believes that UG is in operation but that negative evidence may be a requisite in L2 acquisition although it is not in L1. Others have interpreted the need for negative evidence as a sign that L2 learning is fundamentally different from L1 acquisition and have concluded that second language learners do not rely on UG (because learners no longer have access to it) at all (Bley-Vroman, 1990). Still others do not accept the need for negative evidence in SLA (Schwartz & Gubala-Ryzak, 1992; Schwartz, 1993), holding firmly to the notion that L1 and L2 acquisition processes are the same and can be explained through the theory of UG, which requires positive evidence alone.

So certainly there is a controversy. It might be helpful to recall, however, that SLA theorists are concerned with specifying what is minimally necessary for acquisition to proceed. Second language educators are concerned with maximizing effectiveness. For this reason alone, second language pedagogy should derive comfort from the studies of Tomasello and Herron (1988, 1989), Trahey and White (1993), and most recently, Carroll and Swain (1993), which offer support for the value of negative evidence or feedback in SLA. The Carroll and Swain study is worth summarizing, because their study included several different types of feedback mechanisms. Subjects were divided into five groups according to which type of feedback they received when they made an error in dative alternation in English. Group A subjects were given metalinguistic information when they made an error; Group B subjects were simply told that their response was wrong; Group C subjects were corrected when they erred and were given a model of the desired response; Group D subjects, when they made an error, were asked if they were sure about their response. The fifth group was the control group, which received no feedback at all. What the researchers found was that all four of their experimental groups, which received some sort of feedback when they erred, outperformed the control group, which received only positive evidence of acceptable dative alternation syntax. The authors tentatively concluded that their study "lends empirical support to Schachter's claim that indirect as well as direct forms of feedback can help adult second language learners learn abstract linguistic generalizations" (Carroll & Swain, 1993, p. 373).

Before becoming too complacent about this issue, however, we should note two often-cited observations in SLA: the first has to do with the fact that learners do not receive adequate feedback because only a small percentage of their errors are corrected, and even these are not always dealt with consistently (e.g., All-wright, 1975). The second concerns the question of why learners' errors often seem resistant to revision even in the presence of correction (Cohen & Robbins, 1976). Is it the case, as Schwartz (1993) suggests, that even when negative data are abundant, learners do not necessarily incorporate them into their IL system in order to make changes? Certainly this is counterintuitive and would call into question traditional pedagogical practice. Nevertheless, whether negative data can initiate change in a learner's underlying grammar is an important question and one likely to motivate much future research.[5] The last myth I will discuss in this section of my chapter is Myth 9.

5.3. Myth 9: All Aspects of Grammatical Structures Are Learned in the Same Way

I am aware of no SLA theory that claims explicitly that there is a single mechanism that accounts for the acquisition of all aspects of grammatical structures; however, some models, such as UG theory, seem to imply that this is the case. Calling Number 9 a myth is my way of warning second language educators to avoid presuming that there is a simple solution to an issue as complex as the nature of the grammar acquisition process. Any claim to the effect that all acquisition is the product of habit formation or of rule formation, or today, of setting/resetting parameters or the strengthening of connections in complex neural networks, is an obvious oversimplification of a complex process. The problem is not that our view of acquisition changes or differs. My concern is with the expectation that all of SLA will be explicable by a single process. With language as complicated as it is, why should we expect that a single process will account for all of it (Larsen-Freeman & Long, 1991)?

Some researchers are more circumspect. They acknowledge the complexity by pointing to a modular view of language and warn that we should refrain from generalizing across modules (Sharwood Smith, 1993). Schwartz (1993, p. 159) stated: "The lexicon is learned in a distinct manner from syntax. Indeed, lexical items must be learned. Aspects of syntax are not learned in this sense; they grow." Whether one agrees with this characterization of syntax and lexicon acquisition or not, certainly the underlying assumption of disparate learning processes is sensible. In fact, I have carried this line of reasoning further (Larsen-Freeman, 1991) by arguing that even within a module (here syntax), different aspects are learned through different means. I cannot go into this claim in any detail here, but consider the analysis of the passive voice. I submit that learning how to form the passive voice is different from learning what it means and when and why to use it. As such, I have suggested that we need to teach diverse aspects of grammar structures differently. Meaningful drills contribute to syntactic fluency; they are unlikely to enhance learners' understanding of the semantics or pragmatics governing the choice of particular structures.

---

[5]Of course, as SLA is a complex process, it is unlikely that we will arrive at a categorical answer to this question. It is more likely that we will find that negative evidence is helpful for certain learners, for certain structures (Zhou, 1992), at certain times (Jordens, 1993).

6. SL PEDAGOGY'S CONTRIBUTION
TO SLA THEORY

We now come to reciprocity. I think SL teachers can contribute to SLA theory by constantly reminding theorists of the need to broaden their perspectives. Although it is perfectly acceptable for a theorist to concentrate on one aspect of a problem at a time, a comprehensive theory of second language acquisition must account for a number of phenomena with which language teachers have been acquainted for some time but which current theories have ignored. Teachers are known to draw on a number of theories to create a blend in practice. I do not believe that their eclecticism stems from capriciousness. I think it can be attributed to the fact that teachers confront the complexity of language, learning, and language learners every day of their working lives. This experience reinforces in teachers the conviction that no unitary view of the three will account for what teachers must grapple with on a daily basis.

There are a number of things that teachers know that no current theory of SLA explains.

1. A theory should provide an account of learner differences, including differences in rate of acquisition and ultimate attainment. Although the literature is vast now and grows bigger every day, not much has been noted about success or failure with regard to particular language modules, save for the age differences cited for phonology. But all teachers know that every learner with whom they work is unique. For this reason, as Tomlin (1990) suggested, SLA is a problem of individuals. "A proper account of SLA must be an account of how individuals learn second languages. . . . Thus, statements of the knowledge represented in an IL grammar, of the cognitive processes activated during second language learning, or of the social contexts favoring or inhibiting SLA must be statements that hold true for individuals" (p. 157).

2. The theory should account for the fact that successful learning takes place for some learners regardless of the method employed (Stevick's riddle). As much as we are reluctant to admit it, it is not true that the grammar-translation method or ALM failed to produce communicatively competent individuals. Certainly some students were successful. Why they succeeded when they did needs to be explained in any comprehensive theory of SLA.

3. The theory should account for learning of grammar that does not manifest itself in performance. Every teacher knows that learning is taking place even when it is not visible. But SLA research has traditionally relied on rather arbitrary thresholds in performance data (including grammaticality judgments) for evidence of learning.[6] This is a limitation that must be overcome.

---

[6]I am thinking here, of course, of measures involving some percentage of suppliance in obligatory contexts for a certain period of time.

4. The theory must account for the fact that SLA is not merely a linguistic problem. Although it is true that researchers have been exploring learnability constraints, it is not enough to investigate the relationship between knowledge representations for language and their role in constraining acquisition. One must also identify and describe the cognitive mechanisms that account for changes of state in the individual's interlanguage grammar (Long, 1990). By the same token, it must be acknowledged that cognitive psychological descriptions of second language learning also provide only a partial account of SLA and need to be linked with linguistic theories in order to explain such linguistic phenomena as markedness and linguistic universals (McLaughlin, 1990, p. 126). Furthermore, Wolfe Quintero (1992, p. 42) noted that UG theory must also account for how learners acquire morphological and lexical features of the target language that are language specific and are not instantiations of principles of UG. Currently, morphological and lexical exceptions are considered part of a marked, peripheral grammar, the learning of which is left unexplained within UG theory.

Pointing out that theorists have been selective in their foci is not a criticism, provided that claims that emanate from partial theories are duly modest. Lest we grow too satisfied with our theories, language teachers will be happy to remind us that SLA is a multidimensional phenomenon; by doing so, they will keep us humble. I now turn to the collaborative nature of theory and practice.

7. THE COLLABORATIVE NATURE OF THEORY AND PRACTICE

It is not my intention to call for teachers and researchers to collaborate on research projects because this has already been advocated by others. Instead I propose to treat questions of concern to teachers as items for SLA research agendas. Theorists might have more impact on practice if they dealt with issues that teachers wrestle with all the time. To a certain extent they already do, but more such research is needed. Let me nominate five issues:

1. Learner Readiness. Teachers do not need SLA researchers to tell them that learners only learn when they are ready. What teacher has not had the experience of teaching some aspect of grammar on Friday, feeling reasonably satisfied that the students learned it, and then finding out on Monday that all of the effort was in vain? More important, is there a way to detect when learners are ready to learn? Pienemann's (1984) experiment, in which he showed that Italian schoolchildren made progress in learning subject-verb inversion in German only when they were at the stage to benefit from the instruction they were offered is tantalizing to language teachers searching for the most efficient way to use their limited time with their students. Will Pienemann's "teachability hypothesis" hold up under further scrutiny if it is tested against more subjects than the few in his first two studies (1984, 1986)? And if so, will it help teachers to determine when to provide focused instruction to coincide with the learner's next stage along a developmental continuum? This would truly be a contribution.

2. Focus Selectivity. Teachers know they cannot teach it all. There is too little time for one thing. Are there aspects of structures that if focused upon would yield greater learning efficiency than others? Gass' (1982) experiment teaching relative clause formation is pertinent here. Gass demonstrated that if learners are taught to relativize marked structures (in her case to relativize objects of the preposition in English), they will not only learn to do this but will generalize their learning to being able to relativize unmarked structures as well. Replicating and extending the Gass experiment, Eckman, Bell, and Nelson (1988) showed that generalization of learning is indeed possible from structures that are typologically more marked to those structures that are typologically less marked. The exciting implication of this for L2 pedagogy is, of course, that a strategy of IL intervention could be formulated in which it would not be necessary to teach all structures.

Attractive for the same reason is the idea of clustering in UG. It is predicted by the theory that if the input contains evidence of one aspect of a cluster of properties associated with some parameter, that evidence should be sufficient to trigger all other aspects of the parameter (White, 1992). "Not only is there no one-to-one correspondence between input and acquisition of a construction, but, once the value is set, the acquirer ends up with knowledge that indicates that certain other strings in the language are either possible or impossible as well" (Schwartz, 1993, p. 154). In other words, learners will learn more than they are taught. Wouldn't this be a welcome development in L2 pedagogy if corroborated? Another attractive prediction is that instruction is not necessary if L1 and L2 parameters coincide, or where they differ, if the data needed to reset them are available to learners in the input. Thus, only "where L1 and L2 parameter settings differ and the necessary data to trigger resetting are not present, consciousness raising or instruction would be necessary" (Simblist, 1992, p. 232). If such predictions are borne out, SLA theory might eventually help teachers to focus student attention selectively and thus become more efficient with the time they have.

3. Defossilizing Errors. Of course, it is an empirical question in SLA theory whether a case can be made for errors fossilizing, let alone defossilizing. But certainly teachers can vouch for the fact that some errors in learners' production persist well beyond what one would expect, in spite of the attention the errors receive. What causes these errors to endure? There have been a number of suggestions involving the convergence of L1 differences and L2 inherent complexity, markedness, and so forth. White (1989) suggested that the failure of the Subset

Principle, which forces learners to entertain the most conservative hypothesis, contributes to the fossilization that characterizes L2 acquisition. This suggestion is based upon the observation that learners' interlanguage performances are replete with overgeneralizations and ungrammaticality; like the others, however, White's claim has not been universally endorsed (see, e.g., MacLaughlin, 1991).

Harley (1993a) proposed that teacher-guided crosslingual comparisons could help defossilize some L2 errors for immersion students, especially where partial similarities have encouraged an assumption of complete identity between L1 and L2 items. She cited Lyster's (1993) classroom experiment designed to teach the notion of social register in French to Grade 8 immersion students. According to Harley (1993a), "This study provides evidence that [with] analytic [form-focused] teaching that includes a crosslingual element, it is possible to undo fossilized errors—in this case the typical use of *tu* in all second person contexts by early immersion students, which Swain and Lapkin (1989) found still persisting at the high school level" (p. 250). Although form-focused instruction at a point of interlingual contrast is not exactly a revolutionary pedagogical practice, it would be worthwhile to look further at fossilized errors and see what can be done about them.

4. Role of Practice. This may be a curious addition to my list. After all, practicing grammar forms is a very well established pedagogical procedure. I myself have recently coined the term *grammaring*, asserting that grammar should be seen as a skill like reading and writing rather than an area of knowledge (Larsen-Freeman, 1993). Moreover, for cognitive psychologists such as McLaughlin (1990), practice plays a vital role in SLA. According to McLaughlin, "a complex cognitive skill, such as acquiring a second language, involves a process whereby controlled, attention-demanding operations become automatic through practice" (p. 125). More recently, however, the role of practice has been brought into question. Ellis (1993a) presented arguments in support of a comprehension-based approach to grammar teaching. Pointing to the learnability problem (here that the acquisition of specific grammatical features is constrained developmentally), Ellis (1993b) postulated that structural syllabi serve better to facilitate intake than to teach learners to produce grammatical items correctly. He stated explicitly that "the new rationale for [a structural syllabus] rests on the claim that grammar teaching should be directed at consciousness-raising rather than practice" (1993b, p. 108).

Ellis' preference for consciousness-raising over practice drew support from a study by VanPatten and Cadierno (1993). They reasoned: "Given the rather important role that comprehensible input plays in SLA, the value of grammar instruction as output practice is questionable, if the intent of the instruction is to alter the nature of the developing system . . . It would seem reasonable to suggest that rather than manipulate learner output to effect change in the developing system, instruction might seek to change the way that input is perceived and processed by the learner" (p. 227). In their study, VanPatten and Cadierno compared an experimental group that received an explanation of a grammar point and had experience processing input data with a control group that received the explanation followed by output practice. Pretest/posttest measures revealed significant gains in both comprehension and production of sentences for the experimental group; for those that received traditional instruction, significant gains were made in production only. VanPatten and Sanz (this volume) corroborated the findings of VanPatten and Cadierno by demonstrating that the positive effects for processing input versus no instruction hold for sentence-level tasks. In addition, they report a significant positive effect for input processing as compared with no instruction on a discourse-level task in the written mode, but not in the oral mode.

5. Use of Metalanguage. Teachers often ask if metalanguage is helpful to students and, if so, to what degree it should be used. As Sharwood Smith (1993) noted, "It is still an open question as to how much conscious awareness of the formal properties of language, and hence instruction based on inducing this awareness, actually helps the development of spontaneous language use" (p. 172). It is interesting that in the Carroll and Swain (1993) study cited earlier, Group A, the group receiving explicit metalinguistic feedback, outperformed the other groups. Simply telling subjects that they were wrong, providing indirect feedback, and even providing the right forms did not help as much as the explicit metalinguistic information (p. 372). Such a finding, if it is replicated and if it holds for long-term retention, is clearly important to second language pedagogy. This leads me to my conclusion and final caveat.

8. A FINAL CAVEAT

SLA theory has contributed much to our understanding of the learning/acquisition process. As I pointed out earlier, learners and learning were not receiving much attention when SLA was launched. Second language pedagogy has been well served by second language acquisition theory for this reason alone. And yet, although our understanding of the learning process has been enhanced, it does not necessarily follow that the products of theory are prescriptions and proscriptions for classroom practice. One reason is the reflex fallacy; another is that just as there is more to learning than meets the eye (or ear), there is more to teaching as well.

Teachers are not mere conveyor belts delivering to their students practices/behaviors implied by SLA theory—and teaching is not simply the exercise of classroom activity. The nature of classroom interaction is complex and contingent. Teachers have good reason to say "it depends" when asked whether they would consider adopting a particular practice. Similarly, there are likely to be very few categorical answers forthcoming from SLA research. However, these will not be the measure of the contribution of SLA theory to pedagogy anyway.

I have already suggested a way that pedagogy can benefit theory. Theory can benefit pedagogy in two ways: First, teachers with enhanced understanding of SLA can become more efficient and effective in the classroom by making moment-to-moment decisions that are in harmony with the students' learning. If SLA theory can help expand teachers' awareness of learning beyond the teacher's own experience, can comfort teachers whose students experience backsliding or are not ready to learn, can help teachers to cultivate a positive attitude toward students' errors but can encourage them not to give up on fossilized errors, then it will do a great deal. Teaching does not cause learning, but those who have expanded awareness of it and fascination with it are likely to be better managers of it.

Second, SLA theory will be invaluable if it can help a teacher's sense of plausibility (Prabhu, 1990) to stay alive. If a teacher does not have an active intellectual engagement with teaching and learning, teaching becomes more and more routine and stale. Having one's sense of plausibility challenged by research findings and theoretical hypotheses (even the ones I have called myths here) is one way of keeping it vital. Rather than having a circumscribed role, expanding awareness, enhancing attitudes, and challenging teachers' senses of plausibility are major contributions of SLA theory to pedagogy.

REFERENCES

Allwright, R. (1975). "Problems in the Study of the Language Teacher's Treatment of Learner Error." *On TESOL '75*, ed. by M. Burt and H. Dulay, pp. 96–109. Washington, DC: TESOL.

Andersen, R. (1977). "The Impoverished State of Cross-sectional Morphology Acquisition/Accuracy Methodology," *Working Papers on Bilingualism* 14, 49–82.

———. (1988). "Models, Processes, Principles, and Strategies: Second Language Acquisition In and Out of the Classroom," *IDEAL* 3, 111–138.

Bahns, J., and H. Wode. (1980). "Form and Function in L2 Acquisition: The Case of Do-Support in Negation." *Second Language Development*, ed. by S. Felix. Tübingen: Gunter Narr.

Bell, A. (1984). "Language Style as Audience Design," *Language in Society* 13, 145–204.

Bley-Vroman, R. (1986). "Hypothesis Testing in Second Language Acquisition," *Language Learning* 36, 353–376.

———. (1990). "The Logical Problem of Foreign Language Learning," *Linguistic Analysis* 20, 3–49.

Buczowska, E., and R. Weist. (1991). "The Effects of Formal Instruction on the Second Language Acquisition of Temporal Location," *Language Learning* 41, 535–554.

Carroll, S., and M. Swain. (1993). "Explicit and Implicit Negative Feedback: An Empirical Study of the Learning of Linguistic Generalizations." *Studies in Second Language Acquisition* 15, 357–386.

Clahsen, H. (1987). "Connecting Theories of Language Processing and (Second) Language Acquisition." *First and Second Language Acquisition Processes*, ed. by C. Pfaff. Cambridge, MA: Newbury House.

Cohen, A., D. Larsen-Freeman, and E. Tarone. (1991). "The contribution of SLA theories and Research to Teaching Languages." *Language Acquisition and the Second/Foreign Language Classroom*, ed. by E. Sadtono. Anthology Series 28, Regional English Language Center, Singapore.

———, and M. Robbins. (1976). "Toward Assessing Interlanguage Performance: The Relationship Between Selected Errors, Learners' Characteristics, and Learners' Expectations," *Language Learning* 26, 45–66.

Crookes, G. (1989). "Planning and Interlanguage Variation," *Studies in Second Language Acquisition* 11, 367–383.

Day, E., and S. Shapson. (1991). "Integrating Formal and Functional Approaches in Language Teaching in French Immersion: An Experimental Study," *Language Learning* 41, 25–58.

Doughty, C. (1991). "Instruction Does Make a Difference: Evidence from an Empirical Study of SL Relativization," *Studies in Second Language Acquisition* 13, 431–469.

Eckman, F. (1981). "On the Naturalness of Interlanguage Phonological Rules," *Language Learning* 31, 195–216.

———, L. Bell, and D. Nelson. (1988). "On the Generalization of Relative Clause Instruction in the Acquisition of English as a Second Language." *Applied Linguistics* 9, 1–20.

Ellis, R. (1985). "A Variable Competence Model of Second Language Acquisition." *International Review of Applied Linguistics* 23, 47–59.

———. (1989). "Are Classroom and Naturalistic Acquisition the Same? A Study of the Classroom Acquisition of German Word Order Rules," *Studies in Second Language Acquisition* 11, 305–328.

———. (1993a). "Interpretation-based Grammar Teaching," *System* 21, 69–78.

———. (1993b). "The Structural Syllabus and Second Language Acquisition," *TESOL Quarterly* 27, 91–113.

Flynn, S. (1987). *A Parameter-setting Model of L2 Acquisition.* Dordrecht: Reidel.

Gass, S. (1982). "From Theory to Practice." *On TESOL '81*, ed. by M. Hines and W. Rutherford. Washington, DC: TESOL.

Hammerly, H. (1987). "The Immersion Approach: Litmus Test of Second-Language Acquisition through Classroom Communication," *Modern Language Journal* 71, 395–401.

———. (1992). "The Need for Directed Learning in the FL Classroom: A Response to Collier," *Studies in Second Language Acquisition* 14, 215–217.

Harley, B. (1989). "Functional Grammar in French Immersion: A Classroom Experiment," *Applied Linguistics* 10, 331–359.

———. (1993a). "Instructional Strategies and SLA in Early French Immersion," *Studies in Second Language Acquisition* 15, 245–259.

———. (1993b). "Appealing to Consciousness in the L2 Classroom." Paper presented at the Symposium on the Role of Consciousness in Second Language Learning, Association Internationale de Linguistique Appliquée Congress (AILA), Amsterdam.

———, and M. Swain. (1984). "The Interlanguage of Immersion Students and Its Implications for Second Language Teaching." *Interlanguage*, ed. by A. Davies, C. Criper, and A. P. R. Howatt. Edinburgh: Edinburgh University Press.

Huebner, T. (1980). "Creative Construction and the Case of the Misguided Pattern," *On TESOL '80*, ed. by J. Fisher, M. Clarke, and J. Schachter. Washington, DC: TESOL.

Hulstijn, J., and W. Hulstijn. (1984). "Grammatical Errors as a Function of Processing Constraints and Explicit Knowledge," *Language Learning* 34, 23–43.

Jordens, P. (1993). "Input and Instruction in Second Language Acquisition." Paper presented at the Association Internationale de Linguistique Appliquée Congress (AILA), Amsterdam.

Kellerman, E. (1985). "If at First You Do Succeed . . ." *Input in Second Language Acquisition*, ed. by S. Gass and C. Madden. Rowley, MA: Newbury House.

Krashen, S. (1981). *Second Language Acquisition and Second Language Learning.* Oxford: Pergamon.

———. (1982). *Principles and Practices in Second Language Acquisition.* New York: Pergamon.

———. (1984). "Immersion: Why It Works and What It Has Taught Us," *Language and Society* 12, 61–64.

———. (1985). *The Input Hypothesis: Issues and Implications.* New York: Longman.

———. (1991). "The Input Hypothesis: An Update." *Georgetown University Round Table on Languages and Linguistics*, ed. by J. E. Alatis. Washington, DC: Georgetown University Press.

Larsen-Freeman, D. (1975). *The Acquisition of Grammatical Morphemes by Adult Learners of English as a Second Language.* Doctoral dissertation, University of Michigan, Ann Arbor.

———. (1990). "On the Need for a Theory of Language Teaching." *Georgetown University Round Table on Languages and Linguistics 1990*, ed. by J. E. Alatis. Washington, DC: Georgetown University Press.

————. (1991). "Teaching Grammar." *Teaching English as a Second or Foreign Language*, 2nd edn, ed. by M. Celce-Murcia. New York: Newbury House/Harper Collins.

————. (1993). "Introduction to Teacher's Manual." *Grammar Dimensions: Form, Meaning, Use.* Boston: Heinle and Heinle.

————, and M. Long. (1991). *An Introduction to Second Language Acquisition Research.* London: Longman.

Lightbown, P. (1983). "Exploring Relationships Between Developmental and Instructional Sequences in L2 Acquisition." *Classroom-oriented Research in Second Language Acquisition*, ed. by H. Seliger and M. Long. Rowley, MA: Newbury House.

————. (1991). "What Have We Here? Some Observations on the Influence of Instruction on L2 Learning." *Foreign Language Pedagogy Research: A Commemorative Volume for Claus Faerch*, ed. by R. Phillipson, E. Kellerman, L. Selinker, M. Sharwood Smith, and M. Swain. Clevedon, Avon, England: Multilingual Matters.

————, and N. Spada. (1990). "Focus-on-Form and Corrective Feedback in Communicative Language Teaching: Effects on Second Language Learning," *Studies in Second Language Acquisition* 12, 429–446.

Long, M. (1980). *Input, Interaction and Second Language Acquisition.* Doctoral dissertation, University of California, Los Angeles.

————. (1990). "The Least a Second Language Acquisition Theory Needs to Explain," *TESOL Quarterly* 24, 649–666.

————, and G. Crookes. (1992). "Three Approaches to Task-based Syllabus Design," *TESOL Quarterly* 26, 27–56.

Lyster, R. (1993). *The Effect of Functional-Analytic Teaching on Aspects of Sociolinguistic Competence.* Doctoral dissertation, University of Toronto.

MacLaughlin, D. (1991). "Review of 'Universal Grammar and Second Language Acquisition'," ed. by L. White. *Second Language Research* 7, 245–256.

McLaughlin, B. (1990). "Restructuring," *Applied Linguistics* 11, 113–128.

Meisel, J., H. Clahsen, and M. Pienemann. (1981). "On Determining Developmental Stages in Natural Second Language Acquisition," *Studies in Second Language Acquisition* 3, 109–135.

Pienemann, M. (1984). "Psychological Constraints on the Teachability of Languages," *Studies in Second Language Acquisition* 6, 186–214.

————. (1985). "Learnability and Syllabus Construction," *Modelling and Assessing Second Language Development*, ed. by K. Hyltenstam and M. Pienemann. Clevedon, Avon, England: Multilingual Matters.

————. (1986). "Is Language Teachable? Psycholinguistic Experiments and Hypotheses," *Australian Working Papers in Language Development* 1, 1–41.

Prabhu, N. S. (1990). "There Is No Best Method—Why?" *TESOL Quarterly* 24, 161–176.

Rutherford, W. (1987). *Second Language Grammar: Learning and Teaching.* London: Longman.

————. (1993). "Metacognition and Language Learnability." Paper presented at the Symposium on Metacognition and SLA, Association Internationale Linguistique Appliquée Congress (AILA), Amsterdam.

Schachter, J. (1986). "Three Approaches to the Study of Input," *Language Learning* 36, 211–225.

————. (1988). "Second Language Acquisition and its Relationship to Universal Grammar," *Applied Linguistics* 9, 219–235.

Schmidt, R. (1990). "The Role of Consciousness in Second Language Learning," *Applied Linguistics* 11, 129–158.

Schwartz, B. (1993). "On Explicit and Negative Data Effecting and Affecting Competence and Linguistic Behavior," *Studies in Second Language Acquisition* 15, 147–163.

————, and M. Gubala-Ryzak. (1992). "Learnability and Grammar Reorganization in L2A: Against Negative Evidence Causing the Unlearning of Verb Movement," *Second Language Research* 8, 1–38.

Selinker, L. (1972). "Interlanguage," *International Review of Applied Linguistics* 10, 209–231.

Sharwood Smith, M. (1991). "Speaking to Many Minds: On the Relevance of Different Types of Language Information for the L2 Learner," *Second Language Research* 7, 118–132.

———. (1993). "Input Enhancement in Instructed SLA: Theoretical Bases." *Studies in Second Language Acquisition* 15, 165–179.

Simblist, M. (1992). "Review of W. E. Rutherford's Second Language Grammar: Learning and Teaching'," *Applied Linguistics* 13, 230–233.

Spada, N., and P. Lightbown. (1993). "Instruction and the Development of Questions in L2 Classrooms," *Studies in Second Language Acquisition* 15, 205–224.

Swain, M., and S. Lapkin. (1989). "Aspects of the Sociolinguistic Performance of Early and Late French Immersion Students." *On the Development of Communicative Competence in a Second Language*, ed. by R. Scarcella, E. Anderson, and S. Krashen. Cambridge, MA: Newbury House.

Tarone, E. (1988). *Variation in Interlanguage*. London: Edward Arnold.

Tomasello, M., and C. Herron. (1988). "Down the Garden Path: Inducing and Correcting Overgeneralization Errors in the Foreign Language Classroom," *Applied Psycholinguistics* 9, 237–246.

———. (1989). "Feedback for Language Transfer Errors: The Garden Path Technique." *Studies in Second Language Acquisition* 11, 385–395.

Tomlin, R. (1990). "Functionalism in Second Language Acquisition," *Studies in Second Language Acquisition* 12, 155–177.

Trahey, M., and L. White. (1993). "Positive Evidence and Preemption in the Second Language Classroom," *Studies in Second Language Acquisition* 15, 181–204.

Valdman, A. (1993). Untitled paper presented at Symposium 85: Issues in Conducting Classroom Research, Association Internationale Linguistique Appliquée Congress (AILA), Amsterdam.

VanPatten, B., and T. Cadierno. (1993). "Explicit Instruction and Input Processing." *Studies in Second Language Acquisition* 15, 225–243.

Wagner-Gough, J. (1975). *Comparative Studies in Second Language Learning*. CAL/ERIC/CLL Series on Languages and Linguistics, 26.

White, L. (1985). "Universal Grammar as a Source of Explanation in Second Language Acquisition." *Current Approaches to Second Language Acquisition*, ed. by B. Wheatley, A. Hastings, F. Eckman, L. Bell, G. Krukar, and R. Rutkowski. Bloomington: Indiana University Press.

———. (1987). "Against Comprehensible Input: The Input Hypothesis and the Development of Second-Language Competence," *Applied Linguistics* 8, 95–110.

———. (1989). *Universal Grammar and Second Language Aquisition*. Amsterdam: John Benjamins.

———. (1991). "Adverb Placement in Second Language Acquisition: Some Effects of Positive and Negative Evidence in the Classroom," *Second Language Research* 7, 133–161.

———. (1992). "On Triggering Data in L2 Acquisition: A Reply to Schwartz & Gubala-Ryzak," *Second Language Research* 8, 120–137.

———, N. Spada, P. Lightbown, and L. Ranta. (1991). "Input Enhancement and L2 Question Formation," *Applied Linguistics* 12, 416–432.

Widdowson, H. (1992). "Pedagogic Pragmatics: The Discourse of the Language Classroom." Plenary address at the Eighteenth International Conference of the Japan Association of Language Teachers, Kawagoe, Japan.

Wolfe Quintero, K. (1992). "Learnability and the Acquisition of Extraction in Relative Clauses and Wh-Questions," *Studies in Second Language Acquisition* 14, 39–70.

Zhou, Y. P. (1992). "The Effect of Explicit Instruction on the Acquisition of English Grammatical Structures by Chinese Learners." *Language Awareness in the Classroom*, ed. by C. James and P. Garrett. London: Longman.

Zobl, H. (1985). "Grammars in Search of Input and Intake." *Input in Second Language Acquisition*, ed. by S. Gass and C. Madden. Rowley, MA: Newbury House.

Chapter 10

The Interaction of Pedagogy and Natural Sequences in the Acquisition of Tense and Aspect

Kathleen Bardovi-Harlig
Indiana University

1. INTRODUCTION

The relationship of pedagogy to second language acquisition is complex and is one that is not clearly agreed upon in applied linguistics. The potential influence of instruction on acquisition—both benefits and limitations—is an empirical question. Yet even the empirical evidence is subject to different interpretations. In this chapter I attempt to contribute to the study of the effect of instruction on acquisition by considering the acquisition of tense and aspect in an instructional setting. The study of a single subsystem of grammar facilitates the examination of certain details of acquisition that broader studies may not provide.

The study of the acquisition of tense and aspect is particularly interesting and informative in an investigation of SLA and pedagogy because tense and aspect are central to most second or foreign language curricula. Many language teaching programs include mastery of certain tense and aspect forms in their criteria for advancement from one course to another, and tense and aspect clearly play an important role in grammatically focused pedagogical materials. Here I investigate the effect or noneffect of instruction in which teaching is deliberate and not incidental.

I first outline what it means to acquire a tense/aspect system, then examine patterns of acquisition and the potential effects of instruction on the acquisitional patterns. I then report on two studies of instructional influence on temporal expression, one experimental and one observational. And I close by considering the potential role of instruction.

2. ACQUISITION OF A TENSE/ASPECT SYSTEM

2.1. The Target

For the purposes of language acquisition research, the tense/aspect system of a language is best understood in relation to the more general study of temporal expression in that language (Bardovi-Harlig, 1992b, 1994; Bhardwaj, Dietrich, & Noyau, 1988; von Stutterheim & Klein, 1987). The acquisition of tense/aspect morphology—as well as form-meaning associations—is bound to the acquisition and use of other means of temporal expression (see Section 2.2). If we use English as an example, the inventory of the target system that a learner must master includes linguistic devices

1. *Morphology.* Learners must acquire the appropriate morphology (plus irregular forms): for tense, past (*-ed*) and nonpast (∅, *-s*); for aspect, progressive (*be + ing*); and for perfect (*have + en*);
2. The *morphosyntactics* of the system. Learners come to know the order of these elements in combination, as in the past perfect progressive *had been reading,*
3. Time adverbials (*yesterday* and *in the morning*) and calendric reference (such as *May 5*)
4. Adverbs of frequency (also known as aspectual adverbs),

the temporal semantics of the system, minimally viewed as

5. The meaning of each form,
6. The contrast between the forms,

and finally, in terms of discourse

7. The rules of discourse that govern distribution.

To use Larsen-Freeman's (1990, 1991, this volume) three-way distinction, a learner must master the form (1–4), meaning (5–6), and function (7) of temporal expression.

2.2. The Process: Comparison of Tutored and Untutored Acquisition

In this section I compare the acquisition of tutored and untutored learners with respect to the early stages of temporal expression, formal accuracy, and the distribution of emergent tense/aspect morphology. It should be noted here that in this section I make the comparisons across different populations with the variable of instruction being only one among many. Differences between learners who have immigrated to the host country, on the one hand, and international and domestic students enrolled in second or foreign language courses, on the other, often also include general level of education, socioeconomic status, employment status, contact with native speakers, and living arrangements. Under these conditions (which result from comparing existing studies), common acquisitional stages can be taken as very strong evidence for natural sequences, whereas differences cannot necessarily be attributed directly to instruction.

The early stages of temporal expression in the interlanguage of adult untutored learners of German (Meisel, 1987) and English (Schumann, 1987) have parallel stages in the interlanguage of adult instructed learners (Bardovi-Harlig, 1992b, 1993). Three stages common to both tutored and untutored learners can be identified. In the earliest stage of temporal expression, there is no systematic use of tense/aspect morphology. At this stage learners establish temporal reference in four ways: scaffolded discourse (relying on the contribution of the interlocutor), implicit reference (reference inferred from a particular context), contrast of events, and chronological order in narration (Meisel, 1987; Schumann, 1987). In the next stage, reference to the past is first expressed explicitly through the use of adverbial expressions and connectives. Following the adverbial-only stage, in the third stage verbal morphology appears, but it is not used systematically. At the time of early use of verbal morphology, learners show high rates of use of time adverbials as measured by the ratio of time adverbials to verbs (Bardovi-Harlig, 1992b). As the use of tense morphology increases, the use of time adverbials decreases. This early reliance on temporal adverbials has also been identified in a comprehension study. In a study of foreign language learners of Spanish, Sanz-Alcala & Fernandez (1992) found that when learners were presented sentences in which time adverbials and tense were mismatched (e.g., *yesterday I will go*), the learners responded to the sentences on basis of the adverbs. Because the acquisitional sequences of tutored and untutored learners are virtually identical in the early stages of temporal expression, crosslinguistically and across tasks, the acquisitional sequences in the interlanguage of instructed learners can be attributed to natural patterns rather than instruction.

A fourth stage can also be distinguished. The fourth stage is characterized by high rates of appropriate use of verbal morphology. However, the high rates of formal accuracy and appropriate use that characterize the interlanguage of advanced learners at the fourth stage are not typical of untutored learners. Although classroom learners show the same acquisitional sequences as untutored learners in the early stages, they may surpass untutored learners in terms of formal accuracy. Meisel reports that many of the untutored learners in his study "never use anything which comes close to the German system of verb inflection" (1987, p. 212). The European Science Foundation's 3-year longitudinal study of learners of Dutch, English, French, German, and Swedish found that "all learners develop at least some inflectional verb morphology, but not all of them develop tense contrasts" (Bhardwaj, Dietrich, & Noyau, 1988, p. 206). In contrast, all of the classroom learners achieved high appropriate use of past-tense morphology during the single year of my longitudinal study (Bardovi-Harlig, 1994). The stages can be characterized as a progression from implicit to lexical to grammatical means of expressing temporality (Dietrich, Noyau, Bhardwaj, & Klein, 1988).

Close inspection reveals that in the interlanguage of classroom second-language learners, formal accuracy is not always accompanied by equivalent rates of appropriate use. In fact, the early stages of high formal accuracy are characterized by low levels of appropriate use (Bardovi-Harlig, 1992a). For example, learners may show morphosyntactically correct instances of past progressive, but these forms occur in environments not predicted by the target language.

We have found this to be true in both compositions and structured elicitation tasks. In a study of compositions written by advanced adult learners of English—defined by TOEFL scores of 550—we found that learners exhibited inappropriate use of verb morphology in context but relatively few errors in the forms themselves (Bardovi-Harlig & Bofman, 1989). Learners produced well-formed strings such as *has been developed* and *had jumped*, but used them in inappropriate contexts; in contrast, ill-formed strings such as *had have* and *have been travel* occurred rarely. Even more common forms such as the simple past were used incorrectly. Errors in use were 7.5 times more frequent than errors in form.

In a subsequent study I tested the relation of form to meaning under more controlled conditions (Bardovi-Harlig, 1992a). A cross-sectional study was conducted of 135 adult learners at six levels of proficiency, from beginning to advanced, in which learners completed a cloze passage. The learners were enrolled in the Intensive English Program, Center for English Language Training, Indiana University.[1] The target forms included simple past tense, past progressive, past perfect, and present perfect.

High scores for accuracy of form (over 88%) were reached by low-intermediate proficiency (Level 3; Figure 10.1). Learners at higher proficiency levels did not improve noticeably in their formal accuracy scores. As would be expected from the high scores for formal accuracy, there were relatively few formal errors. Out of 1,890 responses, only 117, or 6.2%, were misformed. The results suggest that learners are aware of what constitutes a grammatical string of English even at lower levels of proficiency. In contrast, the scores for appropriate use were much lower. The scores for appropriate use in context were very low in lower proficiency levels (29.7% and 46.1% for Levels 1 and 2, respectively) and improved gradually to 73% by Level 5. Level 6 showed a slight (statistically nonsignificant) drop to 66%.

Is the predominance of form over meaning caused by instruction? That question must be divided into two parts: (1) Do learners show formal accuracy as a result of

---

[1] In the Intensive English Program, classes meet for 23 hours a week. Students receive instruction in listening and speaking, reading, writing, and grammar. Because the learners received instruction in the host environment, all were potentially contact language learners as well as classroom language learners, although they differed individually in their patterns of contact with native speakers and with other nonnative speakers of different first language backgrounds. In other words, these learners were in what Ellis (1985, 1990) referred to as a *mixed* language environment.

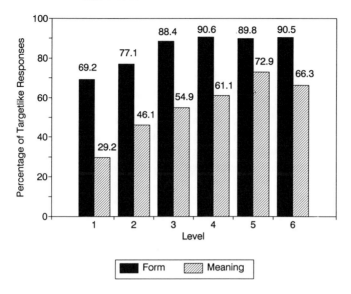

FIG. 10.1. Development of form and meaning by level of proficiency. From "The Relationship of Form and Meaning: A Cross-Sectional Study of Tense and Aspect in the Interlanguage of Learners of English as a Second Language," by K. Bardovi-Harlig, 1992a, *Applied Psycholinguistics*, 13, p. 262. Copyright 1992 by Cambridge University Press. Reprinted by permission.

instruction? and (2) Do learners show higher formal accuracy than appropriate use as a result of instruction? For the first question, regarding the high formal accuracy alone, formal accuracy seems to be a product of classroom language learning. This is the stage at which tutored and untutored learners are distinguished.[2] However, it may be the case that not all instruction results in high accuracy. Dietrich, Noyau, Bhardwaj, & Klein (1988, p. 507) reported that "the influence [of instruction] seems quite limited." Of the 19 learners in the European Science Foundation report, 14 learners had some target-language instruction, ranging from training in the alphabet to approximately one year. This is far less, however, than learners enrolled in an intensive language program receive.

As for the second question, "Do learners show higher accuracy of form than meaning due to instruction?," by virtue of the fact that high accuracy of form is a characteristic of classroom SLA but not a characteristic of untutored SLA, the answer to this question might be "yes." One might attribute the charac-

---

[2]This is not to suggest that high formal accuracy is in any sense a sufficient outcome of instruction. Although high formal accuracy is desirable in instructional settings, it is incomplete from the perspective of linguistic competence. Nor does this suggest that the pattern of high formal accuracy and low appropriate use is the best that instruction can produce. As suggested by Stephen Krashen in his reply to the presentation of this chapter, it is possible that immersion programs or content-based instruction could do better, that is, help learners make the relevant form-meaning associations so that appropriate use rates keep pace with formal accuracy rates.

teristically high accuracy and low appropriate use to lack of attention to meaning and function in the classroom or to lack of relevant comprehensible input. But this clearly requires more investigation, particularly because of other similarities in development. (These will be discussed later.) Interlanguage tense distribution is further unlikely to be the result of instruction, because teachers are largely unaware of the categories that learners intuitively employ.

Among the forces that shape the acquisition of the tense/aspect system are lexical aspectual classes that have to do with the internal constituency of events or situations. The distribution of the simple past tense, for example, shows a decided bias toward lexical aspectual classes. Learners tend to use past-tense morphology first with punctual verbs (achievement verbs) or telic verbs (achievement verbs and accomplishment verbs) and eventually generalize the use of the past throughout the system. Among dynamic verbs, past-tense morphology appears first with achievement verbs, then with accomplishment verbs (verbs that have both endpoints and duration, that is, *build a house*, *write a paper*, or *read a book*), and finally with activity verbs (verbs that have no endpoint but do have duration, e.g. *sleep*, *walk*, and *play*).[3]

Andersen (1986, 1989, 1991) first showed this acquisitional sequence for two child natural learners of Spanish as a second language. A number of studies have since corroborated these findings with instructed and uninstructed adult learners of English as a second language (Bardovi-Harlig, 1992a, 1992c; Bardovi-Harlig & Bergström, in press; Bardovi-Harlig & Reynolds, 1993; Bayley, 1994; Robison, 1990). Spanish as a foreign language (Hasbún, 1993; Ramsay, 1990); and French as a foreign language (Bardovi-Harlig & Bergström, in press; Bergström, 1993, in preparation; Kaplan, 1987). (See also Andersen & Shirai, 1994; Shirai, 1991, for a review of the unpublished research of Andersen's students.) The data on which these studies are based come from a variety of sources, including oral interviews and narratives from the untutored learners and written narratives, expository texts, and controlled elicitation tasks from the instructed learners.

The results of a cross-sectional study that Reynolds and I conducted with 182 instructed learners of English as a second language revealed an acquisition sequence similar to that of Andersen's untutored learners (Bardovi-Harlig & Reynolds, 1993, 1995).[4] Completing a series of cloze passages, the learners showed a significantly greater use of the simple past tense with achievement verbs and accomplishment verbs (verbs with endpoints, often called *telic* verbs or *events*) than with activity verbs (verbs with inherent duration, or *atelic* verbs) as shown in Figure 10.2. Learners at the higher levels eventually used the simple past with all

---

[3]I use the terms *state verbs* and *activity verbs* and so on to refer to the members of the lexical aspectual classes. However, this is a simplification for ease of reference. The scope of lexical aspect is generally considered to be the predicate or verb phrase as in *be tall*, *sing a song*, or *read a book*. Achievement verbs and accomplishment verbs may also group together (Andersen & Shirai, 1994; Bardovi-Harlig & Reynolds, 1993, 1995).

[4]The learners who participated in this study and in the studies following were enrolled in the Intensive English Program, Center for English Language Training, Indiana University.

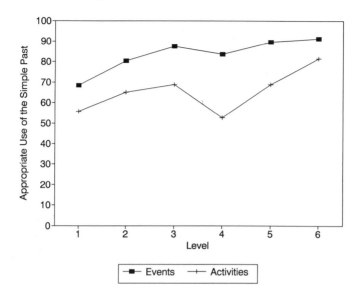

FIG. 10.2. Appropriate use of the simple past by aspectual class. From "The Role of Lexical Aspect in the Acquisition of Tense and Aspect," by K. Bardovi-Harlig and D. W. Reynolds, 1995, *TESOL Quarterly*. Copyright 1995 by *TESOL Quarterly*. Adapted by permission.

predicates in all three aspectual classes, but learners at lower levels began with a system of tense distribution that favored telic verbs. Given the evidence that similar patterns hold crosslinguistically, across environments, and across tasks, it seems clear that the particular distributional patterns cannot be attributed to instruction.

To sum up, tutored and untutored learners follow the same early stages of temporal expression. Tutored learners seem to surpass untutored learners in formal accuracy, an apparent advantage of instruction. However, the distribution of past-tense morphology across aspectual categories is the same for learners in both environments, suggesting that instruction does not change the basic stages of form-meaning associations.

3. PEDAGOGICAL INTERVENTION

In the preceding section I compared the acquisitional sequences exhibited in the interlanguage of tutored and untutored learners. In this section I present two different cases of instruction in which I investigated the influence of pedagogical intervention in the instructional setting. The first case was a pedagogical experiment and the second was a longitudinal observation of the effect of instruction on the use of tense.

3.1. Instruction and the Restructuring of Form-Meaning Associations

Compared to the English system of tense marking, the learner system that dis-
tributes tense by lexical aspectual classes can be interpreted as an undergeneralization of the English system. For example, many learners use the past
progressive with activity verbs (e.g. *was walking* or *was playing*), whereas simple
past tense activities, like *walked* and *played*, are often underrepresented in (or
even absent from) learner grammars. We did an instructional experiment to
learn whether learners could expand their use of the past tense beyond telic
verbs to include activity verbs (Bardovi-Harlig & Reynolds, 1993). According
to the subset principle, a learner grammar that is a subset of the target grammar
should require only positive evidence for acquisition of the target (Berwick,
1985; White, 1989). Positive evidence is any input that shows a learner what
sentences, constructions, or combinations are possible in a language (Sharwood
Smith, 1991; White, Spada, Lightbown, & Ranta, 1991). A learner grammar
that primarily marks telic verbs with the simple past is a subset of a grammar
that can mark all dynamic verbs with the simple past. We thus designed an
instructional unit composed to enhance input to learners in a format that White
(1992) has called *input flooding*. We provided overwhelming positive evidence,
in the form of natural discourse samples, that the simple past tense of activity
verbs, which were underrepresented in the learner grammars, was allowable in
English. The simple past occurred in two conditions: with activity verbs alone
and with activity verbs with adverbs of frequency.[5] Focused noticing that directed
learners' attention to the occurrence of past-tense activity verbs (and to contrasts
between past and past progressive activity verbs) supplemented the presentation
of positive evidence. (See Bardovi-Harlig & Reynolds, 1994, for the instructional materials.) Following Sharwood Smith's (1981, 1991) two-feature description of input, the instruction was elaborate but not explicit. The instruction was
elaborate in that extensive use was made of natural texts and focused noticing
in a 4-hour instructional unit spread over 4 days. It was not explicit, in that the
teachers who participated in our study gave the learners no rules.

On the basis of the results of the cross-sectional study of 182 learners (reviewed
earlier), we chose high beginners (Level 2) and intermediates (Level 4) for
instruction. In the cross-sectional test, Levels 2 and 4 both showed command
of simple-past-tense morphology (unlike Level 1) but did not show the degree
of accuracy reached by the more advanced learners. Level 2 learners seemed to
evidence emergent use of the past tense, and Level 4 learners were experimenting

---

[5]In preliminary investigations (Bardovi-Harlig, 1992a, 1992c) it appeared that learners treat
adverbs of frequency as a strong local cue that overrides global discourse cues to tense. Thus, activities
with and without adverbs of frequency elicited substantially different competing responses from
learners. Both environments were included to test the efficiency of positive evidence in the
pedagogical experiment.

with other past-tense forms such as past progressive and pluperfect. All subjects in the input study were enrolled in the same intensive English program, and they participated through their regular grammar classes. None of the students had participated in the original cross-sectional test that formed the control for the experiment. Both the cross-sectional learners and the experimental learners received instruction in verb tenses according to the established curriculum of the program. Experimental learners received specialized instruction in addition to the established instruction.

The subjects were given a pretest, a posttest immediately following the instruction period, and a retention test four weeks after the instruction period (cf. White, Spada, Lightbown, & Ranta, 1991). Two teachers at each level agreed to participate in the study. Because of the differences in the pretest scores of the different classes, each administration is reported separately. Level 4 subjects were not available for the retention test in the first administration.

The results of the experiment are summarized in Table 10.1. For activity verbs alone in the crosssectional study and in the pretest, past progressive was the chief competitor to the simple past. In the environment of activity verbs with adverbs of frequency, the chief competitor was nonpast (present and base forms). The co-occurrence of nonpast morphology with adverbs of frequency indicates another form-meaning association that constitutes a subset of the target grammar. Learners showed a strong association of adverbs of frequency with the nonpast, whereas English allows adverbs of frequency to occur with past tense as well as nonpast tense. The results show that learners increased their targetlike use of past tense with activity verbs, thus expanding their undergeneralized grammars. Moreover, this increase caused a corresponding retreat from related overgeneralizations.[6] The increase in the rate of appropriate use of the simple past between the pretest and the retention test was accompanied by a decrease in the overgeneralized use of the past progressive in the environment of activity verbs alone and in the nonpast in the environment of activity verbs with adverbs of frequency.

3.2. Instruction and the Emergence of the Pluperfect

A second case of instruction came, not from an experiment, but from observation conducted during a longitudinal study of 16 adult classroom learners of English as a second language (Bardovi-Harlig, 1994). Written samples consisting primarily of daily journal entries were compared to the daily instructional logs completed by the students' grammar and composition teachers to study the relationship between instruction and the productive use of the pluperfect.

---

[6]Potential counterevidence exists in the increase of past progressive in the second administration of the Level 4. However, closer inspection reveals that the use of the pluperfect, which may be regarded as spurious in the established context, is abandoned for the aspectually motivated past progressive. (Recall that progressive is the first marker of activity verbs.) The use of the past progressive declines as the use of simple past increases on the retention test. For further discussion, see Bardovi-Harlig & Reynolds (1993).

TABLE 10.1
Results of Instruction by Aspectual Class and Adverbs of Frequency

A. Activity Verbs without Adverbs of Frequency

Level 2

Administration 1		Past	Nonpast	Past Progressive	Pluperfect
Pretest	(n = 17)	58.5	5.9	19.1	0.0
Posttest	(n = 17)	81.6	2.2	8.8	1.5
Retention	(n = 14)	75.0	3.0	7.1	3.0

Administration 2		Past	Nonpast	Past Progressive	Pluperfect
Pretest	(n = 11)	71.2	10.6	7.6	0.0
Posttest	(n = 11)	83.3	0.0	10.6	1.5
Retention	(n = 9)	78.7	4.6	10.2	0.0

Level 4

Administration 1		Past	Nonpast	Past Progressive	Pluperfect
Pretest	(n = 11)	45.5	0.0	45.5	2.0
Posttest	(n = 11)	76.1	4.6	4.5	2.3
Retention		no test			

Administration 2		Past	Nonpast	Past Progressive	Pluperfect
Pretest	(n = 33)	55.6	4.0	18.2	8.1
Posttest	(n = 33)	60.1	1.0	27.3	1.5
Retention	(n = 28)	69.0	3.9	17.6	0.9

B. Activity Verbs with Adverbs of Frequency

Level 2

Administration 1		Past	Nonpast	Past Progressive	Pluperfect
Pretest	(n = 17)	40.0	42.3	7.1	1.2
Posttest	(n = 17)	73.5	3.0	17.6	0.0
Retention	(n = 14)	67.5	13.5	7.9	2.4

Administration 2		Past	Nonpast	Past Progressive	Pluperfect
Pretest	(n = 11)	58.4	36.4	2.6	0.0
Posttest	(n = 11)	81.8	6.5	11.7	0.0
Retention	(n = 9)	79.4	8.7	3.2	0.0

Level 4

Administration 1		Past	Nonpast	Past Progressive	Pluperfect
Pretest	(n = 11)	74.5	16.4	1.8	3.6
Posttest	(n = 11)	75.0	4.5	11.4	0.0
Retention		no test			

Administration 2		Past	Nonpast	Past Progressive	Pluperfect
Pretest	(n = 33)	61.9	15.2	10.0	7.8
Posttest	(n = 33)	74.0	4.3	10.8	4.3
Retention	(n = 28)	77.8	7.1	6.9	3.8

The pluperfect is one of the linguistic devices used in English to signal deviations from chronological order (*reverse-order reports*; Bardovi-Harlig, 1994). Other devices include the use of adverbials, reported speech or thought, and indicators of causation. The pluperfect is commonly found in the background of narratives to present events that happened before those in the main story line. A typical example of a reverse-order report is "John entered college in 1980. He had graduated from high school five years earlier."

There are two ordered prerequisites for the emergence of the pluperfect: First, a stable use of simple past tense, meaning a rate of appropriate use of past tense in past-time contexts of 80% or more; and second, after the use of past tense stabilizes, the expression of reverse-order reports. The pluperfect emerges later, with slightly higher group accuracy rates for the use of past tense. Although all 16 learners eventually used reverse-order reports, only 10 learners showed productive use of the pluperfect.

The acquisitional sequence is illustrated in Table 10.2. Two rates of appropriate use are given in Table 10.2. The number that appears under the label *ROR* is the rate of appropriate use of the past tense in the sampling period during which the first reverse-order report occurred. The first number gives the percentage of appropriate use, and the number in parentheses is the sum of distinct verb types sampled in the first and second half-month intervals. Because the rate of appropriate use drops for some learners when reverse-order reports first appear, an earlier figure is given that provides the highest rate of appropriate use of past in any sample prior to the emergence of reverse-order reports.

What is the effect on the interlanguage system of teaching the pluperfect? To answer this question, I compared the record of instruction in the teaching logs to the communicative use of the pluperfect in the daily journals kept by the learners.[7] The effect of instruction is predictable on the basis of the stage of the individual learner at the time of instruction. If the learner had not satisfied the prerequisite stages, instruction had no apparent effect. For the majority of the learners the pluperfect was introduced in the first half of the third or fourth month and was reviewed in the seventh month. In Table 10.2, instruction is represented by the shaded squares. The learners divide into three groups: those who used the pluperfect before instruction, those who used the pluperfect after instruction, and those who did not use the pluperfect in any language sample during the study. Four learners used the pluperfect before instruction. This may be an effect of instruction before the student enrolled in the Intensive English Program or of comprehensible input. No more can be said about these cases with respect to instruction.[8]

---

[7]According to the instructional logs, instruction on pluperfect was form focused. For a fuller description see Bardovi-Harlig (1994).

[8]JU's productive use of the pluperfect began at T7.5, one sampling period after the second instructional period at T7.0. It is possible that JU should be classified in the second group in Table 10.2, "PLU after instruction."

TABLE 10.2

Relationship Between the Emergence of the Pluperfect and Instruction

Group	Subject	Language	1	1.5	2	2.5	3	3.5	4	4.5	5	5.5	6	6.5	7	7.5	8	8.5	9	9.5	10	10.5	11	11.5	12	12.5	13
Early PLU	ER	Spanish	ROR+PLU 78 (18)																								
	OS	Spanish		ROR 96 (70)	PLU																						
	HK	Japanese					ROR+PLU 95 (79)																				
	JU	Japanese	ROR+PLU 89 (9)											84 (45)			ROR+PLU 83 (42)										
PLU after instruction	WS	Korean							97 (57)	ROR 96 (56)		PLU 100 (24)															
	IS	Japanese			ROR 86 (68)											PLU 82 (22)											
	RZ	Arabic				84 (19)		ROR 64 (22)					100 (16)			PLU 81 (63)											
	MA	Arabic										ROR 91 (22)								PLU 85 (46)							
	TS	Japanese		ROR 94 (34)					94 (53)														PLU 79 (65)				
	TO	Japanese			ROR 92 (52)				100 (26)				100 (16)	ROR 94 (31)													
No PLU	LU	Spanish	ROR 100 (14)						100 (12)																		
	ST	Japanese				ROR 69 (26)																					
	YJ	Korean												ROR 97 (35)					ROR 90 (10)								
	WA	Arabic													ROR 94 (16)	ROR 87 (37)											
	SA	Arabic							82 (37)												ROR 71 (82)					PLU 86 (57)	
	AR	Arabic																									ROR 37 (41)

▓ Instruction in pluperfect.

ROR Emergence of reverse order reports.
PLU Emergence of pluperfect.
numeral Percentage of appropriate past tense use.
(numeral) Number of verb types sampled in 1 month.

Note. From "Reverse-Order Reports and the Acquisition of Tense: Beyond the Principle of Chronological Order" by K. Bardovi-Harlig, 1994, *Language Learning*, 44, pp. 268–271. Copyright 1994 by the Research Club in Language Learning. Adapted by permission.

Six of the remaining thirteen learners did not use the pluperfect in reverse-order reports in the texts sampled, in spite of instruction. Apparently instruction did not lead these learners to use the pluperfect in the environment under consideration. Four of these learners (SA, AR, WA, and ST) seem not to have reached the requisite developmental stages. Two learners, AR and WA, had not produced reverse-order reports before instruction. They showed use of reverse-order reports only after both periods of instruction, and even then they did not use the pluperfect. The other two, SA and ST, exhibited reverse-order reports before the second period of instruction, but they showed rates of appropriate use of the past at 71% and 69% for that sampling period, respectively, which is under the group mean of 85% for the emergence of the pluperfect. (SA's rate of appropriate use dropped from his all-time high of 82%, shown in Table 10.2, and ST's half-month rate for the sampling period during the instruction was only 55%.) These rates appear to be too low to support the emergence of a new tense. Thus, these learners may be said to have not been ready to acquire a new form because they had not satisfied the previous acquisitional stages. The remaining two learners who did not use the pluperfect, LU and YJ, showed high rates of appropriate use of the past and the use of reverse-order reports prior to instruction, but they did not use the pluperfect.

The remaining six learners did use pluperfect reverse-order reports at some time after instruction. Some learners received repeated instruction on the pluperfect, but produced the pluperfect only after the prerequisites were met.

The observed effect of instruction supports Pienemann's (1989) teachability hypothesis that learners benefit from instruction only when they are at the stage at which they would have naturally acquired the rule in question. (See also Ellis, 1990.) The fact that not all learners who met both prerequisites ever attempted the pluperfect even with (repeated) instruction suggests that meeting the acquisitional stages, with or without instruction, is necessary but not sufficient for the emergence of the pluperfect. One possible reason for this is that learners use other available linguistic devices, such as time adverbials, to express reverse-order reports, and these may be so effective for communication that learners have no need to expand their grammars formally to express this semantic concept. (In fact, independent ratings by native-speaker judges suggest that this is true. (See Bardovi-Harlig, 1994.)

4. THE INFLUENCE OF INSTRUCTION

If we look at the development of the tense/aspect system in the instructional setting, we can ask "Why does instruction appear to have an influence on the acquisition of tense/aspect in some cases and not others?" Ignoring for the moment the difference between the meaning-focused and form-focused instruction that complicates the comparison of the two studies, I submit that the key to the effect of instruction seems to be the timing of instruction relative to interlanguage development.

Taking the second case first, instruction on the pluperfect seemed to be most beneficial for those learners whose interlanguage had reached stability with respect to formal accuracy and appropriate use of the simple past tense, and who had established a semantic environment (reverse-order reports) into which the pluperfect would fit. Thus, they showed readiness both morphosyntactically and semantically. Six out of the eight learners who met these prerequisites responded to instruction with the communicative use of the pluperfect.

Instruction may have contributed to earlier use of the pluperfect in these cases, but there is no way of determining that with certainty. In contrast, for those who had not met the prerequisites for acquisition and thus could be said to not to have been "ready," instruction did not appear to cause the emergence of the pluperfect. This seems to be a clear case of what Ellis (1985, 1990) described as the potential for instruction to change the rate but not the route of acquisition.

In the case of instruction aimed at the undergeneralization of the simple past tense, timing is also important. Instruction was timed to coincide with group scores that reflected mastery of the past tense with telic verbs. At that stage a core understanding of the past could be attributed to the learners. Thus learners could be said to have been ready for instruction that expanded the core meaning of the past, facilitating its generalization throughout the system.

Moreover, the pedagogical approach was based on linguistic analysis of the learner grammar. Viewing the learner grammar as a subset of the target language prescribed a clear pedagogical antidote: the presentation of positive evidence.[9]

Why does instruction focused on expanding undergeneralizations in the association of past tense with aspectual classes seem to work? First, the instruction was based on the availability of comprehensible input. The input flood consisted of positive evidence, which is just the kind that is available in everyday input and that shows learners what is allowable in the language. Essentially, it is the type of evidence that is ambient, although perhaps not always salient or noticeable to learners at earlier stages, as suggested by the results from the cross-sectional study. Put another way, instruction works in the case of undergeneralized form-meaning associations because learners eventually come to make the appropriate form-meaning associations anyway without specialized instruction. This can be seen in Figure 10.2, in which advanced learners (Level 6) use the simple past with activity verbs (82.0%) at a rate that approaches that of accomplishment verbs (91.9%) and achievement verbs (90.9%). Both Level 2 learners and Level 4 learners approximated the level of appropriate use reached by Levels 5 and 6 without input enhancement in the cross-sectional study.

---

[9]Learner production could also be viewed in terms of its errors, which might lead to instruction focused on negative evidence. The bias of the author and colleagues toward interlanguage analysis and the presentation of comprehensible input through authentic texts is evident in the interpretation of the data and the subsequent instruction.

What instruction seems to do in this case is to increase the rate of acquisition. That may not be as interesting theoretically as examining the effects of negative evidence, which is largely unavailable without instruction, but it is pedagogically interesting in terms of helping learners to more quickly achieve targetlike use. Moreover, it is both pedagogically and theoretically interesting, because we were able to use the presentation of positive evidence to cause the retreat of the overgeneralized use of the progressive to mark semantically durative verbs as in the case of the past progressive. In fact, since the past progressive was not the only tense/aspect marker that learners supplied in simple past-tense contexts before instruction (see especially Level 4 in Table 10.1), the presentation of positive evidence is pedagogically *efficient* because all learners have the same target (the use of the simple past tense with activity verbs) but may have individually different alternative form-meaning associations, all of which would need different negative evidence to cause retreat. In addition to the efficiency of focusing on the target rather than on the errors, positive evidence holds another advantage over negative evidence in that positive evidence continues to be available to the learner even after instruction, so that even when instruction ends, input continues to be available. This contrasts markedly with other types of instructional presentations. The advantage of ambient positive evidence shows up in the retention test scores, where learners essentially maintained their improvement in the appropriate use of the past tense one month after instruction.

5. CONCLUSION

The detailed study of the acquisition of a single subsystem of language provides the opportunity to study in depth the influence of instruction on acquisition. Focusing on the expression of temporality has made possible the comparison of specific stages of acquisition across populations, the details of which reveal striking similarities across environments. The similarities are particularly striking when we consider the many potential variables that distinguish the learners in the various studies reviewed here.

It is important to note that although instruction was referred to broadly, instruction is not homogeneous with regard to type, setting, or length or intensity of exposure. When we find that instruction does not affect acquisitional sequences in either intensive second language programs or academic foreign language courses, these findings seem very strong indeed. On the other hand, when the findings suggest that second language learners receiving intensive language exposure are influenced by instruction, the findings cannot be generalized to all cases of instruction (compare, e.g., the differences in levels of appropriate use reported for tutored learners by Bardovi-Harlig, 1994, to those reported by Bhardwaj, Dietrich, & Noyau, 1988).

The study of tense/aspect supports the recommendation of a limited number of pedagogical practices. Many of the recommendations have been made previously by a number of other applied linguists.

1. Acquisitional Sequences Are Important in Instructed Second Language Acquisition. Classroom learners follow natural acquisitional sequences (whether SLA research has identified the orders or not). We can see very clearly from the longitudinal study that learners (in fact, students) who are at different stages of linguistic development (even when they are placed in the same classes), and who received the same instruction, show different instructional effects. Learners who received instruction after meeting the acquisitional prerequisites show positive influence of instruction. For those who were not ready, instruction made no apparent difference (Ellis, 1990; Pienemann, 1989).

2. Meaning Is Important in Instruction. (a) Learners may need help with form-meaning associations. Classroom learners appear to be stronger in form than in meaning or use. The study of the tutored acquisition of tense/aspect provides empirical support for pedagogical recommendations to include meaning and use with instruction on form (Larsen-Freeman, 1990, 1991, this volume; VanPatten & Cadierno, 1994). (b) Semantic environments may need to be established before forms are introduced (as in the case of reverse-order reports and the pluperfect). Often in traditional pedagogical presentations verbal morphology is introduced in isolated sentences with only minimal indication from the context of what it might mean. But environment is crucial, particularly in the case of the tense/aspect system. The establishment of a concept before the introduction of a new form may be a constraint on readiness.

3. Teachers Should Take Advantage of Positive Evidence. Positive evidence that is meaningful to the learners (i.e. comprehensible input) may be particularly worthwhile for helping learners establish form-meaning associations. (The best-known advocate of comprehensible input is Krashen, 1982, 1985, 1992.) Authentic discourse (oral or written) necessarily contains forms used meaningfully. Moreover, positive evidence introduced in the classroom has a real-world correlate, namely, everyday input, which continues the lessons begun in the classroom.

Overall, the patterns of acquisition of tense and aspect in an instructional setting indicate that learners have relatively little difficulty in mastering the form of the verbal morphology related to tense and aspect. What learners do have trouble with, apparently, is establishing targetlike form-meaning associations. We can interpret the acquisitional sequences that we have observed as a needs assessment for pedagogical practice: An emphasis on providing meaningful input is warranted by the data.

ACKNOWLEDGMENTS

The studies reported in this chapter were supported by Grant BNS-8919616 from the National Science Foundation. I thank Dudley Reynolds and Shona Whyte for comments on an earlier version of this chapter.

REFERENCES

Andersen, R. W. (1986). "El Desarollo de la Morfología Verbal en el Español como Segundo Idioma" [The Acquisition of Verbal Morphology in Spanish as a Second Language]. *Adquisición de Languaje/Aquisicao da Linguagem*, ed. by J. M. Meisel. Frankfurt: Vervuert.

———. (1989). "La Adquisión de la Morfología Verbal" [The Acquisition of Verbal Morphology]. *Lingüistica* 1, 90–142. (English version available from the author).

———. (1991). "Developmental Sequences: The Emergence of Aspect Marking in Second Language Acquisition." *Second Language Acquisition and Linguistic Theories*, ed. by C. A. Ferguson and T. Huebner. Amsterdam: John Benjamins.

———, and Y. Shirai. (1994). "Discourse Motivations for Some Cognitive Acquisition Principles," *Studies in Second Language Acquisition* 16, 133–156.

Bardovi-Harlig, K. (1992a). "The Relationship of Form and Meaning: A Cross-Sectional Study of Tense and Aspect in the Interlanguage of Learners of English as a Second Language," *Applied Psycholinguistics* 13, 253–278.

———. (1992b). "The Use of Adverbials and Natural Order in the Development of Temporal Expression," *International Review of Applied Linguistics* 30, 299–320.

———. (1992c). "Adverbs, Aspect, and Tense." *QUILT and QUILL: Achieving and Maintaining Quality in Language Teaching and Learning*, ed. by N. Bird and J. Harris. Institute of Language in Education, Education Department, Hong Kong.

———. (1993). "The Contribution of Classroom Language Learners to Acquisition Research: Evidence from a Longitudinal Study," Paper presented at the Third Conference on Second Language Acquisition–Foreign Language Learning, Purdue University, West Lafayette, IN.

———. (1994). "Reverse-Order Reports and the Acquisition of Tense: Beyond the Principle of Chronological Order," *Language Learning* 44, 243–282.

———, and A. Bergström. (in press). "The Acquisition of Tense and Aspect in SLA and FLL: A Study Learner Narratives in English (SL) and French (FL)." *Canadian Modern Language Review*.

———, and T. Bofman. (1989). "Attainment of Syntactic and Morphological Accuracy by Advanced Language Learners," *Studies in Second Language Acquisition* 11, 17–34.

———, and D. W. Reynolds. (1993). "Adverbs, Aspect, and Tense in the Development of Temporality." Paper presented to the Twenty-Seventh Annual TESOL Conference, Atlanta, GA.

———, and D. W. Reynolds. (1994). "Improving Tense Use Through Input Enhancement." Unpublished manuscript, Indiana University.

———., and D. W. Reynolds. (1995). "The Role of Lexical Aspect in the Acquisition of Tense and Aspect," *TESOL Quarterly* 29.

Bayley, R. (1994). "Interlanguage Variation and the Quantitative Paradigm: Past Tense Marking in Chinese English." *Research Methodology in Second Language Acquisition*, ed. by E. Tarone, S. Gass, and A. Cohen. Hillsdale, NJ: Lawrence Erlbaum Associates.

Bergström, A. (1993). "The Expression of Temporal Reference by English Speaking Learners of French: Report on the Cloze," Paper presented at the Thirteenth Meeting of the Second Language Research Forum, University of Pittsburgh, Pittsburgh, PA.

———. (in preparation). "The Expression of Past Temporal Reference by English-speaking Adult Learners of French," Doctoral dissertation, Pennsylvania State University.

Berwick, R. (1985). *The Acquisition of Syntactic Knowledge*. Cambridge, MA: MIT Press.

Bhardwaj, M., R. Dietrich, and C. Noyau (eds.) (1988). *Temporality* Final Report to the European Science Foundation, vol. 5. European Science Foundation, Strasbourg. (Available from the Max-Planck-Institut.)

Dietrich, R., C. Noyau, M. Bhardwaj, and W. Klein. (1988). "Conclusions." *Temporality*. Final Report to the European Science Foundation, vol. 5, ed. by M. Bhardwaj, R. Dietrich, and C. Noyau. European Science Foundation, Strasbourg. (Available from the Max-Planck-Institut.)

Ellis, R. (1985). *Understanding Second Language Acquisition*. Oxford: Oxford University Press.

———. (1990). *Instructed Second Language Acquisition*. Oxford: Blackwell.

Hasbún, L. (1993). "The Role of Lexical Aspect in the Acquisition of Tense and Grammatical Aspect in Spanish as a Foreign Language." Unpublished manuscript, Applied Linguistics, Indiana University.

Kaplan, M. A. (1987). "Developmental Patterns of Past Tense Acquisition Among Foreign Language Learners of French." *Foreign Language Learning: A Research Perspective*, ed. by B. VanPatten, T. R. Dvorak, and J. F. Lee. Cambridge, MA: Newbury House.

Krashen, Stephen D. (1982). *Principles and Practice in Second Language Acquisition*. New York: Pergamon.

———. (1985). *The Input Hypothesis*. London: Longman.

———. (1992). *Fundamentals of Language Education*. Torrance, CA: Laredo.

Larsen-Freeman, D. (1990). "Pedagogical Descriptions of Language: Grammar," *Annual Review of Applied Linguistics* 10, 187–195.

———. (1991). "Teaching Grammar." Teaching English as a Second or Foreign Language, ed. by M. Celce-Murcia. Boston: Heinle and Heinle.

Meisel, J. M. (1987). "Reference to Past Events and Actions in the Development of Natural Language Acquisition." First and Second Language Acquisition Processes, ed. by C. W. Pfaff. Cambridge, MA: Newbury House.

Pienemann, M. (1989). "Is Language Teachable? Psycholinguistic Experiments and Hypotheses," *Applied Linguistics* 10, 52–79.

Ramsay, V. (1990). "Developmental Stages in the Acquisition of the Perfective and the Imperfective Aspects by Classroom L2 Learners of Spanish." Doctoral dissertation, University of Oregon, Eugene.

Robison, R. (1990). "The Primacy of Aspect: Aspectual Marking in English Interlanguage," *Studies in Second Language Acquisition* 12, 315–330.

Sanz-Alcala, C., and M. Fernandez. (1992). "Native Speakers' and L2 Learners' Processing of Verbal Morphology in Spanish." Paper presented at the Twelfth Meeting of the Second Language Research Forum, Michigan State University, East Lansing, MI.

Schumann, J. (1987). "The Expression of Temporality in Basilang Speech," *Studies in Second Language Acquisition* 9, 21–41.

Sharwood Smith, M. (1981). "Consciousness Raising and the Second Language Learner," *Applied Linguistics* 2, 159–68.

———. (1991). "Speaking to Many Minds: On the Relevance of Different Types of Language Information for the L2 Learner," *Second Language Research* 7, 118–132.

Shirai, Y. (1991). "Primacy of Aspect in Language Acquisition: Simplified Input and Prototype." Doctoral dissertation, University of California, Los Angeles.

VanPatten, B., and T. Cadierno. (1994). "Explicit Instruction and Input Processing," *Studies in Second Language Acquisition* 15, 225–244.

von Stutterheim, C., and W. Klein. (1987). "A Concept-oriented Approach to Second Language Studies." *First and Second Language Acquisition Processes*, ed. by C. Pfaff. Cambridge, MA: Newbury House.

White, L. (1989). *Universal Grammar and Second Language Acquisition*. Amsterdam: John Benjamins.

———. (1991). "Adverb Placement in Second Language Acquisition: Some Effects of Positive and Negative Evidence in the Classroom." *Second Language Research* 7, 133–161.

———. (1992). "On Triggering Data in L2 Acquisition: A Reply to Schwartz and Gubala-Ryzak." *Second Language Research* 8, 120–137.

———, N. Spada, P. M. Lightbown, and L. Ranta. (1991). "Input Enhancement and L2 Question Formation." *Applied Linguistics* 12, 416–432.

Chapter 11

From Input to Output: Processing Instruction and Communicative Tasks

Bill VanPatten
University of Illinois at Urbana-Champaign

Cristina Sanz
Georgetown University

1. INTRODUCTION

Research on explicit instruction in second languages has tended to focus on two questions: (1) whether grammar should be taught and (2) what should be taught. These questions ignore an important aspect of explicit instruction, namely the type of grammar instruction used and the types of processes that the instruction seeks to affect. This chapter is part of a series on an ongoing investigation of the relative benefits of different kinds of instruction.

VanPatten and Cadierno (1993) researched the issue of the type of grammar instruction that should be given to second language learners. Using a model of second language acquisition and use developed by VanPatten (1992, 1995), VanPatten and Cadierno investigated the effects of what they called 'processing instruction' and compared these with the effects of both no instruction and traditional instruction. Processing instruction is an explicit focus on form that is input based. Unlike in traditional instruction, learners do not manipulate or practice structure or form in output (e.g., as in drills or other kinds of guided oral or written practice). Instead, *processing instruction seeks to alter the way in which learners perceive and process linguistic data in the input* in order to provide the internal learning mechanisms with richer grammatical intake.

A major limitation of VanPatten and Cadierno's research, as acknowledged in the discussion section of their paper, is the type of assessment task they used to research the outcomes of instruction. As VanPatten and Cadierno observed, their assessment task was a highly controlled sentence-level production task. In this chapter, we extend VanPatten and Cadierno's line of investigation by comparing the effects of processing instruction on different kinds of language output tasks, ranging from sentence-level tasks to tasks that require the learner to string together sentences to produce a narrative. Our aim is to see whether the general positive effects found for processing instruction as given in VanPatten and Cadierno (1993) as well as in Cadierno (1992) are evident in a wider variety of assessment tasks. First, we will situate processing instruction within a general model of language acquisition and language use. Then we will describe processing instruction as it was used in the present study, and then the research on the effects of processing instruction as measured by various tasks. Finally, we make some recommendations.

2. INSTRUCTION AND SECOND LANGUAGE ACQUISITION

2.1. A Model of Second Language Acquisition and Use

As Long (1990) pointed out, any theory of SLA must acknowledge the role of comprehensible input in the development of the learner's internal grammar. Given the important role of comprehensible input in SLA, SLA can be conceived of as sets of processes as depicted in Figure 11.1 (from VanPatten, 1992). What Figure 11.1 attempts to capture are three (theoretically) distinguishable sets of processes in acquisition. The first set of processes (I) converts input to intake. This is referred to as input processing and is discussed later. From intake the learner must still develop an acquired system, that is, not all intake is automatically fed into the acquired system. The second set of processes (II), then, includes those that promote the accommodation of intake and the restructuring of the developing linguistic system (McLaughlin, 1990; White, 1989). Finally, it is not clear from studies using output data that learner language is a direct reflection of acquired competence. Thus, a third set of processes (III) must be posited to

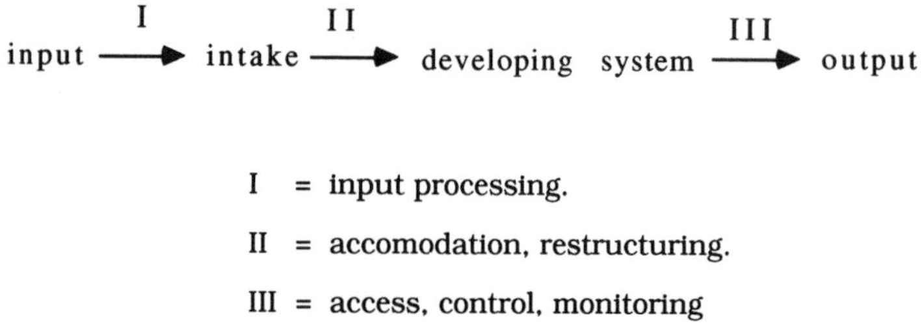

$$\text{input} \xrightarrow{\text{I}} \text{intake} \xrightarrow{\text{II}} \text{developing system} \xrightarrow{\text{III}} \text{output}$$

I   = input processing.

II = accomodation, restructuring.

III = access, control, monitoring

FIG. 11.1. A model of second language acquisition and use (based on VanPatten, 1995).

account for certain aspects of language production, for example, monitoring, accessing, control, and so on (Schmidt, 1992; Terrell, 1991).

Input processing involves the first set of processes, the conversion of input to intake. Although input processing can be examined from a variety of perspectives (Chaudron, 1985; Gass, 1988; Terrell, 1991; VanPatten, 1995), we use the notion of *form-meaning connection* in discussing the processes involved in the conversion of input to intake. In other words, the term *input processing* as it is used here involves those strategies and mechanisms that promote form-meaning connections during comprehension. (See VanPatten, 1995, for a more detailed discussion of the relationship between form, meaning, and input processing.) As the learner processes an incoming input string, it must be tagged and coded in particular ways. If the language is to be learned, the internal processor(s) must eventually attend to how the propositional content is encoded linguistically. We believe that intake is that subset of the input that a learner comprehends and from which grammatical information can be made available to the developing system.

2.1. Questioning Traditional Instruction

Given the important role of input and input processing in second language acquisition, it is reasonable to wonder whether explicit instruction in grammar with a focus on input would be more appropriate than traditional approaches to grammar instruction, in which learners are engaged in production. Current approaches to foreign language instruction involve explanation and output practice, normally moving from mechanical to communicative exercises. What would happen if explicit instruction in grammar involved explanation as well as the manipulation of both input and input processing in some way? What if the input were structured so as to channel the processes responsible for the conversion of input to intake? (See Figure 11.2.) Theoretically this should facilitate the internalization of grammar and would be psycholinguistically compatible with what we know about acquisition (Pienemann, 1987; White, 1989).

To approach grammar instruction in this way we would first need to identify some of the processes and mechanisms that mediate input processing. In a series

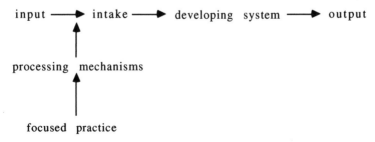

FIG. 11.2. Grammar instruction as the manipulation of input processing (based on VanPatten & Cadierno, 1993).

of papers (VanPatten, 1984, 1985, 1990, 1995), one of the present authors researched and described certain heuristic devices (or processing strategies) used by second language learners during input processing. We discuss two here for purposes of illustration. The first is a word-order strategy. Language learners, it seems, universally tend to process the first noun or noun phrase before a verb as the subject (agent) of the verb (action) and to process the postverbal noun or noun phrase as the object (see also Ervin-Tripp, 1974; Gass, 1989; Lee, 1987; LoCoco, 1987) for second language learners, and Bates et al. (1984) among others for research on first language learners). In languages such as Spanish, where subject nouns and noun phrases may be postposed and object nouns as well as object pronouns may appear preverbally, this processing can result in an incorrect or incomplete coding of the data. For example, it has been shown that a sentence such as *La sigue el señor* is likely to be misinterpreted as 'She follows the man' rather than the correct 'The man follows her'. Likewise, sentences such as *Me gusta el helado* are incorrectly processed as *me* = subject and *helado* = object. This processing strategy also encourages skipping over object markers during input processing such as the case marker *a* in sentences like *Los hijos nuncan llaman a sus padres por teléfono*. Because this processing strategy relies on word order for grammatical relations (i.e., subject, object), the case marker *a* is mere "noise" in the input to the learner of Spanish. Object pronouns that follow preverbal subjects are also likely to be skipped over because they do not fall in the expected spot in the utterance. Thus, with *Mario la conoce bien*, *la* may be ignored by the learner's internal processor, and the learner may simply fill in the object of the verb from context and the universe of discourse. The result is that the intake delivered to the developing system contains the following erroneous information for the learner of Spanish: (a) Spanish is Subject-Verb-Object (just like English), so use word order to mark subjects and objects; and (b) subject pronouns have multiple forms, for example, *ella*, *la*, *se*, *me*, *yo*, and so on. The erroneous conclusion that Spanish is SVO and always marks a subject explicitly in surface structure may be compounded by other input data, for example, a preponderance of simple SVO declarative sentences in teacher talk and in textbooks.

2.3. Processing Instruction

The type of instruction used in the present study is called *processing instruction* because its aim is to alter the way in which learners process input. In other words, its purpose is to direct learners' attention to relevant features of grammar in the input and to encourage correct form-meaning mappings that result in better intake. The input used in processing instruction is called *structured input*. The term *input* is used because, as will soon become clear, learners are not engaged in producing language but are actively engaged in processing input. The term *structured* is used because the input is not free-flowing and spontaneous, like the input one might receive in a communicative interaction. Instead, the input is purposefully prepared and manipulated to highlight particular grammatical features and to push the learners not to rely on their existing processing strategies.

In the preliminary experiments in focusing learners' attention on grammatical features in input we needed to develop some guidelines (Van Patten, 1993):

1. *Teach only one thing at a time.* Break up paradigms and rules into smaller bits and pieces. For example, teach *él/ella* forms of a verb form first and work with them before moving on to *yo* forms, *tú/Ud.* forms, and so on. Work with *estar* + location in isolation from *estar* and its other contexts, and so on.

2. *Keep meaning in focus.* Learners should have to attend to each utterance for a message that it contains and Learners should not be able to successfully complete the activity unless they have understood the content of each utterance.

3. *Learners must "do something" with the input.* Learners must check boxes, complete a survey, indicate true-false, provide one-word responses, provide an answer from a list of alternatives, offer the name of someone else who fits the description, and so on. In other words, learners must be *actively involved in processing the input* and must show this active involvement by responding to the input in some way.

4. *Use both oral and written input.* Because of individual differences in acquisition, some learners benefit more from aural input while others benefit more from written input. A judicious combination of oral and written structured input provides for the widest net possible in directing learners' attention.

5. *Move from sentences to connected discourse.* Early activities in a sequence should focus on isolated sentences. Connected discourse should appear later in the sequence. By starting with sentences, learners have a better opportunity to perceive and process the grammatical item that is in focus. Connected discourse from the instructor or from a lab tape may (a) not allow sufficient processing time for the grammatical item to be attended to, or (b) may result in "noise" that interferes with focal attention and may "drown out" the grammatical item in focus (see VanPatten, 1990, for experimental work). Connected discourse should not be avoided if the purpose is to develop listening skills, but in terms of grammar acquisition, it should be come later in a lesson rather than at the beginning.

6. *Keep the psycholinguistic processing mechanisms in mind.* This guideline serves to ensure that learners' focal attention during processing is directed toward the relevant grammatical items and not elsewhere in the sentence. For example, if you are teaching person-number endings in Spanish, it does little good to have every input sentence contain an explicit subject noun phrase, because the learner is more likely to attend to the subject for person-number information than the verb ending. If you are teaching object pronouns in Spanish, it is not helpful to have every sentence begin with an explicit subject. Rather, sentences should begin with object pronouns.

3. THE PRESENT STUDY

3.1 Motivation and Research Questions

VanPatten and Cadierno (1993) investigated the effects of processing instruction in the teaching of direct object pronouns in Spanish. (For a replication of the study with past-tense morphemes, see Cadierno, 1992). In a carefully designed study, the authors compared three groups: no instruction, traditional (explanation + output practice), and processing (explanation + structured input activities). They gave two assessment tasks: a meaning-based interpretation task to see whether subjects could correctly identify subjects and objects in a series of utterances by matching what they heard to a picture; a meaning-based production task in which subjects had to create a sentence on the basis of a visual stimulus. The results were clear: the processing group performed significantly better after treatment when compared with the traditional and no-instruction groups on the interpretation task; and the processing group performed as well as, if not better than, the traditional group on the sentence production task, although the processing group had never practiced making output with the targeted structure.

A criticism of the VanPatten and Cadierno study is that their tasks did not measure more communicative or discourse-oriented language use, that the tasks used were too focused or too controlled and limited to the sentence level. Our study was a partial replication of VanPatten and Cadierno in which a no-instruction group and a processing group were compared on three output measures: (1) the same sentence-level task as used in VanPatten and Cadierno, (2) a structured question-answer interview, and (3) a video narration task. The basic research question was: Do the observed effects for processing instruction on the sentence-level task also obtain on other language production tasks? This question is not trivial because processing instruction does not engage the learner in language production. If the same effects do obtain, then we will have direct evidence that input does drive the learning mechanism in the learner's head, and we will also have evidence for Krashen's assertion that production can emerge on the basis of input processing alone, although in this case, the input is structured and manipulated.

3.2. Subjects

The subject pool consisted of four classes of students in their third semester of the study of Spanish as a foreign language at the University of Illinois at Urbana-Champaign. At the outset, two classes were assigned to the processing group and two classes were assigned to the no-instruction group. For all subjects, regular instruction was communicatively based with a focus on input and interaction. (At no time during this experimentation did the subjects study the targeted linguistic item as part of their regular class work.) Although we used whole classes during the experimental and instructional phases, in order to be part of the final data pool, the subjects had to fulfill the following requirements: They had to be present during all phases of the experiment; they had to belong to a household where English was the only language of communication; and the accuracy of their performance in the pretest on interpretation (to be discussed later) could not be higher than 60%. Furthermore, the subjects in the experimental group had to show some gain in their ability to interpret object-verb (OV) strings. Thus, not every student in a class wound up in the final data pool. The final number of subjects was 44: 27 subjects in the processing group and 17 subjects in the no-instruction group.

3.3. Instruction

Processing instruction involved a 2-day in-class focus on form as described previously. Subjects did not engage in any out-of-class work at this time. The focus of instruction was the same as that in VanPatten and Cadierno, 1993: preverbal object pronouns. Unlike in English, object pronouns are obligatorily placed before finite verbs in Spanish. The processing instruction consisted of explanation plus structured input activities in which learners first practiced correctly interpreting preverbal object pronouns as objects. They were subsequently engaged in affectively oriented activities in which they responded to the content of sentences. For example, in one activity, students were supposed to think of a female relative or friend. They then had to indicate what sentences were true for them, for example, *I admire her, I respect her, I understand her well*, and so on. At no time during the instructional phase did the subjects in the processing group produce an object pronoun. One of the researchers did the instruction.

The no-instruction group did not receive any special instructional treatment. These subjects continued with their regular classroom activities, and both they and their instructor were unaware of the experimental instruction in the other classes.

3.4. Assessment Instruments

3.4.1. Interpretation Test

As mentioned in Section 3.2, the interpretation test was used as a pretreatment means of eliminating subjects. It was also used as a pre- and posttreatment measure of knowledge gained to ensure that any improvement in accuracy in production was in effect due to an increase in knowledge. The interpretation test included two versions of the same test equally balanced for difficulty and vocabulary. A split-block design was used so that one version was used for one group as a pretest and the other version was used as the posttest and was administered immediately after the instruction. The interpretation test consisted of 26 sentences, of which 20 were critical items and 6 were distractors. A sample item: *Lo mata el hombre* 'The man kills him.' (Him-OBJ kills the man-SUBJ). Subjects selected either a picture of a man shooting a lion or one of a lion killing a man.

3.4.2. Production Tests

Each subject completed three different kinds of production tests. We refer to the tests as the sentence-completion test, the structured interview, and the video narration. The three tests were specifically designed to elicit both oral and written production, because we suspected that mode of production might affect results; namely, that written tests might produce higher accuracy scores than oral tests.

The sentence completion test was based on VanPatten and Cadierno (1993). It involved two consecutive pictures as context that had to be described by two connected sentences. One sentence was given that described the first picture and the subject was required to produce one phrase to describe the second picture. The verb to describe the action in the second picture was provided underneath the image. As an example, one item depicted a man sitting at a table thinking about a woman in the first picture and in the next picture he was shown calling her. The sentence completion was *El hombre piensa en la mujer y entonces* _____ (*llamar*) 'The man is thinking about the woman and then _____ (to call).' An expected correct response was *y entonces la llama* 'and then he calls her'. The task consisted of 14 items: 8 critical and 6 distractors.

The structured-interview test engaged the subject in a dialogue that described a story. A set of 7 pictures and an average of 11 questions provided the context for the story. The subject was required to produce one or two sentences when answering the questions, which were of the type *¿Qué hace el chico con la banana?* 'What is the boy doing with the banana?' These questions require a direct-object pronoun and a conjugated verb in the answer, for example, *La saca de la canasta* 'He is taking it out of the basket.'

The video narration was a storytelling task. The subjects were required to produce a series of connected sentences that described a story they had just watched on a video monitor. Each story contained seven connected events. As an example, one clip involved a man who comes home with his groceries, pulls out a potato, washes it, peels it, cuts it up, fries it, and so on, until he eats it. The instructions specified that the subject should provide as much detail as possible, so that a student in another class could identify the video clip being described from among a series of video clips. This was done not only to elicit as much information as possible but also to provide a communicative context to the task. Each video clip was shown twice and the subjects were required to tell the story only after viewing it the second time. (For more detail on the construction of all three tests, see Sanz, 1994.)

It is important to note that in order to control for test bias, four versions of each test were developed. Thus, not all subjects received the same version of a test. Furthermore, as will be explained later, subjects received the tests in different orders.

3.5. Procedure

Recall that all testing was done with whole classes, that is, subjects were not tested individually but were tested during their regular class. All interpretation tests and written production tests were administered in the subjects' regular classrooms. A television set and a VCR were used to show the video clips as part of the video narration test. The subjects completed the tests by writing their answers in a booklet of blank pages provided at the beginning of the testing session.

The oral production tests were administered in the Language Learning Laboratory; again whole classes were tested at once. Sitting at individual booths with headphones and microphones, the subjects were required to complete all three tests orally, and their answers were recorded for subsequent transcription.

In order to control for test effects, the tests were administered in different orders to each set of subjects. Thus, one class may have performed the tests in the following order: video narration first, structured interview second, sentence completion third; another class may have performed the structured interview first, the sentence completion second, and the video narration third. The other two classes performed the tests in other orders. In order to control for familiarity with the test and the vocabulary, the subjects were provided with a list of pertinent lexical items and a practice item immediately before each test. Finally, the tests were separated by distracting activities consisting of a Spanish–English translation. None of the translation distracting activities involved the use of object pronouns. All pretests were conducted several weeks before the instructional phase, and posttesting was conducted immediately after the instructional phase.

3.5. Scoring

The interpretation test was scored by a simple correct = 1 point/incorrect = 0 point scoring procedure. In order to make the scores for all three types of production tests comparable, all scores were first transformed into ratios. The denominator was formed by the number of of critical items multiplied by two. The numerator was calculated by adding the number of correct responses multiplied by two, the number of incorrect responses multiplied by one, and the number of cases in which the item was not supplied at all multiplied by 0. The scores were then transformed into percentages and the percentages were further transformed using the function $y' = 2 \arcsin (\sqrt{y})$ in order to satisfy the ANOVA normality assumption.

Because of the nature of the video narration test, each subject could produce a different number of sentences with preverbal object pronouns, which means that the denominator in the ratio could vary. To account for this, a special procedure was followed. One native speaker read the protocols and decided on the number of obligatory occasions for the use of preverbal object pronouns generated by the subject. The number of occasions was multiplied by two, and the result, representing the total possible points, was the denominator of a ratio. Two other native speakers independently scored a sample of the protocols. They agreed on 100% of the cases.

4. RESULTS

4.1. Introduction and Overview

Our major question centered on the effects of processing instruction. What was new—aside from the particular type of instruction researched and the theoretical model behind it—was the multiplicity of ways in which we studied the effects of processing instruction. One of the consequences of this approach was the complexity of the design. We first performed analyses of variance (ANOVA) on scores from each task independently, using mode (written vs. oral) as a major variable because, as the reader may recall, we suspected that mode of production might affect outcome. In order to address the question of whether the extent of the effects of instruction would be constant across all tasks, we subsequently conducted two ANOVAs in which we removed mode as a variable but used test type as a variable. Thus, one ANOVA was conducted on the written data and the second was conducted on the oral data. We begin the presentation of results with the outcome of the interpretation test, because we used it as a means to measure whether processing instruction had its desired effect, that is, to alter the way learners process input strings.

4.2. Interpretation Data

Raw scores from the pretest on interpretation were submitted to a nondirectional t test. No significant difference was found between the experimental and the control groups at the onset of the experiment ($t_{42} = 0.24$). Raw scores from the posttest in interpretation were also submitted to a nondirectional t test and a significant difference between the groups was found ($t_{42} = 57.73$) due to a substantial gain in the ability of the experimental subjects to interpret preverbal object pronouns correctly (Table 11.1). We thus replicated the original findings of VanPatten and Cadierno, 1993: Processing instruction had the desired effect of altering the way learners process input strings. We now turn our attention to the production data.

4.3. Production Data: First Analyses

We submitted the data from each test (Sentence Completion, Structured Interview, Video Narration) to its own ANOVA. Each ANOVA involved three factors: Group (processing vs. no instruction), Time (pretest vs. posttest), and

TABLE 11.1
Means and Standard Deviations for the Pretest and Posttests
on the Interpretation Test

Group	Test	M	SD
Processing	Pretest	5.78	.8
(n = 27)	Posttest	11.07	2.61
No instruction	Pretest	5.71	1.10
(n = 17)	Posttest	5.74	1.18

Mode (written vs. oral). Although our question did not include Mode as a variable, recall that we suspected that subjects might perform differentially depending on whether they were asked to write or speak. Thus, we decided to include Mode as a third factor in our analyses. Repeated measures were performed on both Mode and Time. All three analyses yielded the same interaction Group × Time (Sentence Completion, $F_{1,42} = 11.75$, $p < .01$; Structured Interview, $F_{1,42} = 4.90$, $p < .03$; Video Narration, $F_{1,42} = 11.60$, $p < .01$).

Multiple t tests were computed that indicated that the effect for instruction as shown by the interaction Group × Time was due to the following contrasts: the processing group did significantly better on the posttest than the no-instruction group (Sentence Completion, $F_{1,42} = 9.32$; $p < .01$; Video Narration, $F_{1,42} = 8.32$; $p < .01$) and the performance by the processing group significantly improved between the pretest and the posttest (Sentence Completion, $F_{1,42} = 30.07$, $p < .01$; Video Narration, $F_{1,42} = 21.09$, $p < .01$). We found no significant differences when we compared pretest and posttest data of the no-instruction group nor when we compared the pretest scores from the processing and the no-instruction groups.

The significant main effects for Mode yielded by the analyses on the data from the Sentence Completion test ($F_{1,42} = 6.44$, $p < .02$) and the Video Narration test ($F_{1,42}$, $p < .05$) were due to the consistent difference in favor of the written mode (i.e., when averaged across time, both the no-instruction and the processing groups obtained higher scores on the written tests than on the oral tests). Tables 11.2 and 11.3 show the transformed means and standard deviations for

TABLE 11.2
Transformed Means and Standard Deviations for Sentence Completion Test

Group	Test	Mode	M	SD
Processing	Pretest	Written	.67	.91
(n = 27)		Oral	.29	.62
	Posttest	Written	1.22	1.21
		Oral	1.25	1.26
No instruction	Pretest	Written	.56	.76
(n = 17)		Oral	.28	.41
	Posttest	Written	.44	.84
		Oral	.21	.49

TABLE 11.3
Transformed Means and Standard Deviations for Video Narration Test

Group	Test	Mode	M	SD
Processing	Pretest	Written	.29	.48
(n = 27)		Oral	.25	.65
	Posttest	Written	1.12	1.12
		Oral	.64	1.04
No instruction	Pretest	Written	.30	.55
(n = 17)		Oral	.12	.35
	Posttest	Written	.27	.46
		Oral	.15	.34

both groups in the pretest and the posttest as elicited by the Sentence Completion and Video Narration tests, respectively.

The data from the Structured Interview presented a unique problem. Overall, the means on this test were quite low, and although the ANOVA conducted on the data from the Structured Interview also produced a significant interaction Group × Time ($F_{1,42} = 4.90$, $p < .04$), the low means did not reveal any information about Mode. Thus, in order to generate reliable results, we computed gain scores on the Structured Interview and submitted them to t tests. As was the case with the ANOVA, the gain scores from the processing group proved to be significantly higher than those from the control group for the oral version of the task ($t_{26} = 2.87$, $p < .01$) as well as for the written version of the task ($t_{26} = 2.41$, $p < .05$). However, when we compared oral to written data, we found no significant difference (Tables 11.4 and 11.5).

4.4. Summary of First Analyses

Overall, we found a positive effect for processing instruction: Instruction significantly affected the grammatical accuracy with which learners interpreted and produced preverbal object pronouns both orally and in the written mode. This

TABLE 11.4
Transformed Means and Standard Deviations for Structured Interview Test

Group	Test	Mode	M	SD
Processing	Pretest	Written	.04	.14
(n = 27)		Oral	.00	.00
	Posttest	Written	.39	.69
		Oral	.26	.61
No instruction	Pretest	Written	.00	.00
(n = 17)		Oral	.03	.13
	Posttest	Written	.00	.00
		Oral	.00	.00

TABLE 11.5
Transformed Means and Standard Deviations for Gain Scores
Used for the *t* test for the Structured Interview

Group	Mode	Mean Gain Score	SD
Processing	Written	.26	.61
(n = 27)	Oral	.35	.64
No instruction	Written	−.03	.13
(n = 17)	Oral	.00	.00

positive effect held across the three production tests—Sentence Completion, Structured Interview, and Video Narration—although the effect was most evident in the Sentence Completion and Video Narration tests. Our suspicions about mode were only partially substantiated: Written vs. oral production seemed to make a difference on only two tests, the Sentence Completion test and the Video Narration test. We decided to analyze the data in another way—by removing mode as a variable and entering type of test as a main factor.

4.5. Production Data: Second Analyses

In the second set of analyses, we looked for the particular effects of test type as a major variable. Because Mode had been found to be a consistent major variable, we decided to run two sets of ANOVAs: one on the written data and another on the oral data. For each ANOVA, we included three factors, Group (processing vs. no instruction), Time (pre- vs. posttest), and Test (Sentence Completion vs. Video Narration). Because of the low mean scores on the Structured Interview test and the problems it presented for analysis, we decided to eliminate it from the second analysis.

The analysis on the written data revealed a main effect for Group ($F_{1,42} = 4.69$, $p < .04$), a main effect for Time ($F_{1,42} = 6.12$, $p < .02$), a main effect for Test ($F_{1,42} = 4.81$, $p < .04$), and a significant interaction Group × Time ($F_{1,42} = 9.27$, $p < .01$). (See Table 11.6 for the transformed means and standard deviations). In order to investigate the cause of the interaction, we ran multiple *t* tests on the means of the scores from both tasks. The difference on the posttest scores between the no-instruction and the processing groups was significant ($F_{1,42} = 8.67$, $p < .01$). Further, the difference between the pretest and posttest scores for the processing group was significant ($F_{1,42} = 15.42$, $p < .00$). When we compared pretest and posttest scores from the control group, we found no significant difference nor did we find any significant difference between the groups at the onset of the experiment.

The second analysis showed that the processing group produced significantly more accurate written text than the no-instruction group because of exposure to the instructional treatment. We also found that the test that required the

TABLE 11.6
Means and Standard Deviations for the Written Versions
of Sentence Completion and Video Narration Tests

Group	Time	Test	M	SD
Processing	Pretest	SC*	.67	.91
(n = 27)		VN**	.29	.48
	Posttest	SC*	1.22	1.21
		VN**	1.12	1.12
No instruction				
	Pretest	SC*	.58	.76
(n = 17)		VN**	.30	.55
	Posttest	SC*	.44	.84
		VN**	.27	.46

*Sentence Completion.
**Video Narration.

least production, the Sentence Completion test, elicited more accurate speech before and after the treatment overall.

Results from the three-way ANOVA on the oral data reveal a main effect for Group ($F_{1,42} = 5.03$, $p < .04$), a main effect for Time ($F_{1,42} = 9.78$, $p < .01$) a main effect for Test ($F_{1,42} = 7.67$, $p < .04$), a significant interaction Group × Time ($F_{1,42} = 10.95$, $p < .01$), and a significant triple interaction Group × Time × Task ($F_{1,42} = 5.02$, $p < .03$). (See Table 11.7 for the transformed means and standard deviations.) Multiple t tests were computed and revealed that the combined effect for instruction and the assessment test is due to significant differences between the posttest scores from both groups for the Sentence Completion test ($F_{1,42} = 10.44$, $p < .01$). The processing group significantly outperformed the control group when completing sentences in the oral mode. No significant dif-

TABLE 11.7
Means and Standard Deviations for the Oral Versions
of Sentence Completion and Video Narration Tests

Group	Time	Test	M	SD
Processing	Pretest	SC*	.29	.62
(n = 27)		VN**	.25	.65
	Posttest	SC*	1.25	1.27
		VN**	.64	1.04
No instruction				
	Pretest	SC*	.29	.41
(n = 17)		VN**	.12	.35
	Posttest	SC*	.21	.45
		VN**	.15	.34

*Sentence Completion.
**Video Narration.

ference was found when the posttest scores from the Video Narration test were compared; this was the only case in which a comparison of posttest scores between groups yielded nonsignificant results. Instruction seemingly did not significantly improve the accuracy with which the processing group performed on the oral Video Narration test.

4.6. Overall Summary of Analyses

All the analyses suggested that instruction had a positive effect on the subjects' ability to comprehend as well as to produce the target item. In addition, the subjects' production became more accurate when speaking as well as when writing. With the exception of one instance (the scores of the oral Video Narration test), we found that instruction had an effect regardless of test type. In short, we have corroborated the findings of VanPatten and Cadierno (1993) and have shown that the effect of processing instruction is not limited to sentence-level tasks.

5. IMPLICATIONS

The results obtained from the present investigation on the effects of processing instruction are significant in terms of the relationship between SLA theory and language pedagogy. First, we have underscored the important role of input in language acquisition. That the subjects improved their production even at the suprasentential level is notable when we consider that the instructional treatment involved practice in interpreting sentences only. We have shown that altering the processing strategies used by learners when they are processing input leads to a change in knowledge, and that this knowledge is available for use in different kinds of production tasks. Thus, we give additional support to the current idea that explicit instruction works best if it is psycholinguistically motivated on the basis of what we understand about how learners develop grammatical systems.

We also believe, however, that our study has important implications for future research on language acquisition and instruction. Whereas the analysis on the written data produced a two-way interaction between Group and Time and a significant main effect for Test, the analysis of the oral data showed a triple interaction between Group, Time, and Test. In other words, scores are significantly different depending on what assessment test is used. Moreover, the difference depends on whether the subjects performed the tests in the written or in the oral mode. Specifically, when the tests were in the written mode, the effects of instruction were observed equally in all three tests. However, when the same tests were performed in the oral mode, the effects of instruction could be observed only in scores from the sentence completion test. The fact that the structured interview produced such low mean scores in comparison to the other two tests and was eliminated from the second set of analyses offers further evidence that subjects perform differently—perhaps very differently—on different kinds of tests. Thus, the use of single tests to measure the effects of instruction may not be as revealing as one would hope.

The most important implication of our study is the need for the development and implementation of multiple assessment tasks in SLA research as a more informative way of investigating the effects of instruction on SLA. First, the use of multiple assessment tasks is more informative for the teacher interested in knowing what learners can do with what they have learned. Likewise, multiple assessment tasks are more informative for the researcher interested in investigating the full extent of the impact of instruction, that is, the degree of automatization of knowledge achieved by the subject after exposure to the treatment.

Future studies should also consider the long-term effects of processing instruction. VanPatten and Cadierno (1993) and Cadierno (1992) found that the effects of instruction held up for over a month after instructional treatment. We recognized that one of the major limitations of our study is that testing was limited to an immediate posttesting session. Clearly, longer term studies are needed. Nevertheless, we believe that the value of processing instruction is sufficiently clear to warrant continued investigation into both input processing and explicit instruction in grammar.

ACKNOWLEDGMENTS

We thank James F. Lee, Fred Davidson, Terry Ackerman, and Susan Garnsey, at the University of Illinois, for their valuable input. We also thank the instructors and students who gave up their regular class time to participate in this research. This research was made possible by a Thesis Project Grant and a Dissertation Grant from the University of Illinois Graduate College to Cristina Sanz, and by a research award granted to Bill VanPatten by the Research Board of the University of Illinois.

REFERENCES

Bates, E., B. MacWhinney, C. Caselli, A. Devescovi, F. Natale, and V. Venza. (1984). "A Cross-Linguistic Study of the Development of Sentence Interpretation Strategies," *Child Development* 55, 341–354.

Cadierno, T. (1992). "Explicit Instruction in Grammar: A Comparison of Input Based and Output Based Instruction in Second Language Acquisition." Doctoral dissertation, University of Illinois at Urbana-Champaign.

Chaudron, C. (1985). "Intake: On Models and Methods for Discovering Learners' Processing of Input," *Studies in Second Language Acquisition* 7, 1–14.

Ervin-Tripp, S. M. (1974). "Is Second Language Learning Like the First?," *TESOL Quarterly* 8, 111–127.

Gass, S. M. (1989). "How Do Learners Resolve Linguistic Conflicts?," *Linguistic Perspectives on Second Language Acquisition*, ed. by S. M. Gass and J. Schachter. Cambridge: Cambridge University Press.

Lee, J. F. (1987). "Morphological Factors Influencing Pronominal Reference Assignment by Learners of Spanish." *Language and Language Use: Studies in Spanish* ed. by T. A. Morgan, J. F. Lee, and B. VanPatten. Landham, MD: University Press of America.

LoCoco, V. (1987). "Learner Comprehension of Oral and Written Sentences in German and Spanish: The Importance of Word Order." *Foreign Language Learning: A Research Perspective*, ed. by B. VanPatten, T. Dvorak, and J. F. Lee. Rowley, MA: Newbury House.

Long, M. H. (1990). "The Least a Second Language Acquisition Theory Needs to Explain," *TESOL Quarterly* 24, 649–666.

McLaughlin, B. (1990). "Restructuring," *Applied Linguistics* 11, 113–128.

Pienemann, M. (1987). "Psychological Constraints on the Teachability of Languages." *First and Second Language Acquisition Processes*, ed. by C. Pfaff. Rowley, MA: Newbury House.

Sanz, C. (1994). "Multiple Assessment of an Input-Based Approach to Explicit Instruction in Grammar." Doctoral dissertation, University of Illinois, Urbana-Champaign.

Schmidt, R. (1992). "Psychological Mechanisms Underlying Second Language Fluency," *Studies in Second Language Acquisition* 14, 357–385.

Terrell, T. (1991). "The Role of Grammar Instruction in a Communicative Approach," *Modern Language Journal* 75, 52–63.

VanPatten, B. (1984). "Learners' Comprehension of Clitic Pronouns: More Evidence for a Word Order Strategy," *Hispanic Linguistics* 1, 57–67.

VanPatten, B. (1985). "Communicative Value and Information Processing in Second Language Acquisition." *On TESOL '84*, ed. by P. Larson, E. Judd, and D. Messerschmitt. Washington, DC: TESOL.

———. (1990). "Attending to Form and Content in the Input," *Studies in Second Language Acquisition* 12, 287–301.

———. (1992). "Second Language Acquisition and Foreign Language Teaching: Part 2," *ADFL Bulletin* 23, 23–27.

———. (1993). "Grammar Instruction for the Acquisition Rich Classroom," *Foreign Language Annals* 26, 435–450.

———. (1995). "Cognitive Aspects of Input Processing in Second Language Acquisition." *Festschrift in Honor of Tracy D. Terrell*, ed. by P. Hashemipour, R. Maldonado, and M. van Naerssen. New York: McGraw-Hill.

———, and T. Cadierno. (1993). "Explicit Instruction and Input Processing," *Studies in Second Language Acquisition* 15, 225–241.

White, L. (1989). *Universal Grammar and Second Language Acquisition*. Amsterdam: John Benjamins.

Chapter 12

Free Voluntary Reading: Linguistic and Affective Arguments and Some New Applications

Stephen D. Krashen
University of Southern California

1. INTRODUCTION

The case for including free voluntary reading (FVR) in language education programs is, in my opinion, overwhelming.[1] In fact, FVR may be the best educational tool we have for literacy development. In this chapter, I present two arguments for FVR: (1) the language argument: the argument that FVR is a powerful way of developing competence in literacy; (2) the affective argument, the claim that FVR is very enjoyable. In addition, I present some evidence that FVR can be used as a bridge from communicative language competence to academic language competence, and some new applications: how FVR can be used to strengthen bilingual education programs, and how free reading can help in the acquisition of second dialects.

2. FVR: THE LANGUAGE ARGUMENT

The foundation of the language argument is the Reading Hypothesis, the hypothesis that claims that comprehensible input in the form of reading is the major source of our literacy development, that is, our reading comprehension

---

[1] This chapter also appeared in the *Proceedings of the Third Annual Conference on Books in Spanish for Young Readers*, California State University, San Marcos. Reprinted with permission.

ability, much of our vocabulary competence, spelling ability, and writing style, and our ability to use complex grammatical constructions.

The evidence for FVR can be categorized as direct and indirect. Studies providing direct evidence show that more FVR results in greater literacy attainment, and studies providing indirect evidence show that *rival hypotheses*, other proposed means of developing literacy, are not capable of doing the job.

The direct evidence can be further subcategorized into "outside of school" and "in-school" studies. We turn first to the outside-of-school studies, which examine whether those who read more outside of school develop higher levels of literacy.

2.1. Outside of School Studies

Several kinds of outside-of-school studies have been done. Most correlational studies show that those who say they read more read better (Krashen, 1988), write better (Krashen, 1984), and spell better (Polak & Krashen, 1988). West, Stanovich, and Mitchell (1993) have also provided evidence that adults who read more in public and who are familiar with more authors have larger vocabularies. Of course, such correlational evidence does not establish causality. Although this evidence is consistent with the *reading hypothesis*, one could always argue that those who read more also do other things: maybe they write more, study more, or were even "hooked on phonics."[2]

---

[2]Even if the reading hypothesis is true, it does not mean that there is a linear relationship between the amount one reads and literacy development. Several studies have indicated, in fact, that the relationship is nonlinear: there may be an intermediate stage in which a linear relationship is present, but progress eventually slows down and the curve flattens out (Anderson, Wilson, & Fielding, 1988). There are several possible reasons for this: First, it is possible that readers do not continue to read material that is progressively more difficult. If readers stay with the same kind of texts, they will eventually stop encountering new vocabulary, discourse structures, and grammatical structures. Younger readers apparently do expand their reading interests as they get older (LaBrant, 1958), but we have no data on older readers. Second, it may be the case that extensive reading will only guarantee an adequate writing style, not necessarily a superior writing style (Krashen, 1984). I have also argued that reading results in good, but not always perfect, spelling (Krashen, 1985b, 1989). This would also attenuate correlations between reading quantity and writing quality.

These factors help explain why correlations between the amount read and measures of literacy development are usually modest. In a few cases, however, researchers have failed to find significant correlations between reported reading and measures of literacy development. Whenever this has occurred, there have been methodological problems. Hedgcock and Atkinson (1993) reported significant relationships between reported pleasure reading and writing ability among college students in English as a first language, a result consistent with the reading hypothesis. They failed, however, to find a significant relationship between pleasure reading in the second language and second language writing ability, in contrast with previous studies (Gradman & Hanania, 1991, 1992; Janopoulos, 1986). Their dependent variable, however, was a writing test, and it exhibited little variability (SD of .94 on a 0–10 point scale, compared with a larger (but still modest) SD of 1.4 for their English-as-a-first-language study, on an 8-point scale).

A number of case histories of people who have attained high levels of literacy make these alternative explanations doubtful. People such as Richard Wright and Malcolm X attributed their high levels of literacy to reading. As Wright (1966) stated, "I wanted to write and I did not even know the English language. I bought English grammars and found them dull. I felt that I was getting a better sense of the language from novels than from grammars" (p. 275). Although such case histories may not count as hard scientific data, it is difficult to imagine other sources for this literacy development (for more discussion of these cases, see Krashen, 1993).

A recent study of individualized free reading also lends credibility to the hypothesis that it was reading, and not other activities, that resulted in growth. Cho and Krashen (1994) asked four adult second-language acquirers to read for pleasure from the Sweet Valley Kids series, a series of novels written at the second-grade level. Our subjects had studied English as a second language but had never read for pleasure in English. Subjects reported that they enjoyed the reading enormously, and our tests results indicated that they were acquiring impressive amounts of vocabulary, ranging from 7 to 40 words per volume (each volume

---

In addition, subjects read very little in English while in elementary school, which explains why this variable was not a significant predictor. On a 1–4 point scale, where 1 = I don't read this type of material at all, their mean response to "fiction reading in elementary school" was only 1.26, which is not surprising for adult acquirers of English as a second language (in contrast, native speakers of English averaged 2.87 on this question). There was more reported reading of English in high school (1.86 out of 4) and college (2.10 out of 4), but still much less than for native speakers (3.04 and 2.48 in high school and college, respectively).

These restrictions in both the independent and dependent variables help explain why no significant relationship was found between reading frequency and writing ability.

Flahive and Bailey (1993) reported a significant correlation between time spent in non-school-related reading in English and scores on a test of reading comprehension ($r = .49$) for university-level acquirers of English as a second language, but reported no relationship between time spent on pleasure reading and measures of writing, syntactic accuracy, and T-unit length in a writing sample.

There are several possible explanations for these results. First, Flahive and Bailey's subjects reported an extraordinary amount of time spent reading in English, a mean of 5.5 hours per week. In comparison, Christy Lao, in recent unpublished research, asked 171 international science students how much English reading they did weekly. For English fiction, 73.3% reported reading less than 1 hour per week, and only 7% said they read English fiction for 4 hours per week or more. Only 29.7% of her sample said they read English newspapers and magazines for 4 hours per week or more. This suggests that Flahive and Bailey's subjects' estimates included much more than pleasure reading.

Second, as in Atkinson and Hedgcock's study, variability in one of the dependent variables, the essay, was modest ($SD = 1.5$, on a 1–9 scale). Third, the subjects in Flahive and Bailey's study were fairly advanced, with a median TOEFL score of about 525 (Flahive & Bailey, 1993, p. 131). In comparison, Gradman and Hanania (1991, 1992) have consistently reported positive relationships between reported "extracurricular" reading and TOEFL scores and tests of reading and writing among EFL students whose average TOEFL score was about 450. Flahive and Bailey's subjects may thus fall on the part of the curve that had already flattened out. Finally, Flahive and Bailey asked only about current reading. It is quite possible that many students with high levels of competence in English were extensive readers in English years ago but do not read so much now, because they don't have time. On the other hand, some who did little reading in the past may be "born again" pleasure readers with a sudden interest in reading. In comparison, Gradman and Hanania asked students about outside reading in general (as did Atkinson & Hedgcock).

contains about 7,000 words). Two subjects who used the dictionary acquired many more words, but we wonder whether it was worth it, because of the time and effort it required; it might have been more efficient to read more, without the dictionary.

Subjects also reported that their speaking and understanding of English improved. After reading 15 volumes of Sweet Valley Kids, one subject whose spoken English had been very hesitant reported, "Reading helps me understand TV better. I ran across many of the same words and phrases I saw in reading while I was watching TV. I used to be afraid to speak with Americans. But the other day when I went to Disneyland, I enjoyed talking to some American children and their parents who came from Arizona" (translated from Korean by Kyung-Sook Cho). Clearly, it was the reading that made the difference in this case, because no other aspect of our subjects' lives had changed.

2.2. In-School Studies

In-school studies provide very clear evidence for the reading hypothesis, because in these studies, reading is the only treatment. The best known of these are sustained silent reading (SSR) studies, in which a certain amount of time is set aside during the school day for free voluntary reading. In previous publications (e.g., Krashen, 1985a, 1988, 1993), I have concluded that these programs typically work well if they are continued for at least 7 months; students in SSR programs that last that long usually outperform comparison students who spend a similar amount of time in traditional language arts programs.

It is possible, however, to do SSR for a long enough time and still fail, and on the other hand, it may be possible to make short-term SSR work. Maynes (1981) reported no additional gains in elementary students' achievement in reading comprehension after a 1-year SSR program. The children, however, had to read during their lunch period! Pilgreen and Krashen (1993) reported success in a short-term (4-month) SSR study using high school ESL students, with students gaining an average of 15 months on a standardized reading test, nearly 1 month for every week of reading. The reason for this remarkable gain may be that the program was "stacked for success": attempts were made to insure that adequate reading material was available, students were told about the research on free reading, teachers read during SSR, and students were encouraged to read at home in addition to the SSR time in school. Results of this study must be considered tentative, however, because no control group was used.

2.3. Rival Hypotheses

The indirect language argument for the reading hypothesis is that other means proposed for developing literacy do not work. The major rivals to reading are the *instruction hypothesis*, the hypothesis that we can teach literacy directly, and the *writing hypothesis*, the hypothesis that literacy results from writing. One major reason to discount strong versions of both rival hypotheses is that it is clearly possible to attain high levels of literacy without instruction and without writing. In previous publications (Krashen, 1989, 1993) I have reviewed research showing that vocabulary and spelling competence can be increased without instruction and without writing ("read and test" studies), and a number of recent studies confirm that vocabulary acquisition is possible in second language acquisition from reading alone (Day, Omura, & Hiramatsu, 1991; Dupuy & Krashen, 1993; Pitts, White, & Krashen, 1989). In addition, the case histories mentioned earlier strongly suggest that complete literacy development is possible without instruction.

Another strong argument against the instruction hypothesis is the complexity argument. As I have argued previously (e.g., Krashen, 1993), the system is simply too vast, too complicated to be learned and taught one rule or one vocabulary word at a time. In addition, the writing hypothesis suffers because people simply don't write enough, either in school or outside of school, to make any substantial impact on literacy development (empirical data reviewed in Krashen, 1993). Also devastating for the writing hypothesis are studies showing that increasing the amount of writing students do does not significantly increase writing competence. These results hold for first and second language development (Krashen, 1991).

2.4. The Language Argument: Conclusions

The reading hypothesis, the hypothesis that reading for meaning is a major source of our literacy competence, is consistent with the hypothesis that "we learn to read by reading" (Goodman, 1982; Smith, 1988) and is a special case of the more general input hypothesis, the hypothesis that the essential environmental ingredient for language acquisition is comprehensible input, or messages we understand (Krashen, 1985b). Evidence supporting the reading hypothesis thus supports K. Goodman's contention that "reading is natural" (K. Goodman & Y. Goodman, 1982).

3. FVR: THE AFFECTIVE ARGUMENT

In Krashen (1991), I proposed what might be called the *pleasure hypothesis*: Pedagogical activities that promote language acquisition are enjoyable, and those that do not are not enjoyable (and may even be painful). Just because an activity is enjoyable does not mean it is good for language development, but it is interesting that there is strong evidence that free voluntary reading is very enjoyable, even addictive. Recent evidence showing that free reading is pleasant comes from work by Csikszentmihalyi (1991), who introduced the concept of *flow*. Flow is the state people reach when they are deeply but effortlessly involved in an activity. In flow, the concerns of everyday life and even the self disappear—our sense of time is altered and nothing but the activity itself seems to matter.

Crosscultural studies indicate that flow is easily recognized by members of widely different cultures and groups. For example, members of Japanese motorcycle gangs experience flow when riding (Sato, 1992), and rock climbers experience flow when climbing (Massimini, Csikszentmihalyi, & Della Fave, 1992).

Of special interest is the finding that reading "is currently perhaps the most often mentioned flow activity in the world" (Csikszentmihalyi, 1990, p. 117). This finding is consistent with the reports of individual pleasure readers. A resident of Walse in Northern Italy said that when he reads "I immediately immerse myself in the reading, and the problems I usually worry about disappear" (Massimini et al., 1992, p. 68). One of Nell's subjects reported, "reading removes me . . . from the . . . irritations of living . . . for the few hours a day I read 'trash' I escape the cares of those around me, as well as escaping my own cares and dissatisfactions . . ." (Nell, 1988, p. 240). W. Somerset Maugham, quoted in Nell (1988), had similar comments: "Conversation after a time bores me, games tire me, and my own thoughts, which we are told are the unfailing resource of a sensible man, have a tendency to run dry. Then I fly to my book as the opium-smoker to his pipe . . ." (Nell, 1988, p. 232).

Nell (1988) provided interesting evidence showing why bedtime reading is so pleasant. Pleasure readers were asked to read a book of their own choice, while their heart rate, muscle activity, skin potential, and respiration rate were measured; level of arousal while reading was compared to arousal during other activities, such as relaxing with eyes shut, listening to white noise, doing mental arithmetic, and doing visualization exercises. Nell found that during reading, arousal was increased, as compared to relaxation with eyes shut, but a clear decline in arousal was recorded in the period just after reading, which for some measures reached a level below the baseline (eyes-shut) condition. In other words, bedtime reading is arousing, but then it relaxes you.

Consistent with these findings are Nell's results showing that bedtime reading is popular. Of 26 pleasure readers he interviewed, 13 read in bed every night and 11 "almost every night" or "most nights" (1988, p. 250). In view of these results and the positive effect reading has on literacy development, Trelease's suggestion that children be given a reading lamp for their beds at an early age is a good one (cited in Krashen, 1993).

3.1. Fiction as a Bridge

Another argument that supports the case for free voluntary reading is evidence that light reading, especially fiction, can function as a bridge between conversational and academic language competence. On the basis of a factor analysis of a large number of texts, Biber (1988) determined that English genres can be analyzed in terms of a number of underlying dimensions. Following Biber and Finegan (1989) and Biber (1991) (see also Finegan & Besnier, 1989), I focus on three of these dimensions here (all three factors selected from the six identified in Biber, 1988, pp. 126-127, have strong predictive power in distinguishing among genres).

1. *Informational versus involved.* Texts that are informational are characterized by frequent nouns and prepositions, longer words, and attributive adjectives. Texts that are at the involved end of this dimension are characterized by more use of first- and second-person pronouns, "private" verbs (such as *think, consider, assume*), and hedges (*kind of, more or less, maybe*).

According to Biber's analysis, conversational language falls at the extreme "involved" end of this dimension, whereas academic prose falls at the "informational" end.

2. *Elaborated versus situation dependent.* Elaborated texts are more context independent and highly explicit, while situational texts are more context dependent. The former are characterized by Wh-relative clauses, whereas the latter are characterized by time and place adverbials.

Along with academic prose, professional letters fall at the "elaborated" end of this dimension, whereas personal letters and face-to-face conversation fall toward the "situational" end.

3. *Abstract versus nonabstract style.* Abstract texts feature a reduced emphasis on the agent and more on the patient, or the recipient of the action. Abstract texts also feature frequent use of the passive. Academic prose is at the extreme abstract end of this dimension, whereas face-to-face conversation falls at the extreme nonabstract end.

Thus, academic prose can be characterized as informational, elaborated, and abstract, whereas conversational language can be characterized as involved, situation dependent, and nonabstract. Biber's results are quite consistent with the distinction drawn between contextualized and decontextualized language (Cummins, 1989).

Of great interest is fiction's place on these continua. On the informational-involved dimension, general fiction falls near the middle, slightly closer to the informational pole. Science fiction is closer to the informational end, but romantic fiction is closer to the middle of the dimension. On the elaborated-situated dimension, both general and romantic fiction fall at or close to conversation, whereas science fiction is closer to the middle of the dimension. On the abstract-nonabstract dimension, all forms of fiction are at or close to the nonabstract end of the dimension, close to or identical with face-to-face conversation (see Table 12.1).

These results suggest that light reading in the form of fiction may thus be an ideal bridge between conversational and academic language, a bridge that can

TABLE 12.1
Dimensions of English Prose (from Biber, 1988)

	Informational Academic Prose		Elaborated Academic Prose		Abstract Academic Prose
+15					
		+4		+5	
+10					
		+3			
	Science Fiction			+4	
+5					
		+2			
	General Fiction			+3	
0					
		+1			
	Romantic Fiction			+2	
−5					
		0			
				+1	
−10					
		−1			
			Science Fiction	0	
−15					
		−2			
				−1	
−20					
		−3			
			General Fiction	−2	
−25					
			Romantic Fiction/		General Fiction/
		−4	Conversation	−3	Science Fiction
−30					
					Romantic Fiction/
		−5			Conversation
−35	Conversation Involved		Situated		Nonabstract

Note. The numbers are dimension scores, and are derived from a complex factor analysis. For details on the calculation of dimension scores, see Biber (1988).

be crossed in either direction. Language acquirers who have acquired considerable amounts of conversational language but who are lacking in academic language competence will probably find light fiction more comprehensible than academic texts, and reading light fiction will give them at least some of the knowledge that will help make academic texts more comprehensible. Those who have highly developed academic language competence but lack conversational language (e.g., international students and scholars) can move toward conversational language by means of fiction; the fact that fiction has at least some of the characteristics of elaborated texts helps make it comprehensible, and the features it shares with conversation (situated and nonabstract) allow the reader to acquire a substantial amount of language that will be useful in understanding conversation.

The reason fiction provides this bridge is that it contains several subgenres (e.g., conversation, description, narration). This variety aids comprehensibility; those who have acquired one set of subgenres can use this knowledge to help make the nonacquired subgenres more comprehensible (E. Finegan, personal communication, 1993). Thus, someone with more conversational competence will use this knowledge to understand the conversations in a novel, which will help make the descriptive passages more comprehensible.

As noted earlier, the three dimensions considered here are only three of the six dimensions Biber arrived at. It is on these three dimensions that academic language and conversational language fall at end points, with fiction in between. This is not the case with the three other dimensions in Biber's analysis. For example, fiction falls at the extreme "narrative" end of Biber's narrative-nonnarrative dimension, with academic prose at the extreme nonnarrative end.[3]

Research by Hayes and Ahrens (1988) also supports the reading hypothesis for vocabulary, as well as the idea that light reading can serve as a bridge. According to their findings, it is highly unlikely that educated vocabulary can come from conversation or television. Hayes and Ahrens found that the frequency of less-common words in ordinary conversation, whether adult-to-child or adult-to-adult, was much lower than in even the "lightest" reading. About 95% of words used in conversation and television are from the most frequent 5,000. Printed texts include far more uncommon words, leading Hayes and Ahrens to the conclusion that development of lexical knowledge beyond basic words "requires literacy and extensive reading across a broad range of subjects" (1988, p. 409). In Table 12.2, I present a small portion of their data, including two of the three measures they used for word frequency. Note that light reading (comics, novels, other adult books, and magazines), although somewhat closer to conversation, occupies a position between conversation and scientific papers.

4. NEW APPLICATIONS OF FVR

Although it was originally applied primarily to the English language arts classroom, there is good reason to hypothesize that FVR will be of great help in other areas as well.

---

[3]There have been some changes over time in the positioning of fiction along the three dimensions. Biber & Finegan (1989) have shown that in general, 17th-, 18th-, and 19th-century fiction tends to fall more toward the "literate" end of the three dimensions, being more informational, elaborated, and abstract, as compared to current fiction (an exception is 17th-century fiction, which is more involved than current fiction). We might thus predict that those with greater conversational competence would find current fiction more readable, while those starting at the academic end would find older fiction more readable. Such a prediction, however, ignores the role of interest and background knowledge.

TABLE 12.2
Common and Uncommon Words in Speaking and Writing.
Source: Hayes and Ahrens, 1988

	Frequent Words*	Rare Words**
Adults talking to children	95.6	9.9
Adults talking to adults***	93.9	17.3
Prime-time TV: adult	94.0	22.7
Children's books	92.3	30.9
Comic books	88.6	53.5
Books	88.4	52.7
Popular magazines	85.0	65.7
Newspapers	84.3	68.3
Abstracts of scientific papers	70.3	128.2

*Percentage of text from most frequent 5,000 words.

**Number of rare words per 1,000 tokens. A rare word is not among the most common 10,000 words, not counting proper names and numbers.

***College graduates talking to friends and spouses.

4.1. Bilingual Education

Bilingual education has done very well, contrary to public opinion. When programs are set up correctly, children in these programs typically do as well as, and usually better than, children in all-day English programs (for reviews, see Cummins, 1989; Krashen, 1991; Krashen & Biber, 1988; Willig, 1985). Bilingual education, however, could do much better if it took advantage of the power of reading. To see why this is so, we first need to review the components of correctly organized bilingual programs (Krashen & Biber, 1988):

1. *Comprehensible input in English.* It goes without saying that this is important. Comprehensible input is provided through good ESL classes and sheltered subject matter teaching.

2. *Subject matter teaching in the first language, without translation.* Subject matter knowledge, gained through the primary language, makes an indirect but profound contribution to second language development by making second language input more comprehensible.

3. *Literacy development in the first language.* Literacy developed in the first language transfers to the second language. The logic here is simple: If acquiring the ability to read depends on comprehension of the message, or making sense of what is on the page, as argued by Smith and Goodman, it will be much easier to learn to read in a language you already understand. And once you can read, you can read.

There is good reason to add a fourth component:

4. *Enrichment, or continuing development of the first language.* Continuing first language development has practical and cognitive advantages and helps

avoid the damaging syndrome of bicultural ambivalence, shame of the first culture and hostility toward the second culture (Cummins, 1981).

Free reading can help each component enormously:

1. Free reading is an excellent source of comprehensible input in English, and, as I argued previously, it supplies just the kind of input students need to progress to academic language.
2. Free reading is an excellent source of knowledge: those who read more know more (e.g., Ravitch & Finn, 1987; Schaefer & Anastasi, 1968; Simonton, 1988).
3. If the arguments presented in the first part of this paper are correct, free reading is undoubtedly the best way to develop literacy in the primary language. In addition, there is some evidence that the reading habit transfers; readers in the primary language will become readers in the second language. Flahive and Bailey (1993) reported a high correlation ($r = .79$) between time spent reading nonschool materials in the first language and time spent reading nonschool materials in the second language, for college students acquiring English as a second language.
4. Free reading may be the best way of insuring continued development of the primary language.

Books in the primary language, however, are not plentiful. The home environment of many of the children who participate in bilingual education is not print-rich: Rameriz, Yuen, Ramey, and Pasta (1991) investigated the print environment in the homes of children participating in the three types of programs they studied. They were interested in seeing if the home print environment was a potential confounding factor. It was not; children in all three programs had similar numbers of books in the home. What was remarkable, however, was the paucity of books in the homes of children in all three programs: the average number of books in the home that were not schoolbooks was only 22 (immersion = 20.4 books; early exit = 23; late exit = 23.3).

Despite effects to inform school personnel about books in Spanish (e.g., Schon, 1978, 1988), the Spanish print environment in schools is very weak. Schon, Hopkins, Main, and Hopkins (1987) reported that school libraries spend very little on Spanish-language books, and many librarians believe that books in Spanish do not serve an important educational purpose. Pucci (1993) documented that even schools committed to bilingual education have few books in Spanish in their libraries. In the nine schools she studied, schools with heavy Spanish-speaking enrollment, most schools had less than one book in Spanish per child in the school (and usually less than four per child in English). Pucci also found, in agreement with previous research (Krashen, 1993), that children get a large percentage of their reading material from the school library. Moreover, Pucci documented that most schools did not make library use easy for children; they put strict limits on the number of books children could take out and limited access to the library during the school day.

In related research, Constantino, Tai, and Lu (1992) reported that minority parents have little knowledge of public libraries. In their sample of 27 parents, only one parent knew about and used the public library. On the other hand, all seven public school teachers interviewed by Constantino et al. believed that parents did know about the library.

There are thus strong arguments for encouraging free reading in both the first and second language in bilingual programs. The research shows, however, that books in the primary language are not available and that knowledge of libraries is minimal. In fact, it is surprising that bilingual education has done so well working with such a poor print environment. These problems are very easy to solve. I predict that when they are solved, we will see undreamed-of success in bilingual education. If children in bilingual programs are doing well now, without books, with books they will do spectacularly well.

4.2. Acquisition of a Second Dialect

There is widespread agreement that children should be allowed to keep their first dialect while they acquire the standard dialect. The assumption has been, however, that children need to be exhorted to acquire the standard, and that they will learn the standard through direct instruction. Delpit (1986), for example, claimed that whole-language approaches did not help children develop the competence "demanded by the mainstream" and suggested a return to a more skills-based program. Delpit's version of whole language, however, was a program based largely on writing. Her observations are thus consistent with the results I reported earlier in this chapter: language is not developed through output practice.

My hypothesis is that most of the conventions of standard written English can be acquired through reading. This hypothesis is consistent with the case histories cited earlier. If true, it means that we need not exhort students to work hard to acquire standard English; they will acquire it automatically if they read for pleasure.

4.3. Some Objections

One objection that has been raised against free reading is that it is too much fun. Elley, describing a successful "book flood" program in Singapore, reported that in some of the groups he studied, "teachers, principals, and parents expressed concern that children were merely enjoying themselves, rather than learning. Indeed, a few teachers dropped out for such reasons. The assumption that language learning must be hard work is strong in many cultures" (Elley, 1991, p. 403).

Another objection is that if students are allowed to read what they like, they will not read material of high quality; they will read trash. The small amount of empirical research available does not confirm this: Schoonover (1938) reported that children who do extensive free reading eventually choose what the experts have decided are "good books." In addition, the very notion of quality literature can be questioned. Nell (1988) found positive correlations between merit ratings and difficulty ratings of texts, which suggests that subjects were making their merit judgments on the basis of the difficulty of the text; those that were harder to read were considered better quality.

A final objection is that books cost money, and money, these days, is scarce. There are several answers to this objection. First, books are an excellent investment. Lance, Welborn, and Hamilton-Pennell (1993) showed that money spent on the school library is well spent: Better funded school libraries, they found, result in better reading scores. Second, we are currently spending money on equipment and programs that have nowhere near the track record that free reading has: for the price of one computer, a school can add hundreds of books (and thousands of paperbacks) to its library.

I would like to propose another means of solving the money problem: Reduce or even stop standardized language testing. There are good reasons for this. Language tests, unfortunately, hurt language development, because preparation for the tests results in time spent in activities that do not improve language and literacy development. For example, students prepare for vocabulary tests by studying vocabulary in isolation. According to the research, however, reading for pleasure is more more effective, in terms of words acquired per minute, than this kind of study (Nagy, Herman, & Anderson, 1985). Thus, even if tests are reliable and valid, their effect on teachers and students is very negative. In addition, we invest an incredible amount of time, effort, and money on language tests. That money could be spent on school libraries, and the time could be spent reading to children, helping them find good books, and studying literature (discussing good books). This could be the solution to the literacy crisis.

5. CONCLUSION

Rather than end this chapter in the usual way, stating that much remains to be done and that I have raised more questions than I have answered, I will claim that more than enough basic research has been done to justify using FVR much more than we have in language education programs. Furthermore, in a sense FVR answers more questions than we originally thought it would; it is applicable to a wide range of situations. Certainly we currently employ procedures in language education for whose value there is much less evidence. I am not suggesting that we have answered all questions about FVR, but the lack of a research basis cannot be used as an excuse for not using it.

REFERENCES

Anderson, R., P. Wilson, and L. Fielding. (1988). "Growth in Reading and How Children Spend Their Time Outside of School," *Reading Research Quarterly* 32, 285–303.

Biber, D. (1988). *Variation Across Speech and Writing.* Cambridge: Cambridge University Press.

———. (1991). "Oral and Literate Characteristics of Selected Primary School Reading Materials," *Text* 11, 73–96.

———, and E. Finegan. (1989). "Drift and the Evolution of English Styles: A History of Three Genres," *Language* 65, 487–517.

Cho, K. S., and S. Krashen. (1994). "Acquisition of Vocabulary from the Sweet Valley Kids Series: Adult ESL Acquisition," *Journal of Reading* 37, 662–667.

Constantino, R., Y. Tai, and S. Lu. (1992). "Minority Use of the Public Library," *CABE Newsletter* 15, 6.

Csikszentmihalyi, M. (1990). *Flow: The Psychology of Optimal Experience.* New York: Harper Perennial.

———. (1992). "Introduction." *Optimal Experience: Psychological Studies of Flow in Consciousness,* ed. by M. Csikszentmihalyi and I. Csikszentmihalyi, pp. 3–14. Cambridge: Cambridge University Press.

Cummins, J. (1981). "The Role of pRimary Language Development in Promoting Educational Success for Language Minority Students." *Schooling and Language Minority Students,* ed. by California State Department of Education. Evaluation, Dissemination, and Assessment Center, California State University, Los Angeles.

———. (1989). *Empowering Minority Students.* California Association for Bilingual Education, Sacramento.

Day, R., C. Omura, and M. Hiramuatsu. (1991). "Incidental EFL Vocabulary Learning and Reading," *Reading in a Foreign Language* 7, 541–551.

Delpit, L. (1986). "Skills and Other Dilemmas of a Progressive Black Educator," *Harvard Educational Review* 56, 379–385.

Dupuy, B., and S. Krashen. (1993). "Incidental Vocabulary Acquisition in French as a Foreign Language," *Applied Language Learning* 4, 55–63.

Elley, W. (1991). "Acquiring Literacy in a Second Language: The Effect of Book-Based Programs," *Language Learning* 41, 375–411.

Finegan, E., and N. Besnier. (1989). *Language: Its Structure and Use.* New York: Harcourt Brace.

Flahive, D., and N. Bailey. (1993). "Exploring Reading/Writing Relationships in Adult Second Language Learners." *Reading in the Composition Classroom,* ed. by J. Carson and I. Leki, pp. 128–140. Boston: Heinle & Heinle.

Goodman, K. (1982). *Language and Literacy.* London: Routledge & Kegan Paul.

———, and Y. Goodman. (1982). "Acquiring Literacy Is Natural: Who Skilled Cock Robin? *Language and Literacy* (Vol. I), ed. by K. Goodman, pp. 243–249. London: Routledge & Kegan Paul.

Gradman, H., and E. Hanania. (1991). "Language Learning Background Factors and ESL Proficiency," *Modern Language Journal* 75, 39–51.

———. (1992). "The Relative Importance of Reading for Language Learning Programs. *Quilt and Quill: Achieving and Maintaining Quality in Language Teaching and Learning,* ed. by N. Bird and J. Harris, pp. 431–441. Institute of Language in Education, Hong Kong.

Hayes, D., and M. Ahrens. (1988). "Vocabulary Simplification for Children: A Special Case of 'Motherese'?," *Journal of Child Language* 15, 395–410.

Hedgcock, J., and D. Atkinson. (1993). "Differing Reading-Writing Relationships in L1 and L2 Literacy Development," *TESOL Quarterly* 27, 329–333.

Janopoulos, M. (1986). "The Relationship of Pleasure Reading and Second Language Writing Proficiency," *TESOL Quarterly* 20, 763–768.

Krashen, S. (1984). *Writing: Research, Theory, and Applications.* Torrance, CA: Laredo.

————. (1985a). *Inquiries and Insights.* New York: Prentice-Hall.

————. (1985b). *The Input Hypothesis: Issues and Implications.* Torrance, CA: Laredo.

————. (1988). "Do We Learn to Read by Reading? The Relationship Between Free Reading and Reading Ability." *Linguistics in Context: Connecting Observation and Understanding,* ed. by D. Tannen, pp. 269–298. Norwood, NJ: Ablex.

————. (1989). "We Acquire Vocabulary and Spelling by Reading: Additional Evidence for the Input Hypothesis," *Modern Language Journal* 73, 440–464.

————. (1991). "The Input Hypothesis: An Update." *Georgetown University Round Table on Languages and Linguistics,* 1991, ed. by J. Alatis, pp. 427–431. Washington, DC: Georgetown University Press.

————. *The Power of Reading.* Englewood, CO: Libraries Unlimited.

————, and D. Biber. (1988). *On Course: Bilingual Education's Success in California.* California Association for Bilingual Education, Sacramento, CA.

LaBrant, L. (1958). "An Evaluation of Free Reading." *Research in the Three R's,* ed. by C. Hunnicutt and W. Iverson, pp. 154–161. New York: Harper & Brothers.

Lance, D., L. Welborn, and C. Hamilton-Pennell. (1993). *The Impact of School Library Media Centers on Academic Achievement.* Englewood, CO: Libraries Unlimited.

Massimini, F., M. Csikszentmihalyi, and A. Della Fave. (1992). "Flow and Biocultural Evolution." *Optimal Experience: Psychological Studies of Flow in Consciousness,* ed. by M. Csikszentmihalyi and I. Csikszentmihalyi, pp. 60–81. Cambridge: Cambridge University Press.

Maynes, F. (1981). "Uninterrupted Sustained Silent Reading," *Reading Research Quarterly* 17, 159–160.

Nagy, W., P. Herman, and R. Anderson. (1985). "Learning Words from Context," *Reading Research Quarterly* 20, 233–253.

Nell, V. (1988). *Lost in a Book.* New Haven: Yale University Press.

Pilgreen, J., and S. Krashen. (1993). "Sustained Silent Reading with ESL High School Students: Impact on Reading Comprehension, Reading Frequency, and Reading Enjoyment," *School Library Media Quarterly* 22, 21–23.

Pitts, M., H. White, and S. Krashen. (1989). "Acquiring Second Language Vocabulary through Reading," *Reading in a Foreign Language* 5, 271–275.

Polak, J., and S. Krashen. (1988). "Do We Need to Teach Spelling? The Relationship between Spelling Proficiency and Voluntary Reading Among Community College ESL Students," *TESOL Quarterly* 22, 141–146.

Pucci, S. (1993). "Primary Language Free-Reading Resources: A Study of Access and Availability in Los Angeles Public Schools," Doctoral dissertation, University of Southern California, Los Angeles.

Ramirez, D., S. Yuen, D. Ramey, and D. Pasta. (1991). "Final Report: Longitudinal Study of Structured English Immersion Strategy, Early-Exit and Late-Exit Bilingual Education Programs for Language-Minority Students, Vol. I. San Mateo, CA: Aguirre International.

Ravitch, D., and C. Finn. (1987). *What Do Our 17-Year-Olds Know?* New York: Harper and Row.

Sato, I. (1992). "Bosozuku: Flow in Japanese Motorcycle Gangs." *Optimal Experience: Psychological Studies of Flow in Consciousness,* ed. by M. Csikszentmihalyi and I. Csikszentmihalyi. Cambridge: Cambridge University Press.

Schaefer, C., and A. Anastasi. (1968). "A Biographical Inventory for Identifying Creativity in Adolescent Boys," *Journal of Applied Psychology* 58, 42–48.

Schon, I. (1978). *Books in Spanish for Children and Young Adults: An Annotated Guide.* Metuchen, NJ: Scarecrow.

————. (1988). "Recent Children's Books in Spanish: The Best of the Best," *Hispania* 71, 418–422.

————, K. Hopkins, I. Main, and B. Hopkins. (1987). "Books in Spanish for Young Readers in Schools and Public Libraries: A Survey of Attitudes and Practices," *Library and Information Science Research* 9, 21–28.

Schoonover, R. (1938). "The Case for Voluminous Reading," *English Journal* 27, 114–118.

Simonton, D. (1988). *Scientific Genius: A Psychology of Science*. Cambridge: Cambridge University Press.

Smith, F. (1988). *Understanding Reading*, 4th ed. Hillsdale, NJ: Lawrence Erlbaum Associates.

West, R., K. Stanovich, and M. Mitchell. (1993). "Reading in the Real World and Its Correlates," *Reading Research Quarterly* 28, 34–50.

Willig, A. (1985). "A Meta-Analysis of Selected Studies on the Effectiveness of Bilingual Education," *Review of Educational Research* 55, 269–317.

Wright, R. (1966). *Black Boy*. New York: Harper & Row.

Chapter 13

Teaching with Authentic Video: Theory and Practice

Anthony A. Ciccone
University of Wisconsin–Milwaukee

1. THE ARGUMENT FOR AUTHENTIC INPUT

There is now general agreement among foreign language instructors that authentic materials, that is, materials "not designed solely for classroom use but rather for native speakers" (Cummins, 1989), are an essential part of the second language classroom. Teachers may disagree as to the appropriate level of instruction for introducing such materials into the curriculum, their relative importance in relation to more traditional grammar and vocabulary study, and the amount, nature, and necessity of introductory or preparatory activities, but almost all believe that a foreign language curriculum is inadequate if it does not develop in students the ability to read, understand, and respond to authentic language in all its forms.

Recent studies have served to justify this belief. Bacon and Finneman (1990) observed that authentic oral and written input has both cognitive and affective value. Cognitively, authentic materials provide the necessary context for relating form to meaning (decoding) appropriately in the language acquisition process. Affectively, such input increases motivation and can serve to overcome the initial cultural strangeness in foreign language learning. Bacon and Finneman concluded that when students are properly prepared, authentic oral and written materials have a positive perceived effect on comprehension and student satisfaction. Herron and Seay (1991) reported similar cognitive and affective benefits from exclusively oral authentic texts, noting that explicit attention to the development of listening skills improves listening comprehension at all levels of instruction with no negative effect on grammar, vocabulary, or oral skills.

It would be a mistake to infer from these and other studies, however, that authentic input is of such great value to foreign language acquisition that its use is widespread or uncontroversial. Vande Berg (1993) and others noted that despite solid evidence of its benefits, authentic input is often considered too difficult at the lower levels of the curriculum. Not using it at these levels, however, may make student difficulty a self-fulfilling prophecy, because the lack of early exposure to anything other than contrived speech increases students' later frustration and retards their acquisition of the language. Secules, Herron, and Tomasello (1992) agreed that the problems associated with the use of authentic materials derive from the fact that students are often not pushed to their processing limits by more traditional classroom activities and teacher talk. Bacon and Finneman (1990) also suggested that the entire curriculum must be designed and articulated to convince students that learning to deal with authentic input is the true measure of language proficiency. This goal can be reached only if authentic input is an early and important part of instruction. Valuable authentic materials like the satellite newscasts provided by SCOLA (*Satellite Communications for Learning Associated*), which Vande Berg (1993) used in her study, although far removed from the familiar vocabulary, tone, and content of introductory courses, can thus be used effectively if they are implemented in an articulated curriculum and if care is taken in selecting and preparing the materials and in defining the tasks required of the learner.

My own teaching experience supports the view that much of the difficulty students experience can be traced to their lack of familiarity with authentic input, in particular with the processing strategies needed to decode such complex language. When students are given such guidance, most notably when they are shown how to situate the particular authentic input in its context and thus limit the universe of possible meanings, they report greater satisfaction and make better progress. Students with more experience in these processes—for example older students or those in the second and third semester of our three-semester intermediate/advanced language sequence based on authentic reading, video, and audio materials—overwhelmingly report that the intrinsic interest of the materials makes the difficulties in understanding them surmountable. Furthermore, when they are given the opportunity to demonstrate their newly acquired skills in appropriately designed assessment instruments, students learn to process authentic input even more efficiently.

2. AUTHENTIC MATERIALS AND COMPREHENSIBLE INPUT

Much of the interest in the pedagogical value of authentic materials can be traced to Krashen's (1981) work in second-language acquisition and in particular to his now-famous Input Hypothesis. If it is indeed true that humans acquire language principally, if not exclusively, by understanding messages, that is, by receiving and processing "comprehensible input," the main function of the second language classroom should be to provide learners with authentic, comprehensible language that is not otherwise easily available to them. Rather than focusing on form or on memorizing vocabulary, instructors should help learners to develop the processing skills that make possible the manipulation and ultimate decoding of meaningful language. In this theory, moreover, speaking and writing emerge from the improving ability to understand oral and written input. Authentic materials are clearly an essential source of this comprehensible input and thus an important trigger of comprehensible output as well.

Although few now dispute the face validity of this hypothesis and its positive effect on foreign language pedagogy, Krashen has been criticized for not defining $i + 1$ as precisely as some would like (McLaughlin, 1987). The apparent vagueness is perhaps one of the reasons for the wide variety of opinions about where and how authentic materials can best be used in instruction. As I noted earlier, some teachers and researchers see great value in using authentic materials from the outset, whereas others are equally convinced that they can be useful only at more advanced stages of language instruction. Some would argue that authentic materials should be presented only with an extensive array of preparatory activities and significant modifications, while others believe in a "sink-or-swim" approach.

I propose that examining the nature and use of authentic video materials may prove useful in this debate, because it may contribute to the theory of the nature of comprehensible input, as well as suggest how comprehensible input can best be used in the classroom. For example, how does video serve to enhance the comprehensibility of verbal input? What is there about video materials that stimulates the principal activity of language acquisition—understanding meaningful language—and thus the development of the productive skills of speaking and writing? Furthermore, what can the development and implementation of appropriate pedagogical formats for using authentic video tell us about how comprehensible input can be created out of the wide variety of authentic materials we might choose?

3. THE CASE FOR AUTHENTIC VIDEO

Recent theoretical and applied studies have begun to answer the first two questions. Authentic video makes linguistic input more comprehensible by embedding it in a context of extralinguistic cultural cues that assures the transmission of meaning even when complete grammatical and lexical decoding is not likely to be achieved. Anecdotal information from my own students confirms this. Almost all of them report, for example, that they have greater difficulty in understanding audio-only conversations than video materials, despite similarities in topic and preparatory materials. Exposure to authentic video materials also improves the skills necessary for listening comprehension. Secules, Herron, and Tomasello (1992) reported on an experiment comparing a class taught with the *French in Action* video developed by Capretz with a class taught using the Direct Method. They found that the experimental (video) group scored significantly higher on a test of listening comprehension that involved understanding main ideas, details, and inference from a video conversation between native speakers. They obtained these results despite student concerns about rapid speech, the difficulty of the story, and unfamiliar material, indicating that students had developed processing skills from their earlier work with video that students exposed only to oral, nonvideo authentic language had not. Moreover, in his study on the transferability of skills (discussed later), Lund confirmed that video supplies the contextual clues that make decoding oral input more comparable to decoding written texts.

Like other forms of authentic input, authentic video materials clearly produce the positive affective results that are crucial to the definition of comprehensible input. Meunier-Cinko (1992), among others, reported further that video increases student motivation and adds realism to the classroom by integrating context-embedded interactions into it and providing important nonverbal information that increases cultural understanding. Altman (1989) provided further explanation of this superiority of authentic video as comprehensible input: "By displaying language in context, video shows that the meaning of specific words or utterances varies according to the speaker's identity and situation. . . . Video never allows us to forget that full understanding depends on our ability to perceive the reciprocal relationship between the language and the *systems of culture* that it defines and by which it is simultaneously defined" (p. 4).

In other words, video materials stimulate language acquisition and are thus an excellent source of comprehensible input, because they reveal how a culture uses language to make meaning and to transmit it. How does video become usable comprehensible input in the foreign language class? My own teaching experience suggests a number of important factors that may apply to the general nature of comprehensible input as well.

Comprehensibility of input begins with interest on the part of the learner and clear purpose on the part of the instructor. Thus videos chosen first for their visual and conceptual value, and only secondarily for the vocabulary and grammatical structures they might contain, are the most valuable. The most effective video materials are true visual cultural documents that arouse interest and whose multiple meanings are transmitted through a combination of interdependent words, images, and sounds. Comprehensible input, video materials seem to show, needs to be both redundant and meaningful on many levels. Decoding must be possible from several starting points and along several paths.

In keeping with Krashen's notions, the instructor's first purpose should be to improve the student's ability to comprehend authentic language. Focusing attention explicitly on the way meaning is encoded would thus be an important pedagogical strategy. To accomplish this, the video must be presented first from the producer's point of view: What is its organizing principle? Is the creator's purpose to inform or persuade? Is the style descriptive, factual, or interpretive? Questions such as these help focus the discussion on the video mainly as a system of meaning and downplay its unfamiliar vocabulary and grammatical structures. Comprehensible input is, above all, input whose organizing principle has been discerned.

After the learner is interested and the instructor has a purpose, authentic video materials become a source of comprehensible input only if they can be properly adapted to the learner. If, for example, a learner's level is i and the materials are at level $i + 3$, little advantage will be gained through their use. Three issues must be addressed if the gap between the learner's level and the video's level is to be reduced: how to modify the materials, how to prepare the learner, and how to guide the learner toward fuller comprehension.

In the first case, the visual support that the video provides for the language must be determined and, if necessary, enhanced. Altman (1989) recommended isolating and examining key images from the video before viewing it, or creating other visuals based on the video, in order to create a feeling of familiarity with the materials. Segmenting the video into manageable units of no more than two or three minutes, depending on the speed and amount of language, is also essential, although one might easily argue that such segmenting should be used during second and subsequent viewings.

Preparing the learner may be the most important factor in turning authentic video materials into comprehensible input. Two types of activities are particularly useful: those that make learners conscious of what they may already know that will be pertinent to the video and those that provide essential background information that may be lacking. Thus print realia such as charts, maps and surveys, short readings, and short writing or brainstorming activities that supply historical or geographical information, vocabulary, and essential grammar, and activate personal experiences are especially valuable. Connecting the known to the not yet known is the key cognitive principle here.

If language acquisition is really a series of successive approximations of native speech, it might be profitable to think of the development of comprehension as a similar series of increasingly fuller meanings. A program of multiple viewings— at first without sound to organize the images and overall structure through skimming and scanning questions, later with sound to produce a summary, respond to more interpretive questions, or produce another type of appreciation— should be designed to move the learner along the path of greater and greater comprehension.

Finally, Krashen's idea that comprehensible input primes the pump of production implies that the proof that any authentic video materials have indeed become comprehensible input lies in their ultimate value in helping learners to produce comprehensible output. Thus effective video pedagogy would be incomplete without follow-up speaking and writing activities that require exploiting the video model. Such activities should include creating scenarios on related topics using similar language or writing summaries and essays on personal reactions using specific vocabulary and structures. Images are especially effective as prompts for these tasks because they improve recall and encourage imagination.

To sum up, we learn from using authentic video materials that input becomes comprehensible only when we pay attention to the choice of materials, the preparation of the learner, and the definition of the tasks required. Five points are especially important to note: (1) input becomes comprehensible only to interested learners; (2) input must be presented and understood as a coherent system of meaning; (3) input must be redundant and solidly embedded in a meaningful context; (4) existing knowledge and previous experience must be activated; and (5) guided, expansive production must be encouraged.

4. THE CASE FOR COMBINING VIDEO AND READING

I have argued that learners acquire the ability to understand and produce authentic language only by confronting it in its authentic forms. Authentic video materials are valuable sources of this essential comprehensible input because they provoke interest, focus attention on decoding, and encourage productive skills. Moreover, analyzing and implementing authentic video materials clarifies several important issues related to the nature of comprehensible input itself. In many ways, therefore, the use of authentic video materials provides support for Krashen's input hypothesis and the pedagogical strategies that derive from it.

In similar fashion, in his reading hypothesis, a special case of the more general Input Hypothesis, Krashen (this volume) posits that "reading for meaning is a major source of our literacy competence," and suggests that free voluntary reading (FVR), particularly light reading such as fiction, is essential in acquiring comprehensible input and ultimately producing comprehensible output. Does my discussion of authentic video materials provide any support for, or clarification of, the reading hypothesis? To answer this question we must ask two related questions: Can the decoding skills necessary for the comprehension of authentic oral and video materials transfer to reading comprehension? If so, how can authentic video and reading materials be effectively combined in the classroom in ways that would make free voluntary reading even more profitable?

Lund (1991) has examined the transferability of skills and strategies learned in one modality to another. Using purely oral materials in his study, he concluded that the general processes involved in listening and reading comprehension seem to be similar. Both listeners and readers use schema-based processing, although listeners are more likely to depend on this strategy because they cannot pause over words, benefit from more obvious cognates, or exploit other graphic contextual clues (e.g. quotation marks, punctuation). Video, he suggested, may "level the playing field," and I concur. Moreover, by providing analogous clues, video encourages the development of useful reading techniques. For example, video images thats support words or concepts are analogous to written cognates; scene changes often translate notions of chronology, comparison, or contrast not unlike adverbial and conjunctive expressions; and change in voice or actor can provide the aural or visual equivalent of proper names, pronouns, quotation marks, and other identifying graphic features.

Bacon and Finneman (1990) found further similarities in processing strategies. Comparing the tasks of reading authentic materials and listening to a conversation between native speakers, they observed that significant numbers of students listen or look for familiar words (85% when listening, 55% when reading), try to grasp the basic concept first (68% when listening, 67% when reading), and report satisfaction with their ability to understand some of the message (63% when listening, 67% when reading). Moreover, although twice as many students report that they concentrate on each word when reading, only 40% actually do so, and only 34% in either case resort to trying to translate or look up every word as it is perceived. Video, as we have seen, encourages these global strategies.

My own experience indicates that students do see a relationship between video and reading comprehension. When asked, for example, to volunteer any type of comment about the video component of my fifth-semester conversation/composition course, 8 students cited interest, 5 cited value for understanding the accompanying readings, 2 cited culture, and only 3 mentioned difficulty. Although much more work needs to be done in this area, it seems clear that learners use at least some similar strategies when decoding authentic oral and written language.

We may draw two conclusions at this point. First, video increases the comprehensibility of reading materials on similar topics. Thus, combining authentic video materials with authentic reading materials will undoubtedly lead to improved listening and reading comprehension. Second, working with authentic video materials as meaningful, interesting language to be decoded encourages the fundamental processes needed to improve reading comprehension and enhance reader satisfaction.

5. PRINCIPLES FOR EFFECTIVELY COMBINING VIDEO AND READING MATERIALS

The relationship between listening and reading comprehension that the video/reading combination reveals has important pedagogical consequences. If developing strategies to decode meaningful language is our principal instructional goal, and if both video and reading materials can help us reach it, then the problem no longer lies in deciding which type of authentic input to use but rather in discovering how the two can be combined effectively. Furthermore, video in the classroom can be used to promote and improve free voluntary reading.

How can we make them work together pedagogically, that is, how can we use them to develop transferable skills? How can we present video and reading materials in ways that help us reach similar goals?

Helping students turn authentic video and reading materials into comprehensible input requires, first, that we encourage students to avoid word-by-word decoding, especially on the first pass. Listening comprehension is not simply segmenting sounds into words, nor is reading simply assigning lexical meaning to isolated words. For video, this means using techniques such as viewing without sound, presenting and discussing sequences of images first, and inviting conjecture and speculation. For reading, students should be encouraged to look first at what surrounds or jumps out of the text (headlines, pictures, names, form), and to develop hypotheses about the information that the text might actually contain.

Learning to manipulate comprehensible input also involves learning to decode materials for specific purposes. Comprehension does not always require understanding every word or structure; authentic materials are sources of information as well as models of language use. For video, this means learning to view the material, with or without sound, to get specific information. For reading, students should be encouraged to exploit scanning techniques that develop the ability to understand particular threads of meaning in a text. For example, students might be asked to concentrate on the use of color in a particular advertising video, or to categorize the types of adjectives used to describe certain places in a reading passage. In both cases, students are encouraged to consider authentic documents as reference materials in the service of a greater purpose.

Most foreign language teachers would agree that students often lose the forest for the trees when dealing with authentic materials. In all fairness, our pedagogical methods often create this problem; we insist on developing meaning from the bottom up, by connecting small details to each other in the hope of building a coherent picture. A better strategy for dealing with authentic materials would be to encourage students first to use top-down strategies for general comprehension. With video, this means helping them develop the ability to locate the places where organization and structure are most apparent. For example, students should be encouraged to view the video with attention to images that mark change, such as the use of color as opposed to black and white, the arrival and departure of characters, the passage from day to night or indoor to outdoor, rural to city, etc. The corresponding reading skills would include attention to change of speaker or tense and understanding how conjunctions and other expressions such as *on the other hand* or *others might say* both create and set up juxtapositions of meaning.

Another major goal of foreign language instruction is to help students understand the richness of meaning contained in authentic documents and to develop the skill to decode as much of this information as possible. With video, this means creating a coherent program of successive viewings for different purposes or from different points of view. For example, students should be encouraged to view the video as a source of factual information, as an expression of opinion designed to propagandize or persuade, and as an example of a certain style. They should also be asked to imagine how different types of viewers might respond differently to it, for example, men and women, older and younger persons, French people and Americans, and so on. In reading, students should be directed similarly to perform successive interpretations for specific purposes. In the case of literature, for example, students should read the work in the variety of its contexts (social, political, literary criticism, genre theory), and imagine or research how different types of readers might respond to it. In both cases, the purpose is to encourage students to read between the lines for irony, author intent, and connotation by developing the ability to ask questions about choice of words or images and to situate any particular choice in the context of what has come before and what might come later.

Finally, our ultimate goal must be to encourage students to continue to view and read authentic materials on their own, especially after formal instruction. The most obvious way to accomplish this is to cultivate students' ability to respond personally to the materials. With video, this means encouraging students to select and react to particularly striking images. In reading, students should be similarly invited to respond to a surprising turn of events or opinion by relating it to personal experience and expectations. In other words, only by encouraging students to understand that working with authentic materials in not just an "academic exercise" can we hope to have them become lifelong language learners.

APPENDIX A: COMBINING VIDEO AND READING

This is the first video unit used in a fourth-semester French class at the University of Wisconsin–Milwaukee. It is taken from Télétexte : Perspectives sur la France d'aujourd'hui, by Anthony A. Ciccone and Martine D. Meyer (1992a, 1992b). Students have had at least three years of high school or three semesters of college French, or some combination. Some may also have taken an optional placement test.

The materials have been translated into English for this chapter. In class, everything is presented and discussed in French.

As preparation for working with the video, students have completed an introductory reading on the perceptions of the French and France by other nationalities. The video in question relates how one clever farmer manages to have his entire field prepared for planting by the gullible and greedy residents of his rural town.

Students prepare the first section of questions at home before viewing the film in class. These questions establish a context in order to limit the universe of possibilities, orient students to the notion of authorial choice and perspective, bring to the surface what students may already know or think, introduce vocabulary needed to talk about the video, and orient students to visual thinking.

Previewing Assignment

You're going to see a short, 9-minute film that presents a fictitious incident in the life of a small village called Castelnau. The story is extremely simple: A farmer finds a way to convince the other inhabitants of the town to plow his fields for him. There is hardly any dialogue, but the film appears to present a stereotypical idea of certain French people.

- ### *What Do You Think?*

1. There are 26 cities or towns which are called Castelnau or Castelnaud in France, of which 1 has fewer than 100 inhabitants, 10 have between 100 and 500 inhabitants, and 9 have between 500 and 1,000 inhabitants. Why do you think the director chose such a common name? Why such a small town?

2. We all have an image of rural France and French peasants. In each of the following pairs of words, which seems to best represent your image?

young / old	homogeneous / diverse
miserly / generous	intelligent /stupid
worldly / simple	clever / naive
modern / backward	simple / complex
calm / lively	religious / nonreligious
sparsely / heavily populated	different / conformist
conservative / liberal	hard-working / lazy

   What other characteristics could you add to this list?

3. Imagine a French village and draw it. What buildings are there? What are the streets like? The square? Where are the fields?

- ### *Some Vocabulary*

There's very little dialogue in this film, but you'll need these and other words to describe what you'll see. Look up the meaning of the words you don't recognize:

To talk about farmwork: work, plow, cultivate, seed, hoe, make a furrow with a plow, oxen, soil, fields.

To describe the village : streets, square, church, bakery, café, gas station, cemetery, monument to the dead.

While You Watch

- Watch the film once in its entirety and find the following information:

1. Which of these professions are shown?
   baker, pharmacist, priest, mayor, teacher, gas station attendant, cemetery keeper, farmer, lawyer, banker

2. Which of these activities are shown?

    plowing fields, repairing a tractor, going to church, running, buying bread, drinking, reading, eating, harvesting, planting

3. What season are we in? How do you know? What day of the week is it? In what part of France are we?

- Watch the film again and put the following actions in chronological order. Organize your paragraph with expressions like 'Sunday morning', 'Sunday afternoon', 'Sunday evening', 'during the night', and 'Monday afternoon'.

He works in the fields.	He goes past the gas station.
The plow doesn't work.	He talks to the mayor.
He thinks it over.	They leave the café.
He begins to run.	He goes into a café.
They go to the fields.	He goes to sleep.
He shows the mayor three little stones.	He goes back to his place.
	They leave the church.
They begin to dig and hoe.	He looks at his fieds.
He climbs into bed.	He gets up.
He has breakfast.	He seeds the fields.

After a third (optional) viewing, students work alone or in groups on the following series of questions, which have been designed to help them rethink original opinions after new information, interpret the images presented, and reflect on and interpret the choice of images, their organization, etc.

Postviewing

1. Which of your images of the French peasant are shown here? Which are not?

2. What do the townspeople think of the farmer? Are they right?

3. It is clear that the producer has not limited himself to an objective image of the French. Which characteristics of the French does he attack? What does the film say about the French and religion? And work? And conformity?

4. Is the farmer like the other inhabitants? How does the filmmaker show that he is different?

Students now study a fable by La Fontaine on a very similar situation. (The situation is so similar that we're almost certain that the filmmaker started with this fable.)

The film and the fable each shed light on the other. The video provides appropriate images for some of the fable's vocabulary and "reinterprets" the moral; the fable presents another perception of the key concept of social and individual values.

The fable is written in poetry. This is a loose prose translation for the purposes of

the article. Again, students are asked to read the fable twice for specific purposes. Difficult
expressions are glossed in French to discourage dictionary overuse.

Complementary Text : "The Farmer and His Children"

1. Here is a fable by La Fontaine that presents a similar incident but with a
   different moral. During your first reading, notice especially how the farmer's
   children resemble the inhabitants of Castelnau.

   > Work hard, put in whatever effort it takes:
   > These are the resources in which you are most rich.
   > A rich farmer, knowing death was near,
   > Called his children to him and spoke to them in private.
   > "Make sure you don't sell the family land," he told them.
   > "The land our ancestors left us:
   > A treasure is hidden there.
   > I don't know the exact spot, but with a little courage
   > You'll find it; I'm sure you'll succeed.
   > Work the field right after harvest time:
   > Dig it up, turn it over, hoe it well, run the dirt
   > Over and over through your fingers."
   > And so the father died. The sons worked the field
   > Here, there, and everywhere; so well in fact that after a year
   > The land produced much much more.
   > No hidden money, however. But the father had done well
   > To show them, before he died,
   > That work itself is a treasure.

2. How is the father in the fable different from the farmer in the film?
3. How do the sons resemble the villagers?
4. Who comes out on top in the fable? In the film?
5. Do La Fontaine and the filmmaker have the same attitude toward work?
   The moral of the fable is 'Work itself is a treasure' (Le travail est un
   trésor). Can you write a similar sentence to express the moral of the film?

These last questions encourage comparison and contrast, enhance the ability to understand
perspective and author intent, and prepare students to write. A final composition on this
section asks students to develop a detailed comparison of the two works.

REFERENCES

Altman, R. (1989). *The Video Connection: Integrating Video into Language Teaching*. Boston: Houghton
   Mifflin.
Bacon, S., and M. Finneman. (1990). "A Study of Attitudes, Motives, and Strategies of University
   Foreign Language Students and Their Disposition to Authentic Oral and Written Input," *Modern
   Language Journal* 74(4), 459–473.

Ciccone, A., and M. Meyer. (1992a). *Télétexte: Perspectives sur la France d'aujourd'hui*. Boston: Heinle & Heinle.

———. (1992b). *Télétexte chez soi*. Boston: Heinle & Heinle.

Cummins, P. (with assistance of AATF's Commission sur la mobilisation pédagogique). (1989). "Video and the French Teacher," *French Review* 62(3), 411–426.

Herron, C., and I. Seay. (1991). "The Effect of Authentic Oral Texts on Student Listening Comprehension in the Foreign Language Classroom," *Foreign Language Annals* 24(6).

Krashen, S. (1981). *Second Language Acquisition and Second Language Learning*. Oxford: Pergamon.

Krashen, S. (1993). "Free Voluntary Reading: Linguistic and Affective Arguments and Some New Applications." Paper presented at Second Language Acquisition and Pedagogy: Twenty-second University of Wisconsin, Milwaukee (UWM) Linguistics Symposium, University of Wisconsin-Milwaukee.

Lund, R. (1991). "A Comparison of Second Language Listening and Reading Comprehension," *Modern Language Journal*, 75(2), 196–204.

McLaughlin, B. (1987). *Theories of Second Language Learning*. London: Edward Arnold.

Meunier-Cinko, L. (1992). "Interactive French Language Curricula of the Future: A Study of Computer and Video Potential," *French Review* 66(1), 147–153.

Secules, T., C. Herron, and M. Tomasello. (1992). "The Effect of Video Context on Foreign Language Learning," *Modern Language Journal* 76(4), 480–490.

Vande Berg, C. K. (1993). "Turning Down the Fire Hose: Some Techniques for Using SCOLA Broadcasts at the Intermediate Level," *French Review* 66(5), 769–776.

Part IV

OUTPUT: FACTORS AFFECTING PRODUCTION

Chapter 14

SLA Theory and Pedagogy: Some Research Issues

Andrew D. Cohen
University of Minnesota

1. INTRODUCTION

I will look at three issues for research involving the interface between theory and pedagogy in second language acquisition. The issues are (1) the benefits of having teachers instruct their students on how to learn language by providing them with suggestions about strategies for enhancing learning; (2) the effects of having teachers take finely tuned pedagogical insights gleaned from research on gaps in the acquisition of speech act behavior and applying these insights to their classroom teaching; (3) the extent to which language immersion programs create an internal language environment in which the learners' cognitive processing is conducted in the foreign language. The first two issues deal with the facilitation of the language learning process, the first focusing on enhancing that process and the second on filling identified gaps in learning. The third issue covers the consequences of selecting a pedagogical approach that is intended to bring about rapid acceleration of the learning process.

2. LANGUAGE LEARNING STRATEGY TRAINING IN THE LANGUAGE CLASSROOM

Should language learners be left to their own devices or should they receive some form of training in how to learn the language they are studying? In recent years researchers have begun to investigate the results of explicit training in using cognitive strategies for learning second- or foreign-language vocabulary, reading, writing, listening, and speaking. Although research on first language pedagogy has explored learner training in depth, especially reading strategies (e.g., Baumann, 1984; Brown, Palincsar, & Armbruster, 1984; Garner, 1987), parallel research in assessing foreign language strategy training has been more limited (Cohen, 1990; O'Malley & Chamot, 1990; Oxford, 1990).

Such first language strategy training has often included the following sequence of events (Pearson & Dole, 1987):

1. Initial modeling by the teacher, with direct explanation of the strategy's use and importance.
2. Guided practice.
3. Consolidation whereby teachers help students identify the strategy and decide where it might be used.
4. Independent practice.
5. Application of the strategy to new tasks.

Whereas the focus of such L1 training programs has usually been on a limited number of strategies that the researchers considered worthy of extended training, the intention of FL strategy training has often been to expose learners to a large set of strategies at one time. From this larger set of strategies, the learners are asked to identify those that they already use and to become more aware of how they use them. The learners are also asked what strategies they do not currently use and whether they could use them. Then they are to choose which strategies they will use and when. In other words, the training is likely not to be *prescriptive* regarding strategies that the learners are supposed to use, but rather *descriptive* of strategies that they could use if they wished. Planning a research study that includes a variable strategy-selection principle presents more of a challenge than focusing on just one or several preselected strategies that all learners are trained to use.

The L2 learning strategy movement assumes that learners should be made conscious of and responsible for their selection and use of learning strategies, in order to make them more successful language learners by improving their use of classroom time, facilitating their completion of homework assignments, and enhancing their use of the language out of class. The challenge to researchers is to identify approaches to foreign-language strategy training that are feasible for the classroom and at the same time feasible for the researcher to study. The purpose of the research would be to determine whether in the long run there is a need to make foreign language learning so conscious an endeavor.

Weaknesses in previous research on foreign-language strategy training have included the following (Oxford & Cohen, 1992):

1. Lack of clear-cut definitions of strategies.

2. Inadequate pretraining assessment of the learners' needs.
3. Uncertainty on the part of teachers and researchers about whether to integrate strategy training into regular class activities.
4. Too limited a time period for the strategy training itself.
5. Too limited a period over which the effects of the training were assessed.
6. Too easy or too difficult a task.
7. Uncertainty of the learners about whether the training was relevant to their language learning needs.

On the basis of their own research and that of others, O'Malley and Chamot (1990) concluded:

> Strategy training should probably be integrated with regular instruction in order to demonstrate to students the specific applications of the strategies and to promote the transfer of strategies to new tasks. Furthermore, evidence indicates that strategy training should be direct in addition to being embedded. In other words, students should be apprised of the goals of strategy instruction and should be made aware of the strategies they are being taught. (p. 184)

Designing research studies to adequately assess such training poses a challenge. We need to:

1. find motivated subjects for whom strategy training would be fully consistent with their learning goals;
2. conduct adequate pretraining assessment to determine personality and cognitive-style variables;
3. determine which strategies the students already have facility with and which strategies should be included in explicit training sessions;
4. have clear working definitions of all the strategies to be included in the training;
5. have ample time to train the learners in using the strategies;
6. have adequate means for investigating both the training process itself and the effects of the training over time.

Item 6 is perhaps the most problematic because our research methods have tended to reflect traditional testing rather than more innovative means of assessment. Even journal keeping has often produced unfocused verbiage—of little use in determining the effectiveness of a treatment. Suppose that we were interested in training language learners in the use of mnemonic keywords for remembering vocabulary. A key phase of the research would be to determine whether the learners actually use the keywords for both understanding the words when they hear them or read them in text and for producing the words in speaking or in writing. Researchers would probably have to train the learners to record their use of the mnemonic keywords every time they used them—say, by quickly jotting down the event in their pocket diary.

Although it would be desirable for use of a strategy to transfer from a training situation to an actual language use situation, a prominent researcher on L1 reading strategy gives reasons why strategy use may not, in fact, transfer:

1. The learners do not know how to monitor or evaluate their cognitive processing.
2. The learners prefer their "primitive routines" for getting the job done rather than engaging in deep processing.
3. The learners have the strategies but lack the schemata for understanding the content to which they would be applying strategies.
4. The learners do not need to use the strategies for which they received training, in order to successfully outperform others in class.
5. The learners lack sufficient examples of how to generalize the strategy to other contexts. (Garner, 1990)

Because the same factors could arise in foreign language strategy training as well, the research design would need to check for these behaviors, or even to provide extra training to assure that the subjects actually use the strategies for which they received training.

3. EXPLICIT TEACHING OF COMPLEX SPEECH ACT BEHAVIOR

The second issue for research concerns the effects of explicitly teaching complex L2 speaking behavior, like speech acts, rather than leaving learners to acquire these sociocultural and sociolinguistic behaviors from the instructional materials and from out-of-class experiences. Complex speech acts have been shown to be a particular challenge for language learners. The fact that such utterances are routinized helps learning, in the sense that much of what is said is predictable. For example, almost half of the time that an adjective is used in a compliment, the adjective is either "nice" or "good" (e.g., *That's a nice shirt you're wearing*, *It was a good talk you gave*); "beautiful," "pretty," and "great" make up another 15% (Wolfson & Manes, 1980). Yet despite the routinized nature of speech acts, there are still various strategies to choose from—depending on the sociocultural context—and there are often a variety of language forms to choose from for realizing those strategies, especially for complex speech acts such as apologies and complaints. Language learners may tend to respond as they would in their native language and culture and find that what they say is not appropriate for the target language and cultural situation.

The findings from a cross-cultural study by Cohen, Olshtain, and Rosenstein (1986) can serve as an example of gaps between native and advanced nonnative apology behavior in English. The 180 respondents for the study included 96 native speakers of American English studying at one of six U.S. universities, and 84 advanced learners of English, who were native speakers of Hebrew studying at one of five Israeli universities. The basic finding was that nonnatives lacked sensitivity to certain distinctions that natives make, such as between forms for realizing the strategy of expressing apology such as "excuse me" and "sorry." At least one out of every five times a native offered an expression of apology, it was with "excuse me," while few nonnatives used this form. Nonnatives limited themselves to the use of "sorry" in contexts where "excuse me" would also be acceptable and possibly preferable.

Although natives and nonnatives did not seem to differ markedly in their use of main strategies for apologizing, there were striking differences in their modifications of such apologies, especially in their use of intensifiers, such as "very" and "really." Nonnatives intensified their expressions of apology significantly more in one situation (forgetting to help a friend buy a bike) than did the natives. This extra intensity on the part of the nonnatives was not necessarily warranted, given the generally low or moderate severity of the offense in those situations. Not only did nonnatives tend to intensify more but they also used a wider and more indiscriminate set of forms. Actually, the nonnative pattern was either to overgeneralize one of the forms ("very" and "sorry") or to use a variety of forms ("terribly," "awfully," "truly"). The nonnatives did not use "really" as the natives did. They attributed the same semantic properties to the intensifier "very" as to "really," but the natives tended to make a distinction whereby "really" expressed a greater depth of apology and concern. For example, in a situation of "scalding a friend with coffee in a cafeteria," the natives tended to use "really sorry" but nonnatives used "very sorry," which sounded less intensified.

There is evidence that acquisition of nativelike production by nonnatives may take many years (Olshtain & Blum-Kulka, 1984), because the sociocultural strategies and the sociolinguistic forms are not always picked up easily. Hence, the question has arisen as to whether speech act strategies can be taught effectively: whether teachers would be helping their students by explicitly teaching them some of the finely tuned speech act behavior that is not simply acquired over time. The rationale would be that learners do not necessarily have an adequate awareness of what is involved in complex speech behavior. Researchers would learn how to prepare a course of instruction to teach gaps in speech act behavior.

At present, there are only a few published studies dealing with the teaching of speech act behavior, but the findings seem promising. For example, Olshtain and Cohen (1990) conducted a study with 18 advanced EFL learners in Israel, 10 studying in private language schools and 8 in a teachers' college, and with 11 native speakers of American English. The learners were pretested to determine gaps in their apologizing behavior. Then they were taught a set of three 20-minute lessons aimed at filling in the gaps—information about the strategies within the apology speech act set and about modifications of apologies through the use of intensification and emotionals. Finally, they were posttested to determine what they had learned.

The findings suggested that the fine points of speech act behavior, such as (a) types of intensification and downgrading, (b) subtle differences between speech act strategy realizations, and (c) consideration of situational features, can be taught in the foreign-language classroom. Whereas before the instruction, the nonnatives' apologies differed noticeably from those of the native speakers, after instruction advanced learners were somewhat more likely to select strategies for apology similar to those that native speakers used in that situation. For example, in a situation of "forgetting to buy medicine for a neighbor's sick child," the response of one nonnative before training was a weak expression of responsibility ("Unfortunately not yet . . .") and an offer of repair ("but I'll be happy to do it right now"). After training it was an intensified expression of apology ("I'm deeply sorry") and an offer of repair ("I can do it right now"). Furthermore, after training, nonnatives produced shorter utterances, also more in keeping with native behavior.

Before instruction, one learner responded verbosely to a situation of forgetting to meet a friend, with "Did you wait for me? You must forgive me. I could not come because of problems and I tried to warn you by phone but . . ." This response was typical of learners at the advanced intermediate stage of language acquisition who, when uncertain about how to say something, will overcompensate by using too many words (Blum-Kulka & Olshtain, 1986). After training, the utterance was shorter: "Oh, I'm so sorry. It dropped out of my mind." Perhaps the area that met with most success was that of the use of intensifiers. Before training, intensifiers were generally absent in situations like "forgetting to buy medicine for a neighbor's sick child" (only 20% use). After training, intensifiers (e.g., "I'm really sorry I forgot . . .") were used in almost all cases (90%).

Billmyer (1990) studied 9 female Japanese ESL learners tutored in complimenting and responding to compliments and compared them with 9 similar learners who were untutored. He looked not just at the speech act but also at the reply—whether the respondent accepted, deflected, or rejected the compliment, and the types of deflecting moves (a comment, a shift of credit, a downgrade, a request for reassurance, a return). He found that learners who were tutored in complimenting produced a greater number of norm-appropriate compliments, produced spontaneous compliments (which the untutored group did not), used a more extensive repertoire of semantically positive adjectives, and deflected many more compliments in their replies. He concluded that formal instruction in the social rules of language use given in the classroom can assist learners in communicating more appropriately with natives outside of the classroom.

There is another area of investigation that has the potential to impact the teaching of speech act behavior as well—that of finding out more about the processes learners use when producing speech acts and responding to them. What is learned can be used in making choices about the teaching of speech acts and in training learners in speech act strategies.

Research has begun on how learners produce utterances in a speaking exercise, using a replay of a videotape to assist the students in remembering how they arrived at what they said. Cohen and Olshtain (1993), for example, investigated ways in which nonnative speakers assess, plan, and execute such complex speech utterances. The subjects, 15 advanced learners of English foreign language, were given six speech-act situations (two apologies, two complaints, and two requests) in which they were requested to role-play along with a native speaker. The interactions were videotaped, and after each set of two situations of the same type, the videotape was played back and the respondents were asked both fixed and probing questions about the factors contributing to the production of their responses in those situations. The retrospective verbal report protocols were analyzed with regard to processing strategies in speech act formulation.

The researchers discovered that (a) half of the time the respondents made only a general assessment of what was called for in the situation, without planning specific vocabulary and grammatical structures; (b) they often thought in two languages and sometimes in three languages (if trilingual) when planning and executing speech act utterances; (c) they used a series of different strategies in searching for language forms; and (d) they did not attend much to either grammar or pronunciation. As an example of multilingual thinking, in asking the teacher for a lift home, a native speaker of French thought the utterance through in French first, because he was aware that it called for deference to status. Then he translated the utterance into Hebrew, and finally he produced what he thought would be an appropriate English equivalent of that utterance.

Some pedagogical implications were drawn from this study. (1) Learners may have a more difficult time producing complex speech acts than teachers think, because they need advanced knowledge to perform them successfully—sociocultural knowledge about the situation and sociolinguistic knowledge about the language forms that are appropriate. (2) The study gave empirical evidence that some tasks make far greater demands on learners than others. The seemingly simple task of asking the teacher for a ride home, for example, called for the most mental logistics in terms of thought patterns and monitoring for grammar, pronunciation, and so forth. The end product—the learner's utterance—may be the result of extensive thought processes in two or more languages and of repeated internal debate about which lexical word or phrase to choose.

There are important reasons why we need to conduct empirical research on the learning of speech acts. First, there are too few empirical studies on the teaching of speech acts for us to be able to make broad claims. Second, ways of teaching to the gaps, that is, to those areas where untutored language acquisition is not likely to take place (or takes place only slowly), is an important problem to explore. At a time when more empirically based information is becoming available about speech act behavior, there is a concomitant challenge for SLA researchers to conduct studies that help to determine the most productive ways of channeling this information back into the teaching process.

4. THE ROLE OF THE FOREIGN LANGUAGE IN THE INTERNAL LANGUAGE ENVIRONMENT OF IMMERSION STUDENTS

Language immersion programs, which have existed in Canada and the United States for over 20 years, assume that second language acquisition occurs most easily and rapidly when the learners are within the target language environment and culture. Immersion programs attempt to simulate, to some extent, nativelike learning conditions by maximizing the time, intensity, and quality of learners' exposure to the target language and culture. Findings from research on second language immersion programs have shown that students who become bilinguals through such programs make normal or better-than-normal progress in content subjects that are taught primarily in the second language (Cohen & Swain, 1979; Genesee, 1987). There is also evidence that students who develop their bilingual skills in supportive or additive bilingual education environments show enhanced nonverbal abilities (Bamford & Mizokawa, 1991) and problem-solving abilities in science (Kessler & Quinn, 1982; Rosebery, Warren, & Conant, 1992).

How much actual language exposure do learners have within full language immersion programs? Specifically, what *internal language environment* emerges for learners as a result of the *external language environment* created by the teachers and the curriculum? The successful results from immersion research have led to claims that immersion students gain an ability to think in the foreign language. There appears to be an implication that the more adept they are at thinking in that language, the better they will be able to process input and output and consequently function better in that language.

Yet along with the documented success of immersion programs, we realize that there are gaps in foreign-language proficiency, especially in speaking and writing skills. Students sometimes use English-language structures to construct their utterances but substitute foreign-language words, a form of negative transfer referred to as *relexification*. Students also insert native-language words into their utterances, especially adverbs and interjections—a sign that they may be thinking in English and translating as they talk. Finally, the language produced in im-mersion programs has reduced vocabulary and structure (e.g., little or no use of certain complex verb tenses, such as the conditional and the subjunctive), like pidgin languages.

Research on French immersion, for example, has shown that in spite of their having had a number of years of comprehensible input in French, the students' spoken and written French contains numerous morphological, syntactic, and lexical deviations from native-speaker norms (Genesee, 1987; Lapkin, Swain, & Shapson, 1990). In addition, observers of immersion classrooms find that students have relatively little opportunity for the use of extended discourse in class. One study of more than 10 sixth-grade French immersion classes found that when students spoke in teacher-directed activities, their utterances were longer than a clause in length only 14% of the time (Harley, Allen, Cummins, & Swain, 1990; Swain, 1988).

Although in full language immersion programs in the United States the rule has been for students to speak exclusively in the second language in the classroom once they are capable of this, second-grade children in the first U.S. immersion program in Culver City reported using English in the classroom about half of the time (Cohen & Lebach, 1974). And this was in a program in which the teachers scrupulously adhered to their target-language guise and had other teachers provide English language arts in the middle grades. So the fact that students spoke and still speak a considerable amount of English during immersion language classes could have contributed to limitations in their productive skills in the foreign language.

Yet another potential source for a gap between comprehension and production may be the systematic reluctance or inability of the immersion students to perform cognitive operations in the target language, both in and out of the classroom. In essence, the students may not be as immersed as teachers and administrators think they are. Apparently this phenomenon has not been researched at all in immersion classrooms. We might hypothesize that a program that is conducted primarily in a language other than that of the community has the potential to stimulate the performance of cognitive operations largely through the target language both during the processing of academic tasks (*academic language proficiency*) and during social interactions (*conversational language proficiency*) (Cummins, 1991).

In the recent research on cognitive processes and second-language acquisition cited previously, Cohen and Olshtain (1993) provided detailed descriptions of the languages used by nonnatives to perform cognitive operations in their native and target languages while planning and executing utterances in the target language. Discovery of the extent to which speakers perform cognitive operations in their native language during their comprehension and production of target language utterances may shed some light on the acquisition process, because it would give an indication of actual involvement with the target language. Because they immerse youngsters in a target language, early full-immersion programs may provide a rich context for SLA research on the extent to which the target language is used in performing cognitive operations, especially if the research focuses on learners that have been in the program the longest (e.g., 5 to 7 years).

With the benefits of this SLA context in mind, we designed a study to examine the nature of the internal language environment (i.e., how learners process language in their minds) emerging in learners as a result of the specific external language environment in immersion classrooms (Cohen, 1994; Parker, Heitzman, Fjerstad, Babbs, & Cohen, this volume).[1] In the study we investigated the extent to which learners use their L1 and L2 in performing cognitive operations and identified points at which they switched from performing these operations in the target language to performing them in their native language.

We conducted the study at a Spanish full-immersion school in St. Paul, Minnesota. Thirty-two students were selected from Grades 3–6. We collected verbal report data from students as they engaged in school tasks such as solving math problems, reading social studies textbooks, doing science tasks, and writing essays. The primary means of data collection was verbal report, more precisely, through the use of think-aloud (the students' simply thinking aloud without analyzing what they were doing), self-observation (the students' analyzing what they were doing at the time or what they had just done), and self-report (the students' indicating what they tended to do). A team of four University of Minnesota undergraduates and one postgraduate collected the data over a 5-month period.[2]

The finding for the immersion students under study was that English seemed to play a more prominent role in their internal language environment than Spanish. In responding to both numerical and verbal problems in math, for example, students reported favoring English in their cognitive processing and were also observed to be doing so. They would read the problem in Spanish but would shift to English immediately, or as soon as they had some conceptual difficulty. Here is an example:

[Referring to the following problem: *Teri usó la computadora 3 veces más minutos que Sue. ¿Cuánto tiempo trabajó Teri con la computadora?* Teri used the computer three times more minutes than Sue. How long did Teri work with the computer?]

Researcher: When you read these instructions do you understand right away what it says in Spanish or when you read them do you think words in English?

Peter: I try and get them into English, so I can understand them a little bit better. (He reads the problem aloud in Spanish, then continues.) *Sue está aquí, cinquenta y quatro, uno, dos, tres . . . cinquenta . . . OK. ¿Cuánto tiempo . . . ?* [Sue is here, 54, 1, 2, 3 . . . 50 . . . OK. How long?] How many minutes? Three times as many minutes than Sue . . . whoa. OK. Fifty-four times three.

Researcher: What were you thinking before you went "OK"?

Peter: I was thinking that Sue, right there, fifty-four; it says three times more . . . than Sue. So, three times four, twelve. Three times five, fifteen six. A hundred and sixty-two.

---

[1]For a full definition of the internal and external language environments, see Parker et al. (this volume).

[2]For further details of the study, see Parker et al. (this volume).

In this problem, Peter began thinking in Spanish about how to do the problem. He encountered difficulty, and then began to think in English. In other content areas, such as social studies, the students also tended to favor English for solving complex conceptual problems. Some of the most convincing data from the study were the self-report data regarding what the respondents "tended to do." In case after case, the subjects reported tending to use English in a variety of school tasks, especially for performing cognitive operations pertaining to math. If, in fact, this is the case, it may help to explain why full-immersion students in the Twin Cities (and elsewhere) continue to have gaps in their oral and written production in the foreign language even after being immersed for almost 7 years.

The reality may be that the internal language environment of the students is not as intensively foreign-language oriented as the outside observer might think. After all, conclusions derived from observations are based largely on investigation of the external language environment, which seems impressively filled with the foreign language: the teachers speak exclusively in that language and when students are called on by the teachers, they also speak in that foreign language, however briefly. Yet the true picture may be more consistent with the findings from this study—that there is an underground of English-language use, out of earshot of the teacher, in pupils' working groups, and most importantly, in the students' minds, where teachers and course materials do not tread. As one high-achieving fourth-grade student, Bill, put it:

> You usually think that in an immersion school, it's totally in Spanish. If you get caught speaking English, you'll like be in trouble, but that's not really what it is. I mean, you're always thinking in English. I mean they can't really stop you from thinking in English. You can think Spanish, you can act Spanish, you can do everything in Spanish, but you're really not a Mexican.

This resistance to being too immersed in Spanish may be sociolinguistically inevitable, especially for immersion programs that take place in areas of the United States where possibilities for contact with native speakers of the immersion language are limited.

Our study may help to explain why immersion children do not seem to fall behind children in the regular school curriculum. As Lambert and Tucker posited many years ago in an effort to interpret why French immersion students did so well in and through English-language skills:

> (The) children may never have been on "vacation" in English at all. Instead, they may have transferred basic skills of reading, concept development, word manipulation, and verbal creativity *through* French to English by reprocessing in English all the information they received through French, or by simultaneously processing in French and English. The possibility we see in these results (which is only an idea to be tested with further experimentation) is that children of normal intelligence, trained through a second language, process new information encountered

in class both in the second language—thereby developing skill with that language—as well as in the native language. (Lambert & Tucker, 1972, p. 82; emphasis in original)

This phenomenon of *reprocessing* is most likely what we uncovered in the St. Paul immersion study, where the students reprocess in English much, but not all, of the information received through Spanish. It is not so surprising, for example, that the students in this study switched to English to think through their word problems. After 6 or 7 years of immersion schooling, the learners were performing externally or socially in Spanish when necessary, but not necessarily internally—that is, psychologically or cognitively. There are various reasons why learners may wish to reprocess the material in their native language. Some of them are:

- To help them maintain their level of concentration by easing the load on the memory; native-language words are usually more familiar to the learners and are generally stored more easily in memory.
- To help them deal with semantic complexity—sorting out complicated ideas.
- To help them deal with syntactic complexity—understanding how sentences are constructed.
- To provide a comprehension check, that is, to see if they really understood the target language input.

In the St. Paul case, it would appear that all of these reasons for translation applied. Perhaps future research could determine when each of these or other reasons motivates learners to opt for the strategy of translation. So this area needs more extensive research. What we may be finding is that observational studies that have counted the minutes that the target language was being used by students and teachers in the classroom (e.g., Legaretta, 1977), are just getting at the tip of the iceberg. In other words, what goes on externally does not necessarily reflect what goes on internally. More research is needed to tease out the true workings of an immersion classroom. Research is also needed on the internal language environment of students in bilingual classrooms and the possible effects of having teachers model their own thought processes aloud in the target language as they work through school tasks. Perhaps learners need more exposure to the language of thought for them to indulge in it themselves.

One of the major advantages of a full-immersion program is that the students are adept enough at translating from one language to another to be capable of rapid translation so that they can, for example, think through in English a word problem written in Spanish. As illustrated in the math example, this pattern of translation appears to be quite common. One of the reasons why partial-immersion students have been found to be less successful at math than full-immersion students (see Swain, 1984, p. 91) may be that they are not as successful at rapid translation of math concepts into the native language.

Studies in *natural translation* (i.e., translation by naive child translators—bilingual children without any special training in translation) have enlightened us about what may make a fourth- or fifth-grade bilingual youngster a good translator (Malakoff, 1992). Malakoff purposely assigned the students translation tasks involving ambiguity and word/sentence segmentation in which the native- and foreign-language patterns were at odds. The main factor contributing to successful translation appeared to be *metalinguistic awareness*—the ability to step back from the comprehension or production of an utterance in order to consider the linguistic form and structure underlying the meaning of the utterance. It stands to reason that the less facility young bilinguals have with the target language, the more unnatural their translating will be.

In addition to comparing full immersion with partial immersion, we might ask how the language processing of the St. Paul immersion students compares with that of balanced bilingual children. There is at least one study that looked at first- and second-language processing of tasks by subjects who were not native speakers of the dominant language of the society. A study by Saville-Troike focused on nine nonnative English-speaking children during their first 6 months in the United States. She reported that an 8-year-old native speaker of Chinese used English in doing her English-language workbook tasks, but when she worked in her mathematics workbook, her private speech was in Chinese (Saville-Troike, 1988, p. 586). Without extensive data on balanced bilinguals, it is difficult to know how typical or atypical these results with immersion students really are. Perhaps it is unfair to assume that more extensive thinking in the target language is expected or desirable, but if we were to assume this, then perhaps it is unreasonable to expect the level of attainment in the productive language skills to be greater than it is at present.

5. CONCLUSIONS

I have examined three areas for research into whether instruction might enhance second-language acquisition: (1) the benefits of instructing learners in strategies for learning language more effectively; (2) the effects of explicit instruction on the acquisition of speech acts and the issue of what needs to be taught more explicitly because it may not just be picked up along the way through repeated exposure; (3) the pedagogical consequences of using immersion education as an instructional approach for foreign-language acquisition, and the need to explore the internal language environment of the learners.

REFERENCES

Bamford, K., and D. T. Mizokawa. (1991). "Additive-Bilingual (Immersion) Education: Cognitive and Language Development," *Language Learning* 41(3), 413–429.

Baumann, J. F. (1984). "The Effectiveness of a Direct Instruction Paradigm for Teaching Main Idea Comprehension," *Reading Research Quarterly* 20(1), 93–115.

Billmyer, K. (1990). " 'I Really Like Your Lifestyle': ESL Learners Learning How to Compliment," *Penn Working Papers in Educational Linguistics* 6(2), 31–48.

Blum-Kulka, S., and E. Olshtain. (1986). "Too Many Words: Length of Utterance and Pragmatic Failure," *Studies in Second Language Acquisition* 8, 47–61.

Brown, A. L., A. S. Palincsar, and B. B. Armbruster. (1984). "Instructing Comprehension-Fostering Activities in Interactive Learning Situations." *Learning and Comprehension of Texts*, ed. by H. Mandl et al., pp. 255–286. Hillsdale, NJ: Lawrence Erlbaum Associates.

Cohen, A. D. (1990). *Language Learning: Insights for Learners, Teachers, and Researchers.* New York: Newbury House/Harper Collins.

———. (1994). "The Language Used to Perform Cognitive Operations During Full-Immersion Math Tasks," *Language Testing* 11(2), 171–195.

———, and S. Lebach. (1974). "A Language Experiment in California: Student, Teacher, Parent, and Community Reactions after Three Years," *Workpapers in Teaching English as a Second Language,* 8, pp. 33–46. Los Angeles, University of California at Los Angeles.

———, and E. Olshtain. (1993). "The Production of Speech Acts by EFL Learners," *TESOL Quarterly* 27(1), 33–56.

———, and D. Rosenstein. (1986). "Advanced EFL Apologies: What Remains to Be Learned?," *International Journal of the Sociology of Language* 62(6), 51–74.

———, and M. Swain. (1979). "Bilingual Education: The 'Immersion' Model in the North American Context." *Sociolinguistic Aspects of Language Learning and Teaching*, ed. by J. B. Pride, pp. 144–151. Oxford: Oxford University Press.

Cummins, J. (1991). "Conversational and Academic Language Proficiency in Bilingual Contexts," *AILA Review* 8, 75–89.

Garner, R. (1987). *Metacognition and Reading Comprehension.* Norwood, NJ: Ablex.

———. (1990). "When Children and Adults Do Not Use Learning Strategies: Toward a Theory of Settings," *Review of Educational Research* 60(4), 517–529.

Genesee, F. (1987). *Learning through Two Languages.* Rowley, MA: Newbury House.

Harley, B., P. Allen, J. Cummins, and M. Swain. (1990). *The Development of Second Language Proficiency.* Cambridge: Cambridge University Press.

Kessler, C., and E. Quinn. (1982). "Cognitive Development in Bilingual Environments." *Issues in International Bilingual Education: The Role of the Vernacular*, ed. by B. Hartford, A. Valdman, and R. Foster. New York: Plenum.

Lambert, W. E., and G. R. Tucker. (1972). *Bilingual Education of Children: The St. Lambert Experiment.* Rowley, MA: Newbury House.

Lapkin, S., M. Swain, and S. Shapson. (1990). "French Immersion Research Agenda for the 90's," *Canadian Modern Language Review* 46(4), 636–674.

Legaretta, D. (1977). "Language Choice in Bilingual Classrooms." *TESOL Quarterly* 11(1), 9–16.

Malakoff, M. E. (1992). "Translation Ability: A Natural Bilingual and Metalinguistic Skill." *Cognitive Processing in Bilinguals*, ed. by R. J. Harris, pp. 515–529. Amsterdam: North-Holland.

Olshtain, E., and S. Blum-Kulka. (1984). "Cross-Linguistic Speech Act Studies: Theoretical and Empirical Issues." In *Language Across Cultures*, ed. by L. Mac Mathina and D. Singleton, pp. 235–248. Dublin: Irish Association for Applied Linguistics.

———, and A. Cohen. (1990). "The Learning of Complex Speech Act Behavior," *TESL Canada Journal* 7(2), 45–65.

O'Malley, J. M., and U. A. Chamot. (1990). *Learning Strategies in Second Language Acquisition.* Cambridge: Cambridge University Press.

Oxford, R. L. (1990). *Language Learning Strategies: What Every Teacher Should Know.* New York: Newbury House/Harper & Row.

Oxford, R., and A. D. Cohen. (1992). "Language Learning Strategies: Crucial Issues of Concept and Classification," *Applied Language Learning* 3(1–2), 1–35.

Pearson, P. D., and J. A. Dole. (1987). "Explicit Comprehension Instruction: A Review of Research and a New Conceptualization of Learning," *Elementary School Journal* 88(2), 151–165.

Rosebery, A. S., B. Warren, and F. R. Conant. (1992). "Appropriating Scientific Discourse: Findings from Language Minority Classrooms," *Journal of the Learning Sciences* 2(1), 61–94.

Saville-Troike, M. (1988). "Private Speech: Evidence for Second Language Learning Strategies During the 'Silent' Period." *Journal of Child Language* 15, 567–590.

Swain, M. (1984). "A Review of Immersion Education in Canada: Research and Evaluation Studies," California State Department of Education, *Studies on Immersion Education*, pp. 87–112, Office of Bilingual Bicultural Education, California State Department of Education, Sacramento, CA.

———. (1988). "Manipulating and Complementing Content Teaching to Maximize Second Language Learning," *TESL Canada Journal* 6, 68–83.

Wolfson, N., and J. Manes. (1980). "The Compliment as a Social Strategy," *Papers in Linguistics* 13, 391–410.

Chapter 15

Exploring the Role of Foreign Language in Immersion Education

James E. Parker
Shirley M. Heitzman
Amy M. Fjerstad
Lisa M. Babbs
Andrew D. Cohen
University of Minnesota

1. INTRODUCTION

Full Language Immersion Programs (FLIPs), in which students study all or part of their course content in a nonnative language, have become increasingly popular in the United States and Canada over the past 20 years as a form of elementary and secondary education. These programs are predicated on the assumption that second language acquisition (SLA) occurs most easily and rapidly in the target-language environment and culture. Immersion programs thus attempt to duplicate this environment, surrounding the learners with the target language and exposing them to the target-language culture as much as possible. The immersion environment is thought to provide ample incentive and opportunity for learners to acquire both receptive (reading and listening) and productive (speaking and writing) target-language skills (Lapkin, Swain, & Shapson, 1990).

Recent research has shown that students enrolled in immersion programs make normal or better-than-normal progress in content subjects that are taught through a second language (Cohen & Swain, 1979; Genesee, 1987). In addition, research over the past two decades has shown that immersion students' literacy and fluency in their native language does not seem to suffer and may even be enhanced by participation in early total immersion programs (Lambert & Tucker, 1972, p. 203).

But although students in FLIPs have achieved an impressive level of functional communicative proficiency, there appear to be clear gaps in their second language skills. Recent research on French immersion programs in Canada has shown that although students demonstrate very high level receptive skills, they "remain well behind their francophone peers in the productive skills of speaking and writing" (Swain, 1992, p. 644). Despite receiving many years of comprehensible input, students in the French immersion programs produce spoken and written French that deviates from native-speaker norms morphologically, syntactically, and lexically (Genesee 1987). Research conducted by Harley and Swain (cited in Genesee, 1987, p. 60) suggests that although they are communicatively effective, target-language utterances produced by immersion students are less subtle and complex than those of native speakers and tend to be distinctly nonidiomatic.

Learners may also fail to approach nativelike production in the target language if they speak their native language with each other instead of speaking the target language. However, few studies on immersion programs have documented the extent to which learners actually use the native language rather than the target language in the classroom. Cohen and Lebach (1974), in their study of the Culver City immersion program, reported that the second graders in that program reported using English about half of the time in the classroom. However, they collected no observational data on learners' language use in that study. But researchers on the French immersion programs in Canada note that learners seem to use a lot of English with each other. Swain commented: "my own informal observations indicate that most peer-peer interaction that is not teacher-directed is likely to occur in English rather than in French" (1985, p. 246). Again, however, she collected no systematic observational data in that study. In fact, there seem to be few recent studies which address the extent to which learners use the native and target language in the immersion classroom, especially in non-teacher-fronted situations (Swain, personal communication, June 1, 1993).

In recent work on cognitive processes and second language acquisition, Cohen and Olshtain (1993) provided evidence for an interaction between native and target languages in the planning and production of apologies in the target language. Although no systematic study has been made of the role of immersion learners' native and target language systems in the planning and production of task-related target language discourse, it is possible that learners may use their native language in the verbal reasoning processes that accompany classroom tasks. Extensive use of a learner's native language in task-related public and private speech (Vygotsky, 1986) may indicate that a speaker is not fully engaging the target language as a carrier language for communication or intrapersonal reasoning processes. Therefore, although learners in immersion programs are continually surrounded by the target language in theory, they may not actually be surrounded by or be using the target language as much as teachers and administrators think they are.

This study was designed to examine the nature of patterns of language use that emerge in learners as these patterns relate to the nature of the specific internal and external language environments established in immersion classrooms. These environments are defined using the learner as a locus of reference.

The *external language environment* is defined as all language-related elements that influence the learner from *without*: curriculum goals, classroom policies and procedures, classroom materials, the nature of classroom activities, the members of the speech community, the language spoken by members of the speech community, and the nature of communicative exchanges between students, teachers and administrators.

The *internal language environment* is defined as the way learners process language in their minds: their native and second language systems and the role played by each in performing the cognitive tasks that accompany second language use. The internal language environment includes sociolinguistic rules, problem-solving strategies, and decision-making strategies used by the students, as well as their planning for the production of output.

We hope that this examination of the external and internal language environments may shed further light on the true role of the foreign (target) language in the immersion classroom. We asked the following specific research questions: (1) To what extent do learners use their native and target languages to communicate and to perform cognitive tasks in the immersion classroom. (2) During what tasks or learning moments do learners switch from performing cognitive operations in the target language to performing them in their native language?

2. DESIGN

2.1. Sample

Thirty-two pupils, Grades 3–6, were selected from a Spanish-language full immersion program in St. Paul, Minnesota: six at Grade 3, seven at Grade 4, nine at Grade 5, and ten at Grade 6. The sampling began at the Grade 3 level because previous research has shown that learners at this grade level are able to provide reliable verbal reports on their language-using strategies (Cohen, 1992, 1987a; Garner, 1987).

The participants were selected by their teachers and were intended to represent learners at three levels (high, medium, and low) of both Spanish language proficiency and academic achievement. The Spanish language proficiency ratings were based on the teachers' ratings and on the standardized test, *La Prueba Riverside de Realización en Español* (The Riverside Publishing Company, 1964).[1] The academic skills rating was based on the teachers' ratings and on the standardized test, *SRA Survey of Basic Skills* (1985).[2]

---

[1]Subtests included in this test are reading (reading comprehension, vocabulary, study skills), language (grammar, capitalization, spelling, punctuation), and mathematics (math computation, math problem solving.)

[2]Subtests included in this test are vocabulary, reading comprehension, mechanics, usage, spelling, mathematics (computation, concepts, problem solving), reference materials, social studies, and science.

2.2. Setting

2.2.1. Immersion Curriculum

Early Full Language Immersion Programs are designed to serve a pair of goals: the mastery of the elementary-school curriculum and the facilitation of second language acquisition. Content areas covered include mathematics, science, social studies and current events, and English language arts. With respect to the standard elementary school curriculum, the content and activities did not seem to differ significantly from traditional elementary school classrooms.[3]

The immersion program must also meet the additional challenges of teaching a second language. Principal Luz Maria Serano stated that although it was difficult to bring students to nativelike fluency with respect to dialect and idomatic variation, she believed that it was possible to produce learners who were able to speak Spanish that was both grammatical and fluid.

> I tell the parents of our students that their children will be "functionally bilingual." By that I mean that the children will have a good command of the language. If the parents were to take their children to a Spanish-speaking country, the children could lead their parents around and act as an interpreter, but it is unlikely that the children would be mistaken for native speakers. (personal communication, June 17, 1993)

Serano suggested that nativelike fluency in terms of dialect and idiomatic variation may be unrealistic goals for an immersion program situated in a region that is home to so few native speakers of the target language.

It must be noted that all teachers in this immersion program taught both the Spanish and the English sections of the day. This aspect of the immersion program differed significantly from the ideal Spanish immersion program described by Cohen and Swain (1979), where learners have a monolingual Spanish relationship with the Spanish teacher and a monolingual English relationship with the English teacher. It is therefore important to keep in mind that the learners in the St. Paul program had an essentially bilingual relationship with their teacher, probably an influence on the language use of both teachers and learners.

The amount of time devoted daily to English-language instruction in reading and language arts increases as the learners proceed through grades K–6. Learners in Grades K–1 receive no English language instruction, learners in Grades 2–3 receive up to an hour a day, and learners in Grades 4–6 receive up to an hour and 15 minutes each day. These sessions are introduced as soon as school opens in the fall, and their duration remains constant throughout the school year.

---

[3]Non-participant-observations were made in the fifth- and sixth-grade classrooms at the Webster Magnate School in St. Paul, Minnesota, for purposes of comparison.

Thus, participants in this study (Grades 3–6) all spent between 60 and 75 minutes each day in English language arts.

2.2.2. Teaching Staff

Teachers in the immersion program were either native speakers of Spanish or English-dominant bilinguals. We observed classes taught by native speakers and English-dominant bilinguals.

2.2.3. Classroom Situations

The classroom arrangement reflected the teachers' commitment to philosophies that encourage group-work learning. The classroom setup seemed to effectively promote group work, because learners worked together on many tasks that were assigned. However, learners also worked individually. Classroom activity seemed to fall into two types: teacher-fronted and non-teacher-fronted. In a teacher-fronted situation the classroom activity was in a lecture-style format in which the teacher explained parts of the text and then asked the learners questions. During this kind of teacher-fronted situation in the immersion classroom, learners tended to talk to the teacher but not among themselves, and they generally stayed in their seats. However, students sometimes talked among themselves, in whispers or low voices, even during a teacher-fronted situation. In non-teacher-fronted situations, learners worked alone or in small groups. They talked freely with each other and walked around the classroom or stayed at their desks as they needed to.

2.3. Instrumentation

2.3.1. Verbal Report

In order to describe the learner's internal environment, *verbal report*[4] procedures (Cohen, 1987b, 1991) were used to collect data on learners' use of their native and foreign language in performing cognitive operations for solving math problems. More specifically, verbal report procedures included: *think-aloud* (externalizing verbalized thoughts in conjunction with a specific task that one is doing, without analyzing what one is doing), *self-observation* (introspecting about current thoughts and/or retrospecting about something specific that one is doing, has just done, or has done at some earlier time), and *self-report* (indicating what one tends to do, without referring to any specific cognitive activity).

---

[4]Generally, a verbal report will contain samples of each of these three elements. However, respondents were encouraged to do less self-report and more self-observation or self-revelation relating to specific tasks in progress or tasks recently completed.

2.3.2. Classroom Observation

Nonparticipant classroom observation (Bailey, 1985) was used to obtain data on general language use patterns in whole-class, small-group, and paired inter-action—who said what to whom under what circumstances, and in what language.

2.3.3. Questionnaire-Based Interviews

All learners were interviewed initially to elicit self-report data on their abilities, attitudes, and preferences about thinking in Spanish and about using Spanish in speaking with their peers and other adults. Learners were also asked to report on any opportunities to use Spanish within their family or community.

2.4. Data Collection Procedures

A team of five research assistants from the University of Minnesota collected the data over a five-month period from December 1992 to April 1993. Repeated interactions between the research assistants and study participants during this time enabled the research team to establish rapport with the participants and thereby increase the reliability of the findings. Members of the research team were native speakers of English with a range of experience using Spanish: one was a fluent nonnative speaker of Spanish, two were limited speakers of Spanish, and two had no prior experience with Spanish.

2.4.1. Verbal Report Protocols

Most of the verbal report data presented in this study was collected inside of the classroom in non-teacher-fronted situations. The researchers made no effort to direct the students to specific tasks. Rather, they prompted participants to externalize their thoughts or to think aloud in conjunction with whatever task they happened to be engaged in at the time, including numerical and verbal math problems, social studies, science, and essay writing. Researchers sometimes worked with individual learners and at other times worked with learners who were in pairs or small groups.

During interaction sessions, the researchers asked learners to indicate how they used their language systems in comprehending and completing academic tasks. They asked the learners to identify areas in which they had difficulty understanding instructions and content in textbooks and worksheets. They also asked them to indicate points at which they got stuck while speaking in Spanish. From time to time the investigators interspersed questions about the learners' abilities, attitudes, and preferences with regard to using their Spanish and English language systems in the classroom. Research assistants tape-recorded these sessions and encouraged the learners to do their verbal reporting in whichever language they felt more comfortable using at any given moment, even if the investigator did not understand Spanish.

2.4.2. Classroom Observations

Non-participant-observation data was collected on the language used inside and outside of the classroom, in teacher-fronted and non-teacher-fronted situations. The identities of the participants in conversational exchanges and the language used were noted, as well as the nature of the discourse (i.e. task-related or social).

2.4.3. Questionnaire Based Interviews

During individual interview sessions, conducted prior to the onset of classroom observations, we asked learners general questions about which language they used in doing their work and in interacting with other learners and teachers. We asked them about where they got stuck when they used Spanish to perform classroom tasks or to converse with peers or teachers; we also asked them about what strategies they used to overcome these difficulties, and about areas where they had difficulty understanding verbal or written instructions. We conducted these interviews in English and tape-recorded them.[5]

2.5. Data Analysis Procedures

2.5.1. Verbal Report Data

We made written transcriptions of all tape-recorded verbal report data. We organized these verbal report data by subject matter, for example, math, science, reading, and so on, and by the language of verbal cognition used, for example, Spanish, English, or a combination of the two. We also analyzed learners' explanations of language use to find the motivations behind language use. We also coded all data according to type of verbal report: think aloud, self-observation (introspective and retrospective), and self-report, as previously defined. We then coded each instance according to the following criteria: language used (English or Spanish); type of classroom situation (teacher-fronted or non-teacher-fronted); and the orientation of the situation (task or social).

2.5.2. Non-Participant Observation Data

In order to understand how students and teachers used language in various contexts, we tape-recorded non-participant-observation data and prepared written transcriptions from the tapes. Using Schlegloff and Sacks' (1973) concept of adjacency pairs, we counted instances of learner and teacher language use in the

---

[5]These initial intake interviews are the only data in the study for which the researchers explicitly instructed the learners to respond in English.

classroom. An *instance* is defined as a speech set that includes, but is not limited to, at least one adjacency pair. Thus, an instance includes at least one utterance (of any length) from one speaker and another utterance from a second speaker. An example of an instance is a teacher's question to a learner and the learner's response to the teacher. Although some instances we recorded were only one adjacency pair, other instances were composed of many adjacency pairs. We then coded each instance as in Section 2.5.1. Some non-participant-observation data that was not tape-recorded was also collected. This data was also written up and analyzed with the data mentioned previously.

2.5.3. Questionnaire-Type Interview Data

We also prepared written transcriptions of initial interviews with learners. We analyzed these data to find learners' motivations for language use in a particular situation, either in communicating with other people in the classroom or when doing their work.

3. RESULTS

We describe here learners' use of language in the classroom with their peers and teachers, as well as learners' use of Spanish and English as they comprehended and solved mathematical problems individually and in small groups. We also present relevant verbal report data and interview data on language use in the classroom. In all quotes from learners, grade (3, 4, 5, or 6), academic achievement (H, M, L), and Spanish language proficiency (H, M, L) is indicated after the learner's pseudonyms. Therefore, sixth-grader Todd, of average academic and Spanish language achievement, is marked as follows: Todd (6MM). Instances of Spanish use in learner quotes are presented in *italics*.

3.1. Language Use in Immersion Classrooms

Nonparticipant-observation data on learners' language use in the classroom is summarized in Table 15.1. Each line reflects the number of instances of language use that were collected in that context. Each instance was at least one adjacency pair, but it is important to keep in mind that many instances were much longer than one adjacency pair. For example, some instances in English went on for many minutes, whereas others in English or Spanish were very short. Thus, the percentages given are not a reflection of the actual time spent using a language, because the instances lasted different lengths of time.

3.1.1. Spanish Use in the Classroom

In this full-immersion program, learners in the fifth and sixth grades self-reported using Spanish with teachers, and very occasionally with friends, during initial interviews and later interaction sessions. As we see in Table 15.1, non-

TABLE 15.1
Language Use in 5th and 6th Grade Immersion Classrooms

Social and Task-Oriented Teacher-Fronted Situations			Social and Task-Oriented Small-Group Situations		
Language	Number of Instances	% of Instances	Language	Number of Instances	% of Instances
Spanish	7	70	Spanish	4	22
English	3	30	English	14	78
Total	10	100	Total	18	100

Teacher-Fronted, Task-Oriented Situations			Small-Group, Task-Oriented Situations		
Language	Number of Instances	% of Instances	Language	Number of Instances	% of Instances
Spanish	7	88	Spanish	4	27
English	1	12	English	11	73
Total	8	100	Total	15	100

participant-observation results tended to confirm learners' reports about their own behavior. Learners showed a clear preference for speaking Spanish in teacher-fronted, task-oriented situations (7 of 8 instances). On one occasion in Grade 6, Donna (6MM) switched from English to Spanish in the middle of a response to the teacher, possibly in order to comply with this sociolinguistic rule, as seen in 1:

(1) Donna (6MM) was asked a question about how she had worked out the math problem by the student teacher, a native speaker of Spanish from Chile.
Donna responds: If the fraction's not . . . *si no está en forma simple* '[If (the fraction) is not in simple form (reduced).]'

Learners also used Spanish in small-group, task-oriented situations, although they used it much less than in teacher-fronted, task-oriented situations: 27% of the instances in small-group situations compared to 88% of the instances in teacher-fronted situations.

Furthermore, although learners used Spanish in small-group situations, they did not seem to use it equally for task-related and non-task-related purposes. Despite the fact that few social uses of either language were noted overall (five instances of English), it is important to note that we observed no social use of Spanish in this full-immersion program in Grades 5 and 6. Rather, Spanish seemed to be used exclusively for task-related purposes. This finding differs from Cohen and Lebach's findings on second-graders in the Spanish early-full-immersion program in Culver City, CA: "There were no particular things that they said in either Spanish or English . . . Children used Spanish and English in free variation in the classroom" (1974, p. 39). In the St. Paul Grade 5 and 6 immersion classrooms, learners seemed to use Spanish to perform academic tasks rather than talk to their friends socially.

It is also important to note that although learners did use Spanish on task-related activities, they used English much more than they used Spanish. Although we recorded only four instances of the use of Spanish in a small-group, task-related activity, we recorded at least eleven instances of learners using English in the same environment, nearly three times the number of instances of Spanish. These findings suggest that even though learners used Spanish in small-group settings, they used English much more. This conclusion is supported by learner's self- reports. One sixth-grader, Halena (6HH), commented, "Well, most people in our class, when they work together they just talk . . . in English."

3.1.2. English Use in the Classroom

Whereas Spanish seemed to be used almost exclusively for task-related activities, English was used for both task-related and social purposes. Learners reported using English during the English part of the day, during lunch, during recess (even during recess in the Spanish part of the day), and with their friends in general, for a variety of reasons. Learners reported using English because they did not have enough Spanish vocabulary, because speaking Spanish was difficult, and because they worried about making mistakes in Spanish. Learners reported that they used English when they believed their vocabulary in Spanish was not comprehensive enough to talk about things that were not school-related, as Emily reported in 2:

(2) Researcher: Do you ever try to speak Spanish?
Emily (5HH): One day we all said we're only gonna speak Spanish the whole day, but it didn't work, because my friend likes to tell the w-h-o-l-e thing that happens to her and she talks a lot and adds lots of details . . . We would probably get to some words we don't know and because of that English is just easier.
Researcher: Do you think it's important to speak Spanish in the classroom with your friends?
Emily: I don't really think if it's important or not . . . I just talk it cuz it's easy for me. Except when we're talking not about stuff from school but other stuff.

Emily was one of the few students who claimed speaking Spanish was easy for her. However, even this A student said she had difficulty when it came to talking about nonschool "stuff."

Learners also reported using English because they could speak English quickly and with little effort—they considered speaking Spanish all of the time a strain. Some immersion learners, like Allen (5MM), suggested that the extra effort required to use Spanish was a direct result of needing to use English to formulate Spanish utterances:

(3) Researcher: How do you feel about speaking Spanish?
Allen (5MM): I used to like it a lot, but I don't like the Spanish part as much.
Researcher: Why?
Allen: Well, it's a . . . it's a strain.
Researcher: On your head?
Allen: Yeah . . . cuz first you gotta know what you're gonna say in English and then you gotta think what you're gonna say in Spanish and it's really hard, unless you are really good in Spanish.

Learners sometimes believed it was risky to speak Spanish when they were not concentrating on it, because they might make a mistake. Here Daniel (5MH) reported on the language of choice for him and his friends during the school day and why he thought that it was risky to speak Spanish on the playground at school:

(4) Researcher: What do you do on recess? Where do you go?
Daniel (5MH): Out on the playground, right out there . . . that's where kids play football and stuff and we speak English usually. It's just easier to speak English with your friends . . . like you might say something all weird and stuff . . . and it's not right . . . and you know it in English, but you might say it in Spanish and mess it up. You might say *Te-a-soy* (ungrammatical: You [direct object]-to-I am.) and that's like 'You are me' (self-translation). You'd feel all weird.

Thus, in a school where learners were surrounded by other learners who also studied Spanish and would most likely notice a grammatical or pronunciation error, this learner avoided speaking the target language because the possibility of an error, and the concomitant loss of face, was too great.

In fact, non-participant-observation seemed to confirm that the use of English, in contrast to Spanish, tended to be among peers rather than between teachers and learners. Learners almost never used English with a teacher in a teacher-fronted situation. On the one occasion that we observed English used with a teacher in a teacher-fronted situation, the use of English was clearly inappropriate, which was signaled by his classmates' gasps of surprise and muffled laughter:

(5) The sixth grade class was correcting a spelling test. The teacher called on learners to spell words out loud, using the Spanish alphabet. A learner was having difficulty spelling the Spanish word *jornada* ['working day, a day's journey']. In order to spell the word, he said, *Hache, oh*—no, I mean *ge oh*—[(the letter) j, (the letter) o,—]. The learner then simply reverted to English and said 'jay (j)'.

When he did this, the whole class erupted into laughter or talking, indicating the inappropriateness of the response in the English alphabet.

Learners thus tended to follow the sociolinguistic rules described previously: Spanish with teachers in teacher-fronted situations and sometimes for task-related activities in small groups; English with classmates in non-teacher-fronted situations for both task-related and social purposes.

3.2. Language Use in Non-Teacher-Fronted, Task Oriented Settings

Although learners had a greater tendency to use Spanish in small-group task-oriented interactions than in other non-teacher-fronted situations, as we suggested previously, it would appear that learners did not make exclusive use of Spanish either to interact with peers or to engage in self-directed reasoning processes. Significantly, learners appeared to use their Spanish and English language systems to perform coordinate sets of speech acts.

Immersion learners appeared to use Spanish only to perform a rather limited number of task-related speech acts: reading text, rereading or restating information drawn from target-language materials, and producing answer-oriented output. In contrast, many learners seemed to favor English to perform a relatively wide range of task-related speech acts: to perform calculations and verbally based reasoning processes, to facilitate group interaction and confer with peers, to provide other learners with explanations, and to indicate points where they were experiencing difficulty with either the problem or their use of Spanish. In some instances where the learners used English as the principle carrier language for communication, the only Spanish-language items they used were lexical items drawn or derived directly from Spanish-language source materials. In 6, Donna (6MM) and Halena (6HH) were discussing a verbal math problem:

> (6) Halena (6HH): Look, Donna! *Dieciséis millón, seisciento sesenta y seis mil, seisciento sesenta y seis, residuo cuarenta.* [16,666,666 remainder 40.] That should be correct. I don't think that many numbers can fit in a calculator.
> Donna (6MM): OK, *hay cuarenta segundos,* [there are 40 seconds,] that's the first thing. And then there's—
> Halena: *y diez días.* [and ten days.]

In 6 Donna and Halena used a mixed-code interlanguage that is clearly functionally segregated. They used English as their primary carrier language for communication, using Spanish exclusively to refer to intermediate steps in solving the problem and the final answer to the problem.

In the case of Donna (6MM), this pattern of functionally segregated language use was also apparent in one-on-one interactions with the researcher. In 7, Donna (6MM) worked on a verbal math problem:

(7) *Ema, Marcos, José, y María tienen 9, 10, 11, y 13 años. José es mayor que María y menor que Ema. Marcos es menor que José y mayor que María. ¿Qué edad tienen cada uno?*
[Ema, Marcos, José, and María are 9, 10, 11, and 13 years old. José is older than María and younger than Ema. Marcos is younger than José and older than María. How old is each one?]

Donna (6MM): (reads problem to herself) *Ema, Marcos, José, y María tienen 9, 10, 11, y 13 años. José es mayor que María y menor que Ema. Marcos es menor que José y mayor que María. ¿Qué edad tienen cada uno?* (Donna finishes reading and begins to work) *Marcos es menor que José,* [Marcos is younger than José,] OK, that proves that Ema, um, (rereads from the problem) *José es mayor que María, y menor que Ema, Marcos es menor que José y mayor que María.* (end of reread) OK, um, yeah, here, *aquí se parece que Ema tiene trece años, porque nunca es menor que alguien, de los otros tres.* OK, then, *después,* OK, (rereads) *José es mayor que María y menor que Ema, y José es mayor que María,* (end reread) OK, *mayor que María,* [older than María,] uh, I'm trying to think here.
Researcher: In Spanish or in English?
Donna: I'm thinking in English. *José es mayor que María, y menor que Ema,* [José is older than María, and younger than Ema.] José is older than María. OK, it looks here like Marcos is, it looks here like José is eleven, *Marcos es menor que,* [Marcos is younger than,] hang on, and then here, cause it says *menor que* [younger than] um, wait, *Marcos es menor que José y mayor que María,* [Marcos is younger than José and older than María] which would make him ten, so Marcos is ten, and then María is nine.

After her initial reading aloud of the problem, Donna (6MM) produced nine Spanish-language utterances that were at least one clause in length. Of these nine, eight were either rereadings of the problem or restatements of information in the problem. It is crucial to note that in these instances Donna (6MM) used only those Spanish-language forms contained overtly in the given problem. Only once did her Spanish make reference, by way of providing the researcher with an explanation, to verbal reasoning processes:[6]

(8) Donna (6MM): Yeah, here *aquí* [here] *se parece que Ema tiene trece años porque nunca es menor que alguien, de los otros tres.* [it appears that Ema is thirteen years old because never is (she) younger than anyone, than the other three.] OK, then, *después,* [after,] OK . . .

---

[6]This may have been in part due to Donna's (6MM) perception of the researcher's expectations—that is, it is possible that Donna attempted to provide an explanation in Spanish because she believed it was expected of her.

It is interesting to note that Donna (6MM) frequently interspersed Spanish clauses with English words such as 'Wait!' Marina (5HH), working one-on-one with a researcher, displayed a similar pattern while solving a math problem presented in standard Arabic numerals:

(9) Researcher: Can you solve this problem out loud for me?
Marina (5HH): (Marina begins to write while she speaks) *Cinco va en cinco un vez.* [Five goes into five one time.] *Uno por cinco es cinco.* [One times five is five.] *Cinco por cinco es veinticinco.* [Five times five is twenty-five.] *Cinco va en veinticinco cinco veces.* [Five goes into twenty-five five times.] *Veinte* [Twenty] wait! (erases marks on paper) *Cinco va en cinco un* (sic) *vez.* [Five goes into five one time.] *Uno por cinco es cinco.* [One times five is five.] *Cinco menos cinco es cero.* [Five minus five is zero.] (sic) *vez.* [Five goes into five one time.] *Cinco por uno es cinco.* [Five times one is five.] (completes the subtraction) There!

In Example 9 it is apparent that when Marina (5HH) was specifically asked to work the problem out loud, she was able to produce the necessary Spanish language forms. Although the English-language prompt given by the bilingual researcher may have influenced Marina's (5HH) interspersion of English words, further work with this immersion learner suggested that she reverted to English of her own accord when she encountered difficulty in solving math problems. In 10, Marina (5HH) paused twice for substantial lengths of time:

(10) Researcher: *¿Y, la próxima?* [And, the next (problem)?]
Marina (5HH): *Dos va en ocho cuatro veces.* [Two goes into eight four times.] *Cuatro por dos es ocho.* [Four times two is eight.] *Ocho*—[Eight—] (Marina pauses for 14 seconds.) *Ocho menos ocho es cero.* [Eight minus eight is zero.] *Dos va en cuarenta, veinte veces.* [Two goes into forty, twenty times.] (pauses for 12 seconds. Marina begins again from the top, tracing the problem steps with her pencil.) *Dos va en ocho cuatro veces.* [Two goes into eight four times.] *Cuatro por dos es ocho.* [Four times two is eight.] *Dos por dos es cuatro.* [Two times two is four.] *Veinticuatro.* [Twenty-four.]

The researcher replayed the tape of this interaction for Marina (5HH) immediately after she completed the problem, questioning her at length about the pauses. During the questioning, Marina self-reported using English to perform cognitive calculations:

(11) Researcher: You said *ocho* [eight] and then you faded off. What were you doing there?
Marina (5HH): Trying to think.

> Researcher: What were you thinking?
> Marina: I was thinking, 'Wait a minute'!
> Researcher: Did you try to rework the problem?
> Marina: Yes.
> Researcher: Were you using language or just numbers?
> Marina: Language.
> Researcher: What language?
> Marina: English.
> Researcher: If you could describe when the voice in your head changes from Spanish to English, when would that be?
> Marina: When they (math problems) get harder.

In a number of cases similar to those mentioned earlier, learners reported using English-language lexical items to refer to both numbers and mathematical operators (plus, times, etc.) It seems that many learners, like Terry (5LM), used Spanish primarily when their language use, either written or spoken, was to be observed or read by the teacher:

(12) Terry (5LM): I go eight into nine and you put the one up there and you put the eight down here and the one and the six then the eight. Then you just count. I have all the numbers up there.
      Researcher: So that's how you'd normally do it? You wouldn't use the Spanish numerals?
      Terry: No, not a lot of times, unless I'm doing it on the chalkboard. He'll (the teacher) ask me to use the Spanish numerals and say it out loud. So I will.

These examples clearly indicate that learners use both the native and the target languages while solving target-language-based math problems. Learners appeared to use the target language for accessing the target language input and in formulating the target language output. They often preferred the native language when conferring with other learners and when performing verbally based cognitive calculations. Learners were able to use the target language when the teacher was reading the final answers or observing students as they worked problems in front of the class at the chalkboard.

4. DISCUSSION

We discovered several interesting things about how learners use language both as they communicate with their teachers and with other students and as they work on academic tasks. Taken together, these findings suggest that the foreign language plays a more limited role in the immersion classroom than current popular notions about immersion education would indicate.

4.1. Language Use in the Classroom—"Spanish for Special Purposes"

Both non-participant-observation data and learner self-report data suggest that students use Spanish when talking to the teacher in a teacher-fronted classroom situation. In a teacher-fronted situation learners probably feel pressure from the teacher and from their peers to conform to the 'Spanish only' rule of the immersion program. However, the situation changes when students are talking among themselves. In a non-teacher-fronted or teacher-fronted situation where students were addressing each other, the language tended to be English, unless students were working on an academic task. If students were working on an academic task together, they sometimes used Spanish. Students seemed to use Spanish only when working on academic tasks and not for social purposes.

To explain this phenomenon, Elaine Tarone has suggested that learners in an immersion program may be learning an academic Spanish, a 'Spanish for Special Purposes',[7] because there is pressure to produce Spanish only around academic tasks (personal communication, July 6, 1993). She has suggested that learners may not develop an adequate set of social language skills in the target language because they receive little social language input and have little opportunity to practice social conversation within the academic context of an immersion program. That is, as most of the input that learners receive in Spanish and most of the output that learners are forced to produce in Spanish revolve around academic topics, learners may develop only an academic Spanish. As a result, learners may lack the motivation or skills to discuss social events in Spanish, that is, the learners may find it difficult to discuss a television program like *Deep Space Nine* in Spanish because they lack the vocabulary or because they lack practice in discussing such matters in Spanish. Learners may lack the precision of expression that they find in English; they may not know how to say things like, 'neat', 'cool', 'awesome', etc., in Spanish, and they may thus prefer to express these ideas in English (Tarone, personal communication, July 6, 1993).

4.2. Language Use in Non-Teacher-Fronted Problem Solving Interactions

Non-participant-observation, verbal self-report, and verbal think-aloud data all seem to suggest that learners use the target language for purposes even more highly specialized than those suggested by the sociolinguistic rules we have outlined. Immersion learners appeared to use their native and target languages to

---

[7]Many thanks to Elaine Tarone for this explanation of why learners seem to use Spanish exclusively for academic purposes.

perform separate sets of speech acts, the foreign language being used primarily in direct reference to information presented in classroom source materials. Furthermore, immersion learners in the fifth and sixth grades appeared to use a mixed-code carrier language that was functionally highly segregated at both the clausal and discoursal levels, favoring their native language not only in communicative interaction but also during many of the verbalized cognitive processes that accompany the performance of classroom tasks.

Learners using the target language to perform classroom tasks often appeared to switch from the target language to the native language when they were experiencing difficulty with the Spanish language or with the problem itself.[8] This use of the foreign language as but one component of a mixed-code carrier language marks another significant deviation of the language of immersion learners from nativelike fluency.

One possible explanation for the relative absence of the target language in verbalized cognition may be that immersion learners lack the opportunity to witness other target language speakers modeling this type of discourse in the external language environment. In addition, the learners may lack the motivation or opportunity to produce externalized discourse of this nature. The presence of such opportunities may prove crucial in broadening the range of task-oriented target-language speech acts performed by immersion learners. Discussing the sciences and mathematics, Grayson Wheatley (1991) stressed the importance of public conversation in developing internal task-related dialogue, suggesting that class discussion "initiates 'conversations' which students then learn to carry on within themselves." Wheatley further suggested that it is through "continuing the conversations within ourselves" that we "begin to act mathematically" (p. 19). It may therefore be possible to increase the amount of target-language-based verbal cognition present in the internal language environment of immersion learners by using presentation strategies whereby the teacher and the students interact in producing models of problem-solving strategies in the target language.

5. CONCLUSION

Understanding the ways in which learners use the native and target languages with peers and teachers may provide important clues to understanding language-learning processes in immersion programs. In addition, assessing the ways in which immersion learners perform cognitive operations in their native or target language during the processing of classroom tasks may help us to understand SLA processes better by providing insights into learners' real involvement with the target language. Although our results present only an initial view of the

---

[8]For a more extensive discussion of code switching during the performance of classroom tasks see Cohen (1993), Heitzman (1994), and Parker (1994).

language used in the classroom, it is clearly necessary to understand the language that students and teachers choose to use with each other across a variety of situations in order to understand the language-learning processes in an immersion program. A larger empirical study that would document language-use patterns in the classroom more extensively could provide further insights into the motivations for language use in the classroom and shed light on the language acquisition process in immersion education.

ACKNOWLEDGMENTS

We offer our heartfelt thanks to the principal of the Adams School, Luz Maria Serrano, for graciously allowing us to conduct the study at her school. We would also like to thank the teachers, Jane Berg, Lori Dragert, Elizabeth Tabbot, and Concha Hernandez, the pupils, and curriculum specialist Heidi Bernal for their extensive cooperation over the five months of the study. This work was supported in part by grants to Amy M. Fjerstad and Shirley M. Heitzman from the Undergraduate Research Opportunities Program (UROP) at the University of Minnesota.

REFERENCES

Bailey, K. M. (1985). "Classroom Centered Research on Language Teaching and Learning." *Beyond Basics: Issues and Research in TESOL*, ed. by M. Celce-Murcia. Rowley, MA: Newbury House.
Cohen, A. D. (1987a). "Recent Uses of Mentalistic Data in Reading Strategy Research." *Documentacao de Estudos em Lingüística Teóretica e Aplicada* 3(1), 57–84.
———. (1987b). "Using Verbal Reports in Research on Language Learning." *Introspection in Second Language Research*, ed. by C. Faerch and G. Kasper. Philadelphia: Multilingual Matters.
———. (1991). "Feedback on Writing: The Use of Verbal Report." *Studies in Second Language Acquisition* 13(2), 133–159.
———. (1994). "The Language Used to Perform Cognitive Operations During Full-Immersion Math Tasks." *Language Testing* 11(2), 171–195.
———, and S. M. Lebach. (1974). "A Language Experiment in California: Student, Teacher, Parent, and Community Reactions after Three Years," *Working Papers in Teaching English as a Second Language* 8, 33–46.
———, and E. Olshtain. (1993). "The Production of Speech Acts by EFL Learners," *TESOL Quarterly* 27(1), 33–56.
———, and M. Swain. (1979). "Bilingual Education: The Immersion Model in the North American Context." *Sociolinguistic Aspects of Language Learning and Teaching*, ed. by J. B. Pride. Oxford: Oxford University Press.
Garner, R. (1987). *Metacognition and Reading Comprehension*. Norwood, NJ: Ablex.
Genesee, F. (1987). *Learning through Two Languages*. New York: Newbury House.
Harley, B., and M. Swain. (1984). "The Interlanguage of Immersion Students and Its Implications for Second Language Teaching." *Interlanguage*, ed. by A. Davies, C. Criper, and A. P. R. Howatt. Edinburgh: Edinburgh University Press.

Heitzman, S. M. (1994). "Language Use in Full Immersion Classrooms: Public and Private Speech." Summa thesis, University of Minnesota, Minneapolis.

Lambert, W. E., and G. R. Tucker. (1972). *Bilingual Education of Children: The St. Lambert Experiment.* Rowley, MA: Newbury House.

Lapkin, S., M. Swain, and S. Shapson. (1990). "French Immersion Research Agenda for the 90s," *Canadian Modern Language Review* 46(4), 639–673.

Parker, J. E. (1994). "The Language Used to Perform Academic Tasks in Full Immersion Classrooms." Senior thesis, University of Minnesota, Minneapolis.

The Riverside Publishing Company. (1984). *La Prueba Riverside de Realizacion en Español.* [The Riverside Spanish Achievement Test.] Riverside: The Riverside Publishing Company.

Schlegloff, E. A., and H. Sacks. (1973). "Opening Up Closings." *Semiotica* 7(4), 289–327.

Science Research Associates. (1985). *Survey of Basic Skills.* Chicago: Science Research Associates.

Swain, M. (1985). "Communicative competence: Some Roles of Comprehensible Input and Comprehensible Output in its Development." *Input and Second Language Acquisition,* ed. by S. Gass and C. Madden. Rowley, MA: Newbury House.

———. (1992). The Output Hypothesis: A Search for Empirical Evidence in a Classroom Second Language Acquisition Context. *Research Proposal.* Toronto: Modern Language Center, O.I.S.E.

Vygotsky, L. S. (1986). *Thought and Language,* trans. by A. Kazulin. Cambridge, MA: MIT Press. (Original work published 1934)

Wheatley, G. H. (1991). "Constructivist Perspectives on Science and Mathematics Learning," *Science Education* 75(1), 9–21.

Chapter 16

A Variationist Framework for SLA Research: Examples and Pedgagogical Insights

Elaine Tarone
University of Minnesota

1. INTRODUCTION

What does it mean to understand and explain the process of acquisition of a second language from a variationist perspective? In the field of second-language acquisition (SLA), there would appear to be multiple research approaches, and different approaches have different notions of what it means to understand and explain the process of acquisition. What does it mean, then, to take a variationist perspective as opposed to some other perspective?

2. THE NEED FOR A VARIETY OF APPROACHES TO SLA

Tarone (1994) argues that each approach to SLA research is valid for certain uses and not for others. The choice of one over the other is not occasioned by reference to some abstract notion of truth, but rather by the purpose of the research. In this view, no research approach is inherently superior to any other in and of itself. Crucially, however, although the various research approaches in SLA are equally valid for their own purposes, they are typically not interchangeable. To illustrate this, I suggest one of several possible continua along which we might range research approaches in second language acquisition. Following Yule and Tarone (in press) we might look at the Profligate/Conservative, or external-focus/internal-focus continuum in SLA research. At one end of this continuum are those researchers who tend to be profligate, or very open-ended, in the number of categories and constructs they use in interpreting data (the *Pros*) (e.g., Selinker & Douglas, 1985; Young, 1991; Zuengler, 1989). Pros typically focus upon the external and contextualized interactive performance of second language (L2) learners in order to infer something about their underlying abilities. The purpose of this approach is to describe the way in which learners systematically use their interlanguage (IL; cf. Selinker, 1972) in the process of communicating, and to understand and explain the way in which social and interactional forces influence the process of acquisition. At the other end are the conservative researchers (the *Cons*), who tend to be conservative, or parsimonious, in setting up categories for use in data interpretation. Cons typically focus on the learner's internal, cognitive processes, as these are analyzed in the abstract, outside of any particular context; the goal here is to characterize the internal, cognitive processes employed in second-language acquisition.

2.1. The Dispute Over the Role of Variation in Second-Language Acquisition

Some of the tensions between researchers who focus upon one or the other end of this continuum can be detected in the field of SLA. For example, Eckman (1994) described the conflict between Gregg (a Con) and Tarone (a Pro) about whether interlanguage variation should be considered in a theory of second-language acquisition.

2.1.1. *Interlanguage Variation*

Interlanguage variation occurs when, for example, a learner seems to have mastered a given target language (TL) form in one social context, as in a classroom exercise, yet walks out the door and 10 minutes later in another social context, as in a conversation in the hall, systematically produces a quite different (and, in TL terms, inaccurate) variant of that form. Teachers are usually familiar (and frustrated) with this phenomenon. Teachers of course want to know what they can do to help their learners to expand their mastery of such forms to a wider range of social contexts. But should they look to second-language acquisition theories to account for such variation in interlanguage?

2.1.2. *Gregg's Position on Variation*

Gregg (1990) and Tarone (1990) give different answers to the question of interlanguage variation in their attempts to explain the mechanism of second language acquisition. Because Gregg (a Con) focuses upon internal mental processes and models of an abstract (noncontextualized) competence, he discounts the importance of variation in learner performance and argues that it is better to abstract away from variable data in explaining SLA. Contextual variation is a performance factor, and so by definition it is irrelevant to the description of the learner's idealized competence. So Gregg argues that interlanguage variation is not the concern of second language acquisition theorists.

2.1.3. Tarone's Position on Variation

Tarone and other researchers we have called "Pros" focus upon external interactions and L2 learner performance in a variety of social contexts and argue that data on variability (synchronic contextual change) are crucial to explaining the mechanism of SLA, or change in learners' IL knowledge over time. Variation is not a problem for a profligate, open-ended system of analysis; rather it is a source of important information about the way in which interaction in different social contexts can influence both interlanguage use and interlanguage development. Tarone (1990) argues that it is important for second-language acquisition theory to describe variation and explain why it is that interlanguage performance varies systematically from one social context to another. She takes the position that the study of this variation will provide important insights into the mechanisms involved in the development of the interlanguage system over time.

2.1.4. Implications for Pedagogy

The variationist perspective (unlike the position defended by Gregg) promises to address the problem posed by classroom practitioners who want to understand why their learners fail to generalize newly learned patterns to contexts outside the classroom—or, conversely, in second-language contexts, fail to generalize forms used fluently in conversations with peers to more formal classroom situations. If we can identify the external, social forces that influence this style shifting, then we may be able to use those forces for pedagogical purposes to help the student "generalize" the use of the form to a wider range of "discourse domains" (Selinker & Douglas, 1985).

After all, the variationists reason, we must assume that the goal of pedagogy is to enable students to master target language forms and use those forms in communicating in a variety of social situations. The goal of pedagogy is not to foster idealized competence, for example, to enable the student to state the rule for the new form in a classroom quiz. Rather, the goal is to enable the student to use the new form, not just in the classroom but in a variety of social situations outside the classroom.

2.2. The Role of Data in Resolving the Dispute

But what of Gregg's (1990) charge that the study of IL variation can tell us nothing about the L2 acquisition process: the development of ILs? Eckman (1994) argues that the difference in perspective expressed in the Tarone-Gregg debate can be resolved if variationists produce data that show how variation influences acquisition.

3. TWO STUDIES IN A VARIATIONIST FRAMEWORK

3.1. The Markee Study

We could take the position that data alone will not solve the problem. If the essential difference between the opposite ends of the Pro/Con continuum is simply one of focus, then data could be interpreted in different ways depending upon the focus of the interpreter; the choice would be simply a matter of style, or convenience. For example, variationists might see the example of the acquisition/learning of the word *coral* in Markee (1994) as an important piece of data which shows the way in which a series of interactions in English (L2) cause a learner to variably approximate the TL norm. In this study, Markee observed a woman in an English as a second language (ESL) class as the learner participated in a series of group discussions that led up to her presentation in front of the class on the importance of coral reefs in the ecology of the ocean. The learner, in her attempt to internalize the lexical item *coral*, variably approximated the TL norm by gradually eliciting pieces of the definition of this term in a succession of interactions with several interlocutors. At any one point in the conversation, the learner had a tentative and variable notion of what *coral* was (in Tarone's terms, her knowledge itself was unstable in addition to being not equivalent to the TL norm). The learner sought and found additional information about *coral* in her interactions with various interlocutors in small-group discussions, resolved her uncertainty about the meaning of the term, gradually added more information about the term in additional interactions, and finally emerged in her formal presentation with the ability to give a fairly targetlike definition of the term.

A Con might argue that what really matters in this case is the internal processing done by the learner in building up a definition of the term, and that the variable ways she uses the term in her interactions with others are irrelevant, or at best, highly subsidiary, to those internal processes. A Pro would argue that the learner's external negotiated interactions over time with several interlocutors provide the driving force for her variable buildup of an understanding of the term; her variable productions and her interlocutors' reactions to them are central to the acquisition process and in some sense trigger her internal processing.

Clearly, a Pro and a Con would interpret this bit of data differently; in this study there is nothing to persuade us that a study of external interactions engaged in by this learner will shed any light upon our understanding of this learner's internal processing. What is needed are data that can show that the study of interlanguage variation of this sort provides insight, obtainable in no other way, into the mechanisms of second language acquisition. In other words, data are needed that show that the external processes studied by Pros can affect the internal processes studied by Cons in nontrivial ways. The sort of data that can show this kind of relationship are, I would argue, longitudinal case study data in which a learner's IL production in several social contexts is studied over time, so that the relationship between any contextual variation that occurs can be related to the development of the IL system over time. Unfortunately, this sort of data is very hard to obtain and has generally not been gathered and studied with this question in mind. Fortunately, there is one exception to this generalization of which I am aware: a recent dissertation (Liu, 1991).

3.2. The Liu Study

Liu (1991) describes a case study in which the external social interactions of a learner seemed to differentially activate internal acquisition processes.

3.2.1. Description of the Study

Guo-qiang Liu (1991) conducted a 2-year longitudinal study of a Chinese boy named 'Bob', beginning when Bob was almost 5 years old and ending when he was almost 7 years old. Bob acquired English in Australia in four interactional contexts: (1) interacting with preschool peers and supervisory staff, (2) interacting with his teachers in primary school, (3) interacting with primary school peers, and (4) interacting with the adult researcher. Since Bob did not make much progress in preschool, we focus here on his progress in the latter three contexts.

(1) In interacting with teachers at school, Bob was very aware of the importance of doing well and getting good grades; he generally did not initiate interactions, and he focused on presenting himself as a good pupil. In language use, he did not seem to take many risks. Even with T1, an extremely supportive teacher who gave very little negative feedback on his language, Bob took few risks. In the following conversation, the study had been in progress for about a year and a half.

(1) Session 62, 14 December 1987:
    T1:   Bob how's it going?
    Bob: Good.
    T1:   What're you doing? About my truck. When did you do that?
    Bob: Um last week.
    T1:   Who helped you do this one?
    Bob: Miss Back.
    T1:   Really? Can you read it for me please?
    Bob: About my truck. On Saturday my dad has a . . . (pause)

T1:   Got.

Bob: Got a truck. Truck is green. I like my dad truck. I like my wheel.

T1:   Wow! That's great. You were very busy weren't you?

Bob let the teacher take the conversational initiative and limited his responses to very simple utterances.

(2) In interacting with his peers in the classroom at desk work, Bob, as a highly competitive boy, took a much more assertive role, initiating interactions, criticizing his classmates' work, demonstrating the superiority of his own, and speaking more fluently. This interactional context was conducive to giving commands, arguing, and insulting people. In (2), Bob and his three friends, Ben, Shayne, and Simon, are challenged on the quality of their drawing by a rival group, which includes Mark and Paul; this conversation took place in July 1987, six months before the conversation with the teacher in (1):

(2) Session 43, 20 July 1987:

Bob: Look he doesn't know how to draw. (to Ben about Mark)

Mark: I can draw better than both of you.

Ben: Um can you draw peak? (meaning mountain peak)

Mark: Yes I can.

Bob: OK you draw.

Ben: Can you draw school?

Mark: Yes I can.

Ben: Can you draw the whole world?

Mark: Yes I can.

Ben: Ah ha no one can draw the whole world.
      (Paul comes to the table.)

Ben: Can you draw the whole world?

Mark: He would.

Ben: You don't know because you don't know how to draw.

Mark: I don't know how to draw the whole world.

Bob: You don't know.

Ben: Do you know how to draw stars?

Bob: No he don't know.

Mark: I don't know how to draw stars. There's no one in the world knows how to draw stars.

Bob: I know how to draw stars. It's it's very easy. You doesn't know.

Subsequently in the conversation, the competition degenerated into competitive name-calling. Clearly, there were powerful social forces at work among Bob and his peers at desk work that drew Bob into the conversation; he had established a dominant role in his group and he took the initiative in criticizing the work of his rivals and asserting his superiority and that of his friends. The transcript shows a great deal of linguistic modeling being provided by his peers and evidence that Bob both noticed and incorporated those models into his own utterances in the heated exchanges that were recorded.

(3) The adult researcher was a friend of the family and (perhaps more importantly) an adult who knew how to play and was interested in interacting with Bob and drawing him out in a relaxed home environment. Bob's relationship with the researcher changed from a formal teacher-pupil relationship during the preschool period to a more relaxed friendship relationship in which Bob felt free to disobey and even to insult the researcher. The two frequently drew pictures together and played with blocks, talking about their activities as well as about school. Bob tried hard to initiate interactions with the researcher. Bob's attempts to produce English utterances met with the researcher's approval and encouragement (though, interestingly, the latter was often more judgmental than the teachers, giving him more negative feedback on his language than they did). In this third interactional context, Bob used the most complex structures and the widest variety of language functions. The conversation with the researcher in (3) took place at roughly the same time as the conversation with the teacher in (1):

(3) Session 61: 10 December 1987:

    Bob: Now I know what I can do.

    Res: Yeah.

    Bob: I'm not tell you what I'm doing now.

    Res: Tell me what you're doing.

    Bob: I'm not tell you. I draw all of them, so it's complete.

    Res: What do you want to draw?

    Bob: I'm not tell you.

    Res: I know. It's nothing except colors.

    Bob: No. I'm going to draw something. No. I'm not lie to you.

    Res: I didn't say you were lying.

    Bob: I'm just draw a ghost. Can't draw.

    Res: You're drawing a ghost?

    Bob: Yeah. I can draw all of them.

    Res: OK. I'll see what sort of ghost you can draw.

    Bob: I draw a lovely ghost.

Here, Bob produces the most language, initiates more, and produces far more complex sentence structures than in the interaction of Bob with the teacher.

The three interactional contexts just described were engaged in during the same period of time, and so, in Liu's words, during that period, it could be argued that:

> Bob had the same knowledge system of English at his disposal. However, in interaction with the teachers, he only used very simple English, which was a very small part of his knowledge system. In interacting with peers, he made more extensive use of his knowledge by producing more complex English. In interaction with the researcher, he made still more extensive use of this knowledge to the extent of attempting syntactic structures beyond his existing control.

For example, Table 16.1 shows that Bob produced complex structures differentially in these three contexts during the same period of time. In addition, the functions he tried to express varied in a similar way in each of the three contexts, as did the number of initiations he made as opposed to simple responses to the initiations of others. Thus, Liu shows that Bob's interlanguage varied in its general shape from one situation to another: his use of his interlanguage knowledge was affected by the different role relationships in the different social situations. In Gregg's terms, Bob's performance of his competence was different in these different interactional contexts. But such a finding is not new; many other studies have shown that social context, identity of interlocutor, role, and task have an impact on a learner's performance. Does this variation have any impact on the acquisition of the second language?

3.2.2. Two Ways Interactional Context Affects Acquisition

Liu's study goes beyond use and performance to make claims about the way in which interactions in these three contexts differentially affected acquisition. Liu claims that the interactions in which Bob engaged had an impact on his interlanguage development, not only in terms of the *rate* of that development but also on the route of his interlanguage development. Let us examine each of these claims in turn.

TABLE 16.1
Complex Structures Produced by Bob in Three Contexts

Context	Number	Percentage
With teachers	0	0
With peers	40	18
With researcher	177	82
Total	207	

Note. From Liu (1991, Table 8.5, p. 211). Reprinted with permission.

3.2.2.1. Rate. Liu uses Pienemann and Johnston's (1987) framework for the development of English as a second language to examine the development of one aspect of Bob's interlanguage grammar. He focuses upon the developmental stages in Bob's use of interrogative forms:

(4)

Stage 1: Single word

Stage 2: SVO?
   You like number one? (Session 29)

Stage 3: Do-front
   WhX-front
   Why you do that? (Session 36)

Stage 4: Pseudo-inversion
   Y/N inversion
   Where's the monkey? (Session 24)

Stage 5: Aux-2nd
   Suppletion
   What are you doing? (Session 24)

Stage 6: Question tag
   You don't like green, are you? (Session 49)

Liu's data show a clear and consistent pattern whereby more advanced structures appear first in interactions with the researcher and only much later in other settings. For example, Stage 5 interrogative forms initially appear in interactions between Bob and the researcher in Session 23, but do not appear in interactions between Bob and his peers until Session 36. Stage 6 interrogative forms appear first in interactions between Bob and the researcher in Session 49, but do not appear in interactions between Bob and his peers until Session 76, nearly 9 months later. In general, new structures appear first in the interactions between Bob and the researcher, spread to his interactions with his peers, and appear last in his interactions with his teacher. This pattern in the data suggests that different interactional contexts support different rates of development of particular interlanguage features. Further, Liu suggests that if Bob had not had the opportunity to interact with the researcher, the overall rate of development of his interlanguage would probably have been much slower.

Liu's analysis of the differences in IL variety in the three interactional contexts allows us to make some educated guesses about why one of these contexts produced a faster rate of development than the others. Liu shows that Bob took risks with his interlanguage production differentially in different interactional contexts. In interacting with the researcher, as opposed to other interlocutors, Bob spoke in a wider range of styles ranging from narratives to discussions to arguments. Bob also produced a wider variety of forms in interaction with the researcher than in the other interactional contexts. For example, he produced a wider range of Stage 5 interrogative forms with the researcher than with other interlocutors: *What do you need? What color do you like? What do you want to do? What are you doing? Where did I put it? Which do you want to color in? How do you know? How do people go up the top? How can we do it? Who's got long?*

Further, in speaking with this interested and supportive adult friend, Bob's interlanguage was "characterized by inaccurate syntax resulting from his exploitation of his competence in English to its limits. The consequence was that he produced much more complex structures laden with nontarget forms in this context than in any other context" (Liu, 1991, p. 227). For example, by the time Session 35 was taped, Bob was consistently responding to his teacher's questions in the classroom with 'I don't know', but in Session 35 with the researcher he produced responses to questions such as those in 5:

(5) Session 35, 28 May 1987:
    (Bob and the researcher are looking at work done by pupils)

    Researcher: Where's yours?

    Bob: *ni zhi dao na shi hou ma?*
         'You know that time?'
         na shi hou wo hai mei lai ne.
         'It was the time when I hadn't started school yet.'
         Longer longer. I'm not come. Go to go to school. It's. Is not mine.

    Researcher: Longer longer?

    Bob: *shen me?*
         'What?'
         Longer longer. I can't read. I can't draw picture cause I'm not come.

Here Bob initially tried to speak in Chinese to the researcher, who did not respond in Chinese. Then Bob resorted to communication strategies (cf. Faerch & Kasper, 1983; Tarone, 1978). He created some interlanguage vocabulary items, such as *longer longer* for *a long time ago*, and constructions such as *I'm not come* for *I hadn't gone to school yet*. These forms were not related to Chinese sentence constructions, so they were not based on language transfer. They were not targetlike, either. Their creation and use indicated a willingness to take extended turns in interaction and to stretch the interlanguage system beyond safe limits—in short, to take risks with the interlanguage system in attempting to communicate.

What do Liu's data tell us about the way in which interactional dynamics may affect internal L2 acquisition processes? What does interlanguage variation tell us about second language acquisition? One thing such data can do is help us answer this important question: What are the forces that make some learners' interlanguage stay permeable and keep developing? What prevents fossilization? Clearly, there are many cases in which innate, universal cognitive processes alone do not just go into operation in response to input and develop inexorably to the finish. Swain (1985, 1993) has shown that the ILs of immersion children that are exposed to plentiful L2 input data from teachers nevertheless stop developing. She has argued that in situations (like immersion classrooms) where learners are not required to produce L2, their interlanguages fossilize and cease developing. Bob received English input from teachers and peers, but those were not the contexts in which his interlanguage seemed to be most stimulated to move from one stage to another.

Liu's data show us first that interactional demands differ in different social contexts, and further that one context can be identified as the one in which the learner's interlanguage system is most unstable, most variable, and most open to change—and in which the first elements of more advanced developmental stages are produced. There is thus powerful evidence that this is the context in which acquisition occurs. What exactly is it that makes this context so positive for IL development? The answer to this question requires some speculation about the possible cognitive effects of the interactive context. There are at least two possibilities we may be able to explore in a closer examination of data such as these. For example, it is possible that the researcher exemplifies the ideal interlocutor, one who provides the input that is most suited to the learner's developmental needs. The researcher clearly was the interlocutor who was most clearly focused solely upon the learner and communicating with him. Thus, it is possible that the researcher provided the input that was most finely attuned to Bob's needs, and that this explains why the interactions between Bob and the researcher were so productive.

Another possibility is that the key variable was Bob's attempt to produce comprehensible output. Bob was given much more encouragement and opportunity to produce the L2 and to elaborate his utterances in the Bob-researcher context than in the Bob-peer context, where Bob had often to fight to get a word in edgewise. In this view, it is in interactional contexts in which the learner needs to produce output the current interlanguage system cannot handle that the learner pushes the limits of the interlanguage system to make it handle that output, thus keeping that system open to change. In such contexts, the learner functions in much the same way as the learner in Schmidt and Frota (1986), who was struggling to produce output, became conscious of a gap or need for a structure, and then noticed that structure in the input. It can be argued that Liu's data show that it is precisely in those contexts where Bob had to produce output at the limits of his IL that his IL developed fastest, with the richest variety of IL structures and even possibly with structures out of the so-called universal order.

This explanation also allows us to see how communication strategies (Faerch & Kasper, 1983; Tarone, 1978) and interlanguage variation (Tarone, 1990) may be related, both to one another and to the acquisition process. In this view, a learner's use of communication strategies can function to stretch an IL system beyond its current limits, resulting in free variation as the learner tests new hypotheses in the search for an appropriate word or structure. A learner in search of the right word or structure is a learner who is open to noticing such things in the input. Liu's data on rate and variety are very convincing evidence that an exploration of the causes of interlanguage variation will provide important new insights into the process of second language acquisition. The interactions in which Bob engaged had an impact upon the interlanguage structures he was willing to use at any given time and the degree to which he was willing to push the limits of his interlanguage competence. This in turn appears to have had a measurable impact upon the rate and variety of his interlanguage development.

3.2.2.2. Route. Liu argued that certain types of interaction encourage more complete development of certain features in the interlanguage than others. Of course, Selinker and Douglas (1985) have argued this same point, but the sort of longitudinal, context-sensitive data that Liu has gathered provide us with the best evidence yet on this point. Liu uses the development of interrogative forms in Bob's interlanguage as an example. Pienemann and Johnston (1987) claim that there is a universal sequence of acquisition of interrogative forms, such that Stage 4 or 5 features should not appear before Stage 3 features. Although there may be some disagreement on some of the details of Pienemann and Johnston's theory (cf. Hudson, 1993), in fact there is general agreement among SLA researchers on the broad outlines of the sequence of acquisition of questions in English, as noted by Larsen-Freeman and Long (1991): it is generally agreed that questions with noninversion of the SVO pattern (e.g., Stage 3) occur before questions in which inversion occurs (as in Stages 4 and 5). Yet in Bob's case, Stage 4 and 5 interrogative forms did emerge in interactions with the researcher long before Stage 3 forms. That is, interactional context altered the sequence of acquisition.

Liu argues that the researcher's intensive use of Stage 4 and 5 forms in the input, together with an increased opportunity for Bob to produce such forms (Bob took a more assertive role in interactions with the researcher than in the others), influenced Bob to acquire those forms first. Bob's interactions with the researcher gave him a context where there were opportunities and incentives for him to acquire and use Stage 4 and 5 forms before Stage 3 forms. Thus, Liu claims that the interactional context was such that it caused Bob to alter a so-called universal sequence of acquisition in that context.

This is the strongest evidence yet that the study of SLA should include a study of the relationship between internal cognitive processes and external social influences. If internal cognitive processes can be altered by different interactional contexts, then the study of SLA must include the study of IL variation in different social contexts and must relate this variation to the development of IL over time.

It is possible that Pienemann and Johnston's (1987) claim of the universality of this sequence of acquisition of the English interrogative, a sequence developed in the study of learners acquiring German as a second language and not yet fully attested in ESL acquisition, is simply incorrect for English as a second language. In addition, Liu has to date analyzed only this one aspect of Bob's IL grammar in detail. We need to examine the development of other structures in Bob's interlanguage in order to see whether the development of other aspects of Bob's grammar were similarly differentially affected in these three interactional contexts. However, it seems well worth our while to investigate this claim in order to determine the extent to which interactional context may be able to override or alter any claimed innate universal sequence of acquisition.

Liu's study provides us with evidence that a variationist approach to the study of second languages is needed in building a theory of SLA. Clearly, at least one interlanguage (the only one yet studied, to my knowledge, in different social contexts over time) developed differentially in different interactional contexts, as the learner entered into different role relationships and responded to different demands from his interlocutors. Investigations such as these could shed light upon the delicate relationship that is claimed to exist in SLA between internal innate and external contextual forces.

4. SOME PEDAGOGICAL IMPLICATIONS OF VARIATIONIST FINDINGS

I have argued that the variationist framework for SLA research is the only one that promises to address a problem frequently posed by classroom practitioners: Why do L2 learners fail to generalize newly learned patterns to contexts outside the classroom? Or, conversely, in second-language contexts, why do they fail to generalize forms they use fluently in conversations with peers to more formal classroom situations? It has been argued that if we can identify the external, social forces that influence this style shifting, then we may be able to use those forces for pedagogical purposes to help the student generalize the use of the form to a wider range of interactional contexts. Clearly, data such as Liu's must be of concern to second language teachers, particularly those in elementary classrooms, such as ESL and bilingual teachers and teachers in language immersion programs.

4.1. Providing Input to the L2 Learner in Elementary Classrooms

In immersion classrooms, where the students' only well-formed L2 input is from the teacher, that input seems to be restricted to academic topics and possibly to a narrow range of language functions. In fact, it has regularly been noted that immersion students who use L2 with their teachers insist on switching to their native language (NL) in peer-peer interactions and strongly resist teachers' incentives to use L2 in such conversations. But where are immersion students going to be exposed to the wider range of topics and L2 language functions they need for peer-peer desk work interactions such as those engaged in by Bob in his mainstream classroom? If immersion students are never exposed to L2 use in peer-peer interactions (never shown how to compete with, argue with, or insult their peers in L2), how can they be blamed for switching to their native language when they need to perform such language functions in peer-peer interactions? (See Swain & Tarone, in press, for further discussion of immersion issues and pedagogical implications.)

It seems obvious that L2 teachers need to provide learners with exposure to as wide a range of interactional contexts as possible. Certainly, the student needs L2 input in more than just teacher-student interactional contexts. Good models of student-student interactions are needed. In the United States, nonnative speakers of English who are mainstreamed in classes where they must interact in desk work with native speakers are provided with such models. But how can such models be provided for immersion students, whose only L2 model is an adult teacher? It would certainly not be wise for the teacher who needs to maintain control over a classroom to try to provide L2 vernacular models of competition, argument, insults, and so on. Possibly where teacher aides are available, they may be able to establish a more peer-peer relationship with the students (rather as Liu did with Bob), and argue with, compete with, insult, and otherwise use L2 vernacular forms with their young students in L2. Or possibly TV shows are available that show L2 interactions in different age groups. Community language learning techniques might be useful as well; in such techniques, students converse with one another in their NL and may use the full range of language functions and vernacular forms that are natural to peer-peer interactions. The teacher (or aide) standing behind them simply provides the L2 forms they need for the functions they wish to perform, and in this context there need be no threat to the teacher's adult-based control over the classroom. Where native-language-speaking peers exist in the school district, it is possible that assignments might be given that would strongly encourage immersion students to interact with them in L2, thus gaining access to the sort of L2 input they need to acquire L2 for peer-peer purposes.

Once such input is provided, the L2 teacher might find it helpful to provide assignments that require students to look for particular forms in that input. Schmidt and Frota (1986) argue that it is important for L2 learners to consciously notice a new form in input and then to use it. In their view, it is crucial for students to notice the form in the input. How can teachers get students to do this? One possibility is to assign a listening log, in which students are asked to listen for particular forms and note down occasions and contexts where they hear those forms (Trites & Fairchild, 1994). In immersion classrooms, students might be asked to keep listening logs when watching TV situation comedies in which child peer-peer conversations take place. In second language contexts, assignments might be given asking students to listen to conversations in the community as well as on TV.

4.2. Encouraging L2 Output by Elementary Students

It seems clear that L2 students may use a very different range of interlanguage forms in conversing with L2 teachers than in conversing with peers in desk work in L2 classrooms. From an ESL teacher's perspective, this may mean that LEP students are not showing their teacher their most complex and varied interlanguage performance, so that the teacher may underestimate the students' L2 abilities. Thus, there are some problems for language assessment that need to be addressed. L2 assessment measures must elicit language in a variety of types of social interactions. Of even more concern, however, is the possibility that at least some L2 students tend not to take risks in their L2 performance when conversing with teachers. Thus, their IL is unlikely to develop in conversations with their teacher, because they are then unlikely to (in Swain's terms) "push their L2 output." If pushed output is important for interlanguage development, then it is important for L2 teachers to give students opportunities to produce L2 output in conversational interactions that encourage them to take such risks. Possibly community language learning techniques could help in providing such opportunities. Process writing and process speaking assignments (such as the production of a "radio" show, described in Swain, 1985) might provide such opportunities as well. Clearly, teachers need to be creative to develop other opportunities for students to take risks.

5. CONCLUSION

It seems clear that data do exist that show that a variationist framework in the study of second language acquisition is needed. It has been shown that a variationist approach can be helpful in explaining how and why the acquisition processes and the performance of L2 learners might vary in different interactional contexts. Such findings, it has been suggested, have clear implications for pedagogy, and specific recommendations for L2 pedagogy in elementary classrooms have been made.

ACKNOWLEDGMENTS

Portions of this paper were presented at the 22nd University of Wisconsin Milwaukee Linguistics Symposium, on Second-Language Acquisition Theory and Pedagogy, October 9, 1993. I am grateful to Fred Eckman for his encouragement and guidance on this chapter, and to an anonymous reviewer for comments and

270   TARONE

suggested changes which were incorporated. A later version of this paper appears in Tarone and Liu (in press).

REFERENCES

Eckman, F. (1994). "The Competence-Performance Issue in Second-Language Acquisition Theory: A Debate." *Research Methodology in Second Language Acquisition*, ed. by E. Tarone, S. Gass, and A. Cohen, pp. 3–15. Hillsdale, NJ: Lawrence Erlbaum Associates.

Faerch, C., and G. Kasper (eds.) (1983). *Strategies in Interlanguage Communication.* London: Longman.

Gregg, K. (1990). "The Variable Competence Model of Second Language Acquisition and Why It Isn't," *Applied Linguistics* 11 (4), 364–383.

Hudson, T. (1993). "Nothing Does Not Equal Zero: Problems with Applying Developmental Sequence Findings to Assessment and Pedagogy," *Studies in Second Language Acquisition* 15, 461–494.

Larsen-Freeman, D., and M. Long. (1991). *An Introduction to Second Language Acquisition Research.* London: Longman.

Liu, G. (1991). "Interaction and Second Language Acquisition: A Case Study of a Chinese Child's Acquisition of English as a Second Language." PhD dissertation, La Trobe University, La Trobe, Australia.

Markee, N. (1994). "Toward an Ethnomethodological Respecification of Second-Language Acquisition Studies." *Research Methodology in Second Language Acquisition*, ed. by E. Tarone, S. Gass, and A. Cohen, pp. 89–116. Hillsdale, NJ: Lawrence Erlbaum Associates.

Pienemann, M., and M. Johnston. (1987). "Factors Influencing the Development of Language Proficiency." *Applying Second Language Acquisition Research*, ed. by D. Nunan, pp. 45–141. Adelaide, Australia: National Curriculum Resource Centre.

Schmidt, R., and S. Frota. (1986). "Developing Basic Conversational Ability in a Second Language: A Case Study of an Adult Learner of Portuguese." *Talking to Learn*, ed. by R. Day, pp. 237–326. Rowley, MA: Newbury House.

Selinker, L. (1972). "Interlanguage," *International Review of Applied Linguistics* 10, 209–231.

———, and D. Douglas. (1985). "Wrestling with 'context' in Interlanguage Theory," *Applied Linguistics* 6, 190–204.

Swain, M. (1985). "Communicative Competence: Some Roles of Comprehensible Input and Output in Its Development." *Input in Second Language Acquisition*, ed. by S. Gass and C. Madden, pp. 235–253. Rowley, MA: Newbury House.

———. (1993). "The Output Hypothesis: Just Speaking and Writing Aren't Enough," *Canadian Modern Language Review* 50 (1), 158–164.

Tarone, E. (1978). "Conscious Communication Strategies in Interlanguage: A Progress Report." On *TESOL '77: Teaching and Learning ESL*, ed. by H. D. Brown, C. A. Yorio, and R. Crymes, pp. 194–203. Washington, DC: TESOL.

———. (1990). "On Variation in Interlanguage: A Response to Gregg," *Applied Linguistics* 11 (4), 392–400.

———. (1994). "A Summary: Research Approaches in Studying Second-Language Acquisition; or, If the Shoe Fits . . ." *Research Methodology in Second-Language Acquisition*, ed. by E. Tarone, S. Gass, and A. Cohen, pp. 323–336. Hillsdale, NJ: Lawrence Erlbaum Associates.

———, and G. Liu. (in press). "Situational Context, Interlanguage Variation, and Second- Language Acquisition Theory." *Applied Linguistics Principles and Practice: Studies in Honor of H. G. Widdowson*, ed. by G. Cook and B. Seidlhofer. Oxford: Oxford University Press.

———, and M. Swain. (in press). "A Sociolinguistic Perspective on Second-Language Use in Immersion Classrooms," *Modern Language Journal.*

Trites, J., and M. Fairchild. (1994, October). "What is Comprehensible Input? Listening Logs as a Teaching/Learning Tool." Paper presented at the MinneTESOL Conference, St. Paul, MN.

Young, R. (1991). *Variation in Interlanguage Morphology.* New York: Lang.

Yule, G., and E. Tarone. (in press). "Investigating Communication Strategies in L2 Reference: Pros and Cons." *Referential Communication,* ed. by G. Kasper and E. Kellerman. London: Longman.

Zuengler, J. (1989). "Performance Variation in NS–NNS Interactions: Ethnolinguistic Difference or Discourse Domain?" *Variation in Second Language Acquisition: Discourse and Pragmatics,* ed. by S. Gass, C. Madden, D. Preston, and L. Selinker, pp. 228–244. Clevedon, England: Multilingual Matters.

Part V

OUTPUT: PRONUNCIATION

Chapter 17

Markedness in the Acquisition of English /r/ and /l/

John C. Paolillo
University of Texas at Arlington

1. INTRODUCTION

Certain foreign accents of English are so readily recognized that they have become cultural stereotypes for speakers of American English. One widely stereotyped accent is that of native speakers of Chinese. The central characteristic of the stereotype is the substitution of *l* and *r* sounds for each other, as exemplified by alleged pronunciations such as *flied lice* for 'fried rice', and by ethnic jokes targeting such mispronunciations.[1] This stereotype is held not only by laypersons, it also shows up in the literature of second language research. For example, Odlin (1989) groups Chinese, Japanese, and Korean speakers together as having "frequent pronunciation confusions" of /r/ and /l/. The assumption most often made is that the confusion of /r/ and /l/ arises from the lack of phonemic contrast between [r] and [l] in the native languages.

It is true that both Japanese and Korean lack a contrast between /r/ and /l/ (Kim, 1987; Shibatani, 1987). For Chinese, however, the matter is not so simple. For one thing, 'Chinese' actually refers to a group of related languages that differ considerably in their phonology, including the number of liquids they have. Mandarin Chinese (unlike Japanese and Korean) has two liquid phonemes: a retroflex /r/ and a lateral /l/ (Chao, 1968; Cheng, 1973); thus we should expect Mandarin-speaking learners of English to have fewer pronunciation confusions

---

[1]One such joke substitutes /r/ for /l/ in all places in the automobile names Cadillac and Lincoln Continental.

of /r/ and /l/ than speakers of Japanese and Korean. If, on the other hand, comparable /r/ and /l/ confusions are found to exist, then something remains to be explained.

In this chapter I argue that there is more to the acquisition of English /l/ and /r/ by Mandarin speakers than is suggested by the "confusion" stereotype. Specifically, I demonstrate that not only is the distribution of English /r/ and /l/ related to their distribution in Mandarin but that two additional mechanisms interact in the learning of /r/ and /l/. First, the lack of contrast between /r/ and /l/ in a particular position is realized as one of three types of *neutralization*, which correspond to stages of acquisition. Second, the acquisition of a contrast between /r/ and /l/ follows a universal *hierarchy*, such that the contrast is perfected first in certain phonological environments and later in others. These two learning mechanisms operate independently and correspond to two different types of linguistic markedness.

1.1. A Contrastive Sketch

As mentioned previously, Mandarin Chinese has distinct /r/ and /l/ phonemes. These phonemes contrast only in initial position and are distributed in the syllable as in 1:

(1) Mandarin liquids:

Onset	Nucleus	Coda
r	—	r
l	—	—

In the nucleus and coda positions, /r/ and /l/ do not contrast. Both onset and coda are simple in Mandarin (they contain only one consonant), but the nucleus may be complex, allowing for diphthongs and triphthongs, so sequences of consonant-glide, where the glide is part of the following nucleus, are possible. The phone [ɨ], a high, central, slightly retroflex vowel, may occur in any position in the nucleus.

English maintains a distinction between /r/ and /l/ in all three major positions: onset, nucleus, and coda. In addition, both onsets and codas in English may be complex, so two other positions must be distinguished:

(2) English

Onset		Nucleus	Coda	
#__	C__		__C	__#
r	Cr	r	rC	r
l	Cl	ɨ	ɨC	ɨ

There is one more environment to consider, the intervocalic environment, since intervocalic segments sometimes undergo phonological changes different from those of segments in other positions, such as the flapping of English /t/ and /d/ in words like *writer* and *rider*. Again, English has a contrast between /l/ and /r/ in intervocalic position. The Chinese grammars I have consulted do not indicate whether /r/ and /l/ are distinct in this environment.

Comparison of the two systems in 1 and 2 gives rise to certain predictions about Mandarin speakers learning English. We would expect both Mandarin /r/ and /l/ to transfer where they form a simple onset in English. That is, Mandarin speakers should have no trouble differentiating between the words *rice* and *lice*. In other positions, there is no contrast between /r/ and /l/ that can be transferred, and it thus needs to be learned anew, leading to potential difficulties. In the simple-coda position, we would expect /r/ to transfer, possibly rendering that environment somewhat easier than the others. Likewise, in the other noninitial positions, the r-like high central vowel [ɨ] occurring in Mandarin might lead to an earlier appearance of /r/ in these positions. But otherwise we cannot predict through a purely contrastive analysis whether any of the noninitial environments would be more difficult. How then is the distinction between /r/ and /l/ learned in these different environments?

2. METHOD

To investigate this question, I transcribed self-recorded reading passages from 20 Taiwanese graduate business students of the University of Dallas who speak Mandarin Chinese and whose SPEAK test scores were 240 or below.[2] The subjects were instructed to compose a short introduction of themselves in which they would describe their interests and current activities and to record them on cassette tapes, which I collected for analysis. The subjects were allowed to make their recordings at their own convenience, in an environment of their own choosing (typically their homes). The recordings thus tended to vary somewhat in length. In cases where the data from these recordings were not sufficient, I supplemented them with data from pronunciation drill assignments recorded by the same students. I then transcribed the recordings using a narrow phonetic transcription, attending in particular to the phones that represent English /r/ and /l/. A sample transcription appears in 3:

(3) Transcription for subject M:
    ma nẽm iz [name]. may ingiš   nẽ   is kẽⁿˀ. ay kə̃ᵐ frə̃ⁿ taywan.
    My name is [name]. My English name is Kent. I   come from Taiwan
    əv ripabˈɪk   əb čaynə. may fɛmˀli is kəmpozdˀ əv fayv pipoʷ,
    of Republic of China. My family is composed of five people

---

[2]The SPEAK (Spoken Proficiency in English Assessment Kit) test measures pronunciation, grammar, fluency, and comprehensibility, and is scored on a 300-point maximum scale. It consists of several retired test forms of the TSE (Test of Spoken English) to be administered locally by the program requiring the assessment.

 inkʲudī̃   may pɛrɛⁿs   ɛn   c̆u   yan   sɪsɨz.   ay grejuetiv frə̃
including   my   parents   and   two young sisters. I   graduated from
taywan əv   mejɨd   ī̃ stətistiks. ɛbtɨ   ay grejuetiv ay wəz
Taiwan I've(?)   majored   in statistics. After I   graduated I   was
jʲɛbtid tu ami.   tu   yiʲz letɨ ay wɛn into inštins   kəmbəni əzə
drafted to army. Two years later I   went into insurance company as a
kəmpyutɨ pʷʲogʲɛmɨ.   bikɔz   ay əm inc̆ʲɪstɪid ɪn stag mɔkɪt ɛn
computer programmer. Because I am interested in stock market and
doⁿk hɛv ɛni faynešo narij̆
don't have any financial knowledge
ay disaydiʔ tu stədi koporit   faynæ̃s ī̃n yuʔ ɛs ey.
I   decided to study corporate finance in USA.
ay layʔ plenim bæs bow ɛn layʔ lɛsənin   kʲæsᵊkɨ myuzig.
I   like playing baseball and like listening classical music.
ay hob   ðæt ay kɛn nɨn   mɛni əbaw faynešo na'ij̆
I   hɪope that I can learn many about financial knowledge
ī̃ʔ yuʔvɨsti   əv dalɛs ɛn go bɛk wɔ   may kăc̆ʲi.
in University of Dallas and go back work my country.

Subsequently, I culled out from each transcript all of the productions of English words containing /r/ and /l/. These were tabulated according to the phonological environment in which the liquid appears in English. Five environments were considered: postconsonantal (C__), word-initial (#__), intervocalic (V__V), syllabic ([r̩] and [l̩]), and postvocalic (__C/#).[3] The tabulation corresponding to the transcript given in Example 3 appears in Table 17.1. Areas of deficiency, such as word-initial and intervocalic /r/, and postvocalic /l/ for this subject, were supplemented by selectively listening to the pronunciation drill tapes made by each student.

3. RESULTS

3.1. Neutralization

Having tabulated the data for each subject, I then determined whether /r/ and /l/ were neutralized in each environment (e.g. if 'class' and 'crass' were both pronounced as [kræs]). Four different patterns of distribution emerged from this analysis: cases where there was no neutralization and three different patterns showing different degrees of neutralization, depending on the set of phones actually

---

[3]For the Chinese-speaking learners, the five environments listed seemed to be the only important ones conditioning the realization of /r/ and /l/; I found no need to distinguish the preconsonantal (__C) and simple coda (__#) environments. Although I have labeled the combined environment '__C/#' in all of the following discussion, I use the term *postvocalic* to describe it, to avoid using the more awkward phrase "preconsonantal and word-final."

Table 17.1. Tabulation of Words for Subject *m*

	C__	#__	r̪ / l̪	V__V	__C/#
/r/	frã͞n	ripabᵻɪk	yuʔvɪsti	pɛreⁿs	ami
	frã		sɪsɪz	koporit	yiɪz
	greʃuetiv		meʃᵻd		mɔkɪt
	ʃᵻebtid		ɛbtɪ		koporit
	pʷᵻogᵻɛmᵻ		letᵻ		
	inč́ᵻɪstɪd		inšᵻins		
	kãč̃i		kəmpyutᵻ		
			pʷᵻogᵻɛmᵻ		
/l/	ingɪ̃š	lay?	pipoʷ	fɛmᵊli	(pipoʷ)
	ripabᵻɪk	lɛsənin	faynešo	nariʃ	bæs bɔw
	inkᵻudĩ	nᵻn	kᵻæsᵊkɪ	naᵻiʃ	
	plenim			dalɛs	
	kᵻæsᵊkɪ				

Table 17.2. Examples of Distinctness/Neutralization Postconsonantally (C__)

Pattern	Subject	word (r)	gloss	word (l)	gloss
Complete		fᵻã	*from*	ingris	*English*
Neutralization		scᵻi	*street*	pᵻes	*place*
(fig.1)	*h*	progræmɾ	*programmer*	fᵊɔᵻs	*floors*
+		ilæʔcᵻiʔ	*electric*	prenin	*planning*
				əpraylans	*appliance*
Subset		fᵻa	*from*	ingəlɪs	*English*
(fig.2)	*d*	sɛncᵻo	*central*	impoyidə	*employed*
s		pᵻogᵻæ	*program*	pᵻabᵻə	*problem*
		difᵻen	*different*	klæsiz	*classes*
Overlap		fᵻəm	*from*	klaymərəv	*climate of*
(fig.3)		kancᵻi	*country*	klɔk	*clock*
o	2	fwəm	*from*	oʔkᵻok	*o'clock*
		dᵻiw	*drill*	fᵻorida	*Florida*
		epyiw	*April*	plis	*please*
No neutralization		grejuwetɪd	*graduated*	ingəlis	*English*
(fig.4)	*q*	dɪgri	*degree*	plesɛz	*places*
—		incrɛstɪd	*interested*		
		fᵻəm	*from*		

shared between forms containing /r/ and /l/. These four patterns are illustrated for the postconsonantal environment in Table 17.2. In the first pattern, *complete neutralization*, represented by subject H, the two sets of phones completely coincide—in this case both [r] and [ɪ] are shared by /r/ and /l/; the two categories are completely neutralized in that context. In the second situation, *subset neutralization*, exemplified by subject D, the only distinction between the two sets of phones is that one of them has a broader range of variation than the other—here we find that /r/ is represented by only the phone [ɪ]; this phone is shared with /l/, which is also represented by [l] and [əl]. The two categories are thus only weakly distinct. In the third pattern, *overlap neutralization*, represented by subject 2,[4] the two sets of phones are largely distinct, but there is some overlap—here we find [ɪ], [w], and [y] representing /r/, and [ɪ] and [l] representing /l/; the phone [ɪ] is shared

---

[4]Subjects identified by a letter are Mandarin-speaking Taiwanese. Subjects identified by number are from the non-Chinese subject pool. It was not possible to show all four types of neutralization/distinctness for a single environment using only the Mandarin speakers' data.

between the two categories, which are therefore neutralized, but less so than in the second pattern. The fourth pattern, *no neutralization*, illustrated by subject Q, represents a nativelike pattern in which the sets of phones representing /r/ and /l/ do not overlap—we find the phones [r] and [ɹ] for English /r/, and we find [l] and [əl] for /l/; there is no neutralization in that environment. The actual phones used in this pattern may differ from English phones, but a phonemic distinction is maintained. These four patterns may be diagrammed as in Figures 17.1–17.4. In these diagrams, the range of phonetic variation within a given phonemic category is represented by an oval; symbols occurring within it are allophones of that phoneme. Symbols outside the areas of any of the ovals represent possible but nonoccurring phones.

These patterns of neutralization form a natural sequence of acquisition, ordered + > > s > > o > > −. According to this sequence, a phonemic distinction is learned beginning from a stage of neutralization of the two related categories (+); the range of variation of one of the categories is then extended to encompass a greater number of variants than the category it now begins to contrast with (weakly), yielding a subset neutralization (s); the category that has shifted then loses some of its original phones, which still belong to the other category, yielding an overlap neutralization pattern (o); finally the set of shared phones of the two categories is lost, yielding a pattern of no neutralization.

There are two basic arguments in support of this acquisition sequence. One argument is that the sequence intuitively reflects an increasing strength of phonemic contrast, from a total lack of contrast through stages of increasing contrast to a complete contrast. The other argument comes from distributional evidence. If the sequence is correct, then in cases of subset neutralization (Fig.

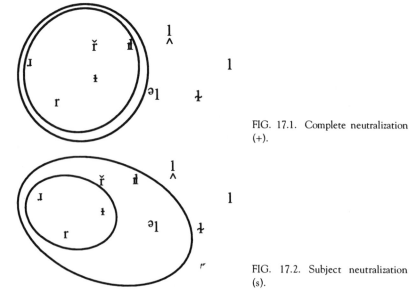

FIG. 17.1. Complete neutralization (+).

FIG. 17.2. Subject neutralization (s).

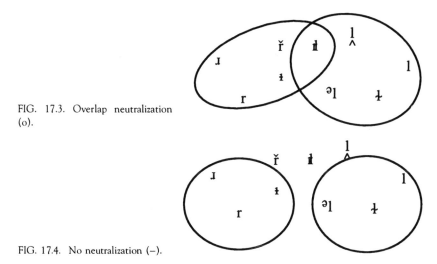

FIG. 17.3. Overlap neutralization (o).

FIG. 17.4. No neutralization (–).

17.2), the shared core of phones should be closer to the older, transferred category, and the stretched area of the more widely varying category should be made up of newer phones. Mandarin has r-like phones in all the relevant positions, which we expect to transfer and to be older than the l-type phones which have to be learned in most environments. Thus, we should expect the core area of /r/ and /l/ to be composed of r-like phones and the stretched area to be composed of l-like phones. This is exactly what is found in the data of the Mandarin learners reported in Table 17.2: there are more instances of subset neutralization where r-type phones are shared (82%) than those where l-type phones are shared (18%). The data are thus consistent with the proposed order.

3.2. A Hierarchy of Environments

When the neutralization patterns for the different environments are compared, more interesting patterns are revealed; these are summarized in Table 17.3. Of the 20 subjects, only 3 (subjects N, K, and U) lack a contrast between /r/ and /l/ in initial position; the majority of subjects show positive transfer from Mandarin in observing the contrast in this position. Only two subjects showed neutralization in all noninitial environments, suggesting complete transfer of the Mandarin system. The other subjects appear to have undergone some degree of learning the English /r/–/l/ contrast.

As ordered in Table 17.1, the environments in which /l/ and /r/ are neutralized exhibit a strong implicational relationship, with a scalability factor of 96%.[5] The few cells that are out of order are also those for which the least data is available.[6]

---

[5]The value reported was calculated counting the four "–" cells of subjects n and k as out of order; the reason for this procedure was that there was clearer evidence of neutralization in the word-initial environment than of no neutralization in the syllable nucleus and intervocalic environments. Calculated the other way, the scalability factor would be 98%.

Table 17.3. Patterns of Neutralization of /r/ and /l/

Subject code	SPEAK	#__	ɾ/ḷ	V__V	C__	V__C/#
q	240	–	–	–	–	–
i	175	–	–	–	–	s
d	170	–	–	–	s	o
c	160	–	–	–	s	o
g	170	–	–	–	s	s
s	185	–	–	–	+	s
h	165	–	–	–	+	o
b	170	–	–	–	+	o
e	170	–	–	–	+	o
o	190	–	–	–	+	o
m	145	–	–	s	s	s
a	175	–	–	s	+	s
r	170	–	–	s	+	s
p	185	–	–	s	+	o
f	140	–	–	s	+	o
t	170	–	s	s	s	o
j	190	–	+	s	s	s
n	145	s	–	–	s	o
k	135	+	–	–	n/a	o
u	n/a	o	s	s	s	o

The implicational scale governing the environments in which /r/ and /l/ are neutralized is given in 4.

(4) #__ << syllabic ɾ/ḷ << V__V << C__ << __C/#

That is, if speakers neutralize /r/ and /l/ in a particular environment (e.g. inter-vocalic), then they will also neutralize /r/ and /l/ in all environments to its right on the scale (e.g. postconsonantal and postvocalic). Note that the rankings according to the implicational scale do not correspond especially well to the subjects' SPEAK test scores: those with the neutralization in only the last two environments (postconsonantal and postvocalic) have a mean SPEAK score of 172.5 with a standard deviation of 10.69; those with the last three environments neutralized have a mean SPEAK score of 163, with a standard deviation of 17.1. Thus, the pattern observed does not appear to be a consequence of any kind of global proficiency difference among the students.

The ordering of the environments on the scale can be accounted for by considering the factors that contribute to the salience of /r/ and /l/ in each environment. First, liquids like /r/ and /l/ are distinguished by their acoustic formant structures. These are salient in the syllable nucleus and nonsalient in all other, more transitory environments. Second, segments nearer the beginning of a word or syllable, that is, in the onset, will be more salient than those in

---

[6]Subjects N and K had the shortest recordings of the entire group and no pronunciation drills to supplement their data. These recordings yielded particularly small numbers of tokens of /r/ and /l/ in syllable-nucleus and intervocalic positions, those being the positions in which their data is out of order.

Table 17.4. Relative Salience of the Environments

	#__	ɾ/ḷ	V__V	C__	__C/#
Nucleus	–	+	–	–	–
Onset	+	–	+/±	+	–
Simple	+	+	+	–	+/–

other positions. Third, simple segments are more salient than complex segments, for example, consonant clusters. Table 17.4 shows how these universal criteria for salience, labeled 'Nucleus', 'Onset', and 'Simple Segment', respectively, apply to each environment. The overall salience of each environment according to these criteria corresponds quite closely to the order of the environments in which the /ɾ/–/l/ contrast is learned.

In Table 17.4, we can see that the word-initial and the syllable-nucleus positions have the greatest salience. These are followed in ranking by the inter-vocalic position, which is intermediately ranked for Onset (±) if ambisyllabicity is possible (an ambisyllabic consonant is ambiguously both onset and coda), and positively (+) if it is not. In other words, we predict that this environment may pattern one of two ways: either with the word-initial environment, or independently and ranked less salient than the word-initial and syllable-nucleus environments. Next come postconsonantal and postvocalic positions; if we assume that salience with respect to Onset is ranked higher than salience with respect to Simple Segment, then the postconsonantal environment will be ranked greater than the postvocalic in salience. In postvocalic position, we frequently find a zero alternant for both /ɾ/ and /l/. The majority of the overlap neutralizations exhibited in this environment are due to the zero alternant. The overwhelming tendency for deletion (and consequently neutralization) in this position can be explained by its low phonetic saliency.[7]

The lack of relative ranking of the word-initial and syllable-nucleus positions is of interest, since these are only weakly ranked by the data in Table 17.3. If this order can be maintained empirically, then the criteria of Onset and Nucleus may need to be ranked relative to each other to make the right predictions, so that Onset would be ranked higher in salience than Nucleus. Alternatively, the prototypical functions of /ɾ/ and /l/ may play a role. Liquids occur more commonly as consonants crosslinguistically than as vowels. Vocalic and consonantal contrasts are linguistically quite different, so a direct comparison between these two environments may not be appropriate. Note too that Mandarin has a contrast between /ɾ/ and /l/ in word-initial position but not in the syllable nucleus. We

---

[7]Note that this is also a position in which /ɾ/ and /l/ are often deleted in dialects of English.

Table 17.5. Markedness and Relative Difficulty

Markedness Relation		
L1 > L2	L1 ≈ L2	L1 < L2
easy	easy	hard

Note: Degree of markedness ≈ degree of difficulty

should therefore not be surprised to find a more robust /r/ and /l/ contrast in word-initial position than in the syllable nucleus.

Another way of stating these generalizations is to say that the implicational scale in 4 corresponds to a universal scale of markedness for /r/–/l/ contrasts. Markedness in this sense refers to what is rare crosslinguistically; those elements that are common to more languages are relatively less marked. The more marked elements in the world's languages can be seen as being somehow inherently more difficult for human beings to learn. This is the essence of Eckman's Markedness Differential Hypothesis, stated in Example 5 and Table 17.5.

(5) The Markedness Differential Hypothesis (MDH)
     The areas of difficulty that a language learner will have can be predicted on the basis of a systematic comparison of the grammars of the native language, the target language and the markedness relations in universal grammar. (Eckman, 1987, p. 61)

With respect to the contrast between /r/ and /l/, environments on the right of the implicational hierarchy in Example 4 are relatively more marked and should be relatively more difficult to learn, whereas those on the left are less marked and should be relatively less difficult to learn. Although Mandarin has a contrast between /l/ and /r/ only in initial position, a contrastive analysis of Mandarin and English (Section 1.1) could not predict which of the other environments the /r/–/l/ contrast would appear in first. Given the account of the implicational order in Example 4 in terms of the criteria for salience in Table 17.4, we can now make such predictions for other languages. The acquisition of phonemic contrasts between /r/ and /l/ should follow these criteria so that the contrast is learned in the least marked (or most salient) environments first. To the extent that these predictions are borne out, the scale in 4 could provide further support for the proposals of Eckman (1987a, 1987b) and Broselow (1987) that universal principles of markedness may be used together with contrastive analysis to predict the difficulty of acquisition of L2 features.

One prediction that we may want to test is the placement of the word-initial environment in the implicational hierarchy. As can be seen from Table 17.3, subjects N and K neutralize /r/ and /l/ in this environment but appear to maintain

Table 17.6. Neutralization of r/l for Native Speakers of Other Asian languages

Native Lang.	Subject	SPEAK	r / l	#__	V__V	C__	V__C/#
Indonesian or Javanese	3	165	–	–	–	–	o
	4	180	–	–	–	–	o
	10	170	–	–	–	–	o
	11	180	–	–	–	–	o
Thai	5	175	–	–	–	+	o
	2	180	–	+	+	o	–
	1	170	–	+	+	+	o
	7	165	–	+	+	+	o
	6	130	o	+	+	s	+
	8	165	o	+	+	+	o
	9	155	o	+	+	+	o
Korean	14	170	o	+	+	o	s
	13	145	o	+	+	s	+
Japanese	12	145	o	+	+	+	+

the /r/ and /l/ contrast in other environments. This appearance should not be accepted uncritically, given that the data samples for these subjects were limited.[8] We must ask, therefore, what the ranking is of the word-initial and syllabic environments.

3.3. Non-Chinese Patterns of English /r/ and /l/

One might reasonably ask whether the patterns I have described merely concern speakers of Mandarin Chinese, or whether they apply to learners of English more generally. Is the implicational ordering of the environments of the /l/–/r/ contrast in fact a universal pattern? To address this question I examined 14 additional subjects using the same analytical procedure described. These subjects were speakers of other Asian languages (Indonesian, Thai, Japanese, and Korean). The results of the analysis are given in Table 17.6.

This group of subjects is easily grouped according to the native language of the learners. Japanese and Korean, both of which lack a phonemic contrast between /r/ and /l/ (Kim, 1987; Shibatani, 1987), show some degree of neutralization in all environments. The Indonesian speakers seem to observe a contrast in all positions, except in the most difficult, postvocalic position.

The most interesting learners are the Thai learners, because /r/ and /l/ have an interesting status in Thai. According to Hudak, both /r/ and /l/ occur in Thai, and both can even appear in initial clusters (pr, pl, pʰr, pʰl, tr, tʰr, kr, kl, kʰr, kʰl). Yet "the phonemic status of /l/ and /r/ in Thai appears to be in a state of

---

[8]They also shared other peculiar phonological patterns that were not shared by the majority of subjects. For example, for subject /r/, a glottal stop systematically replaced /s/ in all /sC/ clusters, a substitution I hadn't seen in other subjects' data when I first did the coding. I included subject U when I found that her SPEAK test data included a similar substitution; her data show some degree of neutralization in all environments. The clearer and more complete data of subject /l/ appear to show that if /r/ and /l/ are neutralized in the word-initial environment, then they should be neutralized in all other environments.

flux . . . In fast speech . . . /r/ freely alternates with /l/ although certain forms occur more with /l/ than with /r/ . . . Linguistic hypotheses suggest that this lack of a stable contrast may signal a sound change in process" (Hudak, 1987, p. 791). It appears that either this same process is showing up in the transfer of the /r/–/l/ contrast in the Thai speakers' English or that they, like the Mandarin speakers, are at different stages of learning the English contrast.

The Thai speakers are also crucial in demonstrating an ordering of the environments in which /r/ and /l/ contrast, other than postvocalically. For them, the best ordering appears to be that given in Example 6, with a scalability factor of 98%.

(6) syllabic r/l $<< \begin{Bmatrix} \#_ \\ V_V \end{Bmatrix} << $ C_ $<<$ _C/#

Note that in this ranking, the initial environment is ranked lower than the syllabic environment, the opposite ordering from the Mandarin speakers' pattern, and the syllable-initial and intervocalic environments appear to be identical— they might profitably be treated as a single environment for the Thai speakers (e.g., prevocalic without a preceding consonant). This situation is somewhat different from that of the Mandarin speakers, and requires explanation.

With regard to the ranking of word-initial and intervocalic environments, there is nothing universal that requires these environments to be treated differently. One of the possibilities allowed by the rankings in Table 17.4 is that word-initial and intervocalic environments could pattern identically. The fact that the Mandarin speakers treat the environments differently suggests that some additional phonological pattern is being transferred from Mandarin in the learning of the English contrast.

What is more problematic is the ranking of the word-initial and syllable-nucleus environments. The different rankings for the Thai and Mandarin speakers might be affected by the nature of the contrast involved. The apparent contrast between /r/ and /l/ in the syllable nucleus for some of the Thai speakers could be due to the neutralization of /l/ with other categories, especially /o/, in that position. The Standard English phone for /l/ in the syllable nucleus is a velarized lateral [ɫ], acoustically much like a back vowel, which explains the prevalence of [o] representing /l/ for both the Thai and Mandarin speakers (Ard, 1989). For the Thai speakers, we do not find any lateralized phones in this environment; thus, there is no firm evidence that we are seeing a contrast between two liquids /r/ and /l/ in syllable-nucleus position, and we might guess that /l/ has not become distinct from /o/ in this environment. For the Mandarin speakers, the same situation holds, although there are some examples of lateralized phones representing /l/ in the syllable-nucleus position. Thus, the data regarding /r/ and /l/ in the syllable nucleus might not be relevant to the markedness hierarchy of /r/ and /l/ contrasts but to some other hierarchy of vocalic contrasts. This issue could be resolved by a focused study of vocalic contrasts using the methodology employed here.

The combined data from all of the subjects thus supports the revised marked-ness hierarchy given in 7. The brackets surrounding the intervocalic environment indicate that this environment is optionally available in the hierarchy, depending on the phonological patterns of the learner's native language; when present, it occupies the indicated position on the hierarchy.

$$(7) \quad \left\{ \begin{matrix} \text{syllabic } r \, / l \\ \#\_\_ \end{matrix} \right\} \quad << \quad (V\_\_V) \quad << \quad C\_\_ \quad << \quad \_\_C/\#$$

3.4. Two Types of Learning

One potentially troubling pattern remains to be interpreted in Tables 17.3 and 17.6: why is it that the environment that is last to be learned (postvocalic) shows some evidence of contrast (i.e. either subset or overlap neutralization) for all of the Mandarin speakers and a majority of the others, when the less-marked environments show complete neutralization? If the environments are learned according to the acquisitional sequence in Example 7, then we should expect that when learning is going on in less marked positions, there should be no contrast of any kind in the most difficult, postvocalic position. The answer to this question seems to reside in the frequency of occurrence of /r/ and /l/ in each of the environments. Input frequency is known to exert influences on the order of acquisition of other aspects of L2 (Larsen-Freeman, 1976; Long, 1981), quite apart from other linguistic influences. The expected frequency of the /r/–/l/ contrast in the learners' English can be used to give a rough index of the need for the contrast. Table 17.7 shows the counts of words containing /l/ and /r/ in the Mandarin-speaking subjects' self-introductions.[9] Among all the positions, postvocalic position is most frequent (29%), followed by syllable-nucleus (25%), and postconsonantal position (22%).[10] In addition, /r/ and /l/–containing words occur in nearly equal frequency in postvocalic position (53% /r/ and 47% /l/), unlike the postconsonantal and syllable-nucleus positions, which are heavily skewed toward /r/ (containing 72% and 77% /r/, respectively). In these latter positions one could adopt a strategy of using r-like phones throughout and be assured of being correct about 75% of the time. In the postvocalic position, such a strategy would produce an error about 50% of the time, creating an impetus to adopt a different strategy.

These observations invoke another sense of "markedness," distinct from the typological sense employed by Eckman (1987a) and Broselow (1987). In this second sense of markedness, what is least marked is what is most common *in a particular language*; I will call this *language-specific* markedness. Although crosslin-guistic recurrence and language-internal frequency are both used in linguistic

---

[9]The pronunciation exercise sentences are excluded from these counts.

[10]Even if the word-initial and intervocalic environments were combined (e.g., as "simple syllable onset"), the combined environment would only rank third, at 23% of occurrences.

Table 17.7. Uses of /r/ and /l/ by Mandarin-Speaking Subjects

	C__	#__	r/ l	V_V	_C/#	Total	
r	146	40	182	56	142	566	(60%)
l	58	64	52	55	125	354	(40%)
Total	204	104	234	111	267	920	(100%)
	(22%)	(11%)	(25%)	(12%)	(29%)	(100%)	

typology as criteria for identifying typological markedness relations (Croft, 1990; Greenberg, 1966), it is widely recognized that these two criteria may diverge. Thus it may be useful to distinguish between the two criteria and the kinds of markedness they represent. We may also expect their effects to be manifest in different ways in language acquisition.

Regarding the patterns observed, the /r/–/l/ contrast in postvocalic position is very frequent, carries a high functional load, and is therefore relatively less marked in the language-specific sense than the /r/–/l/ contrast in other positions, even though it is highly marked crosslinguistically. Consequently the subjects appear to have begun learning the /r/–/l/ contrast in postvocalic position before attempting some of the typologically less marked (but less frequent) ones, adopting production strategies that lead to subset or overlap neutralizations. The contrast in postvocalic position is more difficult, however, and is learned completely later than in other, crosslinguistically less marked environments.

We have therefore two different kinds of markedness—language specific and crosslinguistic—which correspond to two different patterns of learning observed simultaneously in the same data. Language-specific markedness corresponds to the degree of functional load that a contrast has in a particular environment in a particular language, and consequently to how early or late a learner may *begin* learning that contrast. Crosslinguistic markedness corresponds to the inherent difficulty of a contrast in a particular environment and dictates the relative order in which a learner may complete learning the /l/–/r/ contrast in different environments. Since these two principles concern different aspects of language acquisition (i.e., inception vs. completion of learning), neither need take precedence over the other.

4. CONCLUSIONS

The English interlanguage data from both Mandarin speakers and speakers of four other Asian languages appear to support the markedness hierarchy in 7, with the contrast between /r/ and /l/ being least marked in syllabic or prevocalic position, and most marked in postvocalic position. Learners appear to follow this hierarchy in the process of acquiring phonemic contrasts between /r/ and

/l/. In addition, we have strong evidence that the contrasts in the learner's native language are transferred, so that speakers of a language with a more robust set of contrasts (e.g., Indonesian) have a significant advantage over those with a more reduced set of contrasts (e.g., Mandarin, Thai, Korean, and Japanese, in increasing order of difficulty). We have in effect demonstrated a case of Eckman's Markedness Differential Hypothesis, i.e., that the difficulty that a language learner has in learning the pronunciation of the L2 can be predicted by a comparison of the L1 and L2 and the markedness relations in universal grammar. We must add one important qualification to this hypothesis, however; learners may *begin* acquiring the more frequent contrasts earlier, *even if they are more marked crosslinguistically*. The acquisition of these contrasts is not complete, however, until the crosslinguistically less marked contrasts are fully learned.

The results of this study have clear implications for second language teaching. First, they suggest that strategic use of minimal pair exercises could be beneficial in teaching pronunciation. Minimal-pair exercises have fallen out of favor during the "communicative" vogue of language teaching. Beebe (1987) even suggested that minimal pairs have no real use in language teaching. This may be true if the learner is in a stage of learning where s/he cannot effectively utilize the contrast being taught. Learning pronunciation is like learning many other features of a language: learners must first achieve a particular stage of learning before they are able to use the input that will lead to another stage of learning. The evidence here suggests that the phonemic contrast between /r/ and /l/ must be learned in word-initial or syllable-nucleus position first, next in intervocalic position, next in postconsonantal position, and finally in prevocalic position.

A common problem with minimal-pair exercises is that often a phonemic contrast is not illustrated in all the positions in which it must be learned. For example, Trager and Henderson (1983) and Baker and Goldstein (1990) treat /r/ and /l/ in initial and final position, but not explicitly in intervocalic or postconsonantal position. Other texts, such as Esary (1977), Gilbert (1983), Grant (1993), and Hagen and Grogan (1992), do not systematically discriminate any of the environments recognized here, although most environments receive at least a few examples. In the worst case, a text may provide only examples of a contrast in initial position. These methods effectively ignore the needs of Mandarin speakers, who already have the contrast in initial position but need to learn a similar contrast in other positions.

In addition, all of the texts seem to assume that the teaching of a contrast like that of /l/ and /r/ can be dealt with as a single unitary phenomenon, without internal stages or structure. Pronunciation texts are designed with a unit for each sound or sound contrast to be learned. This practice, undoubtedly borrowed from structuralist grammatical description, presumably makes the task of text writing easier for the text author. But it shows no sensitivity to what any given learner's needs might be and fails to assist the teacher in determining them. My research shows that the learning of /r/ and /l/ passes through a range of related but distinct stages, and that any given class of learners at a comparable level of proficiency is likely to be composed of individual learners with quite different learning needs. Teaching of pronunciation therefore needs to be strategic in two ways: it must target the individual learner, and it must target the stage of learning s/he is currently at. None of the currently available texts or teaching manuals appears to do that.

This problem could be rectified by employing the methodology of this study as a diagnostic for assessing learners' stages of acquisition. Short oral introductions like those used here are easily prepared at home or in a language lab, and they reveal much about the stage of development of the learner's pronunciation. Alternatively, one could construct a reading passage containing pairs of words contrasting /r/ and /l/ (or other sounds) in all relevant environments to determine the next environment in which each individual learner is most likely to learn a contrast, and then target that environment for individual teaching emphasis. The resulting patterns of contrast and neutralization would indicate the stage of learning of each student. Vocabulary and minimal pairs could then be chosen strategically to address the needs of each student. A carefully constructed diagnostic like this would be more useful to ESL teachers than tests like SPEAK and TSE in identifying problem areas and teaching needs, since it addresses the strategic requirements of teaching pronunciation.

Finally, we must reconsider the stereotype that instigated this investigation. It is true that speakers of Mandarin Chinese neutralize English /r/ and /l/ and that this neutralization is due in part to transfer. However, speakers of Mandarin exhibit patterns of neutralization different from those of speakers of other Asian languages, and the so-called confusion of /r/ and /l/ is consistently and significantly patterned. Speakers of Mandarin learning English are far less likely to neutralize /r/ and /l/ in initial position than speakers of Japanese or Korean, and neutralization of /r/ and /l/ in Mandarin English is almost always in the direction of /l/ going to [r]. The *flied lice* pronunciation stereotype, in fact, is not a characteristic of the English of native speakers of Mandarin. Furthermore, patterns of neutralization in Mandarin English observe both language-specific and typological markedness hierarchies that are also found in the interlanguage of other learners of English.

ACKNOWLEDGMENTS

My thanks to Susan Herring for providing many helpful comments on an earlier version of this paper. All errors and omissions are the responsibility of the author.

REFERENCES

Ard, J. (1989). "A Constructivist Perspective on Non-Native Phonology." *Linguistic Perspectives on Second Language Acquisition*, ed. by S. Gass and J. Schachter, pp. 243–259. Cambridge: Cambridge University Press.

Baker, A., and S. Goldstein. (1990). *Pronunciation Pairs: An Introductory Course for Students of English*. Cambridge: Cambridge University Press.

Beebe, L. (1987). "Myths About Interlanguage Phonology." *Interlanguage Phonology*, ed. by G. Ioup and S. Weinberger, pp. 165–175. New York: Newbury House.

Broselow, E. (1987). "An Investigation of Transfer in Second Language Phonology." *Interlanguage Phonology*, ed. by G. Ioup and S. Weinberger, pp. 261–278. New York: Newbury House.

Chao, Y. R. (1968). *A Grammar of Modern Spoken Chinese*. Berkeley: University of California Press.

Cheng, C.-C. (1973). *A Synchronic Phonology of Mandarin Chinese*. The Hague: Mouton.

Croft, W. (1990). *Typology and Universals*. Cambridge: Cambridge University Press.

Eckman, F. (1987a). "Markedness and the Contrastive Analysis Hypothesis." *Interlanguage Phonology*, ed. by G. Ioup and S. Weinberger. New York: Newbury House.

———. (1987b). "On the Naturalness of Interlanguage Phonological Rules." *Interlanguage Phonology*, ed. by G. Ioup and S. Weinberger. New York: Newbury House.

Esarey, G. (1977). *Pronunciation Exercises for ESL*. Pittsburgh: University of Pittsburgh Press.

Gilbert, J. (1983). *Clear speech: Pronunciation and Listening Comprehension in North American English*. Cambridge: Cambridge University Press.

Grant, L. (1993). *Well Said: Advanced English Pronunciation*. Boston: Heinle & Heinle.

Greenberg, J. (1966). *Language Universals, with Special Reference to Feature Hierarchies*. The Hague: Mouton.

Hagen, S., and P. Grogan. (1992). *Sound Advantage: A Pronunciation Book*. Englewood Cliffs, NJ: Regents-Prentice-Hall.

Hudak, T. (1987). "Thai." *The World's Major Languages*, ed. by B. Comrie, pp. 757–775. Oxford: Oxford University Press.

Kim, N.-K. (1987). "Korean." *The World's Major Languages*, ed. by B. Comrie, pp. 881–898. Oxford: Oxford University Press.

Larsen-Freeman, D. (1976). "An Explanation for the Morpheme Acquisition Order of Second Language Learners," *Language Learning* 26, 125–34.

Long, M. (1981). "Input, Interaction, and Second Language Acquisition." *Native Language and Foreign Language Acquisition*, ed. by H. Winitz. *Annals of the New York Academy of Sciences* 379; 259–78.

Odlin, T. (1989). *Language Transfer: Cross-Linguistic Influence in Language Learning*. Cambridge: Cambridge University Press.

Shibatani, M. (1987). "Japanese." *The World's Major Languages*, ed. by B. Comrie, pp. 855–880. Oxford: Oxford University Press.

Trager, E., and S. Henderson. (1983). *PD's: Pronunciation Drills*. Englewood Cliffs, NJ: Regents-Prentice-Hall.

Chapter 18

Foreign Accent and Phonetic Interference: The Application of Linguistic Research to the Teaching of Second Language Pronunciation

Robert M. Hammond
Purdue University

1. INTRODUCTION

Since the decline in popularity in the 1960s and 1970s of the Audio Lingual approach (ALM) to second language instruction, many new methods of teaching second and foreign languages have been introduced. Most of these more popular post-ALM second language methodologies can readily be classified as communicative approaches to second language acquisition. All of the communicatively based language teaching models have several major points of agreement: (1) they stress the meaningful use of a second language for the purposes of true communication in the classroom; (2) they require the presence of a maximally high amount of what Krashen (1981) called comprehensible input; (3) again in Krashen's terms, they stress the creation of a classroom environment that produces a maximally low affective filter. However, another common thread running through all communicatively based teaching methodologies is the fact that none of them makes any genuine effort to deal with the teaching of pronunciation in the second language classroom. Although none of them explicitly states that pronunciation is not to be taught, they do largely imply that by not including any type of pronunciation explanations or activities in their methodologies. Krashen (1985) commented in passing that speaking emerges on its own after the student has been exposed to comprehensible input and after a sufficient amount of acquisition has taken place. After a very brief discussion of pronunciation, Krashen and Terrell (1983, pp. 89–91) concluded ". . . we do not place undue emphasis in early stages on perfection in the students' pronunciation, but

293

rather concentrate on providing a good model with large quantities of comprehensible input before production is attempted." It is particularly surprising that proponents of the so-called proficiency movement, although they place a great deal of emphasis on linguistic accuracy in the nascent stages of second language acquisition (to avoid what they term 'fossilization'), they include no provision for the teaching of pronunciation in the classroom (see, e.g., Omaggio, 1986). After surveying various communicative methodologies, Terrell arrived at the same conclusion: "Communicative approaches likewise have not known what to do with pronunciation" (Terrell, 1989, p. 197).

The question that a linguist, especially a phonologist, might ask at this point is why none of these new language teaching methodologies has chosen to include the teaching of the sound systems of second languages, in view of the fact that one of the important aspects of linguistics is the study of the association of sound with meaning. Putting aside the spurious question of fossilization, there seem to be three principal reasons why methodologists have chosen not to include the teaching of pronunciation in current communicative methodologies. Many believe that:

1. The teaching of pronunciation appeals only to learning and not to acquisition, and is therefore of no value in a system that is attempting to get students to acquire language.

2. The constant reference to correct pronunciation or to the correction of student pronunciation errors will inhibit students from speaking by raising their affective filters.

3. Since most second language instruction in the United States involves learners who have passed the so-called ideal age for language acquisition, these methodologists believe that adult students have already lost much of their innate capacity to acquire a nativelike pronunciation in a second language.

Because of the issues raised by these three points, the research in this paper was undertaken to attempt to begin to assess the significance for second language pronunciation acquisition of each of the following:

1. There is a relatively large body of phonetic research that shows adult language learners are capable of perceiving, imitating, and learning fairly subtle and precise phonetic distinctions present in target languages.

2. Phonologists have demonstrated that the acquisition of second language phonology is governed by universal principles of phonology.

3. We need to determine the significance of phonetic and phonological research such as that discussed in this chapter for the acquisition of pronunciation in a second language.

4. We need to discover how this information can be incorporated into the theoretical framework of communicative teaching methodologies and into the actual classroom situation.

2. THE PHONOLOGICAL AND PHONETIC RESEARCH

Previous research has established that adult foreign language learners may produce speech sounds in a foreign language according to the sometimes inappropriate phonetic norms of their native language, and also that they are able to detect foreign accent in the speech of others (Barry, 1974). Previous phonetic research has likewise shown that there are measurable physical differences between the speech of native and non-native speakers that can be revealed by instrumental analysis (see, e.g., Flege, 1980; Flege & Eefting, 1987; Suomi, 1976). In this chapter I will discuss three phonetic and phonological studies that demonstrate both the perceptual and learning abilities of second language students and the effect of phonological theory and universal grammar on second language pronunciation acquisition as representative examples of linguistic research interacting with second language acquisition.

2.1. Voice-Onset Time in the Acquisition of Spanish

In two earlier studies (Flege & Hammond, 1982; Hammond & Flege, 1988), experiments were carried out to determine if American adult language learners studying Spanish as a second language might be aware of different nonsegmental phonetic aspects of foreign accent. A paradigm was designed in which native speakers of American English attempted to imitate a foreign accent. If Americans imitating Spanish-accented English produced some of the nonsegmental phonetic differences that are known to distinguish native and Spanish-accented English, in addition to the more obvious segmental substitutions, this would indicate that even naive listeners without special training in phonetics are aware (at least at some level) of some of the purely phonetic aspects of foreign accent.

In these experiments, Flege and Hammond asked adult subjects to read English sentences with what they considered to be a typical Spanish accent. The test material consisted of 21 English sentences of the form 'The _____ is on the _____'. The utterance-medial and utterance-final blanks in this carrier sentence were filled with a number of different C(C)VC test words, all nouns, for example, 'The *phone* is on the *book*'. Present in each of the test words was one of six different English sounds that are known to be replaced by inappropriate sounds in the speech of at least some Spanish speakers of English.

From the larger population, two groups of speakers were chosen: the ten subjects who produced the greatest number of sound substitutions and the ten who had produced the fewest. Also, for purposes of comparison, a control population of ten speakers producing unaccented English was established. These speakers produced the same sentences previously produced by speakers imitating a Spanish accent.

An instrumental analysis of voice-onset time (VOT) phonetic differences in the speech of Americans imitating a Spanish accent was performed. VOT is a readily measurable acoustic parameter that often serves to distinguish categories of stop consonants (Lisker & Abramson, 1964, 1967) and that may provide a sufficient perceptual cue to the phonological contrast between English syllable-initial voiced and voiceless stops occurring before stressed vowels (Abramson & Lisker, 1970, 1973). VOT may be defined as the interval of time between the release of a stop closure and the onset of voicing (glottal pulsing) for the following segment. The stops found in human languages generally fall into three distinct VOT categories, although the actual VOT values of the stops representing those categories may vary somewhat from language to language (i.e., these values are relative; Lisker & Abramson, 1964). From a perspective of acoustic correlates, a stop is said to have been produced with lead VOT when voicing onset precedes stop release; with short-lag VOT when voicing begins at or shortly after stop release; and with long-lag VOT when voicing onset is delayed until considerably after stop release. The perceptual correlate of VOT is aspiration; hence stops produced with long-lag VOT are heard as being (heavily) aspirated.

Adult foreign language learners often seem to have difficulty in producing the stops of a foreign language correctly if their VOT specification differs from that of stops found in their native language (Flege, 1980; Jones, 1948, 1972; Suomi, 1976). The voiceless unaspirated /ptk/ of Spanish differ from the voiceless aspirated /ptk/ of English in that the voiceless stops of Spanish are produced with short-lag VOT, but English aspirated voiceless stops are articulated with long-lag VOT values (Lisker & Abramson, 1964; Williams, 1977; Zlatin, 1974). As a result of such cross-language phonetic differences, English speakers may tend to produce Spanish /ptk/ with too much aspiration (that is, with VOT values that are too large), whereas Spanish speakers may seriously underaspirate English /ptk/ (producing them with VOT values that are too short by English standards) (Dalbor, 1980; Stockwell & Bowen, 1965; Williams, 1979).

To very briefly summarize the analysis of the VOT data produced by subjects trying to imitate a Spanish accent, adult language learners are indeed aware of at least some nonsegmental phonetic characteristics of a foreign accent in addition to the more obvious segmental differences between native and accented speech. The subjects in these studies produced VOT values that typify Spanish-accented English (Williams, 1979). Thus, these subjects apparently could modify laryngeal timing patterns to produce stops with VOT values that were not characteristic of their native language. Both the speakers who were relatively successful and those who were unsuccessful in imitating a Spanish accent (as measured by the number of segmental substitutions produced) made the VOT of /t/ much shorter than normal for an English /t/.

2.2. The Acquisition of French VOT Values
by Adult Speakers of Mandarin Chinese

In a paper read in February 1993 at the Third Second Language Acquisition-Foreign Language Learning Conference, Rochet (1993; see also Rochet & Chen, 1992) presented the results of an experimental study, also involving voice-onset time, that was designed to establish the validity of three questions of importance to the theory underlying the acquisition of second language pronunciation:

1. Is it possible to teach adult second language learners to perceive fairly subtle phonetic differences between the native language and the target language?
2. If second language students can be taught to perceive such phonetic differences between L1 and L2, is there a carryover to an improvement in their second language production in these same areas?
3. If improved perception leads to improved L2 production, is there a transfer or extension to other phonologically related categories in L2 pronunciation?

Mandarin Chinese and standard French are similar with respect to the VOT values just discussed for American English and Spanish. As in Spanish, the voiced stops of Standard French are produced with lead VOT (since voicing onset precedes stop release), and the voiceless stops of Standard French are produced with short-lag VOT values. Like English, Mandarin Chinese has aspirated voiceless stops that are articulated with long-lag VOT values and unaspirated voiceless stops that are articulated with short-lag VOT values. As was the case for Spanish and English, the crossover boundaries between French voiceless and voiced stops and Mandarin unaspirated voiceless stops do not coincide, so some degree of perceptual and articulatory difficulty can be predicted for Mandarin speakers learning French.

In order to answer these three questions, Rochet set up an experimental study that first pretested the ability of native speakers of Mandarin Chinese to discriminate voiced and voiceless stops articulated by native speakers of standard French. This pretest contained both an imitation task and a perceptual task. In general terms, the pretest showed, as expected, that native speakers of Mandarin had difficulty both in perceiving and in producing French stops according to the VOT norms of standard French.

The second portion of his study involved a series of six one-half-hour training sessions in which the adult subjects worked with various sets of acoustic stimuli consisting of a labial stop follow by the vowel [u]. The first set of the training materials contained labial stops with maximally opposed VOT values, and each subsequent set of materials gradually and systematically decreased the differences between the VOT values of the stops. The training sessions involved only perception of stops according to French VOT norms, and each subject completed all training sets with a minimum success rate of 95%. After the completion of the training sessions, subjects were given a post-test that again evaluated their abilities to accurately perceive and produce French stops. The data from the post-test were compared to those of the pretest, and subjects showed improvement in perceptual accuracy in identifying voiced and voiceless stops according to French norms. Furthermore, the same subjects also showed improvement in the correct articulation of all six French stops.

Rochet showed, therefore, that the perceptual performance of L2 students can be improved by means of instruction in specific areas related to those acoustic categories, that an improvement in perceptual performance can in turn lead to an improvement in production performance within the scope of those same categories, and finally that, in following the notion of pattern congruity, a transfer of training from a specific context to a more general environment is also possible.

2.3. Universal Phonological Principles and Coda Consonants in English Interlanguage

In another paper presented at the Third Second Language Acquisition - Foreign Language Learning Conference (as well as in another recent study), Eckman and Iverson (1993, 1994) analyzed consonant pronunciation errors in syllable codas in English made by adult native speakers of Cantonese, Korean, and Japanese. The casual speech of these subjects was recorded, and the errors made involving English single-consonant codas were tabulated.

Eckman and Iverson hypothesized that the phonetic errors made by their subjects could be predicted and largely accounted for by applying principles of phonological theory, markedness, and universal grammar. They further predicted that the quantity and types of errors made by these subjects could not be accounted for by the principles of contrastive analysis or L1 interference. With respect to syllable codas, Eckman and Iverson based their predictions on the phonological principles of markedness, internal syllable structure (Clements & Keyser, 1983), the Sonority Sequencing Generalization (Selkirk, 1982), and the Sonority Hierarchy (Clements, 1990; Selkirk, 1984). In an analysis of the pronunciation errors made by their subjects in English syllable codas the authors confirmed their hypothesis that a combination of these phonological principles would account for the greater difficulty their subjects had in pronouncing some English syllable codas (such as obstruents over sonorants). They then combined those principles of universal phonological grammar with L1 phonotactic rules to account for all coda pronunciation errors.

Their Cantonese subjects had much more difficulty with obstruent codas than nasal codas, thus confirming the validity of the phonological principles of markedness in codas and of the Sonority Sequencing Generalization, since obstruents are more highly marked than nasals in syllable codas. Of the total number of coda pronunciation errors made by the Cantonese subjects, 77% involved obstruents. Their remaining coda pronunciation errors were distributed as follows: Liquids, 20%; nasals, 3%; and glides, less than 0.5%. Since Cantonese permits obstruents (unreleased voiceless stops), nasals, and glides in coda position, an explanation based only on native language interference would not account for these errors. Native language interference would account for the relative difficulty these subjects had pronouncing liquids in syllable codas but would not explain why they experienced much more difficulty with obstruents in codas than with nasals and glides.

In this same vein, of the total number of coda pronunciation errors made by the Korean subjects, 84% involved obstruents, 13% liquids, 2% nasals, and less than 1% involved glides. Since Korean allows stops and nasals in codas but excludes both liquids and glides, once again phonological analysis accounts for these facts much more completely than native language interference. L1 interference can predict the difficulty these subjects had with liquids in codas, but it fails to account for obstruents being more difficult in L2 than nasals, and would be completely off target if it predicted extreme difficulty with codas containing glides.

Finally, their Japanese subjects showed the same difficulty with pronouncing obstruents in codas as the Cantonese and Korean subjects. Of the total number of the Japanese subjects' coda pronunciation errors, 59% involved obstruents, 21% liquids, 19% nasals, and less than 1% glides. Since Japanese phonotactics excludes liquids, glides, and the bilabial nasal in syllable codas and allows only alveolar nasals in this position, the syllabic markedness hypothesis again accounts for the relative degrees of difficulties the Japanese subjects had with each of these three consonant groups. It also predicts that these subjects would have relatively little difficulty acquiring the more sonorous glides in coda position. As was the case with the Korean subjects, an L1 interference account incorrectly predicts that Japanese speakers would have profound difficulty pronouncing English codas containing glides.

Eckman and Iverson showed that when concepts such as syllable structure and consonant sonority are taken into consideration, it becomes clear that pronunciation acquisition depends largely on where a segment occurs within an internal syllable structure, and that accounts based on native language interference are of only minor importance in accounting for L2 pronunciation acquisition difficulties. Their study therefore suggests that it *is* possible to teach pronunciation because it is governed by universal phonological principles.

3. THE SIGNIFICANCE OF LINGUISTIC RESEARCH FOR SECOND LANGUAGE PRONUNCIATION ACQUISITION

These six studies analyzing the phonetic parameter of VOT and the phonological structure of English syllable codas are only representative examples of phonetic and phonological research that is related to our understanding of the acquisition of second language sounds and sound systems—at least on a theoretical level. These types of phonetic studies make it clear that adult second language learners are capable of both perceiving and articulating subtle phonetic distinctions that are not present in the native languages. Phonological studies of this nature also make it clear that the acquisition of second language sound systems is governed by universal phonological principles.

4. THE INCORPORATION OF THE PHONETIC RESEARCH INTO THE SECOND LANGUAGE CLASSROOM

Because phonetic and phonological research clearly indicate that adult second language learners can hear and articulate both segmental and nonsegmental phonetic differences that are known to distinguish native and target-language sound systems, and because of the existence of universal phonological principles that underlie the acquisition of second language sound systems, it should be possible to teach second language pronunciation.

Our questions, then, are: How can the objections to including pronunciation instruction in communicatively based second language classrooms be overcome? And how can underlying phonetic and phonological principles be incorporated into L2 methodology?

4.1. The Error Correction Objection

The most troublesome and valid of the three objections is that constant reference to accurate pronunciation in the second language classroom and the overt correction of student pronunciation errors will inhibit students from speaking by raising their affective filters. Clearly, continual attention to form will instill in L2 students the idea that correctness is more important than communication. Conventional wisdom, although never empirically tested, seems to suggest that the earlier ALM-type methodology, which consisted of intense pronunciation drill, practice, and overt correction of student pronunciation errors, did lead to an improved L2 pronunciation; however, it did little to improve communicative abilities in the L2. On the other hand, the notion imparted in communicative methodology texts, that merely providing a correct model is sufficient for L2 students to acquire a reasonably accurate target language pronunciation, seems equally misguided. It appears, then, that instruction in pronunciation and the correction of student pronunciation errors, while apparently useful or even necessary in teaching second language pronunciation, should not take place in the communicative classroom setting.

4.2. The Critical Age Objection

Data from the phonetic studies cited here indicate that the notion that students beyond some critical age can no longer accurately perceive and/or produce L2 sounds that are significantly different from the sounds of their native language is erroneous. Whether the phonetic learning and articulation abilities exhibited by the adult subjects in these studies can actually be carried over into their everyday use of their target languages remains an open question.

4.3. The Acquisition Versus Learning Objection

If the Krashen distinction between learning and acquisition is absolute, then explicit instruction in pronunciation can be of no value in the second language classroom because such instruction results only in learned information and not acquisition. Furthermore, if, as Krashen has hypothesized, learned information cannot cross over to become acquired behavior, then, once again, explicit pronunciation training would be of no value in teaching a second language. However, these notions remain only hypotheses and have never been empirically tested. Therefore, to rule out any value of pronunciation instruction on the basis of these ideas would be premature, because the validity of the hypotheses has yet to be determined.

4.4. Pronunciation Instruction
within a Communicative Framework

Because phonetic research indicates that adult second language learners can accurately perceive and produce the sounds of a target language, and because phonological research suggests that pronunciation can be taught, it would seem appropriate at this point to ask how a communicative methodology could include explicit pronunciation instruction without inhibiting the classroom communication atmosphere. One possible method of accomplishing this would be to make explicit pronunciation instruction part of the overall communicative methodology without actually including it within the communicative classroom. Many second language curricula still include a weekly laboratory session at the beginning and intermediate levels, primarily as a residual of earlier ALM-type methodologies. Since communicative methodologies do not use repetition drills, pattern practice, transformation drills, and other types of aural/oral activities that are easily delegated to audiotape programs, the role of the traditional language laboratory in communicative methodologies has not been well-defined. However, in programs with a traditional weekly language laboratory, it seems that the time could easily be redefined as one of analysis and explicit pronunciation instruction. In language programs with other organizational patterns, some specific time period per week could be set aside for pronunciation instruction. The other regular weekly class hours could then be preserved expressly for communicative second language acquisition activities. The advantage of this dichotomy is that clearly acquisitional activities could then be kept separate from learning activities. Another advantage of this approach is that it could be carried out with a minimum of paperwork and red tape. This type of modification would involve only a change in activities but no schedule changes and curriculum revisions.

5. CONCLUSIONS

Most language instructors seem less than completely satisfied with their students' L2 pronunciation. Therefore, researchers should investigate how best to modify communicative methodology in order to improve the teaching of second language pronunciation. The research presented in this chapter suggests that pronunciation can be taught. The question of HOW it can best be taught, whether by explanations, drills, or exercises, awaits further research.

REFERENCES

Abramson, A., and L. Lisker. (1970). "Discriminability along the Voicing Continuum: Cross-Language Tests," *Proceedings of the Sixth International Congress of Phonetic Sciences*, ed. by B. Hala, M. Romportl, and P. Janota, pp. 569–573. Munich: Hueber.

———, and L. Lisker. (1973). "Voice Timing Perception in Spanish Word-Initial Stops," *Journal of Phonetics* 1, 1–8.

Barry, W. (1974). "Language Background and the Perception of Foreign Accent," *Journal of Phonetics* 2, 65–89.

Clements, G. (1990). "The Role of the Sonority Cycle in Core Syllabification." *Papers in Laboratory Phonology I*, ed. by J. C. Kingston and M. E. Beckman. Cambridge: Cambridge University Press.

Clements, G., and S. Keyser. (1983). *CV Phonology: A Generative Theory of the Syllable.* Cambridge, MA: MIT Press.

Dalbor, J. (1980). *Spanish Phonology: Theory and Practice.* New York: Holt, Rinehart & Winston.

Eckman, F., and G. Iverson. (1993). "Pronunciation Difficulties in ESL: Coda Consonants in English Interlanguage." Paper presented at the Third Conference on Second Language Acquisition and Foreign Language Learning, Purdue University, West Lafayette, Indiana.

———. (1994). "Pronunciation Difficulties in ESL: Coda Consonants in English Interlanguage." *First and Second Language Phonology*, ed. by Mehmet Yavas, pp. 251–265. San Diego, CA: Singular.

Flege, J. (1980). "Phonetic Approximation in Second Language Acquisition." *Language Learning* 30, 117–134.

———, and W. Eefting. (1987). "Production and Perception of English Stops by Native Spanish Speakers," *Journal of Phonetics* 15, 67–83.

———, and R. Hammond. (1982). "Mimicry of Non-Distinctive Phonetic Differences between Language Varieties," *Studies in Second Language Acquisition* 5(1), 1–17.

Hammond, R., and J. Flege. (1988). "Attitudes, Experience, and the Mimicry of Sounds—Implications for Second Language Acquisition." Paper presented at The Seventh International Symposium on International Perspectives on Language, Literature, and Culture, George Mason University, Fairfax, Virginia.

Jones, D. ([1948] 1972). "An Outline of English Phonetics." Cambridge, England: Cambridge University Press.

Krashen, S. (1981). *Second Language Acquisition and Second Language Learning.* Oxford, England: Pergamon.

———. (1985). *The Input Hypothesis.* London: Longman.

————, and T. Terrell. (1983). *The Natural Approach.* Hayward, CA: Alemany.

Lisker, L., and A. Abramson. (1964). "A Cross-Language Study of Voicing in Initial Stops: Acoustical Measurements," *Word* 20, 384–422.

————, and A. Abramson. (1967). "Some Effects of Context on Voice-Onset Time in English Stops." *Language and Speech* 10, 1–28.

Omaggio, A. (1986). *Teaching Language in Context: Proficiency Oriented Instruction.* Boston: Heinle & Heinle.

Rochet, B. (1993). "The Role of Auditory Training in Teaching Non-Native Speech Contrasts." Paper presented at the Third Conference on Second Language Acquisition and Foreign Language Learning, Purdue University, West Lafayette, Indiana.

————, and F.-X. Chen. (1992). "Acquisition of French VOT Contrasts by Adult Speakers of Mandarin Chinese." *ICSLP 92 Proceedings, International Conference on Spoken Language Processing,* vol. 1, ed. by J. J. Ohala, T. M. Nearey, B. L. Derwing, M. M. Hodge, and G. E. Wiebe. University of Alberta, Edmonton.

Selkirk, E. (1982). "The Syllable." *The Structure of Phonological Representations, Part II,* ed. by H. Van der Hulst and N. Smith. Dordrecht: Foris.

————. (1984). "On the Major Class Features and Syllable Theory." *Language Sound Structure: Studies in Phonology Presented to Morris Halle by His Teacher and Students,* ed. by M. Aronoff and R. Oehrle. Cambridge, MA: MIT Press.

Stockwell, R., and D. Bowen. (1965). "The Sounds of English and Spanish." Chicago: University of Chicago Press.

Suomi, K. (1976). "English Voiceless and Voiced Stops as Produced by Native Speakers of Finnish and English." *Jyvaskyla Contrastive Studies* 2. Jyvaskyla, Finland: Jyvaskyla University Department of English.

Terrell, T. (1989). "Teaching Spanish Pronunciation in a Communicative Approach." *American Spanish Pronunciation—Theoretical and Applied Perspectives,* ed. by P. Bjarkman and R. Hammond. Washington, DC: Georgetown University Press.

Williams, L. (1977). "The Voicing Contrast in Spanish," *Journal of Phonetics* 5, 169–184.

————. (1979). "The Modification of Speech Perception and Production in Second Language Learning," *Perception and Psychophysics* 26, 95–104.

Zlatin, M. (1974). "Perceptual and Productive Voice-Onset Time Characteristics of Adults," *Journal of the Acoustical Society of America* 56, 981–994.

Chapter 19

A Study of the Effect of the Acculturation Model on Second Language Acquisition

Doris Hansen
University of Wisconsin–Milwaukee

1. INTRODUCTION

Not long after Lenneberg first introduced his Critical Period Hypothesis (CPH) and its concomitant theory of lateralization in 1967, it was extrapolated to second language acquisition (SLA) and accepted by many linguists, including Oyama (1976), Lamendella (1977), and Scovel (1981) as the most probable explanation for accented speech in adult SLA. "The extent of the foreign accent is directly correlated with the age at which the second language is acquired" (Lenneberg, 1967, p. 9).

Oyama investigated the relationship of two variables, the immigrant's arrival age and length of stay, with degree of accent. Oyama used 60 Italian males, all of whom had studied some English in college. Using Labov's social dialect techniques, she elicited a variety of speech samples, ranging from spontaneous first-person narratives to monitored paragraph readings. These samples were then rated on a 5-point scale for degree of accent by two graduate students in linguistics. Although the data revealed no correlation between length of stay and degree of accent, they did reveal a strong inverse correlation for the age-of-arrival variable.

Although there is a wide acceptance of the generalization that the younger people are when they arrive, the greater the likelihood of an accentless phonology, the CPH is limited. It fails to account for the exceptions, those individuals at both ends of the spectrum who either maintain accents despite having arrived when young, or, of greater interest and concern to researchers, those individuals who achieve nativelike phonation after puberty.

Somehow exceptional learners access some strategy or combination of strategies that enables them to extend or override biological constraints, which predict that postpubescent second language learners will not be able to speak without an accent. An analogous situation might be seen in intelligence. Although the range is genetically programmed, the individual's interaction with environment determines the individual's specific IQ. Because the biological explanation fails to account for the successful (no-accent) postpubescent learner, there must be some other, perhaps supplemental, explanation of Selinker's (1972) estimated 5% of adult learners who master a nativelike second language phonology.[1]

Of the various affective-based SLA models, Schumann's Acculturation Model (1978, 1986), an 11-point taxonomy of variables, is perhaps the most comprehensive. He posits both social (group) and affective (individual) variables as the primary causative variables. Acculturation refers to the learner's positive identification with, and hence social and psychological integration with, the target language group. "[T]he learner will acquire the second language only to the degree that he acculturates" (1978, p. 29). I focus on the exceptional second language learners and investigate the effect of the Acculturation Model on their success.

Like Oyama, I used Labov's social dialect interview techniques to tape subjects reading a short paragraph with some acknowledged difficult phonemes for nonnative speakers of English. I then had them narrate a "close to death" experience, of which only the last minute is used. The first task calls for careful speech, the second for spontaneous speech, since it is designed to involve the speaker emotionally. Then judges that were native speakers of English evaluated the subjects' accents on Neufeld's (1978) 5-point scale.

However, this study differs from Oyama's in a number of ways. Whereas her subjects comprised a homogeneous group of professional Italian males, all with some university education, the subjects of my study comprised a group of 20 Germans of both sexes, with little if any university education. All had been in the United States for over 20 years. Instead of two judges, there were six. Finally, my study investigated the correlation between the subjects' degree of accent and their scores on a questionnaire based on Schumann's Acculturation Model.

2. GENERAL DESIGN

To test Schumann's hypothesis that degree of accent correlates with degree of acculturation, I studied a group of German second language learners following Oyama's (1976) design. I used one principal independent variable, age of arrival

---

[1]Whereas Selinker estimates that 5% of adult speakers have nativelike phonation, Seliger puts that figure at 7% of the population. The accuracy of these figures, however, is not a concern of this chapter.

in the United States. Oyama had also analyzed number of years in the United States, but since all the subjects had been here for 22–37 years, there seemed little need to analyze this variable. Although the first three age-of-arrival intervals were based on Oyama's: prepuberty (ending at age 10), early adolescence (age 11–15), and late adolescence (age 16–20), a fourth group was added.

Although Oyama's study did not include individuals who arrived after age 20, my study included 5 subjects who arrived at ages 21–33. Although this group could have been included under the parameter of postpubescent learners, I treat it as a separate subgroup for two reasons. The first is to see if there are any postpubescent exceptions, since puberty, according to Oyama, is the pivotal point after which non-native language ". . . acquisition results in linguistic functioning [which] differs from that of native speakers . . ." (Oyama, 1973, p. 25). The second reason is to see if the pattern of Oyama's data, increasingly greater degree of accent with each successive group, is maintained with the final and oldest group. Although Lenneberg's hypothesis that the older people are when they arrive, the greater the degee of accent, has gained general acceptance among linguists, it makes no attempt to explain the exceptions other than to recognize them as outliers. Another purpose of my study, then, is to seek explanatory variables in an attempt to determine, ". . . what constellation of characteristics may be ascribed to such exceptions" (Seliger, 1978, p. 55).

2.1. Subject Selection

The subjects were 20 German-born immigrants, 9 females and 11 males, whose arrival ages ranged from 6 to 33. Most of the subjects were drawn from the middle class and none had a university education. They had taken English classes in the United States mainly within a vocational context, typically for a year or two, to acquire necessary survival skills and to pass citizenship tests. Although 4 subjects had studied English before they came to the United States, the other 16 had not. Most of the male subjects were craftsmen or tradesmen, whereas most of the females did some type of clerical work. Three subjects owned their own businesses. None would be considered professionals on Labov's occupational scale as adapted by Oyama.[2] The three native-speaking Americans who comprised the control group were chosen to reflect the same age range and educational and social backgrounds as the experimental group.

2.2. Procedure

Subjects were seen on an individual basis and told that they were participating in a study that attempted to reveal how people approached learning second languages. Their participation would consist of an oral part and a written part.

---

[2]Oyama adapted Labov's (1966) occupational scale: 0—student; 1—manual, craftsman, foreman; 2—clerical, sales; 3—managerial, proprietor, official; 4—professional, semiprofessional.

The oral part required first the reading of a paragraph and then the narration of a story about a time when the subject was in a life-threatening situation. The written part required the filling out of two questionnaires, one biographical, the other about the subject's approach to language.

2.3. The Measures

2.3.1. Paragraphs

Pronunciation was scored on the basis of two taped speech samples based on Oyama's (1976) study, which, in turn, was loosely based on Labov's 1966 study of social dialects in New York. Labov's purpose was to correlate the people's linguistic patterns with their social class. To that end, Labov designed various techniques for eliciting a range of responses, from casual to formal (Labov, 1966). Asking the subject to read a paragraph into a tape recorder results in a monitored, consequently formal, speech sample because the individual tends to be self-conscious about pronunciation. All subjects were asked to read the same paragraph.

2.3.2. Narratives

The second taped sample was designed to elicit a more casual, less monitored speech pattern. Speech tends to be casual when either the situation is informal or some emotional element, such as danger, excitement, fear, or fatigue, comes into play. Labov's method of eliciting casual speech was to have the subject narrate a "danger-of-death sequence." This method was used by Oyama and consequently in my study.

Control samples were randomly mixed in with tapes of the paragraph readings and narratives. The tapes were then divided into a paragraph half and a narrative half. After listening to six warmup samples, each judge rated each speaker's accent according to written instructions adapted from Oyama's study, which was loosely based on Neufeld's (1978) study as follows:

1 point: no foreign accent.
2 points: faint foreign accent.
3 points: moderate foreign accent.
4 points: pronounced foreign accent.
5 points: heavy foreign accent.

Six judges were used in all. Two had masters degrees in linguistics; two were high school language teachers; and two had no linguistic backgrounds. Whereas Oyama used only two judges—graduate students in linguistics—I was interested in seeing how different linguistic backgrounds would affect perception and recognition of accents.

2.3.3. Questionnaires

Each subject completed two written questionnaires. The first was designed to gather demographic information on possible factors involved in language learning. The second questionnaire was based on Schumann's Acculturation Model. Schumann identified seven social, or group, variables, and four affective, or individual, variables. Although I spent a good deal of time looking, I was unsuccessful in locating any standardized questionnaire. With the exception of a few questions I found in other linguists' studies (Seliger, Krashen, & Ladefoged, 1975), I wrote my own, based on the Acculturation Model. To ensure content validity, I sent a copy of the questionnaire to Schumann for his approval and suggestions.[3]

There were at least two questions per variable. All question stems and responses were refined through five versions with a psychometric judge.[4] Each question stem had four possible responses, scaled from one to four points: the higher the number, the greater the acculturation. Finally, the questionnaire was used in a pilot study of three subjects for face validity. An example of a question on motivation, an individual variable, is:

Which of the following was the biggest reason for you to learn to speak English?

a. To become an American.
b. For day-to-day living.
c. To communicate with Americans.
d. To get a job.

3. RESULTS

Combined accent scores from six judges for each taped speech sample ranged from 6 to 28 (out of a possible 6–30 range) with a mean of 2.83 and a standard deviation of 1.41. As in the case of Oyama's data, the first three mean cell scores increase with arrival age, 1.06, 2.87, 3.35. However, Cell 4 showed a mean of 3.11, a reversal of the pattern and an apparent exception to Lenneberg's Critical Period Hypothesis, which claims a direct incremental correlation between age of arrival and degree of accent. These results can be reconciled with Lenneberg's hypothesis only if (a) the results from the present study are not representative of the larger population from which the subjects are drawn, or (b) a ceiling

---

[3]John Schumann responded promptly, stating that it was one of the better questionnaires of its type he had seen.

[4]Timothy J. Van Susteren received his PhD in educational measurement and evaluation from Michigan State University in 1986. He edited the question stems and responses to ensure that they were clear, objective, and consistent with proper test formatting.

exists after which language acquisition in general is not age-influenced. Although the former possibility suggests that the sample may be too small, or that the subjects are somehow atypical, the latter possibility can be explored only with further research.

Aside from this salient difference from Oyama's results, the range of standard deviations indicates a surprisingly high degree of variation, especially among the postpubescent subjects. Two in particular stand out, a 16-year-old arrival in Cell 3 and a 31-one-year-old in Cell 4. Together, they received scores of 1 in 22 out of 24 judgments. Although the scores are remarkable, both (female) subjects had taken English classes in Germany. The 16-year-old had taken 3 years of English beginning at Age 12; the 31-year-old had taken 9 years beginning at Age 6. Subsequently neither took English classes in the United States; instead both began working upon arrival.

All of Oyama's subjects had received some college education in the United States. Oyama's rationale was twofold: First, she hoped to have fluent English speakers; second, she hoped to eliminate stylistic or dialect variation. Presumably, most of her subjects had also had some presecondary education in the United States. My results, however, indicate not only that there were postpubescent exceptions but also that these exceptions existed without the benefit of instruction in English in American schools.

3.1. Analysis: Narratives

With the exception of the fourth cell, which Oyama did not have, my pattern of results mimics hers. Accent scores based on narratives paralleled paragraph scores, ranging from 6 to 28.4 (6 to 30 range) with a mean of 2.75 and a standard deviation of 1.47. As expected, the first three cell scores increased with arrival age, 1.11, 2.5, and 3.27, respectively; however, the fourth cell score was also 3.27. Although Cells 1 and 4 showed increases (greater degree of accent) over paragraph scores, consistent with Labov's expectation of greater deviation from the standard English norm with the more informal speech of the narrative, Cells 2 and 3 showed decreases.

To account for the performance of Cells 2 and 3, Oyama posited that immigrants, already very self-conscious about their speech, were likely to be even more self-conscious reading the paragraph than recounting a familiar story. Another possibility, she concluded, was that judges were willing to be more lenient about phonological precision on the narrative than on the paragraph. Another possibility, based upon my study, is that the oral interview began with the reading of the paragraph, at which time almost all of the subjects seemed very self-conscious and ill at ease. As the interview progressed, the subjects seemed to relax and ostensibly performed better on the second speech sample. A final possibility is that the judges, although they were asked to make a judgment on one sample before moving on to the next, considered previous samples before making their decisions, because all subjects read the same paragraph. Obviously it would be more difficult to make comparisons across 20 different narratives. Furthermore, judges could have focused more on the extralinguistic content of the narratives at the expense of the linguistic.

Of the 20 subjects' scores, 4 remained the same on both tasks: 6 had greater degree of accent scores on the narratives (consistent with Labov's theory), and 10 had lesser degree of accent scores. An analysis by gender reveals that 4 females had greater degree of accent scores on the narratives, 4 less, whereas 2 males had greater and 6 had less. These results suggest that females as a group more closely approximated nativelike phonation than males. Additionally, 2 out of 3 speakers rated native by all 6 judges were female, whereas a third female received means of 1 on her paragraph and 1.17 on her narrative, and a fourth female received a 1.25 on her paragraph and a 1 on her narrative. Overall mean performance for females as a group was 2.72 for both the paragraphs and narratives: for males, it was 3.47 and 3.35, respectively. It would be interesting to see future research devoted to assessing the impact of gender on second language acquisition.

In conclusion, perhaps the most noteworthy observation was the considerable variation within the sample, as evidenced in the relatively high standard deviations of the mean cell scores, ranging from .098 to 1.56. Although the results of my study parallel Oyama's pattern of graduating scores on the first three cell groups, the performance of the oldest subjects in Cell 4 and the wide range of individual scores suggest that any generalization about a one-to-one correspondence between age at arrival and degree of accent is inappropriate.

3.2. Analysis: Survey Questionnaire

The survey consisted of 25 questions with 4 possible answers scaled from one to four: the higher the number, the greater the acculturation. With a possible total score of 100, subject scores ranged from 59 to 89. The mean score was 74.3, with a standard deviation of 8.03. Pearson product-moment correlation coefficients yielded $r = -.1235$, $p < .43$, suggesting that age of arrival was not significantly correlated with acculturation. In contrast, when the dependent variable of accent scores was compared with the questionnaire score, the correlation was $r = -.585$, $p < .01$. Not only were the correlations significant but all were negative: the higher the subject's survey score, the less the degree of accent. The results are consistent with Schumann's Acculturation Model prediction.

Pearson product-moment correlation coefficients were then computed between each acculturation factor and the accent scores, for both group and individual factors, to determine which specific factors yielded the highest correlations. Group factors include dominance, integration strategies, enclosure, cohesiveness and size, congruence, attitude, and length of stay. Individual factors include motivation, language shock, culture shock, and ego permeability. The most significant group factors were enclosure, $r = -.56$, $p < .01$, and cohesiveness and size at $r = -.47$,

$p < .05$. In general, group variables correlated at $r = -.555$, or at $p < .01$. Overall, group factors correlated at $r = .92$, $p < .001$, or a 99% probability that the results were not by chance. Although only one of the individual factors, language shock, correlated at $r = .72$, $p < .01$ as a whole, individual factors correlated at $r = .52$, $p < .01$.

4. DISCUSSION

The purpose of my study was to investigate two hypotheses: that accent correlates with age of arrival and acculturation, or affective variables. Specifically, I posited that acculturation rather than age of arrival correlates with nativelike phonation of the successful, older-arrival-age speakers. Although the results confirmed the arrival age hypothesis in general, there were both individual and group exceptions. Whereas it is the exceptions that render an exclusively biological age constraint hypothesis unacceptable, it is the tremendous variation across all cell groups that suggests the need for an alternative or at least a supplementary explanation. I first discuss the similarities between the results of Oyama's study and mine, and then focus on the differences.

The most salient similarity between the two studies is the pattern of increasing mean cell scores with older arrival age. As with Oyama's results, my first three mean cell scores rose for both paragraphs and narratives, consistent with Lenneberg's prediction of greater accent with older arrival age. Another similarity between Oyama's data and my study was the tendency for scores to be lower on the narratives than the paragraphs, with the notable exception of the youngest subjects' scores, which increased from 1.06 on paragraphs to 1.11 on narratives. This contradicts Labov's prediction of greater deviation from the standard English norm in informal, casual speech. To account for this discrepancy, Oyama surmised that the youngest arrival group would probably perform closest to native speakers in an informal context.

Had my study been identical to Oyama's, I would have to draw the same conclusions, because the pattern of the first three cells was the same. However, my addition of the fourth cell, not present in her study, presented some unexpected results and significant differences. First of all, the fourth group (Ages 21–33) scored lower than the preceding younger group (Ages 16–20) on the paragraph (3.11 and 3.35, respectively). On the narratives, the two groups had identical means of 3.27. Not only are the results of my study inconsistent with Lenneberg's CPH but they also suggest the need for further research to determine if an age-related ceiling exists for SLA.

Second, the pattern of greater accent on the narrative (informal speech) than on the paragraph (formal) speech, mimics the youngest-arrival-age group. Oyama's hypothesis that the youngest arrival group's performance most closely resembles that of native speaker performance obviously cannot be applied to the oldest group and points to the need for an alternative explanation.

One alternative explanation is that the groups are somehow atypical, which could only be verified by more research. Another possible explanation is that older subjects with low accent scores were more acculturated to American ways and people, as reflected in the subjects' survey scores. An analysis of mean survey scores by cell groups reveals the following: Cell 1 = 79.3, Cell 2 = 74.2, Cell 3 = 70.3, and Cell 4 = 75.2 As might be expected, the youngest subjects had the highest mean acculturation scores. Not only does the score suggest that they were the most Americanized but it also offers an alternative explanation for the generally acknowledged superior performance of the youngest second language learners. Predictably, the pattern of lower accent scores and higher acculturation scores increases progressively with the next two cells. Cell 4, the oldest group, however, deviates from the pattern by having the second-highest acculturation score.

If acculturation were the most significant factor in nativelike phonation, then it would be reasonable to expect the oldest group to have the second-lowest accent score, right behind the youngest group, which had the highest acculturation score and lowest accent score. That this is not the case suggests that acculturation alone does not correlate with degree of accent any more than arrival age alone does. It does suggest, however, that degree of accent correlates with a combination of arrival age and acculturation.

Next, the accent scores were compared with the questionnaire for an overall negative correlation: the higher the accent score, the lower the acculturation score. All group variables had a negative correlation, even if they were statistically insignificant. Length of stay, for example, at $r = -.14$ proved to be insignificant, consistent with Oyama's data which investigated length of stay as an independent variable. Specifically, there were two variables that had high negative correlations, cohesiveness and size, and enclosure. Both cohesiveness and enclosure refer to the degree to which the immigrant group shares the same churches, schools, clubs, recreational facilities, crafts, and trades with the target language group. It seems fairly obvious that immigrants who are more involved in intra- rather than intergroup activities are not going to become acculturated or identify with the target language group, and that a relatively higher degree of accent is the expected by-product. Conversely, immigrants who have immersed themselves in the target language culture will benefit from the additional exposure to the second language. For such individuals, approximating nativelike phonation is the best possible way of showing their solidarity with the target language group.

Of the remaining individual factors, only language shock, the adult learner's fear of embarrassment, criticism, or even ridicule in speaking the target language, showed a significant negative correlation with accent. Surprisingly, motivation was not a statistically significant variable. Perhaps this result is a reflection more of test error than reality. It might be interesting to note, however, that the 16-year-old (rated as a native speaker in 10 out of 12 judgments) wrote unsolicited, next to the question about motivation, "It was extremly [sic] important to me to learn to speak correctly: I worked very hard at it.". Apparently her performance on the paragraph (mean score of 1) benefited from her motivation, but her more casual speech (mean score of 1.17) gave her away as a nonnative speaker. However, her performance is consistent with Oyama's hypothesis of more nativelike performance of the youngest second language learners.

One final noteworthy difference between my study and Oyama's was her assertion that she found substantial differences between the controls and even the youngest subjects: "On no measure did controls fail to perform significantly better than the experimental subjects."[5] This is a surprising revelation in light of the fact that even though my study had only 20 subjects, as compared to 60 in Oyama's study, 3 subjects received mean scores of 1 on both the paragraph and narrative criterion. In addition to the three perfect scores, another 3 subjects, with arrival ages of 6, 12, and 16, scored well. The 6-year-old scored a mean of 1.17 on the paragraph and a mean of 1.33 on the narrative; the 12-year-old, 1.25 and 1, respectively. The 16-year-old's scores mimicked the youngest age-of-arrival subjects' performance in both Oyama's study and mine. It is also interesting to note that the subjects' scores have a pattern exactly the reverse of Lenneberg's prediction of higher degree of accent with older arrival age.

The fact that there were two postpubescent subjects who were rated as native speakers by the judges on 22 out of 24 ratings is noteworthy, even though they had taken English classes in Germany. In the case of the 16-year-old, her English classes did not begin until after Age 12, which by innatist standards is probably already too late for accentless speech. In the case of the 31-year-old who received a 1 on all 12 ratings, her instruction was over a period of 9 years, but from non-native speakers of English, with British accents.[6] In both cases, the likelihood of native-speaker competence being acquired through classroom instruction from non-native speakers with British accents seems remote at best. In fact, Seliger, Krashen, & Ladefoged (1975) stated that English learned from nonnative speakers in their native countries will limit the second language learners' ability to learn English after their arrival. They see this situation as analogous to unlearning one dialect pronunciation and learning a new one—"a task that appears to be beyond the ability of most adult learners" (1975, p. 22).

Anyone who has ever taken foreign language courses before visiting a country, can attest to the general difficulty not only of functioning on a daily basis but of using the language so as to be indistinguishable from native speakers. Age, in the case of these two subjects, does little to account for their lack of accent. Both received high scores on their acculturation questionnaires, the 31-year-old scoring 77, the 16-year-old scoring 89, the highest score.

---

[5]Although Oyama's control subjects rated a mean score of 1 on the paragraph reading, they rated a mean of 1.05 on the narrative.

[6]This subject decided that her British accent was a liability and subsequently obtained coaching in American English not long after she arrived in the United States. None of the six judges detected any type of accent or dialect whatsoever in her English.

The sample in my study was composed of individuals who had been exposed to English for a long period of time, even though they had not had college educations. Although their overall performance on the measures seemed to be at least in part age related, the fact that the oldest group had a lower accent score and a higher acculturation score than the preceding younger group indicates that affective variables can override the biological age constraint. Obviously, there is a need for further research to discover what leads to native speaker phonation.

The biggest shortcoming of my study is the small sample size. It would be interesting to see whether data support the theory of greater degree of accent in successively older arrival age groups, specifically between the postpubescent (Ages 16–20) and adult learners (over Age 20).

More work needs to be done, too, to create and refine instruments such as the one used in this study, because as far as I was able to ascertain, no such standard instrument exists. In particular, there is a need for more reliable measures of assessing what individual acculturation factors correlate with nativelike phonation. The gender-specific performance my study revealed suggests the possibility of largely unexplored research areas. Finally, it would be interesting but difficult to find and analyze successful second language learners who had not taken English in their native countries in an attempt, to borrow Seliger's (1978) phrase, to discover what "constellation of characteristics" is responsible for postpubescent nativelike phonation.

REFERENCES

Labov, W. (1966). *The Social Stratification of English in New York City*. Washington, DC: Center for Applied Linguistics.

Lamendella, J. T. (1977). "General Principles of Neurofunctional Organization and Their Manifestation in Primary and Nonprimary Language Acquisition," *Language Learning* 27, 155–193.

Lenneberg, E. H. (1967). *Biological Foundations of Language*. New York: John Wiley and Sons.

Neufeld, G. (1978). "On the Acquisition of Prosodic and Articulatory Features in Adult Language Learning." *Second Language Development, Trends, and Issues*, ed. by Sascha W. Felix, pp. 137–149. Tubingen, Germany: Gunter Narr Verlag.

Oyama, S. C. (1973). "A Sensitive Period for the Acquisition of a Second Language." Doctoral dissertation, Harvard University, Cambridge, MA.

———. (1976). "A Sensitive Period for the Acquisition of a Nonnative Phonological System," *Journal of Psycholinguistic Research* 5, 261–283.

Schumann, J. H. (1978). "The Acculturational Model for Second Language Acquisition and Foreign Language Teaching." *Second Language Acquisition and Foreign Language Teaching*, ed. by Rosario Gingras, pp. 28–50. Arlington, VA: Center for Applied Linguistics.

———. (1986). "Research on the Acculturational Model for Second Language Acquisition," *Journal of Multilingual and Multicultural Development* 7(5), 379–392.

Scovel, T. (1981). "Discussion of 'Exceptions to Critical Period Predictions: A Sinister Plot.'" *New Dimensions in Second Language Acquisition Research*, ed. by Roger W. Andersen, pp. 58–61. Rowley, MA: Newbury House.

Seliger, H. W. (1978). "Implications of a Multiple Critical-Periods Hypothesis for Second Language Learning." *Second Language Acquisition Research*, ed. by W. C. Ritchie, pp. 12–19. New York: Academic Press.

———, S. D. Krashen, and P. Ladefoged. (1975). "Maturational Constraints in the Acquisition of Second Language Accent," *Language Sciences* 36, 20–22.

Selinker, L. (1972). "Interlanguage," *International Review of Applied Linguistics in Language Teaching* 10, 209–231.

Author Index

Subject Index

A

Accent, see Speech, accented
Accessibility Hierarchy, 14–15, 101–102, 104
Acculturation Model, 306, 309, 311–315
Acquisition sequence, 153, 156, 280, see also
    Development, stages of
Adjacency pairs, 241–242
Adjuncts, 104–105
    clauses, 92
Adverbials
    clauses, 48–49
    time, 152–153
Affect and SLA, 306, 312–313, 315
Arguments of verbs, 104–105
Aspect, 151–152, 154, 165
Aspiration, 296–297
Assessment, 25
Avoidance, 108–109

B

Barrier, 85
Behaviorism, 46
Bilingual education, 196, 198
    and reading development, 196–197
Binding
    anaphors, 66–67

    local, 71, 74
    long distance, 9–11, 15, 66–67, 71, 74
    non-local, 75
    Principle B, 65, 67, 70, 80, 84–85, 88, 91,
        93
    reflexive, 9–11, 15, 65–70
    theory, 84
Branching direction, 49

C

C-command, 91–92
C-test, 36
Chinese, 50, 52, 264
Classroom language learning, see tutored
    learning
Cognitive process, 236–237, 248
Collaborative learning, 24–25
COLT (Communicative Orientation to
    Language Testing), 138
Communication strategy, 265–266
Competence, 256–257, 262, 264, 266
Complementation
    infinitival, 81, 85, 87, 89
    subjunctive, 81–83, 85–89
    verb, 81–82, 90
Comprehensible input, 34, 187, 191,
    196–197, 236

323